UNIVERSITY OF HAWAI'I PRESS
HONOLULU

EDITED BY STEPHEN SNYDER
AND PHILIP GABRIEL

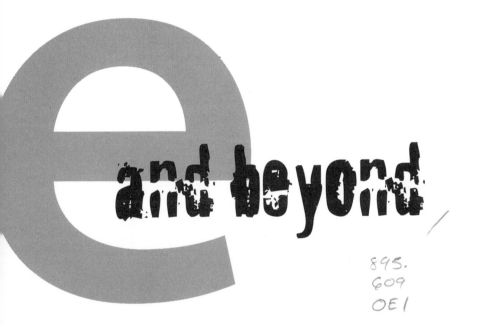

FICTION IN
CONTEMPORARY JAPAN

© 1999 University of Hawai'i Press
All rights reserved
Printed in the United States of America

04 03 02 01 00 99 5 4 3 2 1

LIBRARY OF CONGRESS CATALOGING-IN-PUBLICATION DATA
Ōe and beyond : fiction in contemporary Japan / Stephen Snyder
and Philip Gabriel.
     p.   cm.
  Includes index.
     ISBN 0-8248-2040-1 (cloth : alk. paper). — ISBN 0-8248-2136-x
(paper : alk. paper)
     1. Japanese fiction—1945– —History and criticism. 1. Snyder,
Stephen, 1957– . II. Gabriel, J. Philip.
PL747.8.O34   1999
895.6'3509—dc21   98–41900
                                                            CIP

University of Hawai'i Press books are printed on acid-free paper and
meet the guidelines for permanence and durability of the Council on
Library Resources.

Designed by Diane Gleba Hall
Printed by The Maple-Vail Book Manufacturing Group

CONTENTS

ACKNOWLEDGMENTS

The idea for this volume came from a panel organized for the Western Conference of the Association for Asian Studies meeting held in Mexico City in 1993. The editors were fortunate to be joined on the panel by Van Gessel, and Sharalyn Orbaugh served as discussant and voice of reason. We would like to express our thanks to them and all the other friends and colleagues who subsequently agreed to contribute chapters to this project for their patience and good humor through the editing process. We are also grateful to Sharon Yamamoto at the University of Hawai'i Press whose intelligent and clear-headed advice was in many ways responsible for this volume finding its way into print. During the production process, Sandy Adler in Boulder, Don Yoder in California, and Masako Ikeda in Honolulu were enormously helpful and made important contributions. We would also like to thank the two anonymous readers for suggestions that substantially improved the volume. Finally, we are grateful to our families and to our respective teachers, Professors Edwin McClellan of Yale University, Brett de Bary and Karen Brazell of Cornell University, and Asai Kiyoshi formerly of Ochanomizu Women's University for their support and guidance.

INTRODUCTION

Stephen Snyder and Philip Gabriel

On the evening of October 13, 1994, as reporters began to gather outside Ōe Kenzaburō's home in suburban Tokyo, a cycle in Japanese literary history was coming to an end. With the awarding of the Nobel Prize for literature, a writer whose career had been marked by literary resistance and (at least symbolic) marginality was officially installed as an icon of mainstream mass culture. It required, however, an outside force, the Nobel committee, to accomplish this repositioning, and it is a measure of Ōe's commitment to his role as social conscience that he rejected the Order of Culture the government tried to award him shortly after. Ironically, in the months that followed, thanks to the publicity associated with the prize, Ōe's works finally began to undergo the process of commodification that he had so consistently criticized in relation to the works of writers such as Murakami Haruki and Yoshimoto Banana.[1] New editions of *Kojinteki na taiken* (A Personal Matter) and other novels were brought out to fill emptied bookstore shelves, and *Kaifuku suru Kazoku* (A Healing Family, 1995) became an enormous best-seller. Yet Ōe has used the enhanced visibility conferred by the prize, in part, as an occasion to distinguish his "serious works of literature" from "those novels which are mere reflections of the vast consumer culture of Tokyo and the subcultures of the world at large."[2] (Ironically, the term "subculture novel" was perhaps first used two decades earlier by Ōe's erstwhile literary opponent, Etō Jun, in a similarly uncomplimentary description of Murakami Ryū's *Kagiri naku tōmei ni chikai burū*.)[3] Elsewhere, Ōe is more explicit as to who and what he means by this term:

> Serious literature and a literary readership have gone into a chronic decline, while a new tendency has emerged over the last several years. This strange new phenomenon is largely an economic one, reflected in the fact that the novels of certain young writers like Haruki Murakami and Banana Yoshimoto each sells several

hundred thousand copies. It is possible that the recent sales of the books produced by these two authors alone are greater than those of all living novelists combined. . . . In contrast to much postwar writing which fictionalized the actual experience of writers and readers who, as twenty- and thirty-year-olds, had known war, Murakami and Yoshimoto convey the experience of a youth politically uninvolved or disaffected, content to exist within a late adolescent or postadolescent subculture. And their work evokes a response bordering on adulation in their young readers. But it is too early to predict where this trend will lead as they grow older. Will the audience brought together and cultivated by people like Murakami and Yoshimoto come more generally to be the mainstay of Japanese fiction? Or will this readership, along with its favored writers, vanish with its own subculture?[4]

These are clearly questions worth asking. Later in the same essay, Ōe mentions other writers whose work he much prefers, including Nakagami Kenji, Tsushima Yūko, and Shimada Masahiko. But the same questions might be asked of them: Will they, in time, be said to have created an audience (in Japan and abroad) and a literature that is the new "mainstay of Japanese fiction"? Or will they simply fade away like the reputations of a number of the postwar writers Ōe himself would have identified as significant and "serious"? Do they, in fact, constitute any sort of coherent school or movement? Or is their work collective evidence of the end of serious fiction? The present volume poses these questions in relation to some of the most significant contemporary Japanese writers and seeks to provide answers, tentative though they must be, that will constitute a mapping of the current literary landscape in Japan.

The temptation to periodize, to create schools, and to label movements is, of course, always with us, naming being one of the few powerful practices accorded the critic. In the present case, the catchall category of the "postmodern" is the likely candidate to provide some context for a literature that defines itself, or is defined, against the work of a (self-defined) modern such as Ōe. But the postmodern, as is now all too evident, is a category or concept that has the—perhaps fortunate—quality of deconstructing its own definitions, denying its own possibility, disowning the various attempts at its theorization—and in precisely this sense, it might indeed be said to have much in common with the work of the writers studied in the essays that follow. While recognizing the inadequacy of such a term, it will be used to mark a fissure in the cultural landscape the existence of which, if not its nature, is agreed upon by those on both sides of what Andreas

Huyssen calls the "Great Divide" between the modern and the postmodern cultural moments.[5]

If labels for movements or schools or even periods have lost some of their salience, how do we characterize—that is, make sense of—the contemporary Japanese literary scene without the advantage of perspective? Kobayashi Hideo offers an impressionistic but useful rule of thumb:

> Any period has a tone and a coloration distinctive to it. But to the end this remains just a tone or a coloration, not a landscape that we can see clearly. What happens vividly before us is just a structure of various signs given birth by that period's color and tone.[6]

The task, then, is to first determine the "tone and coloration" of contemporary Japanese literature, after which we can begin to provide a hermeneutics for the structure of signs that tone and coloration engender. Only then will the landscape begin to emerge in outline. Ōe's comments, and his experience, are useful once again in this respect, though they delineate what might be called a fault line in recent Japanese literary history, rather than an outline of it. If the one-time enfant terrible has reached an age and stature at which he feels alienated from, rather than connected with, the present generation, then clearly he stands at some critical remove from the contemporary aesthetic. If Ōe is, as he suggests,[7] the last of the postwar generation of writers, then those who come after, the so-called post-postwar generation, invent and inhabit a world with a very different coloration and tone and based on a very different experience—one, however, that is perhaps not, a priori, reducible to that of the "vast consumer culture of Tokyo."

The essays in this volume examine a broad range of works by Ōe and his contemporaries, as well as by the "post-Ōe" generation, to delineate what specific writers have to say about the contemporary Japan they inhabit. The oldest author considered, Endō Shūsaku, is a generation older than Ōe, yet he remained very active and in many ways quite "contemporary" until his recent death; Yoshimoto Banana, however, would not be born for another six years when Ōe won the Akutagawa Prize in 1958. While the approaches represented by the individual studies vary widely, each attempts to give a concrete sense of the nature of the writer's work and to situate its themes and techniques in a larger critical framework.

The literary and epistemological debate being enacted among the various essays and writers here is not, in a sense, new. At the heart of these discussions, as they have been at the heart of literary discussions in Japan since the Meiji period, are the knotted questions of the self and its representation. To read these essays, with their various thematic concerns and critical approaches, is to be reminded that the debate begun in the pages of the naturalist mouthpiece *Keiō Bungaku* and its rival, the antinaturalist *Mita Bungaku*, and continued by, among many others, Akutagawa and Tanizaki in the 1930s is still alive today and still a central concern, tacit or explicit, of a broad cross section of the Japanese literary world and, by extension, of the culture as a whole. Since the Meiji period, narrative fiction in Japan has been construed by a large segment of the writing population as a medium for embodying the content of the personal "self."[8] This assumption gave rise initially to the Japanese version of naturalism *(shizenshugi)* and then to the *shishōsetsu,* or "I-novel," which has been the dominant form of novelistic discourse in Japan throughout the modern century. It is a form that is only marginally associated, in name at least, with the work of postwar-generation writers such as Ōe Kenzaburō or Endō Shūsaku. In the context of the current debate between the postwar generation and their postmodern successors, however, it becomes apparent that this old conflict—between fiction that purports to represent the sincere "self" and fiction that denies that possibility or its desirability—is flaring up yet again, this time in the guise of a generational skirmish between modern and postmodern aesthetics.

The battle lines, however, are somewhat more complex this time around—due in large part to the fact that the combatants are more diverse in terms of background and, in particular, gender. Ōe and Endō can be seen as representative of postwar (male) writers who are, as Susan Napier says in Chapter 1, "implicitly or explicitly engaged in a search for an ineffable something that Ōe himself terms the 'sublime.' " Theirs is a literature of mistrust of dogma and institutions and national identities, but it is finally a fiction with a very moral (if oppositional) vision and a commitment to the notion of the individual in society. Ironically, we find Napier arguing for the "deeply spiritual, even overtly religious" quality of Ōe's writing despite his reputation as an iconoclast and agnostic, while in Chapter 2 Van Gessel calls for a reevaluation of Endō, suggesting that his usual pigeonholing as a Catholic writer is less important in understanding his work than Endō's war experience. Ōe's work, in particular, is increasingly concerned with the chronicling of his experience and that of his family, with the *shishōsetsu*-like presentation of self as the apparent purpose of works as diverse as *Pinchrunner Memorandum* and *A Healing Family.* The one inviolable principle in Ōe's fiction is the sanctity of the individual. To this pair of writers might be added Hayashi Kyōko, whose work, like Ōe's and Endō's, is, as Davinder Bhowmik describes it in Chapter 3, an attempt to make sense of the senseless (her experience as a *hibakusha*)—to represent the unrepresentable horrors of atomic warfare. Again like Ōe and Endō, in her role as self-described *kataribe,* or "tribal narrator," she seeks to give expression to a moral, if marginal and oppositional, vision for her "self" and her collectivity.

Following Ōe and this company of immediate postwar writers are three others discussed here (part of the so-called *senchū-ha*). Although these writers too experienced the war, in the cases of Ohba Minako, Takahashi Takako, and Kurahashi Yumiko the experience does not play in quite the same terms, nor perhaps could it have. They represent a transitional moment. Kurahashi's background, as Atsuko Sakaki points out in Chapter 7, closely parallels Ōe's. Both were born in Shikoku in 1935, studied French at college, wrote graduation theses on Jean-Paul Sartre, and made something of an impression on the literary world while still at school. Yet her career has been characterized by a pointed literary debate with Ōe over the purpose of literature—a debate in which she has often been cast (anachronistically, it would appear) in the role of postmodern writer and subject to criticisms from Ōe (and, ironically, Etō Jun) that are quite similar to those more recently leveled against Murakami Haruki and Yoshimoto Banana: her work is not "original" and does not demonstrate a commitment to her world—that is, it lacks a "moral" component. As Sakaki characterizes her fiction, Kurahashi is writing a kind of antinovel, one that operates on principles of pastiche, parody, and narrative self-consciousness that are characteristic of postmodern fiction. Thus while Kurahashi might well have become a canonized member of Ōe's generation, factors in her writing and the fact of her gender have mitigated against inclusion and moved her work in the direction that would be followed by later writers.

No doubt the same can be said of Takahashi Takako and Ohba Minako, both of whom were born before Ōe but did not establish their literary reputations until the 1970s—and then only with literary sensibilities that are quite different from those of the immediate postwar generation. Takahashi shares the Catholic faith with Endō, but her splintered narrative perspective that Mark Williams describes in Chapter 5 can be read as an early attempt to jettison the monologic configurations of the self that are the hallmark of the traditional I-novel. Likewise, in Chapter 4 Adrienne Hurley finds that Ohba's fictions constitute an "alternate form of community building" that crosses the national boundaries of the Japanese literary imagination. Her work dismantles standard national identities and imagines transnational ones in their stead, a possibility that is, clearly, already quite postmodern.

There is, however, a sense in which these writers remain on Ōe's side of the "Great Divide." Their work, like Ōe's, Endō's, and Hayashi's, is readily identifiable as *junbungaku* (pure literature). The "anxiety of contamination" by mass culture that Ōe evinces in the essays quoted earlier, as well as the "strategy of exclusion" by high art of the popular, would tend to position their work near Ōe's in the literary constellation.[9] It is only among writers born after the war whose careers begin well into the 1970s that a new relationship between high and mass culture ("anxiety-free," as it were), as well as a new attitude toward the representation of self, can be seen. This new literature operates, as Huyssen puts it, "in a field of tension between tradition and innovation, conservation and renewal, mass culture and high art, in which the second terms are no longer automatically privileged over the first."[10] The fascinating aspect of this tension in the Japanese case, of course, is that it has existed in various guises at least since the Tokugawa period, when "contamination" between low and high cultures was endemic and pervasive; but the role of high modernism has been to insist on the exclusionary strategies, the defense of *junbungaku,* that have made the departures of the post-postwar generation appear so pronounced.

The essays in the latter half of this volume describe writers who differ as radically, perhaps, from one another as they do from the earlier generation of writers. Their works do, however, share a commitment to the reexamination of both their medium and the integrity of the psychic entity, or "self," it purports to represent. The eldest of this group, Kanai Mieko and Nakagami Kenji, both born in 1946, grew up in the immediate aftermath of the war and came of age in the period of high growth. Their careers, like those of all the writers in this group, can be read as reactions—and to varying degrees resistances—to a world where commodity came to dominate, and eventually replace, lived experience, what Guy Debord calls the "society of the spectacle."[11] Nakagami (the only author considered here besides Endō who is no longer living), as Eve Zimmerman suggests in Chapter 6, produced his elaborate verbal constructs as "challenges to established order," yet at the same time, and by the same mechanism, he reaffirmed an almost mythic patterning. This order, however, is not the redemptive one to which Ōe has come; rather, it is an "ongoing cycle of transgression, violence, and retribution." Though Ōe and Nakagami share a commitment to marginal subject positions (the small town in the woods of Shikoku, the *buraku* "alley" of Shingū), it is as if Nakagami, the child of a "spectacular" society whose function is the "concrete manufacture of alienation,"[12] is unable to envision the community or a "self" in it that serves as an underpinning for Ōe's work. Instead, the violence and transgression in Nakagami's fiction at best serve to disrupt the order, or image of order, that had totalized itself by the time of his early short stories. Nakagami's contemporary, Murakami Ryū, considered in Chapter 9, takes this process a step further by creating marginalized characters and "extreme" narrative situations designed to oppose the "accelerating flow of everyday life" in contemporary Japan. Moreover, in Ōe's evocation of the margins—Shikoku, Hiroshima and the *hibakusha*, Okinawa, the handicapped—we have, in essence, an opposition based on privileging the margins over the center, an inversion that tends to reify difference over a previously reified center. In the works of Nakagami, Murakami Ryū, or Yoshimoto Banana, we find instead the representation of the margins (the *buraku*, an S&M hostess, the *shōjo*) without the privilege. As Linda Hutcheon puts it: "Postmodernism does not move the marginal to the center. It does not invert the valuing of centers into that of peripheries and borders, as much as *use* that paradoxical doubled positioning to critique the inside from both the outside and the inside."[13]

Similarly, Kanai Mieko's work, as Sharalyn Orbaugh characterizes it in Chapter 11, takes a "complicated, even deconstructionist view of fiction" and goes further still in questioning the givens of *shishōsetsu* narrative structure—namely, the inviolability of the narrative consciousness. Kanai creates rare and disconcerting communal "we" narrators who undermine notions of identity and generally shake loose "the cognitive strictures that accompany gender." Rather than seeing identity and subjectivity as facts of nature, she construes them as negotiable and performative. Again, it seems useful to read this iconoclasm as a possibility "engendered" by gender; as for Takahashi, Kurahashi, or Banana, it is in part the blockage and closure of opportunities to be voiced in the context of the (male) Japanese literary establishment that encourages Kanai to seek new routes to expression—routes that, by definition then, no longer conform to accepted literary practices. In this context, however, it is interesting to observe what Ann Sherif describes in Chapter 12 as recent attempts by establishment critics to recuperate Banana's *shōjo* literature as "oppositional and utopian." As the boundaries shift and a new generation assumes the cultural cartography, will the definitions and categorizations of "pure" literature shift with them?

Perhaps nowhere in Japanese contemporary literature is the notion of the "spectacular" or "infantile" nature of Japanese commodity culture explored more consciously or in greater depth than in the works of Shimada Masahiko discussed by Philip Gabriel in Chapter 10. Here we see the sinister side of infantilization and "free play," of the totalization of identity as performance, of a blissful immersion in the "Nonsense Zone" of the sort that Ōe fears despite his admiration for Shimada's work, as well as the possibility of an ethical movement within the postmodern characterized by the "continual resistance to a fixed identity." Thus, in its extreme form, it might be possible to imagine a kind of morality *within* postmodernism's "doubleness," one that in essence posits the immorality of the fixed, *shishōsetsu*-like subject position. And it is only in the tentative light of such a morality, perhaps, that one can view truly "spectacular" writers such as Murakami Haruki and Yoshimoto Banana, the objects of both Ōe's disapprobation and nearly universal reader adulation.

The charge that these most contemporary and most popular writers lack seriousness is, as Linda Hutcheon points out, somewhat predictable:

> In the debate about postmodernism, as soon as a critic (of any political persuasion) invokes either mass consumer culture or late capitalism, the second step seems always to be to condemn the postmodern as their expression (rather than contestation). And the next step is almost always to lament the "unserious" nature of ironic, parodic postmodernism, conveniently ignoring the history of art that teaches that irony and parody have always been used as potent political (and very serious) weapons by satirists.[14]

Jay Rubin's reading of Murakami in Chapter 8 flies in the face of Masao Miyoshi's warning that we must not take these texts too seriously or look too deeply for their symbolic structure (lest we find there is none). In examining Murakami's symbols (sheep, poor aunts), Rubin finds that, as Murakami himself suggests, their significance is to be located precisely in the fact that even the author is not sure of their meaning. What this examination of Murakami's texts reveals, however, is once more a concern with the nature of self-representation. But this time the self to be represented is a far more tenuous, negotiated entity: the "story of who each of us is," as Rubin puts it, "an inaccessible, fragmented narrative that transcends time and that we can only know through images." Still, the self gets narrated, though no longer in the context of some coherent (national) discourse. As Susan Napier suggests in Chapter 1: "Unlike Ōe, Murakami turns not to collective myth and memory but to the inviolateness of the individual and the insistence on the right of the individual to loneliness and separation."

Finally, however, it seems that in all these formulations it is narrative itself that is reaffirmed. Whether the self to be represented is the more coherent, skeptical self of the postwar writer on the margins or the fragmented, commodified, lonely self of the writer after the postmodern divide, it is the urge to narrate it that remains constant and remains the keystone of contemporary Japanese fiction as a fitting successor to the modern period. Perhaps the best evidence of this ongoing urge is the sheer volume of fiction that continues to be produced by many of the writers considered here and many others as well. Murakami Haruki, Yoshimoto Banana, and Murakami Ryū publish several books each year, with Haruki's fiction, in particular, growing more bulky with each additional title. And, most tellingly, Ōe himself, after ostensibly ending his career as a fiction writer with the enormous *Burning Green Tree* trilogy, was able to refrain from the novel form for less than a year before beginning work on yet another ambitious project. This volume collects a number of statements on the various projects of important writers in the postwar era. Our object as editors has been to trace the contours of the literary landscape, so often a fascinating shadow map of the "real," and to delineate what it is now, and what it is likely to become, beyond Ōe.

NOTES

1. At the same moment that Ōe's Nobel Prize was being announced, a nearby suburban department store was mounting a survey-cum-exhibit to gauge the relative popularity of a "Gang of Four" singled out for their sales figures: Yoshimoto, Murakami, Yamada Eimi, and Murakami Ryū (unpublished reader survey data from Parco Kichijōji, autumn 1994).

2. Ōe Kenzaburō, *Japan, the Ambiguous, and Myself* (Tokyo: Kodansha International, 1995), pp. 121–122. The speech defines Ōe's literature (and politics) not only in opposition to those who come after him (Yoshimoto and Murakami) but also to those who come before: Kawabata, whose title and speech are parodied, and Mishima, who for obvious reasons is a regular target of Ōe's criticism.

3. Etō Jun, "Murakami Ryū, Akutagawa-shō jushō no nansensu," *Sandee Mainichi,* July 25, 1976; pp. 136–138.

4. Ōe Kenzaburō, "On Modern and Contemporary Japanese Literature," in *Japan, the Ambiguous, and Myself,* pp. 49–50.

5. Andreas Huyssen, *After the Great Divide: Modernism, Mass Culture, Postmodernism* (Bloomington: Indiana University Press, 1986).

6. Kobayashi Hideo, *Literature of the Lost Home,* transl. and intro. Paul Anderer (Stanford: Stanford University Press, 1996), p. 24.

7. Ōe Kenzaburō, "Japan's Dual Identity: A Writer's Dilemma," in *Japan, the Ambiguous, and Myself,* p. 98.

8. Masao Miyoshi has argued persuasively that the *shōsetsu* (*shi-* or otherwise) is a form which is fundamentally different in kind from the novel and that its insistence on the self, the "I," is a convoluted admission that no "I" exists as a possible object of representation:

"Art is hidden, while honesty and sincerity are displayed. Distance is removed, while immediacy is ostensible. The rejection of individualism in Japan is thus compensated for by the dominance of the first person. What makes the *shōsetsu* fascinating is this complex negotiation between the formal insistence on the 'I' and the ideological suppression of the self." See Masao Miyoshi, "Against the Native Grain," in *Postmodernism and Japan,* ed. Miyoshi and Harootunian (Durham: Duke University Press, 1989), p. 155. Although he sees Ōe (and Takahashi Takako, among others) as opposed to the current "postmodern" cultural moment characterized by consumer subject positions, he would, I think, still position Ōe in the camp of those whose work is centrally concerned with this question of self, however baroquely conceived.

9. Huyssen, *After the Great Divide,* p. vii.

10. Ibid., pp. 216–217.

11. Guy Debord, *The Society of the Spectacle,* trans. Donald Nicholson-Smith (New York: Zone Books, 1994). "The spectacle," Debord writes, "corresponds to the historical moment at which the commodity completes its colonization of social life. It is not just that the relationship to commodities is now plain to see—commodities are now *all* that there is to see; the world we see is the world of the commodity" (p. 29).

12. Ibid., p. 23.

13. Linda Hutcheon, *A Poetics of Postmodernism* (London: Routledge, 1988), p. 69.

14. Ibid., p. 210.

1

ŌE KENZABURŌ AND THE SEARCH FOR THE SUBLIME AT THE END OF THE TWENTIETH CENTURY

Susan J. Napier

Ōe Kenzaburō (b. 1935), Japan's second Nobel Prize winner in literature, was born in a small village amid the mountains of Shikoku, the smallest of Japan's four major islands. Too young to serve in the Pacific War that would engulf his country until 1945, Ōe was still deeply impressed by the emperor-centered ideology that was taught to all schoolchildren. Although, after the war's end, the young Ōe became a firm believer in democracy and even a carnivalesque form of anarchy, he still vividly remembers promising his teacher as a young child that he "would cut open his belly and die for the emperor."

Besides this imperialist ideology, Ōe's other main influence was his grandmother and the wild natural setting in which he lived. Ōe's grandmother and other older village members regaled the young boy with myths and stories concerning the village's inhabitants and its many *kami* or deities. The villagers viewed their history as outside and even in confrontation with the authoritarian policies of imperial Japan. Ōe's work has retained this confrontational stance throughout his life, on the one hand celebrating the marginal and on the other hand excoriating imperialist ideology.

An excellent student, Ōe left Shikoku to study at Tokyo University, Japan's most prestigious university. There he studied French literature, writing his thesis on imagery in the fiction of Jean-Paul Sartre and also publishing his first stories. In 1958 he won the Akutagawa Prize for the short story "Shiiku" (Prize Stock), which launched him on his literary career. The story of a black American soldier held hostage in a remote Japanese village, "Prize Stock" was followed by other works with themes of rural violence and the sacrifice of the innocent during wartime, such as *Memushiri kouchi* (Nip the Buds, Shoot the Kids, 1958). Called "pastorals" by the critics, these stories contrasted markedly with subsequent works from his early period such as "Sebunchin" (Seventeen, 1961) and *Warera no jidai* (Our Era, 1959), which dealt with urban and political issues often involving the emperor.

Married in 1960 to Itami Yukari, Ōe might well have continued to write political or pastoral novels indefinitely had it not been for the birth of his first son, Hikari, in 1963. Hikari's difficult birth (he was diagnosed with a brain hernia and was not expected to live), subsequent development as a severely retarded child, and recent flowering as a composer of classical music vitally influenced Ōe's fiction and essays from that time on. Two superb fictional works from the time of Hikari's birth, *Kojinteki na taiken* (A Personal Matter, 1964) and "Sora no kaibutsu Aguii" (Aghwee the Sky Monster, 1964), memorably explore the reactions of a young father to the birth of his brain-damaged child.

While Hikari has remained a mainstay of Ōe's inspiration, the author has not abandoned his earlier political or pastoral themes. Often he combines these three elements, as in his 1967 novel *Man'en gannen no futtobōru* (The Silent Cry), which follows the tumultuous adventures, both political and sexual, of a young family's attempt to return to their native village to raise their mentally handicapped son.

Ōe's later fiction reworks many of his basic themes but also includes apocalyptic and fantastic elements. His 1972 novella *Mizukara waganamida o nuguitamau hi* (The Day He Himself Shall Wipe My Tears Away) is an angry parody of the novelist Mishima Yukio's emperor-obsessed life and works. Ōe's 1976 *Pinchirannaa chōsho* (The Pinchrunner Memorandum) follows the increasingly fantastic adventures of a man and his brain-damaged son as they take on the Japanese establishment's nuclear policies. His complex 1979 novel *Dōjidai geemu* (The Game of Contemporaneity) is an attempt to tell a mythic version of Japanese history from the point of view of those who live on its margins.

In 1994 Ōe received the Nobel Prize in literature. This supreme accolade has not dimmed his political or intellectual ardor. Shortly after winning the Nobel, Ōe made headlines again in Japan for refusing the Imperial Order of Culture, the highest honor the emperor can confer on a subject. Ōe continues to test the literary frontier as well. His most recent series of novels, a trilogy called *Moegaru midori no ki* (The Burning Green Tree, 1992–1995), combines deeply spiritual themes with many intertextual references to Western humanist writers to produce a spirited call to arms. Besides being a stunning creator of modern myths, Ōe remains a fiercely engaged human being, relentlessly trying to awaken not only his countrymen but the world.

■

And after the concrete outer walls had radiated in the fierce heat the shock waves would probably echo in his son's ears. At that time Isana wanted to hear his son say, as if whispering quietly, "It's the end of the world, you know."
— Ōe Kenzaburō, *The Floodwaters Have Come Unto My Soul*

It was a bright, quiet garden without striking features. Like a rosary rubbed between the hands, the shrilling of cicadas held sway. There was no other sound. The garden was empty. He had come, thought Honda, to a place that had no memories, nothing.
The noontime sun of summer flowed over the still garden.
— Mishima Yukio, *The Decay of the Angel*

The whole town was dead in an energetic lifelike way. I decided not to think anymore about who could or would survive.

—Abe Kōbō, *The Ark Sakura*

"Please," cried the chubby girl. "If you don't get up, the world is going to end!"
—Murakami Haruki, *Hard Boiled Wonderland and the End of the World*

"It's the end of the world as we know it and I feel fine."

—R.E.M.

∎

When Ōe Kenzaburō won the Nobel Prize for literature in October of 1994 he became only the second Japanese writer to win the prize. The first winner was Kawabata Yasunari, who received the award in 1968. Twenty-six years may not seem such a long time in Nobel history (many countries still have not been honored), but they demarcate a clear change in Japan's literary generations. Ōe's complex, resolutely intertextual, and frequently grotesque works radically contrast with Kawabata's exquisite elegies to a lost Japanese past. Critics in both Japan and the West see Ōe as representing a new "international" Japan, a Japan with a new identity on the world stage.[1] The question remains, however: Is Ōe's voice representative of his postwar generation or is he unique? And who will follow Ōe in the "post-postwar" generation?

Ōe has given his own answers to these questions. In his Nobel acceptance speech, Ōe strives to differentiate himself from Kawabata's Zen-inspired traditionalism, putting himself instead at the "end of the line" of the postwar generation of writers whom he describes as "deeply wounded by the war yet full of hope for rebirth."[2] He firmly distinguishes this generation from that of the younger writers who grew up after the war and who write novels that Ōe calls "mere reflections of the vast consumer culture of Tokyo."[3]

In fact, Ōe is notably pessimistic on the subject of recent literary trends. He calls 1970 "the year in which the curtain fell for postwar literature,"[4] citing the bizarre suicide of his fellow writer Mishima Yukio in 1970 as the turning point. Ōe considers Mishima's attempted coup d'état and subsequent suicide to have been simply a performance and refers to Mishima as a "baleful ghost" whose posturing shadow he sees affecting the new generation of shallow, consumer-oriented writers.[5] But Ōe also blames "today's grotesquely bloated consumer society" of modern Japan. As he explains it: "Lack of activity in the realm of *jun-bungaku* (pure literature) can be substantiated objectively when we compare the volume of its publication with that of other literature such as popular historical novels, science fiction, mysteries and various nonfiction categories."[6] To Ōe, pure literature is being elbowed out by contemporary Japan's increasingly prominent popular culture.

Is Ōe correct? Is he simply a representative voice of a dying literary tradition, a tradition which was unique to the set of circumstances that produced the society of immediate postwar Japan? And what does Ōe offer as a solution for this crisis? This essay attempts to answer these questions. Yes, Ōe is indeed representative —if not in style then certainly in the thematic obsessions of postwar literature. Ōe shares with these writers, but perhaps feels more intensely, a need for some form of transcendental spiritual experience, an experience which Ōe himself terms the "sublime" and which he offers as a possible solution for some of the ills afflicting modern Japan. I would suggest, however, that this desire for the sublime is not restricted only to authors of Ōe's generation. A search for transcendental experience characterizes not only some of the best of recent Japanese literature but can also be found in some of the most prominent products of popular culture, notably comic books *(manga)* and animation.[7]

What is the sublime? In Ōe's vision it is far more than the dictionary definition of "noble, awe-inspiring" (echoed almost word for word in *Kōjien*'s definition of *"koso,"* the Japanese word for "sublime"). In a 1993 conversation recorded in *Boundary* between Ōe, Donald Pease, and Rob Wilson, Ōe is clearly searching for a Japanese sublime in contrast to what Wilson has developed as an American sublime of power. Wilson's "American sublime" includes America's awesome garrison of nuclear weapons, the power of the American landscape (from mountains to the "commodity infinitude of shopping malls"),[8] and even a sublime of transnational cyberspace. Ōe suggests that Japan too needs a "sublime," which he links with Pease's concept of a "visionary compact." Further linking the sublime with Freud's notion of the "unheimlich" or uncanny, he states that "we've reached this point where it is crucial for the Japanese to think seriously about the question of the Japanese sublime, of the Japanese visionary compact."[9] Ōe's linkage of the sublime with the surreal notion of the "uncanny" and the interactive notion of a "compact" suggests the breadth of his notion of the sublime. For Ōe the sublime experience seems to be one that has unearthly or extreme aspects but is still rooted in the world around us.

Confining ourselves to his fiction, we can identify three major paradigms in which Ōe seems to be locating the sublime. The first is a vision of violence, often of an apocalyptic type, sometimes linked with the Japanese emperor or with the Japanese past: a vision of wholesale destruction that both terrorizes and liberates his characters runs through a number of Ōe's novels. The second is Ōe's notion of a human collectivity tied to a natural setting. Often this sublime is a rural village located in a liminal space that may or may not be Ōe's own homeland of Shikoku and composed of marginals and outsiders such as Ōe's own mentally handicapped son, Hikari. These outsiders are engaged in a frequently carnivalesque confrontation with established authority. Although they often lose the fight, the process of violent confrontation itself seems to liberate them, thereby connecting this paradigm with that of the apocalyptic sublime. The third site of the sublime is the body, usually in its sexual aspect, but also in relation to violent action. Many of Ōe's characters engage in grotesque and sometimes violent sexual activity. As with the previous two paradigms, however, the very extremity of the process often conveys a form of freedom to the participants.

Ōe is not alone, of course, in his search for the sublime. Writers of his own generation, such as Abe Kōbō and Mishima Yukio, as well as more recent writers such as Murakami Haruki, share a common sense of the spiritual emptiness of postwar Japan and a concomitant desire to fill that emptiness with some aspect of sublimity. Like Ōe, they tend to use the quest format (usually in absurdist guise) and a variety of defamiliarizing techniques, most notably the use of the grotesque and the fantastic, both to explore the emptiness and to present some form of alternative to it. Also like Ōe, they frequently privilege the body as a site for potential sublimity, either through sexual liasons or its own destruction. Finally, these writers also share a fascination with the disastrous and the apocalyptic in the form of dystopian visions of the end of Japan or indeed the end of the world itself.

One caveat remains: Despite all the similarities in themes and structures, Ōe's final vision is unique. Unlike the other writers cited here, Ōe's search for the sublime does not end in a nihilistic celebration of emptiness (Mishima, Abe) or resignation (Murakami). Instead his search is a never-ending quest that has as its object redemption and rebirth. Indeed, since its very beginning, his writing has shown a strongly spiritual aspect, as is demonstrated in works such as the 1958 "Shiiku" (Prize Stock), which emphasizes themes of sacrifice, and the 1964 *Kojinteki na taiken* (A Personal Matter), which explores the potential for redemption. This spiritual element has deepened in recent years as novels such as *Kōzui wa wagatamashii ni oyobi* (The Floodwaters Have Come Unto My Soul, 1973), *Reintsurii o kiku onnatachi* (Women Who Listen to the Raintree, 1982), and most obviously his final trilogy *Moegaru midori no ki* (The Burning Green Tree, 1992–1995) embed their stories within frameworks of suffering, sacrifice, and hope for salvation. Frequently Ōe encapsulates his spiritual themes in lengthy intertextual references to Western writings, ranging from the Bible to *The Inferno* to the poetry of Blake and Yeats.

This essay explores Ōe's search for the sublime in terms of the three paradigms described earlier: the apocalyptic, the body, and the collectivity. In examining Ōe's use of these paradigms in comparison with the fiction of Abe, Mishima, and Murakami, we may be able to answer the questions posed at the beginning of this chapter regarding Ōe's "representativeness" and the alternatives Ōe offers to the emptiness he so brilliantly describes.

ŌE, ABE, MURAKAMI, AND DEATH BY WATER

Within the trope of the apocalypse can be found all three of Ōe's paradigmatic sublimes, so it is perhaps not surprising that some of Ōe's most significant fiction plays with the notions of wholesale destruction.[10] But Ōe is not alone in his fascination with a vision of endings—of a world, of a culture, or simply of a self. Postwar Japanese literature and popular culture have been dominated by images of destruction to a remarkable extent. The reasons for this are not hard to find: Most obviously, Japan is the only country so far to have suffered nuclear bombing, and many writers and artists have explored this shadow of imminent destruction.[11] Ōe in particular was deeply affected by a trip in the summer of 1963 to Hiroshima, the same year his eldest son Hikari was born with massive brain damage. Ōe's concern for the innocent victims of Hiroshima, often linked with the image of his innocent son, has led him to write numerous essays on Hiroshima. The most important of these is *Hiroshima Notes,* in which Ōe maintains, "As long as the A-bomb victims' lives and cries are this urgent, who can sweep Hiroshima from his or her consciousness?"[12]

While Ōe's essays straightforwardly lament the horror of nuclear destruction, his fiction contains examples of a more ambivalent engagement with apocalypse, sometimes verging on a Menippean celebration of destruction.[13] Nowhere is this complex attitude toward apocalypse clearer than in his long 1973 novel *Kōzui wa wagatamashii ni oyobi* (The Floodwaters Have Come Unto My Soul), a work whose premise is based on human confrontation with a variety of apocalyptic imaginaries. *Kōzui* may usefully be compared with Abe Kōbō's 1984 *Hakobune Sakuramaru* (The Ark Sakura), another vision of potential worldwide destruction, and both of these works stand in intriguing contrast to Murakami Haruki's 1985 novel *Sekai no owari to Haado boirudo wandaarando* (Hard Boiled Wonderland and the End of the World).

To turn to Abe's novel first: Although *The Ark Sakura* was written eleven years after *Kōzui,* certain elements of the plot are so similar that, in many ways, the work can be seen as an Abe-esque rewrite of Ōe's earlier novel. As their explicitly biblical titles suggest, both works center on a vision of wholesale destruction in which water plays an important part. Ōe's *Kōzui* takes its title from Psalm 69: "Save me O God, for the waters are come in unto my soul." The psalm mixes apocalyptic imagery of a great flood, "I sink in deep mire where there is no standing. I am come into deep waters, where the floods overflow me" (v. 2), with a plea for the total destruction of the speaker's enemies: "Let their eyes be darkened, that they see not. . . . Let their habitation be desolate" (vv. 23–25). The psalm ends, however, with a vision of salvation in which God saves the righteous and "heaven and earth praise him" (v. 34). Abe's title, with its use of the term *"hakobune"* or "ark," also evokes the biblical—in this case, Noah's vessel of salvation from the great flood. In contrast to Ōe's use of the Bible for spiritual solace, however, Abe ironically conjoins the term "ark" with the notion of the *"sakura,"* or shill, that is, the person hired by salespeople to deceptively promote a product. Mired in a world of consumer deception, Abe's "ark" offers only the illusion of salvation.

Both novels are set in the near future and belong to the dystopian genre of novels offering a warning of future disaster—in this case ecological and nuclear. But Ōe's work presents a possibility of escape, or at least positive confrontation with disaster, through human collective action and human links with the natural world. In fact, *Kōzui* offers visions of all three versions of Ōe's sublime: sexual (bodily) fullfillment is achieved through the protagonist's linking up with a group of outsiders (the collectivity), who assert their identity through a vision of apocalypse.

Kōzui's protagonist is Ōki Isana (Big Tree Brave Fish), a middle-aged man who has abandoned bourgeois life to assume what he considers to be his true responsibilities as representative of "the whales and the trees," two species that Ōe sees as the principal victims of human depradation. Hiding in an abandoned nuclear shelter with his brain-damaged son awaiting a final day of destruction, Isana forms a bond with a group of idealistic young terrorists who call themselves Freedom Voyagers. Ultimately he becomes especially close to a female member of the group named Inago (Locust), with whom he experiences hitherto undreamt of moments of sexual fulfillment. The Freedom Voyagers have also created a hideout away from the city where they are building a schooner in which they intend to escape when some future disaster lets loose a flood upon Tokyo. They never complete the schooner, however. At the novel's end most of the young terrorists, along with Isana, die in a shootout with the Japanese Self-Defense Forces, an apparent contemporary reference to the Japanese government's battles with the Japanese Red Army during the 1970s.

Despite its protagonists' end, *Kōzui*'s vision of apocalypse is not completely downbeat. Though at times poignant and even tragic, at other moments the novel's mood is carnivalesque as the terrorists glory in their self-imposed confrontation with stronger forces. Indeed, Isana's vision of the end of the world is largely a welcoming one that is encapsulated in the quotation at the beginning of this chapter in which Isana dreams of hearing his son announce, "It's the end of the world, you know." In fact, Isana dies before any apocalypse actually occurs. But in his last moments he has a vision of the whales and the trees and announces to them "All is well" before the final nothingness surrounds him.

Whereas *Kōzui*'s vision of the last day is a transcendent one, metonymically associated with the half-built schooner whose graceful beauty promises something beyond the simple survival offered by an "ark," Abe's work deconstructs the whole notion of salvation and survival. *The Ark Sakura* documents the increasingly absurd adventures of a man nicknamed Mole (or sometimes Pig) who, like Isana, possesses his own fallout shelter built in an abandoned mine. Mole styles this shelter his "ark" and, at the novel's beginning, is searching for a few select people to whom he can give tickets to the ark so long as they acknowledge his captaincy.

Despite the nautical imagery, Abe's vision of survival has nothing to do with cleansing water but is instead linked to excrement. Two of the central images in *The Ark Sakura* involve feces. The first concerns the presumably mythic eupcaccia, an insect from "Epicham Island" that survives by ingesting its own feces. The second image is that of the lavatory. As a child, Mole was chained to the toilet by his father. At the end of the novel, his leg becomes stuck in the shelter's special toilet with virtually no hope of escape. In his use of excrement-related images Abe parodies the whole notion of survival, reducing it simply to an insect eating its own feces. Although sexuality remains (like Isana, Mole lusts after one of his fellow survivalists but she does not respond), the real bodily focus here is on Mole's anguished leg—a leg that still bears the scars of his father's chains. While Isana is able to enjoy sexual fulfillment with Inago in the shadow of apocalypse, Mole's body is only an agent of pain, humiliation, and entrapment.

Water and nature, which in *Kōzui* were cleansing and redeeming elements, are only part of a larger maze of deceptions that bind Mole. Ōe's positive natural imagery of "Big Tree" and "Locust" are replaced here by images of the pig, another creature that eats its own feces, and the mole, an earth animal that survives through blind tunneling. *The Ark Sakura* ultimately links the image of the tunnel to water, although in a negative fashion, when Mole finally dynamites his own hideout in order to free his leg. Although water flushes out, releasing his leg, his next step is only downwards, into the metaphorical bowels of the mine that contain his secret escape route.

Unlike Isana, Mole apparently survives, but in a form that is virtually ghost-like. Crawling to the end of his escape tunnel, he drags himself out into the town, planning to take a "souvenir photograph" (commemorating his own survival perhaps?), only to find that

> everything was too transparent. Not only the light but the people as well: you could see right through them. Beyond the transparent people lay a transparent town. Was I transparent, then, too? I held a hand up to my face—and through it saw buildings. . . . The whole town was dead in an energetic lifelike way. I decided not to think anymore about who could or would survive. [pp. 334–335]

In opposition to Ōe's celebratory vision of nature revenging itself on humanity, Abe presents a vision of a town full of living ghosts. While the ghostly images of trees and whales in *Kōzui* suggest a supernatural potential for change and hope, the spectral Mole only problematizes the meaning of survival. The body that had pained and trapped Mole has now been rendered transparent, without feeling, either positive or negative. Mole has survived but not in any transcendent way. Instead he is simply part of a dead town where survival and escape have no more meaning.

The image of shadowy people in a dead town brings me to another vision of the end of the world—that presented in Murakami Haruki's *Sekai no owari to haadoboirudo wandaarando* (Hard Boiled Wonderland and the End of the World). Although Murakami, perhaps the best-known writer of the post-postwar generation, at first glance seems to differ radically from Ōe, his best work deals with an apocalyptic notion of the sublime, one that similarly privileges the body and a form of interactive responsibility as well. That said, it must be admitted that Murakami's exploration of these paradigms in *Hard Boiled Wonderland* is fascinatingly unique—an exploration whose differences from Ōe suggest important generational changes. While not so nihilistic as Abe's work, *Hard Boiled Won-*

derland's vision of apocalyptic destruction is deeply solipsistic and privileges a collectivity that exists only in the mind of one man.

A richly realized fantasy, Murakami's novel is based on the notion of two interlocking worlds: the "Hard Boiled Wonderland" and the "End of the World." The "Hard Boiled" half of the book is set in the dystopian near future in which Japan is controlled by two authoritarian information organizations, the System and the Factory. While "Hard Boiled" has obvious cyberpunk as well as classic dystopian science fiction references, the "End of the World" part of the novel is a pure fantasy featuring unicorns, a gatekeeper, and a walled European-style town. As the reader eventually comes to learn, the two worlds are linked: The "End of the World" exists only within the brain of the nameless protagonist whose surface existence takes place in the "Hard Boiled" world. Eventually the protagonist must decide whether to escape the "End of the World," which he has created inside his own brain, or stay there and accept what amounts to a kind of death in his "real" "Hard Boiled" world. Throughout much of the novel, the reader assumes he will try to escape, since life inside the Town of the "End of the World" is a strangely passive and unemotional affair: although the protagonist connects on a limited level with the Town's female librarian, most of his time is spent as a "Dream Reader" exploring old memories in the skulls of unicorns.

As in Ōe's and Abe's novels, water is an important instrument of both salvation and destruction in *Hard Boiled Wonderland*'s apocalyptic scenario. The protagonist's one hope of escape in the "End of the World" is a whirlpool at the edge of the Town.[14] Urged on by his shadow, which represents his memory and his real-world identity and which had been severed from him when he entered the Town, the protagonist contemplates jumping into the whirlpool. Ultimately, however, he decides to stay in the Town. Although by now he knows that the Town is a creation of his own mind, the protagonist insists that he has "responsibilities . . . I cannot forsake the people and places I have created" (p. 399). In the novel's strangely poignant final passages, we see the self in the "End of the World" embracing his aloneness as he watches his shadow slip under the waters of the pool, a separation that may ultimately cut him off from all memory or engagement with others:

> Long after the Pool had swallowed my shadow, I stand staring at the water until not a ripple remains. The water is as tranquil and blue as the eyes of the beasts. I am alone at the furthest periphery of existence. Here the world expires and is still. [p. 400]

It is fascinating to contrast the endings of these three apocalyptic novels. Murakami's apocalypse is ultimately solipsistic: the death of the self, or at least the retreat of the self from engagement with outside responsibilities and society.[15] Cut off from the body, which lies dying in the real world, the self in "End of the World" speaks of his "responsibilities," but these are not responsibilities to an outer collectivity of other human beings. Water becomes the avenue to a solipsistic sublimity, a means of flushing away the irritating protestations of the still-sentient social "shadow." The end of the world becomes a self-created "Town," a collectivity inside the head.[16] In *The Ark Sakura,* Abe uses water to transport his protagonist down to a netherworld of dead shadows. In this novel's deeply nihilistic ending, the Mole is left resignedly alone with a transparent, impotent self, cut off from both past and future. Unlike the protagonist of *Hard Boiled Wonderland,* he has no connections, even to himself, and is left an alien in a Town that is not even of his own making.

Only in Ōe's work does apocalyptic destruction bear a poignantly positive aspect. In his final moments inside the shelter as water begins to pour in, Isana, rifle in hand, waits expectantly for his own death while looking forward to the renewal of the world:

> Like a blind man he opened his eyes into the darkness, listening to the voices of the whales and the sound of the water gushing in. Still speaking to the spirits of the whales and the trees, as if in a kind of prayer, he waited. I wonder what's happening on the ground above? Since I went inside the shelter has there been a nuclear blast? Or maybe there's been a huge movement in the earth's crust and the land is being visited by tidal waves or floods? After all, the water's already over my knees inside the shelter. Perhaps this great water will wipe out the human race and will give new life to the whales who are now, thanks to humanity, on the verge of extinction. Perhaps even now the whales are swimming in great groups on the earth's surface with their comrade trees. . . . I have styled myself the representative of the whales and the trees but now on the ground above, the whales who are establishing their supremacy, the trees that are fluttering their tops above the water, they'll probably be seeing me as one of their enemies.
>
> Because I myself should be wishing for that to happen. I have wanted to denounce the atrocities of humanity toward the trees and the whales. . . . As the last of the humans, my body=consciousness suspended in mid air will explode and then there'll be nothingness. At that time o Whales you will surely face you o Trees, no one but you, and will sound out the great chorus "ALL IS WELL."

... falling once more into the already deep water he lets out a fourth shot. Everything was suspended and in the distance nothingness lay bare. Turning toward the "spirits of the trees" and the "spirits of the whales" he makes his final salutation. ALL IS WELL. The thing that comes in the end to every human came to visit him. [pp. 200–201]

The floodwaters that Isana loves to imagine may finally liberate the only entities he respects: the trees and the whales. And for Isana himself, the possibility of wholesale destruction has allowed him to go beyond the fragmented individual self to bond with a greater collectivity, symbolized on the bodily level by his sexual relationship with Inago, on the human level by his alliance with the Freedom Voyagers, and on the most transcendent level by his love for the trees and whales. Although not explicitly religious, it is clear that Isana looks forward to sacrificing himself in atonement for the "atrocities" of humanity.

The contrast with both Murakami and Abe could not be more striking. Abe's apocalyptic paradigm suggests the impossibility of collective action. Mole's new friends simply humiliate and betray him, and there is no one to help him escape when he is trapped in the toilet. Mole's final eerie vision of a transparent world is not a hopeful sublime; it is totally nihilistic. While Isana trumpets the resuscitation of the whales and trees, Mole decides "not to think anymore about who could or would survive." Abe's work, while nihilistic, is also clearly angry. Mole has tried very hard to fight against a fate over which he has no control, encapsulated in the image of a father who would chain his son to the latrine, but ultimately he fails. Like Ōe, Abe shares with the writers of the immediate postwar generation a desire for political action. In Abe's case it is the frustration of action, or even the absurdity of action, which fuels both his plots and his anger. In contrast, Murakami's version of apocalypse seems to welcome the denial of action and privileges an inward turning. The end of the world is reduced to meaning the end of one character's life. And although the protagonist insists that he will take responsibility for his own actions, he is clearly unconcerned and perhaps even hostile to any wider social collectivity. In his detachment from the world and even from his own body, Murakami's character seems to show major generational differences from Ōe and Abe. Born after the war's end, Murakami shows a discomfort with collective responsibility, while his willingness to show the body as separate and fragmented suggests an affinity with cyberpunk science fiction or even the more apocalyptic visions of *manga* and animation.

ŌE AND MISHIMA: THE MOON AND THE TREE

Ōe's vision of apocalypse is complex, however. His depictions of a final catastrophe are sometimes more specifically related to the death of traditional Japan and the demise of the emperor system, an end that Ōe applauds. One of his most extraordinary depictions of this kind of apocalyptic sublime is in his 1972 novella *Mizukara waga namida o nuguitamau hi* (The Day He Himself Shall Wipe My Tears Away). In this angry work he parodies the death of Mishima Yukio, who committed ritual suicide after a failed coup in the emperor's name. *The Day* contains an obviously apocalyptic vision of the emperor's destruction—envisioned as a purple chrysanthemum-like aura spreading over the sky above Tokyo.

But what Ōe is really critiquing here is not simply the emperor system but Mishima's whole conception of traditional elite Japan's history as an entity to be longed for and whose disappearance Mishima insisted on seeing as the end of the world. Ōe's most recent fictional work, the trilogy *Moegaru midori no ki* (The Burning Green Tree), is not only an important creation in itself but also his most sustained literary reaction to Mishima's credo, especially as it was expressed in Mishima's final work, the tetralogy *Hojo no umi* (The Sea of Fertility).[17] Like Ōe, Mishima was clearly preoccupied with a search for a Japanese sublime. But in Mishima's case, this sublime frequently encompassed a recovery of an idealized and elite Japanese past. Ultimately it appears that Mishima decided this past was a chimera, and this realization may have been one of many reasons behind his suicide. Certainly the apocalyptic notion of a dead and finally unrevivable Japanese past was the foundation of his *Sea of Fertility*.

Comparing Mishima's tetralogy with Ōe's trilogy *Moegaru midori no ki*, we can easily find important similarities. Both authors clearly saw these works as major statements concerning modern Japan. Both works contain many instances of each author's vision of a sublime. But Ōe's work may also be seen as a conscious response to Mishima: an attempt to offer a message of redemption within destruction in opposition to Mishima's final vision of emptiness. *Moegaru midori no ki* is a summing-up of Ōe's principal themes and topoi. As Yoshida Sanroku says of it: "Ōe is very close to completing the mythic elaboration of his native village in Shikoku, a myth that now encompasses the cosmos."[18] *The Burning Green Tree* recovers and reworks characters, incidents, and concerns from all of Ōe's previous work. As the titles of the three books suggest—*Sukuinushi ga nagurareru made* (Until the Savior Is Beaten Up, 1993), *Yureugoku/Bashireshon* (Vacillation, 1994), and *Ōi naru hi ni* (For the Day of Greatness, 1995)—it is also a dense and complex vision of a world crying out for salvation.

As his use of Yeats' poem hints, Ōe's is a vision based upon antinomies. Indeed the first verse of Yeats' poem "Vacillation," which provides both the overall title of the trilogy and the title of its second volume, expresses this clearly:

> Between extremities
> Man runs his course
> A brand, or flaming breath,
> Comes to destroy
> All those antinomies
> Of day and night,
> The body calls it death,
> The heart remorse
> But if these be right
> What is joy?

Joy in the face of death and ugliness is, in Ōe's fictional cosmos, the only response to the human condition. (Thus his trilogy ends with the English word "rejoyce.") But as we have seen in *Kōzui*, it is a joy that can appear only through an acknowledgment, even an embracing, of the most painful aspects of the human condition: death, destruction, and all the "antinomies of day and night." This joyful acknowledgment contrasts starkly with Mishima's nihlistic vision. At the same time, however, both trilogy and tetralogy contain visions of the sublime that are based on the three paradigms we have been examining. Ultimately, however, Mishima's sublime is a deceitful illusion, while that of Ōe is a call to action.

This difference is clear even in the titles of the two works. Each is based on a paradox. Mishima's *Sea of Fertility* refers not to a genuine sea but to the Mare Foecanditus on the moon and is, of course, an ironic reference to the sterile state of modern Japan, a world whose consumer cornucopia hides a spiritual desolation. Ōe's title of *Burning Green Tree,* from the second verse of "Vacillation," involves a contradiction, as well, a tree that emblemizes both life and destruction. The verse goes as follows:

> A tree there is that from its topmost bough
> Is half all glittering flame and half all green
> Abounding foliage moistened with the dew
> And half is half and yet is all the scene;
> And half and half consume what they renew

And he that Attis' image hangs between
That staring fury and the blind lush leaf
May know not what he knows, but knows not grief.

In implicit (and perhaps explicit) opposition to Mishima's sterile sea of fertility stands Ōe's and Yeats' burning green tree. In Ōe's perception, the antinomy of burning and greenery is a positive one, suggesting the potential for life and hope in the heart of destruction. For Ōe the notion of hope in desolation is a vital conception related to the birth of his brain-damaged child in 1963 and to his sub-sequent visit that summer to Hiroshima. Ōe's image of the tree is his most com-prehensive and evocative vision of salvation from the midst of chaos. The tree has been a central image for Ōe from at least the time of his *Reintsurii o kiku onna-tachi* (Women Who Listen to the Raintree) and is linked both to his fascination with Malcolm Lowry's cabalistic Tree of Life and to Ōe's own veneration of trees, given explicit voice as early as *Floodwaters*.[19] The Yeatsian image of consump-tion and renewal connects with the idea of sacrifice, a notion we saw expressed in Isana's willingness to die for the whales and trees. This contrasts with Mishima's vision of the world of empty consumption and nonrenewal—vividly portrayed in the last novel of his tetralogy in the image of an empty beach, site of the *Nō* play *Hagoromo*, now full of the litter of postwar affluent society.

Both *The Sea of Fertility* and *The Burning Green Tree* can be seen as the sum-mation of each author's vision of modern Japan—a society that both writers find to be in desperate lack of any higher cause or meaning. To realize these visions, Ōe and Mishima use the fantastic theme of reincarnation as a framework around which the novels' action unfolds. Both works treat the theme of sacrifi-cial early death of the "supernatural" protagonists. Both also deal implicitly and explicitly with questions of faith and hope and the sublime.

But here, of course, we come to some major differences. Mishima's sublime —related to the body, the Japanese emperor, and self-immolation—is clearly delineated in each of the first three volumes of the tetralogy, only to be finally sub-verted in the final volume, *Tennin gosui* (The Decay of the Angel, 1971). In *Haru no yuki* (Spring Snow, 1969), the first volume of the work, the protagonist, the aristocratic Kiyoaki Matsugae, both epitomizes and searches for the sublime romantic beauty in the fallen world of Meiji Japan. In the second volume, *Honba* (Runaway Horses, 1969), Isao Iinuma, Kiyoaki's presumed reincarnation, searches for nobility and purity through political murder and a suicide supposedly in the name of the emperor, the ultimate ideological sublime in Mishima's universe. In the degraded postwar world of the third volume, *Akatsuki no tera* (Temple of the Dawn, 1970), the protagonist is reincarnated as a beautiful Thai princess named Ying Chan who seems to live only for sensual pleasures. All three characters attest to Mishima's consistent privileging of an elite based on birth and body in sharp contrast to Ōe's sublime of a collectivity of the marginal.

The last volume of the tetralogy, *The Decay of the Angel,* explicitly takes up the question of faith—only to give an answer suggested by the novel's title, an ironic reference to the Nō play *Hagoromo* about an angel who comes to earth and begins to "decay." In the play the angel is allowed to return to heaven by a generous fisherman. In Mishima's last novel, however, the "angel" of Japanese culture has decayed: the reincarnations, which the reader had been led to believe were real, turn out to be false, and we are left with nothing in which to believe. This discovery is made by Kiyoaki's boyhood friend Honda, initially a skeptical rationalist, who has tracked the incarnations in ever-increasing hope that they are actually true. Honda's aged, disillusioned figure as he stumbles out into a temple garden, empty of memories or hope, is the final image that Mishima left to his readers. (See the epigraph at the beginning of this chapter.)

Ōe's sublime, although it too is problematic as to whether it can actually exist, is never totally subverted. *Moegaru midori no ki* offers the reader one of Ōe's most carefully detailed visions of the sublime. The plot revolves around the attempt by Gii, one of the main characters, to build a church in the midst of rural village in Shikoku. In doing so, the village collectivity becomes a place of refuge, but also of violence, for a variety of marginalized and exiled characters. The most important of these are Gii, the son of a diplomat who, although Japanese, had grown up abroad, and Sacchan, the novel's narrator, a hermaphrodite who "switched" from male to female but retains both sets of sex organs.

As in Mishima's tetralogy, the action of Ōe's trilogy is set in motion by the apparent possibility of revitalizing the dead. But this vision of the dead returning is not the artificial sort of "reincarnation" privileged by Mishima. Rather it is giving the dead a chance to speak again. As Ōe says of another instance of reincarnation in his writing, it is a process of "making an act or even an individual come to life in the here and now." In Ōe's trilogy, a form of literal reincarnation is also presented. The ancient matriarch of the village, Oba (Granny), dies of cancer early on in the story. Refusing to cremate her, some of the villagers, including Gii and Sacchan, bury her in the forest and burn an empty coffin in order to deceive the rest of the village. They do this supposedly in order to preserve her mysterious powers of healing. During the burning of the coffin a hawk lands on

Gii, who is then surmised by the villagers to have taken on Oba's healing powers. In Mishima, reincarnation is simply another false promise; in Abe or Murakami, the characters' problematic survival only underlines the isolation and unreality of modern life; in Ōe this reincarnation is seen as something that will contribute positively to others' lives.

The presumed revitalization of Oba in Gii is not without its problems, however. Gii is hesitant to use his alleged powers but is drawn into playing the role of healer by the needs of his fellow villagers. At the end of the first novel, *Until the Savior Is Beaten Up,* he is severely beaten by the villagers, who are enraged upon hearing of Oba's false burial. Gii does not give up, however, and is in fact inspired to formally found a church, giving it the symbol of the burning green tree from the Yeats poem that Sacchan had read to him. But Gii's role is not entirely spiritual. His body, both as a vessel of sacrifice and as a means of connection, is vitally important as well. This becomes clear in an extraordinary sexual encounter described at the end of the first novel. Severely battered from his beating, Gii is comforted by the hermaphrodite Sacchan. Gii asks Sacchan to have intercourse with him, and she acquiesces in a memorable scene in which the hermaphrodite experiences both male and female sexual pleasure but also, and more importantly, a sense of mutual understanding:

> Caressed tenderly by Gii's fingers and his lips which soon joined in, there came a moment when I felt liquid welling out in minute amounts like drops of sweat, from a certain spot within the folds of my femaleness. . . . When Gii's finger started a more perpendicular movement I began to anticipate pain or at least a sensation of some unpleasant foreign body. Although I felt I must accept it as a kind of desired self sacrifice, I also felt a sort of cold shuddering sensation. Unexpectedly, however, my sexual organ started a pulsating motion as if to welcome in Gii's finger. And Gii's moist mouth sucked in my penis as if returning the favor.
>
> All this time Gii's eyes were riveted on the entire expanse of my genitalia, caressing them, invading them, almost as if his eyes themselves were touching me. I cried out and came with my penis, and in the heightened aftermath came with my female organ as well. Painfully, Gii changed his position and mounted my shuddering body but instead of inserting his penis where his fingers had been, he forced himself into my anus, wet with my secretions and Gii's spit. Then gently, slowly, as if to fill me up, Gii's semen flowed into my anus to the farthest possible reaches. And then Gii spoke in Japanese in a tear filled voice like that of a small child:

I . . . I'd always dreamed of this kind of sex . . . always, a marvellous man and a marvellous woman have sex and I could be invited in. And to be a person who could experience three types of sex in one body . . . even though I knew that kind of sex was impossible, I always dreamed of it. Having this kind of sex . . . [pp. 314–315]

This kind of tripartite sex not only satisfies Gii, it also gives Sacchan a new sense of self-worth and an awareness of the strange ways in which life courses can intersect. She muses:

The kind of bizarre sex that Gii had dreamed of during his childhood in all those different countries . . . some event or other must have caused that dream to take shape I guess. But then he came to Tokyo and piled up painful experiences on top of that and after that he came to live in this village. So that was the independent course that his life took.

And on the other hand, I too had my life course, my "switch." I had tried to reject my memory of the pain, but honestly, it had been a terrible, cruel experience. And that had been my independent life course.

But those life courses, Gii's and my own, those independent single lives, had been tied together through our mutual desire. I had been able to fulfill Gii's bizarre dream, and at the same time had been able to find in my heart a meaning for my "switch." And with that realization my heart was swept with a sense of relief, as if the knots in my soul had come untied. . . .

I had anticipated only to live out my life in the house in the woods, expecting to live a miserable, aimless existence as a weird "manwoman," growing old as a "manwoman," dying as a "manwoman." And now I had been given the chance to live for this lonely helpless "savior" lying in deep sleep at my side, his battered body emitting a poignant heat. [pp. 316–317]

This passage mixes self-abnegation, sexuality, tenderness, and pain and links them to a form of heart's desire: "what I have always dreamed of." Unlike Abe, for example, who uses grotesque sexuality as one of his most forceful expressions of the impossibility of human connection, Ōe has explored "deviant" sexuality as a means to self-renewal in many other works. These include most notably the sodomization of Himiko in *A Personal Matter* and the grotesque but strangely poignant threesome with cucumber episode in *Reintsurii*. But the coupling of Sacchan and Gii in *Until the Savior Is Beaten Up* is surely the most explicit and perhaps most extreme manifestation of sexuality as an avenue to the sublime in all of Ōe's work. The notion of sacrifice combined with pleasure implicit in Himiko's pain in *A Personal Matter* is here given a more positive treatment in that Sacchan feels no pain but experiences sensual pleasure while at the same time she feels the satisfaction of having found some "meaning" to her existence in the very extremity of sexuality. In this notion of combining the physical with the spiritual Ōe echoes Yeats, whose Crazy Jane poems from the same collection as "Vacillation" celebrate the potential for truth in "bodily lowliness." Or as Crazy Jane says to the Bishop: "But Love has pitched his mansion in / The place of excrement / for nothing can be sole or whole / that has not been rent."

A comparison with the treatment of sex in Mishima's tetralogy is enlightening here. Mishima too uses sexuality for its metaphoric potential throughout his oeuvre; but toward the end of *The Sea of Fertility*, sexuality takes on largely negative resonances as a powerful symbol of yet another form of lost or false sublime. Thus in the climactic ending of the third novel, *The Temple of Dawn*, the lonely intellectual protagonist Honda feels his innate urge for voyeurism taking hold of him again:

> The palpitations were signs of welling desire. Manifestly only ugliness and disgrace lay in store, yet these palpitations had the richness and the brilliance of a rainbow; something indistinguishable from the sublime burst forth.
>
> Something indistinguishable from the sublime! That was the villain. Nothing was more unattractive than the fact that both the force moving one to the noblest or most just of deeds and that inspiring the most obscene pleasure and the most ugly dreams should spring from the same source and be accompanied by the same warning palpitations. . . . Perhaps the root of temptation lay not in carnal desire but in this pretentious illusion of silvery sublimity, this vague and mysterious half-hidden peak among the clouds. It was the birdlime of "sublimity" that first ensnared a man and then made him yearn with unbearable impatience after the vast light. [p. 295]

As in Ōe, this "sublimity" (*koso*) is related to sexuality and constructed from contradictions—such as the "noble" and the "base" or the "just" and the "ugly" —but Mishima finally denies any potential for synthesis, deconstructing the sublime into a "pretentious illusion." This is made abundantly clear as Honda peeps at his friend Keiko and Kiyoaki's presumed reincarnation Ying Chan having lesbian sex:

When the envisioned summit, that unknown golden limit was manifest, the scene was completely transformed, and Honda could see the two women entangled beneath his gaze only in their suffering and torture. They were battered by the dissatisfaction of the flesh, their gathered brows were filled with pain, and their hot limbs seemed to writhe as though trying to escape from what seared them. They possessed no wings. They continued their futile thrashings to escape from their bonds, from their suffering . . . [p. 295]

Rather than finding beauty or sublimity in what is essentially Mishima's version of a tripartite sex scene (the two women lovers with Honda as voyeuristic participant), Mishima can only delineate "suffering and torture." Each participant remains, finally, alone, "wingless" and unable to escape. No knots are untied here. Rather, the participants continue their lonely suffering. To underline the essential "odiousness" of the reality Honda has discovered, his house burns down a few hours later, incinerating another pair of illicit lovers. Gazing at the flames reflected in his swimming pool Honda has a sudden memory of the religious revelation he had experienced in Benares:

Flames reflecting in the water . . . burning corpses . . . Benares! How could he not have dreamed of recapturing the ultimate he had seen in that holy land? [p. 306]

Mishima's implicit point is that the "ultimate" is not some sublime pinnacle of life and love. Rather, it is the awareness of emptiness, the Heian Buddhist belief that life itself is merely a burning house, incandescent with desires that must be escaped or transcended. Or as the text puts it: "The house had turned into kindling and life had become fire. All triviality had turned to ash" (p. 306).

Ōe and Mishima understand not only the human search for the sublime but also the disappointment that is almost inevitable in that search. Mishima deconstructs the search, revealing its emptiness and meaninglessness to the point where in his final work in the trilogy he leaves his readers in an empty garden where magic and memories are notable only for their absence. Ōe too understands the hopelessness of the search but describes the continuous process of the quest— insisting that it is the process itself, the unextinguishable human desire for unattainable "dreams," that distinguishes and ultimately elevates the human condition.

Thus Ōe's fascination with bizarre and deviant sex is a far cry from Mishima's superficially similar interest. Mishima's depiction of lesbian sexuality, with the heterosexual Honda looking on, simply underlines the isolation and the gulf between the sexes. For the intellectually powerful but physically unprepossessing Honda can never join in. Ōe's use of Sacchan, by contrast, who combines male and female sexuality, as his narrative voice suggests a self-reflexive attempt to literarily and literally transcend the isolation imposed by heterosexuality and the fact of the body itself. Ōe's impossible dream of sex becomes an expression of the imagination, of the place where contradictions and impossibilities are somehow transcended, where all knots are untied and a tree can burn and remain green.

Endō Shūsaku, himself one of Japan's few avowedly Christian writers, has suggested that Ōe's works are "characterized by the quest for salvation without God."[20] Ōe has replied to Endō's assertion with the following soul-searching statement: "I don't know whether there is a god or not; possibly there is. The most important thing for me is the orientation of the soul or the heart to something beyond our world. . . . With God or without God I don't know. But our concentration on something over and beyond our reality is most important."[21] Ōe is one of the few major Japanese writers explicitly concerned with religion, but he is certainly not the only writer concerned with "something over and beyond our reality."[22] Unlike most of his peers, however, he still believes in at least the possibility of finding that something and achieving sublimity on both an individual and a collective level.

In his insistent call for action to find/create a Japanese sublime, Ōe may seem a lonely voice in modern Japanese literature. Yet his concerns clearly affect and inspire other writers. In a discussion between Tsuge Teruhiko and Wakamori Hideki on Murakami, Mishima, and Ōe, Tsuge mentions the three writers' need for mythic structures to serve as narrative frameworks for their novels.[23] Wakamori goes on to suggest that Murakami's *Hard Boiled Wonderland* is actually a response to Mishima's *Sea of Fertility*, which announced what Mishima considered to be the death of Japan. More broadly, Wakamori argues, "*Hard Boiled Wonderland* is a kind of response to the question of how do we live after the end of that world."[24]

While Wakamori's comment is acute, illuminating some of the generational differences between Murakami and older writers, it seems to me that *Hard Boiled Wonderland* emphasizes "the end of the world," not "how do we live." The older Ōe, however, still appears to see the end as a possible beginning. In the final volume of his trilogy, rival religious factions set upon Gii and kill him.[25] This ending, however, is not an invitation to despair. Unlike Mishima, whose dead protagonists leave the living only with a feeling of betrayal and emptiness, or Abe, whose characters survive in misery, and above all unlike Murakami, whose protagonists commit a sort of suicide to the outside world, Ōe gives us a vision of the outside world revitalized by the sacrifice of a body. The followers of Gii do not give up. Instead they cry out, "Rejoice."

NOTES

1. *The Economist* has a particularly interesting discussion of Ōe's role as a spokesman for the "new" Japan. Commenting that "there would hardly be a better symbol of Japan's intellectual change [than Ōe]," the journal mentions how in Ōe's Nobel acceptance speech "he spoke in English with smatterings of French, and paid tribute to *The Adventures of Huckleberry Finn,* George Orwell, and W. H. Auden." *The Economist* goes on to conclude: "The Orientalism of Kawabata is giving way to the universalism of Mr. Ōe. . . . Mr. Ōe aims to be a bridge. He is steeped in western literature and yet is self-consciously Japanese; he wants to graft his universalism on to Japan's insular past, producing something that is distinctively Japanese but free of obscure mysticism" (*Economist,* January 14, 1995, p. 19). *The Economist* is certainly correct in pointing to Ōe's "universalism." As this essay will attempt to show, however, although far from "obscure mysticism," there is a strongly spiritual side to Ōe as well.

2. Ōe Kenzaburō, *Japan, the Ambiguous, and Myself* (Tokyo: Kodansha International, 1995), p. 118. Ōe also sees himself as part of a more cosmopolitan literary tradition—the Western humanism of Yeats, Rabelais, and Blake.

3. Ibid., pp. 121-122.

4. Ōe Kenzaburō, "Japan's Dual Identity: A Writer's Dilemma," *World Literature Today* 62(3) (1988):363.

5. Ibid.

6. Ibid.

7. In recent literature, besides Murakami Haruki I would also cite Murakami Ryū and Yoshimoto Banana as seeking a highly contemporary sublime. In terms of animation and *manga* comics, I would offer Miyazaki Hayao and Otomo Katsuhiro, whose *manga* and animated films frequently show characters in search of some kind of transcendent experience.

8. Rob Wilson, "A Conversation with Ōe Kenzaburō," *Boundary 2* 20(2) (1993):4.

9. Ibid., p. 9.

10. Besides *Kōzui wa wagatamashii ni oyobi* and *The Day He Himself Shall Wipe My Tears Away* discussed in this essay, other notable works by Ōe containing apocalyptic elements include the 1976 *Pinchirannaa chōsho,* the 1982 *Reintsurii o kiku onnatachi* (Women Who Listen to the Raintree), and his two-volume science fiction work *Chiryōtō* and *Chiryōtōwa-kusei* (Tower of Healing and Tower of the Healing Planet), published in 1990 and 1991, respectively.

11. For a detailed discussion of the role of apocalyptic thinking in Japanese culture see my article, " 'It's the End of the World You Know': Images of Apocalypse in Japanese Culture," in Tina Pippin, ed., *Teaching Apocalypse* (Atlanta: Scholars Press, 1998).

12. Ōe Kenzaburō, *Hiroshima Notes* (Tokyo: YMCA Press, 1981), p. 23.

13. Ōe has been fascinated for over two decades by the notion of carnival and the revolt of the marginals found in the genre of Menippean satire as explored by Mikhail Bakhtin. This protean genre privileges the fantastic, the grotesque, and, most important, the notion of carnival as an almost mystical inversion of accepted reality in which the low are lifted above the rulers and protagonists are often sacrificed or martyred; see Mikhail Bakhtin, *Problems of Dostoevsky's Poetics* (Minneapolis: University of Minnesota Press, 1984), pp. 112–127. I see Ōe's novel *Kōzui wa wagatamashii ni oyobi* (The Floodwaters Have Come Unto My Soul) as a particularly brilliant example of modern-day Menippean satire. For an extensive discussion of Ōe's use of carnival and grotesque realism in relation to his reading of Bakhtin see Michiko Wilson, *The Marginal World of Ōe Kenzaburō: A Study in Themes and Techniques* (Armonk, N.Y.: Sharpe, 1986).

14. There is also a scene involving water in the "Hard Boiled" section of the novel. In this case the water is a fearsome flood threatening the protagonist and his female helper as they make their way through vast underground tunnels beneath Tokyo. This flood is therefore very different from the cleansing inundation in Ōe's novel. While Ōe's work posited a flood-induced rebirth on the surface of the earth, *Hard Boiled Wonderland's* flood, like the water in Abe's *Ark Sakura,* evokes only images of entrapment, darkness, and death.

15. Murakami's vision of what might be called an "internal apocalypse" is not unique to him. Robert Jay Lifton has examined case studies of schizophrenics, especially those traumatized in World War I, many of whom were profoundly affected by personal visions of the end of the world. Psychiatrists refer to this kind of inner disintegration as "soul murder." Lifton describes this kind of schizophrenic in the following terms, intriguingly reminiscent, I believe, of the split protagonist in *Hard Boiled Wonderland:* "At the ultimate level, his absence of connection beyond the self leaves him with the feeling that life is counterfeit, and that biological death is unacceptable and yet uneventful because psychic death is everywhere. This combination of radically impaired meaning and constant threat of annihilation is at the heart of the schizophrenic's imagery of the end of the world"; see Robert Jay Lifton, "The Image of 'The End of the World': A Psychohistorical View," in *Visions of Apocalypse: End or Rebirth?* ed. Friedlander et al. (New York: Holmes & Meir, 1985), pp. 151–165. While Murakami's "post-postwar" generation has hardly experienced a trauma close to either World War I or their parents' experiences in World War II, images of fragmented, dissociated selves occur not only in Murakami's fiction but in works by Banana Yoshimoto, Murakami Ryū, and Kono Taeko.

16. For a discussion of *Hard Boiled Wonderland and the End of the World* in relation to utopian and dystopian paradigms, see my *The Fantastic in Japanese Literature: The Subversion of Modernity* (London: Routledge, 1996).

17. For an in-depth discussion of Ōe in comparison with Mishima, see my *Escape from the Wasteland: Romanticism and Realism in the Works of Mishima Yukio and Ōe Kenzaburō* (Cambridge, Mass.: Harvard Council on East Asian Studies, 1991).

18. Sanroku Yoshida, "The Burning Tree: The Spatialized World of Kenzaburō Ōe," *World Literature Today* (1995): 6.

19. Lowry's vision of the Tree of Life was related to his interest in the mysticism of the Jewish cabala. As he explains it: "The Tree of Life which is its emblem [that of the cabala] is a kind of complicated ladder with Kether or Light at the top and an extremely unpleasant abyss some way above the middle"; Malcolm Lowry, quoted in Douglas Day, *Malcolm Lowry* (New York: Oxford University Press, 1973). Ōe became interested in Lowry, especially his novel *Under the Volcano,* about the time he was writing the "Raintree" stories, which ultimately became the 1982 book *Reintsurii o kiku onnatachi* (Women Who Listen to the Raintree).

20. Endō Shūsaku, quoted in *The Observer,* November 6, 1994.

21. Ōe Kenzaburō, quoted in *The Observer,* November 6, 1994.

22. Besides the writers mentioned in this essay I would suggest that in popular culture, as well, there are many artists searching for "something over and beyond our reality." Among the most interesting are two *manga* (comic book) and *anime* artists, Otomo Katsuhiro and Miyazaki Hayao. Otomo's 1980's *manga* serial and subsequent animated film *Akira* delineate a variety of searches for this "something," including psychic power and apocalypse. Miyazaki's works such as *Kaze no tani no Nausicaa* (Nausicaa of the Valley of the Wind) and *Tonari no totoro* (My Neighbor Totoro) present a variety of sublimes from postindustrial apocalypse to a Shintoesque vision of nature spirits.

23. Tsuge Teruhiko in Tsuge Teruhiko and Wakamori Hideki, "Shinka suru tekisuto," *Kokubungaku* 40(4) (1995):7.

24. Ibid., p. 8.

25. As Hirano Hidehisa points out, in some ways Ōe's trilogy "anticipates the tragic activities of the Aum Shinrikyo of the mid 1990's" (the group responsible for the Tokyo subway gas bombing incident); Hirano Hidehisa, "Ōe Kenzaburō," in *Japanese Fiction Writers since World War II,* ed. Van C. Gessel (Detroit: Bruccoli Clark Layman, 1997). Intriguingly, Murakami has written a nonfiction work on the gas bombings, consisting of interviews with the survivors, titled *Andaaguraundo* (Tokyo: Kōdansha, 1997).

2

THE ROAD TO THE RIVER: THE FICTION OF
ENDŌ SHŪSAKU

Van C. Gessel

Endō Shūsaku (1923–1996) was perhaps the most influential and popular Christian writer in postwar Japan. He was born in Tokyo but spent his early youth with his family in Manchuria, where his father was working for a Japanese bank. Taken back to Japan by his mother after she divorced her husband, Endō followed his mother's example and was baptized a Catholic at the age of eleven. Recurrent lung problems kept him from military service during World War II, but he was subject to taunts from his classmates for adhering to the enemy faith. After lackluster performance in secondary schools, Endō was able to gain admission to the French literature department at Keiō University after the conclusion of the war. His studies enabled him to become part of the first group of Japanese allowed to study overseas during the occupation. He spent over two years in Lyon, between 1950 and 1952, studying French Catholic writers, but a relapse in his lung condition forced him to cut short his stay and return to Japan. He completed his college work, married, and began his career as a literary critic. Soon, however, the literary success of some of his friends inspired him to write his own creative work, a novella titled *Shiroi hito* (White Men, 1955). Its companion piece, *Kiiroi hito* (Yellow Men, 1955), garnered Endō the Akutagawa Prize for new writers.

Most of Endō's early works examine the Japanese sense of moral guilt in contrast to that of the Christian West. *Umi to dokuyaku* (The Sea and

Poison, 1957; trans. 1972) documents the brutal vivisections Japanese doctors performed on captured American pilots during the war. In 1959, Endō wrote the first of many humorous novels that would gain him a wide following among Japanese readers. But his health took a dramatic turn for the worse in 1960, when he developed a severe case of pleurisy while traveling in Europe. He spent the next three years in Japanese hospitals and endured three major operations that ultimately left him with only one lung. Out of his physical and emotional pain came his greatest novel, *Chimmoku* (Silence, 1966; trans. 1969), which examines the tortures and faith of Japanese Christians in the early seventeenth century.

With improved health and the success of *Silence,* Endō became a prolific writer of "entertainment novels" that earned him the title "the Japanese Graham Greene" and became involved in many extraliterary activities, including the formation in 1968 of Kiza, the largest amateur theater company in Japan. He spent a time as editor of his alma mater's literary journal, *Mita Bungaku,* and in 1973 published his idiosyncratic biography of Jesus, called *Iesu no shōgai* (Life of Jesus; trans. 1979). A series of historical novels examining the lives of Japanese Christian warriors from the seventeenth century followed.

The next major serious novel, *Samurai* (The Samurai, 1980; trans. 1982), which earned him the Noma Prize, led to his election to the Geijutsuin, the Japan Academy of Arts, and played some role in his election as president of the Japan P.E.N. Club, where he served from 1985 to 1989. He received honorary degrees from three Catholic universities in the United States and in 1988 was named a Person of Cultural Merit by the Japanese government. His last two major novels were *Sukyandaru* (Scandal, 1986; trans. 1988) and the moving *Fukai kawa* (Deep River, 1993; trans. 1994), the publication of which raised speculation that he would be the next Japanese novelist to receive the Nobel Prize for literature. In 1995, as he was recovering from a stroke, Endō was awarded the highest cultural decoration of his country, the Bunka Kunshō (Order of Culture).

Other works that have been translated into English include *Obakasan* (Wonderful Fool, 1959; trans. 1974); *Kazan* (Volcano, 1960; trans. 1978); *Watashi ga suteta onna* (The Girl I Left Behind, 1964; trans. 1994); *Ryūgaku* (Foreign Studies, 1965; trans. 1989); and *Kuchibue o fuku toki* (When I Whistle, 1974; trans. 1979).

■

I have been attempting for some time now, mostly in vain, to argue that the Christian context is not the sole—and, in some ways, perhaps not the most valuable—framework in which to examine the novels of Endō Shūsaku. While I would not suggest for a moment that the Christian substance of Endō's writings is inconsequential, I think we will have pigeonholed an important writer if we look exclusively at the religious implications of what he has written. Unless we are content to stereotype Endō as a one-theme author, therefore, we must strip him of his title as the "Japanese Graham Greene," return him to the generation of Japanese writers to which he belongs, and examine his works as documents of the experience of a man who lived, like many others, through the intellectual suppression of the late thirties, the war, the defeat and occupation, and the attempts to rebuild Japanese society after the war without the benefit of spiritual roots. The fact that he emerged from that tortuous period as a Christian writer adds many layers of texture to his work, but it would be a mistake, I think, to dismiss the generational context in which he matured and learned the lessons of life that he would later view through the Christian lens.

Contemporary literary fashion rejects outright the familiar "life and works" approach adopted in so many dissertations on modern Japanese literature. The "life" of an author is a dead issue when it comes to studying the texts, the argument goes, and the "works" must stand on their own merits independent of the author's personal experience. Yet how are we to comprehend as rich and powerful a novel as Endō's *Chimmoku* (Silence, 1966; trans. 1969) if we examine it merely as a fictional recreation of the tortures of seventeenth-century Christians in Nagasaki? Is it utterly irrelevant to us as readers that Endō has identified himself so closely with the apostates of that era that he can publicly declare "Kichijiro is me"?[1] Is it none of our business, as independent interpreters of the novel, that Endō's personal struggles with his adopted faith are displayed on the pages of *Silence* and other works or that the manner in which his Christianity was draped over him, and the shame with which he wore his "foreign suit of clothes" during the war years, had a profound effect on the subjects he chose to write about, the way he wrote about them, and the manner in which he retailored that foreign suit to accommodate his rather gawky Japanese body?

At this point in my reading of Endō's novels, I find it impossible to separate the text from the author without doing major damage to the meanings of the texts. Not that the author's experience is the single key to interpreting the fiction, but a familiarity with that experience deepens the quality of the reading. I am increasingly persuaded that it is at least as important to remember that Endō was a member of the *senchū-ha,* the war generation, and that his wartime experience was dramatically defined by his affiliation with Christianity, as it is to consider the impact of his faith upon his writing. In searching for the roots of one of the dominant motifs in Endō's fiction—a rejection of all human institutions, which are depicted as enemies of the individual, destroyers of the weak, and obliterators of human feeling—it is far more instructive to look to the sentiments he shared with other *senchū-ha* survivors than it is to compare his attitudes with those of other Japanese Christians. The image of a maternal Christ that Endō painstakingly fashioned in his novels is, yes, a theologically charged response to the "paternal" Christianity of Europe; it is likewise, as Endō himself discovered in reading Etō Jun's writings on *Silence,* an idealized portrait of Endō's own mother, who brought him to Christianity; and it is, at the same time, an image of warmth, forgiveness, unconditional love, and compassion for the weak that must have appeared in the dreams of many terrified youths in Japan during the war years.

Tracing Endō's anti-institutional sentiments to his personal experience is not particularly taxing. Baptized a Catholic at the age of eleven in the mid-1930s at the insistence of his mother, Endō was, in essence, unconsciously beginning an inner journey in a direction very different from that which his native land was pursuing with its growing emphasis on ultranationalism and militaristic expansion. (It might be worthwhile to point out that he spent the years between the ages of three and ten with his family in Manchuria and had no memories of Japan until he returned there with his mother after her divorce.) Endō, of course, had no notion that he was choosing the Prince of Peace as though the adoption of Christianity were some form of protest against Japan's warmongering. But the taunts hurled at him by classmates during the war years would serve as one reminder that he was walking a path leading in a very different direction from those around him.

The *fumie* in *Silence*—that almost omnipresent reminder of human pain in the form of an image of Christ or Mary that suspected Christians were forced to trample upon to prove they had abandoned the foreign faith—must, in some respects, represent within the author's experience the unenviable choices that were forced upon him during the Pacific War. As one after another of his contemporaries was called up for military service, he was asked whether his own choice, when that day arrived, would be to serve Japan's divine emperor or to follow the enemy's God. It is not difficult to imagine the skepticism, fear, and distrust aroused in any young man—particularly a young man who had already persuaded himself that he was a physical coward—toward a country that demanded such choices be made by the weak of spirit.

And yet, in a country that has historically allowed its citizens a limited range of choices in moral matters, Endō did not have the ease of simply rejecting his bellicose nation and choosing the kingdom of his adopted God. Although Endō dealt little with the issue in his fiction,[2] his distrust of the church as an institution started during the war, when he thought the Catholic authorities in Japan had buckled under pressure from the government and compromised the purity of their teachings—particularly the prohibition on killing in the Sixth Commandment—by allowing Japanese Catholics to serve in the military. Pressured on the one hand by his political leaders and betrayed on the other by his spiritual teachers, Endō ultimately elected, I think, to create through his writing an image of a Christ stripped of ties to the powers of both earth and heaven, a Christ who can do nothing more than love, empathize, and forgive. It was an image that sustained Endō through the trials of the war years, the challenges of the postwar era (when he was anointed in 1950 to represent all Japanese Christians as the first Catholic exchange student to France), and the mounting dissatisfactions he felt with the direction Japanese society adopted—seeking riches before all else—during the period of economic recovery.

For a writer too easily dismissed by some as just another Pollyanna Christian author reeking of the rancid foreign smell of butter, there is an awful lot of depravity, despair, loss, and alienation in Endō's fiction. We would do well to remember—as we try to expand our definition of him so that he can be seen as both a Christian writer and a postwar writer—that the slender, faintly illuminated path toward faith and hope in his writings comes into view only momentarily— and only after we have passed through harrowing infernos of torture, betrayal, murder, and barbarity. How else can one explain the fact that Endō's attempts to understand the impact of Christianity on the Western world have been filtered through his almost too painstaking studies of the Marquis de Sade or the fact that his look at the Christian century in Japan is a focus, not upon the ranks of the faithful martyrs, but upon the cowardly apostates?

From the very beginning, Endō's novels examined with an almost morbid fascination the acts of human cruelty that would appear to the casual observer to give the lie to the very notion of a God that was clearly so important to Endō himself. His first novella, *Shiroi hito* (White Men, 1955), concerns itself with betrayal and torture in the French Resistance. Its companion piece, *Kiiroi hito* (Yellow Men, 1955),[3] once again turns on a betrayal within the Japanese church and concludes with the suicide of an apostate foreign priest. While *Yellow Men* is usually read as a Christian's condemnation of the Japanese preference for moral vagueness and situational morality—certainly Endō criticizes the characters in the novella who can commit crimes without suffering pangs of conscience—he is less than enthusiastic about the radiance of Western Christian dogmatism.

The Japanese Christians in *Yellow Men,* most of them apostates, claim to have "none of the grave, inflated concerns like an awareness of sin or of nothingness" that the foreigners have: "All we have is weariness—a profound weariness."[4] One young Japanese apostate, Chiba, becomes sexually involved with his cousin after leaving the church. To the foreign priest who tries to bring him back into the fold he says: "You white men are able to create tragedies and comedies in your lives. But for me the drama does not even exist. . . . I never had any idea what sin was. Or maybe it would be more accurate to say that I never had any sensitivity to sin."[5]

On the other hand, Endō portrays his Western apostates as suffering all the torments of hell their minds can conjure up. The only essential difference between apostates east and west is that the Japanese are able to avoid the perpetual stabs of conscience, while for Durand, a priest cast out for committing a mortal sin with a Japanese woman, his sense of guilt ultimately drives him to suicide. Kimiko, the Japanese woman who lives with the outcast priest, cannot understand the tragic drama he creates within his own mind: "Why can't you . . . forget about God? It would be better for you if you could forget. You gave up the church, didn't you? Then why is that the only thing that constantly weighs on your mind? Buddha, who would forgive you if you'd just utter his name, would be so much better."[6]

Hearing these words, Durand mutters to himself: "Today for the first time I understood the happiness of the stranger—of those, that is, who are strangers to God. I can't actually declare whether they are happy or not. But I feel at least that I have understood the secret of those narrow, murky eyes peculiar to the yellow race—eyes like Kimiko's, or that young man named Chiba who came by the other day. . . . They are eyes apathetic to God and to sin, eyes unmoved by death."[7] Durand becomes almost envious of the Japanese ability to remain numb to the hellish torments of sin. Just before he kills himself he declares:

> While I have rejected God, I cannot deny His existence. . . . And yet . . . the Japanese are able to handle everything without God. They are able to live with their ambiguity, showing no feeling for or interest in the church, in the torments of sin, in the yearning for salvation—in all the things we white men have thought to be the fundamental requirements to live as a human being. How can this be? How can this be?[8]

If Endō is to be labeled merely as a "Japanese Christian writer," the only convenient way to do so is to put the focus exclusively upon his condemnations of Japanese moral "ambiguity" compared with the all-too-clear prescriptions and proscriptions of Western Christianity. Many passages in his earliest writings can be cited to justify such a classification. But as the passages from *Yellow Men* I have quoted suggest, the focus of Endō's criticism is not directed solely toward the Japanese. There are indications, even in these early works of fiction, that Endō is uncomfortable not only with the shortcomings he sees in Japanese moral attitudes and that his writings do not lend themselves easily to appropriation by the Catholic Church to persuade the heathens of the wrongness of their ways. Certainly this pattern continues in his next major novel, *Umi to dokuyaku* (The Sea and Poison, 1957; trans. 1972), which, lest we be too easily taken in by the smiling image of Endō in television advertisements for Nescafé and Casio *kanji* calculators, is about vivisections performed in wartime Kyushu on captured American pilots. As proselytizing tracts proffering evidence that God moves in a mysterious way his wonders to perform, Endō's novels fail with nearly miraculous regularity.

By the time *Silence* comes along, we have become almost numbly immune to the tortures, betrayals, murders, and apostasies that fill its pages. Many readers, I suspect, are almost ready to dance on the face of the *fumie* themselves, if only that will bring us relief from a litany of barbarous acts that seem designed primarily to persuade us to curse God and die. Equally disturbing about this fabled book is the fact that, for readers of the English translation and the tiny flock of the faithful in Japan as well, the novel seems to have as a fundamental premise the necessity of crushing Western ideas about Christianity as a precondition for fashioning a regenerated faith in the Japanese setting.

Silence seems clearly to be yet another step along the path that Endō began walking with the publication of *Yellow Men* a decade earlier: a path that leads away from Japan's vague pantheism but at the same time in a different direction from the uncompromising self-assuredness of the West's clear-cut dogmatism. It is all too easy a matter for Westerners to sit back comfortably and read *Silence* as a cataloging of Japan's spiritual crimes. Not only do several characters in the novel give voice to the notion of Japan as a "mud swamp" that swallows up and transforms all foreign ideas, but the violence of the Japanese authorities (which we can look forward to seeing in all its horrifying visuality in Martin Scorsese's promised film version) is so strong a focus of the novel that its subtler messages are hidden away in the shadows.

I strongly suspect, though I am not now and have never been a Japanese reader myself,[9] that the tendency on the part of Japanese readers of the novel (who have, evidently, distorted the interpretation of *Silence* so badly that Endō felt it necessary a few years ago to break his own silence about the novel and collaborate in the production of a video to clarify his motives in writing) is to emphasize the manner in which Rodrigues, who comes bearing the rigid absolutism of Western Christianity on his back, is finally broken and submits to the "superior" values of the Orient. Such an interpretation must delight the purveyors of the myths about Japanese "uniqueness" and serve as a reaffirmation to many, including the American hippies of the 1960s and the 1990s, that the Eastern meditative tradition must be "in" because it is so "far out."

It seems doubtful, however, that *Silence* should be so blithely interpreted as yet another example of the Japanese penchant for importing foreign ideas, such as Christianity, and then subjugating them—not, ordinarily, through brute force but through the powers of transformation. The portions of the novel dealing with this transformative nature of indigenous Japanese culture owe something to the ideas expressed by Akutagawa Ryūnosuke in his 1922 story, "Kamigami no bishō" (The Smile of the Gods). In this work Akutagawa sets up a debate between Padre Organtino, a Catholic missionary who helped build the Nambanji Church in Kyoto in 1578, and an old man who represents the Japanese gods. In a manner that should make us suspicious of the motives governing the presentation of such debates by either Akutagawa or Endō, Organtino is depicted as an ignorant buffoon who is looking forward to the day when he can flee Japan and return to the comfort and safety of Lisbon,[10] while the old god is a veritable encyclopedia of knowledge about Japanese cultural interactions with "the foreign." The god argues that every alien cultural artifact—the writing system, the poetry, or the

43

philosophical ideas imported from China; the Buddhism and Confucianism brought over from the Asian continent; the Christian teachings brought by the "red-haired, long-nosed" fathers—will inevitably be transformed by the power of the Japanese gods "who witnessed the dawning of the world" and remade into something palatable to the Japanese. As he bids a ghostly farewell to Organtino, the old man warns: "What I want to tell you is that, of all those who have come to this land, like your Deus, not a single one of them has been victorious. . . . It may well be that your Deus himself will be transformed into a native of our land. China and India changed. The West too must change." [11]

In appropriating this argument in *Silence,* Endō employs the image of a butterfly trapped in a spider's web: its inner substance rotting while its outside appearance remains unchanged. The transformative power of the Japanese moral "mud swamp" is described in similar terms. Such vivid metaphors reinforce the interpretation that the passion of Rodrigues, as he follows in the footsteps of his Master, is relating essentially the same story: priest comes to Japan bearing foreign ideas, is trapped in the mud swamp of the land, and by trampling on the *fumie* is finally transformed by his encounter with the essence of Japanese spirituality and changes his own beliefs about Christ. It is worth noting, however, that Endō's own interpretation of the novel seems utterly apathetic toward the question of "which side wins" the battle between Christian absolutism and Japanese religious relativism. [12] While the surface drama of the novel—the portion that captures the most attention—may seem to focus on the larger question of whether Christianity or transformative pantheism will win the battle for souls in Japan, the activities in the shadows, among the weak and groveling, are of far greater significance to the novel's creator.

The high dramatic event in *Silence* is, of course, Rodrigues' struggle as he is seduced into stepping on the *fumie.* What lingers in the brain are the adroitly phrased debates that rage back and forth between a desperate Rodrigues and his chief tormentor and former mentor, the apostate priest Ferreira. The two of them, trained so effectively in the persuasive logic of proselytization, have a field day with one another, twisting reason and positing new arguments to vanquish the opponent. Both are in fine form. And though Rodrigues has been physically drained by his suspension in an odious pit, the battle of words seems to revive his sense of himself as a man called to convert the unbeliever.

But we must not forget the groans. Far more important in *Silence* than the question of whether the broken Ferreira or the soon-to-be-broken Rodrigues will emerge victorious in the verbal Crusades is the issue of those groans breaking the "silence," as if they were the voice of God attempting to break through the hard, egotistic shells of these two foreigners. While catechismic conflicts are being waged between the rational Western prelates, the common people are suffering. No theological debate that ignores the cries of the Japanese peasants moaning from the pit has any efficacy in the view of the human condition presented in Endō's fiction.

Therein lies the superlative (and powerfully Christian) irony of the novel—that in giving up himself by placing his foot on the face of Christ, Rodrigues is setting aside all the religious debates that lead only to conflict and is performing an act of compassion that will succor the weak and help bind the wounds of the suffering. By "losing his life" as a Catholic priest, Rodrigues has found the meaning of his mission to Japan, which is simply to make the lives of the humble and the powerless bearable. And the ultimate enemy to such a simple act of charity is none other than the institutions of the mundane world—the brutal Japanese government, the dogmatic church organization—that would grind individual sufferers under their feet in order to achieve their aims.

In this sense, the "Japanese" side does not win out over the "Western" side in *Silence*. The only winners are the losers who no longer care what the social instruments of oppression demand of them; their only concern is sharing the pain of others. This is not "simply" a Christian view but also a very *senchū-ha* sort of view of the human situation. In rejecting Japanese institutions—whether they choose, depending upon the climate of the times, to maim or merely to transform—as well as Western institutions—which come across in the novel as equally willing to persecute the individual who does not conform to their notion of what is right—Endō is as much a product of his experience during the war as he is of his religious conversion. Like others of his generation who have become writers and cast a cynical eye on the parade of "isms" that have captured the attention of the Japanese masses over the last several decades,[13] Endō seems unwilling to offer his unconditional allegiance to any. The path along which Endō proceeds in writing *Silence* becomes increasingly solitary as he turns his back on the two main sources of his heritage: the physical homeland of Japan that betrayed him with its ruthless warmongering and the spiritual homeland of the West that spawned Christianity and then betrayed the religion's ideals.

Viewed in retrospect through the lens of such novels as *Samurai* (The Samurai, 1980; trans. 1982) and Endō's last religious novel, *Fukai kawa* (Deep River, 1993; trans. 1994), *Silence* on one level certainly seems to be undertaking a dismantling of both the non-Christian society of the Japanese and the un-Christian society of foreign missionaries who came to Japan with colonializing attitudes and supercilious egos. Like the fascinating juxtaposition of Horikawa and Yoshihide in Akutagawa's "Jigokuhen" (Hell Screen, 1918; trans. 1948)—in which it soon becomes impossible to determine which of the protagonists is a more vile example of self-absorbed passion—in *Silence* it is often difficult to determine whether the enlightened heathens in the Japanese government or the naively pompous Catholic missionaries are the cause of the greater suffering among the simple peasants who have accepted Jesus as their new master.

Seen from that angle, *Silence* clearly points us in the direction that *The Samurai* leads us a few years later. No human institution, whether political or religious in intent, survives Endō's, shall we say, "vivisection." Church and government become no better than self-perpetuating bureaucratic monsters that thrive by trampling upon the individual. We almost find ourselves back in pre-Hobbesian days: the novel seems to suggest that a person could get along just fine in this world, realizing personal goals and finding sources of hope and consolation, were it not for all those social structures designed solely for the purpose of robbing him of everything. And Endō certainly seems catholic as he passes judgment on all human institutions, castigating Western and Japanese bureaucratic systems alike with equal venom. After dragging the envoys to Italy, desperately hoping for an audience with the pope that will help him achieve his selfish aims, Father Velasco meets with Cardinal Borghese, who in a voice tinged with sadness rejects Velasco's pleas to help the tiny flock of believers in Japan. Borghese comments: "If in searching for the one lamb the other sheep are exposed to danger . . . the shepherd has no choice but to abandon that lamb. It cannot be helped if one is to protect the organization." [14] Wherever they go, the characters in the novel hear the same message: "Protect the organization; sacrifice the one." When the envoys return to Japan after failing to accomplish their assigned mission, they are informed that, insofar as the government authorities are concerned, "something that was good four years ago has to be judged evil if it has no use today. . . . Government is as fierce as a battle. Wars can't be fought if a general has to worry about the private grief of his lance-corporals." [15] Advised by his patron to live "unobtrusively," Hasekura, the low-ranking samurai who has been sent on this journey against his will, mentally retraces the steps of his journey: "The wide world, the many countries, the great oceans. Yet no matter where they went, people were the same. Contentions raged everywhere and manipulation and intrigue were at work. That was the case in both the castle of His Lordship and the sectarian world of Velasco." [16] Endō's rejection of both native and imported institutions makes the closing martyrdoms of Hasekura and Velasco that much more poignant and that much more balanced. If nothing else, *The Samurai* offers a clue that Endō's intentions as a writer are not to bring the West to its knees but to hammer all human institutions into abject prostration.

What does all this have to do with Endō's generational background? If these scorched-earth activities have some object other than the conversion of the world to an apocalyptic Christian vision, what inspires and informs them? These questions bring me back to my original contention: that Endō has to be studied as a writer who passed through some of the same experiences as Yasuoka Shōtarō, Shimao Toshio, and many of those who now determine political and social orthodoxy for contemporary Japan. These are writers who have devoted much of their energies to a depiction of the disillusionment attending the experiences of war and defeat and the emergence of a spiritual wasteland in postwar Japan. In an interesting literary paradox, many of them focus upon the losses of the recovery period and the collapse of human relations in the shadows of the economic rebuilding.

Endō himself continued to detail the betrayals and losses of the war and postwar eras in his 1986 novel *Sukyandaru* (Scandal; trans. 1988). But I think his most compelling portrait of human alienation appears in *Deep River*. In this final literary testament, Endō focuses on five separate human tributaries that eventually flow into the Ganges, one of several rivers of his title. In separate chapters he traces the lives and experiences of these individuals and then, in the simple framework of his story, brings them all together as members of a Japanese tour group that is traveling to India to tour the Buddhist holy sites.

Fearing, perhaps, that readers both in Japan and the West might miss the allusion in his title if he called the novel simply *Fukai kawa*,[17] Endō glossed the Chinese characters with the phonetic symbols for "Diipu Ribaa." And in his epigraph to the novel he quotes from the Negro spiritual of that title: "Deep River, Lord: I want to cross over into campground." Despite all these efforts, one has to wonder how many readers in any language are familiar with the source of the quotation. Endō in essence adds a third layer of meaning to the words of the hymn. Just as the children of Israel wandering four decades through the wilderness sought their spiritual repose on the opposite banks of the River Jordan, the black slaves of the American South likewise yearned for release from their mortal trials. But for this latter group of the oppressed, salvation was not to be hoped for in this life: the Jordan had been transformed into the barrier separating mortality from the welcome comforts of paradise, where the lashes and torments of this life could no longer afflict the weary. In his capping layer of meaning, Endō transforms the river into the Ganges: the fountainhead of Asian spirituality and the source of respite for millions of suffering Hindus who make the final pilgrimage of their lives in order to liberate their souls from their mortal bodies on its banks. In his novel, Endō's main characters make both a physical and a spiritual journey—as does Hasekura in *The Samurai*—aimed at bringing them release from the deprivations and tortures of life in a world of conflict that has its origins in the egotistical clashes of institutional greed. In common with the wandering Jews and the shackled slaves, these characters share the yearnings expressed in the words of the spiritual: "Deep River: my home is over Jordan. Deep River, Lord: I want to cross over into campground."

Each of the five main characters in *Deep River* is a case study in loss and emptiness. Isobe, the first of the five to flow into the narrative (four of the five main characters in the novel have names relating to "water"), loses his wife to cancer early in the novel and has been so absorbed in his profession that he has nothing to cling to once she is gone. He becomes so desperate for a human tie that he begins to believe in his wife's dying words, which promise him that she will be reincarnated and beg him to search for her. A large part of his motivation for traveling to India is to seek out a young Indian girl who claims that she lived her previous life in Japan.

Mitsuko, the character given the most detailed attention in the narrative, is also the most alienated. She has lost faith in everything and in her despondency has succumbed to playing games with the lives of others—seeking out imitations of love and warmth and honest contact, sleeping with men she picks up in bars, volunteering at a local hospital but deep in her heart wishing she could strangle the miserable old women for whom she "cares." Having studied French literature at school, she likens herself to two of the most despairing characters she has encountered in her reading: Julien Green's Moïra and Mauriac's Thérèse. These two novels were, it is worth mentioning, highly influential on Endō's views of the function of religious literature. What makes Mitsuko the most interesting character in the novel is that, despite her almost consciously maintained isolation from others, one of the primary reasons she travels to India is to see and talk with a man she toyed with, humiliated, and then jilted in her college days. That man is Ōtsu, the religious bungler who shows up in virtually every Endō novel. Here Ōtsu, after a meaningless youthful sexual fling with Mitsuko that betrays his Catholic upbringing, decides after she abandons him that he must accept the inevitable embrace of his God and begin training for the priesthood. But just as he was despised and rejected by Mitsuko, so is he rebuffed by the foreign priests under whom he trains in Japan, in France, and later in Israel. Ōtsu is too pantheistically eager to find God in every phenomenon—too willing to locate traces of God's love in any religion and any human act of compassion, no matter how humble. Although he is finally ordained, he cannot find acceptance in any monastic order and ultimately winds up in Vārānasī, dressed like an outcast, carrying the bodies of the dead to the cremation grounds beside the holy river.

Two characters of lesser importance are Kiguchi, who saw all the horrors and degradation of human existence—including cannibalism—along the Highway of Death in Burma toward the end of the war,[18] and Numada, who has endured both separation from his loved ones and the pains of critical illness, finding his consolation in nature and his writing of children's stories about birds and dogs. The links between all these diverse characters are their shared feelings of hollowness, their separation from other people, their lack of hope. Beaten down by assaults from nature and from the institutions framed by human hands, they set out on their pilgrimages to India searching for something—anything—that will restore some glimmer of hope or even just *feeling* to their lives.

Characteristically, Endō denies them much consolation. As they proceed on their pilgrimage through India, the sights that greet them are only visions of illness, poverty, starvation, and death. Though ostensibly they have come to visit Buddhist holy sites, their Japanese tour guide, Enami, who knows both the profound and the horrifying faces of this womb of Asian civilization, leads them with almost perverse pleasure to see the statue of a Hindu goddess, Chāmundā. This goddess, almost the antithesis of the regal Virgin Mary in its abjectness, represents the forgiving, accepting Mother who endures all the burdens that mortality can heap upon her and who continues to suckle her offspring, knowing all the while that they, too, must suffer in this life. Enami takes his charges into a dark, steamy subterranean cavern and leads them to the image:

"This goddess is called Chāmundā. Chāmundā lives in graveyards. At her feet you can see human corpses that have been pecked by birds and devoured by jackals."

A large droplet of sweat from Enami's body coursed like a tear to the floor that was dappled with gobs of candle wax.

"Her breasts droop like those of an old woman. And yet she offers milk from her withered breasts to the children who line up before her. Can you see how her right leg has festered as though afflicted with leprosy? Her belly has caved in from hunger, and scorpions have stung her there. Enduring all these ills and pains, she offers milk from her sagging breasts to mankind."[19]

Chāmundā is clearly to be cataloged alongside other maternal images in Endō's fiction. And like the motherly Jesus he creates elsewhere, she has no power to respond to the various prayers and entreaties of these Japanese visitors. All she can do is embrace them and suffer along with them. The individual quests of the leading characters are, of course, frustrated. Isobe can never find the girl who is supposedly the reincarnation of his wife. Mitsuko is reunited with Ōtsu, but she can only shake her head at the pointless futility of his labors among the dying in India. Kiguchi is disappointed in his attempts to hold a memorial service to appease the tormented souls of his dead war comrades. Numada can never quite accept the duality of nature in India, with its combination of sweeping beauty and dank obscenity.

At the end of the novel, Ōtsu is attacked by a mob during the riots following the assassination of Indira Gandhi. Mitsuko, who has bought herself a sari and has been bathing in the Ganges, kneels helplessly over his broken body and watches while some Indian outcasts prepare to carry the critically wounded man to the hospital:

> "You're a fool. You're really a fool!" Mitsuko shouted as she watched them carry the litter away. "Really a fool! You've thrown away your whole life for this God of yours! Just because you've tried to imitate your God doesn't mean that this world full of hatred and egotism is going to change! You've been chased out of every place you've been, and now in the end, you break your neck and get carried away on a dead man's litter. When it comes right down to it, you've been completely powerless!"
> Crouched to the ground, she pounded her fists futilely on the stone steps.[20]

Mitsuko seems to recognize that her words are reflected back onto her own meaningless life as much as she wants them to apply only to Ōtsu. By this point in the novel she must sense the enormous gap separating her "imitations of love," which have only hurt others, and Ōtsu's earnest but, yes, ultimately powerless acts of selflessness on behalf of total strangers.

Mitsuko's feeling of frustration is shared by virtually every character in *Deep River*. Endō spares no one and makes no attempt to mute his characters' desperation and impotence. He suggests that the human condition will never improve and that human life will inevitably flow toward the final act of separation— death—which provides the welcome and only true release from human complicity in acts of inhuman cruelty. Once again we are reminded of the novel's title and epigraphic reference to the slaves' hymn and the yearning to "cross over into campground" on the opposite banks of the river. Whether the human undertaking is the nurturing of family, the earning of a living, the seducing of the simple, the waging of war, the writing of literature—in the end, it makes no difference what the involvement is. When the conflict has ended, all those activities converge into the flow of the deep river.

It is worth noting, I think, that all five protagonists in this novel belong to the same generation, the *senchū-ha,* or war generation. And all share not only their wartime experiences but also their contempt for younger Japanese, their distrust for any political or moral philosophy, whether of native or foreign origin, and their inability to define the sources of their own feelings of debilitating emptiness. They all, in a way, long for an answer or two in their lives, but they have despaired of finding any and now long only to pass into the peace of oblivion.

Near the end of the novel Isobe, drowning himself in alcohol to diminish the agony of losing his wife, sits alone on the banks of the Ganges:

Every once in a while, the sound of tumult echoed from the city. . . . [For] Isobe, who had lived through the war and postwar periods in Japan . . . , the vague feeling that he could never believe in anything had come to rest permanently at the bottom of his heart. He had ultimately got along well with everyone in his company, but he had not been able to believe sincerely in any of them. He had learned through experience that egoism resided in the hearts of every individual, and that a man's insistence on his own good intentions and the propriety of his actions was merely an attempt to gloss over his egoism. He had tried to live an unassuming life himself, tempered by his understanding of human nature.

But now that he was all alone, he had finally come to understand that there is a fundamental difference between being alive and truly living. And though he had associated with many other people while he was alive, he had to admit that the only two people he had truly formed a bond with in his life were his mother and his wife.

"Darling!" Once again he called out toward the river. "Where have you gone?"

The river took in his cry and silently flowed away. But he felt a power of some kind in that silvery silence. Just as the river had embraced the deaths of countless people over the centuries and carried them into the next world, so too it picked up and carried away the cry of life from this man sitting on a rock on its banks.[21]

What makes *Deep River* a moving record of Endō's own generational inability to accept any school of dogmatic conviction is the novel's ultimate rejection of Christianity's presumed monopoly on truth. Not even his own faith, fashioned through much effort in his earlier novels, is able to overcome Endō's inherent refusal to place his trust in anything other than the certainty that all human undertakings will fail and that the only true strength lies in weakness. Like the Ganges itself, Endō reaches out in this novel to embrace the fragile significance of any human being who can suffer on behalf of another. He offers a memorable, sharply etched portrait of selfless service in *Deep River* in the form of a cowed but determined priest who has fallen from favor among his brethren. That priest, of course, is Ōtsu, a man who, like the Jesus he worships, has been rejected by his comrades and who concludes that the only thing of any worth in a world like ours is the performance of an act of abject love. The picture of a spurned Catholic priest dressed in rags and wandering the streets of Vārānasī to pick up the bodies of beggars and carry them to the funeral pyres is almost unbearably powerful:

Ōtsu's chappals slapped along the stone pavement soiled with filthy water and dog droppings, then came to a stop. At his feet, an old woman leaning against a wall peered up at Ōtsu. Hers were eyes bereft of feeling, like the eyes of the cow that had looked at him and then sauntered away. Her shoulders heaved as she panted for breath. Crouching down, Ōtsu took from the bag on his shoulder an aluminum cup and a bottle filled with water.

"*Pāni. Pāni.*" He gently encouraged the woman. "*Āp mērē dost hain.*" Water. Water. I am your friend.

He placed the aluminum cup to her tiny mouth and slowly poured the water in, but it merely moistened her chin and soaked the tattered clothing that wrapped her body. In a faint voice she muttered:

"*Gangā.*" The Ganges.

When she spoke the word Gangā, a look of entreaty flickered in her eyes, and finally a tear flowed down.

Ōtsu nodded, and in a loud voice asked, "*Tabiyat kharāb hai?*" Do you feel ill? "*Koyi bat nahin.*" There is no need to fear.

From his bag he took an Indian-style sling he had woven from rope, wrapped her frail body in it, and lifted her on to his back.

"*Gangā.*" With her body resting on his shoulders, the old woman repeated the word over and over in a weeping voice.

"*Pāni chahiye?*" Do you want to drink of the waters? Ōtsu responded as he began to walk.

By now the morning light had begun to trickle into the city, as if to suggest that God had finally noticed the sufferings of man. Shops opened their doors, and flocks of cows and sheep, the bells around their necks tinkling, crossed the streets. Unlike Japan, here no one gave Ōtsu a strange look as he passed by with the old woman on his back.

How many people, how much human agony had he taken on his shoulders and brought to the River Ganges? Ōtsu wiped away the sweat with a soiled cloth and tried to steady his breathing. Having only a fleeting connection with these people, Ōtsu could have no idea what their past lives had been like. All he knew about them was that each was an outcast in this land, a member of an abandoned caste of humanity.

He could tell how high the sun had climbed from the intensity of the light that struck his neck and back.

O Lord, Ōtsu offered up a prayer. *You carried the cross upon your back and climbed the hill to Golgotha. I now imitate that act.* A single thread of smoke already was rising from the cremation grounds at the Manikarnikā Ghāt. *You carried the sorrows of all men on your back and climbed the hill to Golgotha. I now imitate that act.*[22]

As has been the case with many of the Christian literary images Endō has embedded within his narratives, it is likely that few of his non-Christian Japanese readers detected the symbolic codes packed into this passage. The offering of water as a gift of life is perhaps a universally recognizable image, but the connection with Christ as the "living water" is less self-evident. The links between the waters and the names of the characters or the waters and the Ganges are, of course, obvious. When Ōtsu asks the old woman "Do you want to drink of the waters?" the kind of salvation he offers seems to bear more than a single meaning. The light of morning begins to illuminate the many scenes of agony that litter the streets beside the ghat, "as if to suggest that God had finally noticed the sufferings of man." And certainly the depiction of Ōtsu hoisting the dying woman onto his back and carrying her to her final resting place is, as he himself recognizes, reminiscent of Jesus bearing the cross to the spot where his passion reached its culmination.

But the light that shines faintly in the morning does not linger for long. It is the world of reality—or brutality, as Endō might have it—that is depicted in the novel, and each glimmer of light is quickly supplanted by a scene of darkness. After Ōtsu is carted off to a leper's hospital, his neck broken, the Japanese tourists pack their bags and prepare to flee from this incredible misery they have paid good money to view. They seem almost heartless as they scurry to catch their flight back to Japan, more than ready to get back to "civilization." Even at the airport they cannot escape depressing images. An old woman is leaning against a wall, yellow foam spurting from her mouth. Two nuns from Mother Teresa's Home for the Dying rush to aid the dying woman, and in response to Mitsuko's query as to why they bother (she still seems to miss the point of her experience), a nun responds innocently: "Except for this . . . there is nothing in this world we can believe in."[23] Mitsuko has difficulty hearing the nun and wonders whether she has actually said "except for this" or "except for him."

And yet the final line of the novel throws us back into our uncertainty about whether *anything* is worth the effort. Enami phones the hospital to inquire about Ōtsu's condition, and the novel ends with his report: "He's in critical condition. About an hour ago he took a sudden turn for the worse."[24] In Endō's literary world, things seem always to be taking "a sudden turn for the worse." The gentle and kind can never quite overcome the violent and the foul; love never quite seems to conquer selfishness. Whether Ōtsu lives or dies, his life will have been a pathetic example of one who chose the path of the weakling, the "imitations of Christ" rather than the "imitations of love" by means of which Mitsuko repeatedly attempts to anesthetize her conscience.

Perhaps at the end of the novel, Ōtsu stands on the banks of a river gazing longingly toward the other shore. Perhaps he realizes that his home—the only place where he can belong and find acceptance—lies, as it did for the slaves who sang of Jordan, in a world other than this one. Judging from the thrust of the narrative in *Deep River,* it may be that all who attempt to bring maternal understanding and love into this vicious world must be annihilated: the suffering goddess Chāmundā; Indira Gandhi, eulogized as the "Mother of India"; Christ, whose love is defined in Endō's cosmology as that of a forgiving Mother; and Ōtsu, whose only wish is to imitate the acts of the man he follows. Each of them is brutalized. And in *Deep River* each becomes a confluent segment of this narrative of human life as the Ganges takes everything into its embrace and carries it into the next world. There is, no doubt, a quiet hope in that notion. But it is a hope that is like the bubbles on the surface of the river: they are not the first to attract our notice, nor are they the part of the river that will last the longest. All that remains after the tumult is merely the river: the deep river that takes into its flow every good act, as well as evil, delivering them to the peaceful, embracing ocean.

A little over a year after *Deep River* was published in Japan, rumors spread through Europe that Endō was a serious contender for the 1994 Nobel Prize in literature. Since the award to Kawabata Yasunari in 1968 was the only time a Japanese had received such international recognition, speculation was high that Japan's turn had again come around. On the eve of the announcement of the newest recipient on October 13, 1994, a cluster of Japanese reporters gathered outside Endō's apartment in the heart of Tokyo, waiting for him to emerge after the announcement to accept their congratulations and give them a pithy quote for their morning editions. Then came the announcement that a Japanese novelist had indeed won the Nobel Prize. The recipient was none other than Ōe Kenzaburō, a self-proclaimed enemy of Endō's and a highly politicized writer, a man thirteen years Endō's junior with only three novels available in English translation.

The Japanese reporters, before racing off to Ōe's residence, decided they must get a quote from Endō about his victorious archrival and demanded that he come outside and utter something fit for publication. Endō, nearly seventy-two years old and very frail from a lifetime of ill health, emerged from his apartment leaning on his cane, no doubt disappointed and less than eager to have tape-recorders and microphones thrust in his face. Nobel Laureate Ōe Kenzaburō, said Endō, is a superb novelist who writes about "the search for salvation in a world without God."

For what must have been a spur-of-the-moment reaction to unwelcome news, the remark says a great deal about Ōe and the fundamental ways in which Endō differs from him. Ōe does in fact write about the hope for salvation—but his is a salvation that comes from making courageous political choices, not from decisions to follow God. Ōe assaults his readers verbally and morally to awaken them from their nihilistic apathy, and he embraces an existential assurance that the only meaningful action in a world bereft of God involves protest against the ruling order. In Endō's literature, too, the "ruling order" is an enemy to be confronted, but Endō holds out little hope that the individual will win in that confrontation. His pessimism derives largely, I think, from his experiences as a member of the Japanese war generation. But salvation in Endō's cosmology is "not of this world." His characters carry their burdens and sorrows upon their backs as they stagger toward the river—toward death, toward God—knowing that the world will never let up in its assaults.

And so, for me, the image of Ōtsu standing alone and unheeded on the banks of the Ganges, performing his silent acts of service, is easily interchanged with an image of Endō himself, an isolated voice in the Japanese literary "world" who did not live long enough to receive the same accolades as his colleagues who write of existence without God. No bells will toll for such a writer. But Endō might have preferred it that way. His entire literary career was an attempt to create characters that could capture a portion of the reflection of Christ: the portion that rejected the glories this world has to offer and was, in turn, rejected by them. Perhaps, with no bells tolling in our ears to drown out the whispers of those who suffer all around us, we are in a better position to hear the voice of God breaking the silence, urging us to reach out to help, but to expect no rewards, at least on this side of the river. This is the image of Christ I have seen and heard in Endō's literature; and this, for me, has been the reward of studying his work.

NOTES

1. Endō made this comment at a symposium held at John Carroll University on May 18, 1991. The symposium, titled "Silences and Voices," was held the day before Endō received an honorary doctorate degree from the university. Following presentations given by Michael Gallagher, Van C. Gessel, and J. Thomas Rimer, Endō offered a response. In the question period, he was asked by a member of the audience why the American critics of his work put such weight on the apostate character of Kichijiro. In a moving reply, Endō stated: "To answer simply, Kichijiro is me. Kichijiro's weaknesses are my weaknesses. I loved Kichijiro as I created him." The conference proceedings were published in *Journal of the Association of Teachers of Japanese* 27(1) (April 1993): 57–89.

2. One prominent exception where this issue comes to the forefront is *Onna no isshō: Sachiko no baai* (Tokyo: Asahi Shimbunsha, 1982).

3. I know of at least two unpublished translations of this novella; one was done by Linda K. Keehan, the other by Gary Stoneman. For the purposes of this essay I have done my own translations of the passages cited.

4. Endō Shūsaku, *Kiiroi hito* (Tokyo: Shinchōsha, Shinchō Bunko, 1960), p. 87. This "profound weariness" was cited by Murakami Hyōe as a fundamental characteristic of the Japanese *senchū-ha*.

5. Ibid., p. 86.

6. Ibid., pp. 129–130.

7. Ibid., p. 130.

8. Ibid., p. 148.

9. Much less was I a Japanese left-wing college student in the sixties, the group that turned *Silence* into a best-seller in Japan. Evidently they saw in the novel a metaphorical depiction of the tortures and false confessions their spiritual predecessors in Japan, the Marxists of the 1930s, had had to endure in the *tenkō* phenomenon when so many leftists were tortured or even killed as the government attempted to enforce an "intellectual conversion" upon them.

10. In reality, Organtino became quite conversant in Japanese language, history, and culture and among the padres of the Christian century was one of the most insistent that the Japanese were, in all ways but their religious beliefs, superior to Europeans. He dressed like a Japanese and urged the other priests in Japan to adapt themselves to Japanese ways "in everything as much as possible." He was much beloved by his Japanese converts. See Neil

S. Fujita, *Japan's Encounter with Christianity: The Catholic Mission in Premodern Japan* (New York: Paulist Press, 1991).

11. Akutagawa Ryūnosuke, "Kamigami no bishō," *Akutagawa Ryūnosuke zenshū,* 12 vols. (Tokyo: Iwanami Shoten, 1977), 5:187.

12. I base this interpretation on Endō's comments in the video titled "Haha naru mono —Ningen no dōhansha" (Mothers—companions to mankind) and on any number of conversations I have had with him or overheard.

13. One well-known example is Endō's contemporary, the late Yoshiyuki Junnosuke, who wrote: "During the war, I couldn't bring myself to sacrifice my life for the sake of any single philosophy, even if its ideals might be realized at some point in the future. Many willingly made the sacrifice, but the very thought repelled me. . . . Communism enjoyed a great wave of popularity shortly after the war. . . . But the innate resistance I felt toward that philosophy was the same resistance I had felt toward the militarism of the war years. I could not bear the thought of putting on another uniform when I had just taken off the previous one and thereby liberated my individuality"; *Watakushi no bungaku hōrō* (Tokyo: Kōdansha, Kōdansha Bunko, 1976), pp. 26–27.

14. Endō Shūsaku, *The Samurai,* trans. Van C. Gessel (New York: Harper & Row/Kodansha International, 1982), p. 193.

15. Ibid., pp. 236–237.

16. Ibid., p. 245.

17. In a conversation Endō made it very explicit to me that as he was writing he kept in mind not only his Japanese readers but also the readers in the West who would read *Deep River* in translation. This statement contrasts sharply with the comments Ōe Kenzaburō made both before and after receipt of the Nobel Prize, to the effect that he writes only for his contemporaries in Japan. The conversation *(taidan)* between Endō and myself has been published in *Endō Shūsaku to Shusaku Endo* (Tokyo: Shunjūsha, 1994), pp. 88–120; see p. 116 for this comment.

18. Kiguchi is the only one of the five main characters whose name does not include some suggestion of water. One is prompted to wonder whether the horror of his wartime experience has drained him of all redemptive moisture, leaving him parched. The water imagery, of course, ties the characters to the Ganges but surely also is intended as a link to the biblical description of Christ as the "living water."

19. Endō Shūsaku, *Deep River,* trans. Van C. Gessel (London: Peter Owen, 1994), pp. 139–140.

20. Ibid., p. 212. I have made a minor change from the published translation for the sake of clarity. In the novel, Mitsuko at one point tells Ōtsu she is tired of hearing about God; since Ōtsu cannot stop talking about God, however, he suggests they come up with a name acceptable to her, and they agree upon *tamanegi,* an onion. Taken out of context, the conversation quoted would be ludicrous, so I have replaced "onion" here with "your God."

21. Ibid., pp. 188–189.

22. Ibid., pp. 192–193.

23. Ibid., p. 215.

24. Ibid., p. 216.

3

TEMPORAL DISCONTINUITY IN THE
ATOMIC BOMB FICTION OF HAYASHI KYŌKO

Davinder L. Bhowmik

Hayashi Kyōko established her career as an atomic bomb writer with the publication of her 1975 autobiographical novella *Matsuri no ba* (Festival Place). This Akutagawa Prize winning work presents a painfully detailed account of August 9, 1945, and the two months that follow in the forever bifurcated life of a fourteen-year-old first-person narrator who experienced the bombing at a Nagasaki munitions factory, 1.4 kilometers from ground zero. Although the bombing is the story's central event, Hayashi weaves in bits and pieces of news, medical and scientific data, and personal history, making a narrative about a single moment in the past extend indefinitely toward an unknowable future. Frequent temporal shifts and a strong sense of continuity, both positive and negative, lie at the heart of Hayashi's atomic bomb fiction. Due to the tenacious hold the disaster has had on her life and her writing, Hayashi has called herself the reciter of the atomic bombing of Nagasaki *(hachigatsu kokonoka no kataribe)*.

Born in 1930 in Nagasaki, Hayashi moved before her first birthday to Shanghai, where her father, an employee of Mitsui Trading Company, was posted. Together with her parents and three sisters Hayashi enjoyed a comfortable life in cosmopolitan Shanghai until the spring of 1945, when anti-Japanese hostilities escalated, forcing the family to evacuate. Hayashi's fourteen years of relative peace and tranquility in China ended with her return to Japan in March 1945. In order to attend Nagasaki Girls High School, she boarded in Nagasaki while her mother and sisters lived in Isahaya, 25 kilometers to the east. As a member of the student mobilization program, Hayashi was assigned to a munitions factory along with 323 of her classmates. When the bomb exploded on August 9, 1945, Hayashi was inside the factory. She suffered no major external injuries but experienced severe radiation sickness for two months and has since remained in frail health. After graduating from high school, Hayashi briefly enrolled in nursing school, went to Tokyo in 1951, and married a newspaper reporter with whom she had a son. Now divorced, Hayashi lives alone in Zushi, a resort town near Kamakura.

Hayashi's writing career began in 1962 when she joined authors such as Nakagami Kenji and Tsushima Yūko in the coterie magazine *Bungei Shuto* (Literary Capital). Since the critical acclaim of *Matsuri no ba*, Hayashi's fiction and essays have regularly appeared in Japan's leading literary journals. Much of her fiction is autobiographical, inspired largely from her experience as a *hibakusha* (atomic bomb survivor) or from memories of her childhood in Shanghai. Hayashi's three major atomic bomb works are her novella *Matsuri no ba* (Festival Place, 1975), the short story collection *Giyaman biidoro* (Cut Glass, Blown Glass, 1978), and the full-length novel *Naki ga gotoki* (As If Nothing Happened, 1981). Hayashi's important Shanghai works are the short story collection *Missheru no kuchibeni* (Michelle's Lipstick, 1980) and *Shanhai* (Shanghai, 1983), a nonfiction book of essays.

■

The writings of Hayashi Kyōko primarily concern the atomic bombing of Nagasaki and its aftermath. Hayashi was born in Nagasaki and was present at its destruction on August 9, 1945. A striking feature of Hayashi's atomic bomb works is the commingling of past and present within her narratives: although these writings typically focus upon the devastating moment of the bombing and the ensuing confusion, these past events are then generally coupled with facts or incidents from the narrative present. The juxtapositions in time are patently evident, even jarring at times, yet the temporal discontinuity that characterizes Hayashi's writing does not disorient the reader. On the contrary, the glaring gap between past and present in Hayashi's narratives offers a harrowing view of the nuclear-threat-filled world that, we often forget, we inhabit. Behind Hayashi's narrative device of revealing the past while simultaneously alluding to the present lies a sense of urgency. Hayashi's own position regarding the past is that its distance from the present is problematic.[1] This distance creates a strained relationship between past reality and a literary representation of the past. The deep abyss that separates past from present keeps Hayashi, a most prolific writer of atomic bomb themes, from putting her pen down.

Hayashi's wartime experience began in Shanghai long before the bombing of Nagasaki. As a young girl, Hayashi witnessed atrocities—in both China and Japan—that she would never forget. In her essay "Shanhai to hachigatsu kokonoka" (Shanghai and August Ninth) she observes the following about her writing: "When I write about August Ninth or Shanghai . . . I want to guard those moments in time and forever protect their purity . . . , but it is difficult to resist the movement of time. The more relentlessly I write about myself in the midst of those times, the more those events are changed by the illumination of the present."[2] One of Hayashi's concerns as a writer of atomic bomb fiction is that the passage of time makes human memory malleable. In her writing she strains to resist the distortions that time effects by augmenting her stories with historical facts, scientific data, shifting points of view, and interjections of the present. As problematic as time is for Hayashi, however, what finally makes her writing successful is the conspicuousness of time in her atomic bomb narratives. Hayashi tells her stories of the past while rooting them securely in the present.

Three atomic bomb narratives—the novella *Matsuri no ba* (Festival Place,[3] 1975), a collection of thematically related short stories entitled *Giyaman biidoro* (Cut Glass, Blown Glass, 1978), and Hayashi's first full-length novel, *Naki ga gotoki* (As If Nothing Happened, 1981)—demonstrate how Hayashi employs time in her writing. These works have established her as a leading contemporary writer of atomic bomb fiction in Japan. Hayashi began her career as a writer in 1962 with contributions to the coterie journal *Bungei Shuto*. Among her literary colleagues in this enterprise were Nakagami Kenji and Tsushima Yūko, two distinguished contemporary writers.[4] Hayashi's first published work was titled "Aoi michi" (Blue Road, 1962). Because of her responsibilities as a mother and wife,

Hayashi published little between her debut and her seventh piece, *Ritual of Death,* the work that brought her fame when it was published in 1975. She received the Gunzō Prize for new authors in April 1975 and three months later won the Akutagawa Prize, Japan's most coveted literary award. Both prizes were for *Ritual of Death.* While one may argue that the profusion of literary prizes in Japan results in accolades for less than finally remarkable works, for *Ritual of Death* to win the Akutagawa Prize was notable—the first time an atomic bomb work was so richly awarded.[5]

Hayashi has called herself "the chronicler of August Ninth" *(hachigatsu kokonoka no kataribe),* and it is by this cognomen that she is known in the literary establishment.[6] She has secured her place in Japanese letters as a firmly seated second-tier writer by publishing innumerable stories and essays about the atomic bombing in Japan's most prominent literary journals, such as *Gunzō, Bungakukai,* and the quarterly arts issues of *Chūō Kōron.* Hayashi continues to write about Nagasaki, as well as Shanghai. More recently, family issues stemming from her divorce, the death of her father, and the aging of her mother have become themes in her work.

By 1975, when Hayashi received awards for *Ritual of Death,* many other writers had written about the devastation that visited Hiroshima and Nagasaki. Some of the more noteworthy works were Hara Tamiki's *Natsu no hana* (Summer Flowers, 1947), Ōta Yōko's *Han-ningen* (Half-Human, 1954), and Ibuse Masuji's *Kuroi ame* (Black Rain, 1966). The atomic bomb was already an established theme, but Hayashi added a new dimension by introducing a fourteen-year-old's viewpoint of a disaster so total that it ended her days of innocence and made her cynical beyond her years. Adolescence, an emotionally charged and trying period under ordinary circumstances, was undoubtedly more painful for Hayashi. The intensity of the age was compounded by feelings of guilt for surviving when many of her classmates had died. Survivor guilt, a theme that infuses the texts of other atomic bomb writers, appears in Hayashi's works as well.[7] In addition to presenting a penetrating vision of irreversibly altered youth to the genre of atomic bomb literature, Hayashi makes the residual effects of radiation in survivors and their children a matter of great consequence in her narratives. Beginning with *Ritual of Death,* this theme of the never-ending taint of radiation is a perpetual motif in Hayashi's atomic bomb works. Nuclear contamination manifests itself in the works through recurring references to blood and the fear of blood, children and the fear of bearing children, and—most important for the purposes of this essay—time and the expressed fear that "time equals oblivion."[8]

At this point a brief account of recent critiques of historicism and their impact on our conceptions of time is essential. Theorists of late have brought to our attention certain assumptions about history. These views presume that time is synonymous with historical time. History is inextricably linked with time, and time with narrative. A characteristic aspect of the narratives that inform our lives is the convention of historical time, a convention that is inspired by a major, generally unexamined article of cultural faith: the belief in a temporal medium that is neutral and homogeneous and therefore permits the mutually informative measurements between one historical moment and another that support most forms of knowledge in the West.

In *Sequel to History: Postmodernism and the Crisis of Representational Time,* Elizabeth Deeds Ermarth writes: "History has become a commanding metanarrative, perhaps *the* metanarrative in Western discourse."[9] She argues, further, that history may be the West's greatest modern product and that the medium of historical time is a construct and itself "a representation of the first magnitude."[10] Although exhaustive critiques of Western metaphysics and its discourses have been made in recent years, historical time is one construct that has remained incompletely theorized.[11] The subject of time has been addressed in new ways by theorists from Heidegger to Kristeva, but in most current literary and philosophical studies time is still discussed in the same terms employed by Western scholars in the seventeenth century.

For hundreds of years historical time, owing to its links between past and future, has resulted in the preeminence of linear development. The modern idea of history—with its view of time as a neutral, homogeneous medium where mutually informative measurements can be made between past, present, and future—offers but a single-point perspective. All relationships are explained in terms of a common horizon. The historical conventions of temporality assert the fundamental and powerful idea that the neutral medium of experience, which extends to infinity and opens to an individual mind the vast power of generalization, is a product of consensus.[12] This historical consciousness that allows for the formation of generalizations and universal laws makes its way into narratives in the figure of the omniscient narrator who tells the past and intimates the future for the passive reader.

In "Women's Time," Julia Kristeva describes historical time as "totalizing" in its broad sweep and "totalitarian" toward what it excludes as "nonessential or even nonexistent."[13] Kristeva is one of a group of theorists who are endeavoring to reformulate ideas about time. In *Modern Fiction and Human Time: A Study in Nar-*

rative and Belief, Wesley A. Kort couples his (re)vision of time with such musical metaphors as rhythm, polyphony, and melody. Kort posits that narrative time is composed of these three instrumental elements, although a principal pattern emerges in any given text.[14] In her study of time, Ermarth demonstrates how postmodern narrative language undermines historical time and replaces it with a new construction of temporality she identifies as rhythmic time.[15] The workings of time as presented in these new formulations are perceived to be more complex than the unrelenting linearity of historical time. The visual images frequently associated with historical temporality—train tracks and roads—give way to the nonvisual metaphor of rhythm in recent constructions of alternative forms of temporality.

In historical time the present is continually forsaken for the future. Rhythmic time, with its emphasis on recurrent temporal alterations, restores the present. In narrative, rhythmic time allows each moment its own definition. Time is no longer neutral or indefinite. Moments regain their significance because the present is no longer dematerialized. Narratives in which rhythmic time figures prominently are filled with events and nonevents that follow no predetermined order. Associations between the past and present are many; linear plotting is minimal. Language in these narratives is less syntactic than paratactic; that is, rather than marching inexorably forward, narration swings to and fro, juxtaposing discontinuous temporal moments. Rhythmic time is a more natural medium for narration because its discontinuities resemble the processes of human thought. Memory, triggered by sensation, lets in startling discontinuities between past and present, offering to the consciousness the old as new. Memory is nonuniform and dynamic in its ordering, as is rhythmic time.

The totalizing nature of historical time so unsettling to Kristeva was noted much earlier by the surrealists, who frequently made time obsession the subject of their paintings. Salvador Dali's *Persistence of Memory,* with its melting timepieces, is perhaps the most famous example. Less well known is René Magritte's *Time Transfixed,* in which a railroad train charges full steam out of a fireplace. The yoking of two contrasting images is shocking; but more disturbing, from the surrealists' view, is the idea of time moving relentlessly forward. Thus the train —surely the most recognizable modern metaphor for time—is thrown off its track. Precision and progress come screeching to a halt. The surrealists are joined today by theorists who strive to formulate new alternatives for a temporality that will similarly derail historical time.

Trains and timepieces, products that link synchronicity and mechanics, are superseded in sophistication by the atomic bomb—this century's mechanical juggernaut. In narratives that make the atomic bombing their theme, an author's words are overshadowed by the herculean power of the bomb. The sheer force of the bombing and its effects cannot be mitigated, but in writing about it an author can elect to subvert historical time with its twin limitations of neutrality and transcendence. In Hayashi's atomic bomb stories, rhythmic time, not historical time, serves as the medium of narration. The substitution of this new alternative temporality in the place of historical time undermines the omnipotence of the atomic bomb, at least in narrative.

Contemporary works have new realities with which to contend: writers must represent the devastating horrors of the twentieth century without recourse to concepts such as "dignity" and "humanity," words that have become as naturalized as other suspect concepts such as "history" and "time." Rhythmic narrative that exhibits a new temporal configuration is one instance of a type of writing that does not rely on these radioactive terms. The three aspects of time—past, present, and future—are no longer constrained by linearity in rhythmic narrative; instead they are discontinuous.

Hayashi exemplifies many of these aspects of rhythmic time in "Buji" (Safe, 1982), an ironic story that first appeared in *Gunzō*. The subtitle of the work, "Seireki 1981—Genbaku 37" (1981 A.D.—Atomic Bomb Year 37), is a brilliant encapsulation of Hayashi's wish to bring the past and its particular significance into an ever forgetful present. The protagonist of this eerie story, a Nagasaki *hibakusha* (atomic bomb victim), is a female reporter who goes to Hiroshima to write a feature story for a women's magazine. As the airplane begins to land, the *hibakusha* imagines another aircraft, the *Enola Gay,* cruising above Hiroshima. As she walks through the Peace Park, the woman relives the day she was bombed in Nagasaki. Comparisons between the two cities are made throughout the story, yet ultimately the differences are only topical. The fact that the two bustling cities were former wastelands is indelibly engraved on the protagonist's mind.

The most serious moment in this disturbing story occurs when the woman eventually reaches the Atomic Bomb Dome. Weary from the walk, she sits down on a bench in front of the dome. Looking up, she sees the dome shimmering in the heat of the day and wonders: "Are the glass shards from August Sixth still intact or have they turned to dust in the wind? And more importantly, is this uninhabited A-Bomb Dome to which people are forbidden entrance our past or our future?"[16]

Time is so important to Hayashi that she reorganizes it in "Buji" in a way that makes sense to herself and other *hibakusha* whose lives were permanently scarred by the atomic bombing. Nineteen forty-five becomes, at once, the inaugural year for the nuclear age *(genbaku gannen)* and the zero-degree marker from which time proceeds. In this radical new system, embraced not by scientists, but rather by a *hibakusha* whose thoughts can never escape the day of the bombing, the past is no longer a static entity; it is fused with the present.[17] The bomb that fell on Nagasaki at 11:02 A.M., August 9, 1945, was a force so total that it, and the radiation which followed, has seeped beyond the past into the present-day lives of second-generation *hibakusha*. For Hayashi, time is forever ruptured by the bombing. Her secure childhood in cosmopolitan Shanghai is singularly displaced by the unimaginable bomb that fell on her in Nagasaki. Critics such as Karatani Kōjin and Nakagami Kenji call Hayashi's innumerable tellings of this experience "fetishism,"[18] but for Hayashi to fulfill her role as Nagasaki's *kataribe*, she must persist in writing stories of the bombing. Unlike Ōta Yōko, who strove in her A-bomb writings to "fashion a 'single literary work'—single in the sense of comprehensive, literary in the sense of possessing lasting value"—Hayashi realizes soon after writing *Ritual of Death* that her experience was only one among countless others.[19] She recalls that her memory of the bombing involved her escape from the munitions factory in Nagasaki over Mount Konpira to her home in Isahaya. She only witnessed what could be seen on a single route between the charred city and the verdant countryside. To broaden this narrow, though credibly horrific view, Hayashi writes and rewrites the same story, each time interjecting another fact, an alternative point of view, or more time through which the events of the past are filtered. Thus, in Hayashi's narrative world, the bombing of Nagasaki becomes a mantra and not, as Karatani and Nakagami would have it, a fetish.

In her atomic bomb works Hayashi does not employ historical time to narrate events. Linearity disappears as Hayashi manipulates past, present, and future in a dazzling disarray of continuity. In *Time and the Novel,* Patricia Drechsel Tobin describes how the shape of writing is altered by powerful forces:

> Once the novel's historical time becomes contaminated or haunted or enriched by the mythical and the primitive, the one impossible distance from beginning to end is a straight line; thereafter, the novel must depart from the lineal coercion of narrative and entice myth into structure through new schemes of accommodation that will most certainly participate variously in the atemporal.[20]

In Hayashi's works the atomic bombing described time and time again takes on mythic proportions. This is not to say that what Hayashi so ardently writes about has diminishing value in the real world; rather, the cumulative effect of her variations on the atomic bomb theme is the levitation of the historical event from its constrained position. Free-floating in Hayashi's writings, the atomic bombing rests wherever narration lies: past, present, or future.

Thirty years after the atomic bombings, Hayashi wrote *Ritual of Death*, a fictional documentary of the nuclear devastation of Nagasaki. This novella has become a classic in the genre of atomic bomb literature, ranking among other seminal works by such authors as Ōta, Hara, and Ibuse. *Ritual of Death* is the story of a fourteen-year-old girl's escape from the burning city of Nagasaki to the relative safety of her family's home in the country. Though this painful journey lasts just three days, Hayashi records the teenager's two months of grave illness (August and September 1945); and at the same time, by adeptly incorporating contemporary facts and emotions into the narration, no fewer than thirty years (1945 to 1975) are encompassed in this single work.

The critical reception of Hayashi's debut was overwhelmingly positive and resulted in a number of awards; yet, interestingly, a closer look at the kind of praise Hayashi garnered exposes the biases of the *bundan* (literary establishment). Inoue Mitsuharu, Haniya Yutaka, Endō Shūsaku, and Fukunaga Takehiko each single out the vivid, intense force of Hayashi's personal experience as the basis for their favorable praise.[21] While these critics are affected by the weight of the facts Hayashi presents in her story and overwhelmed by the author's lived experience, they denounce *Ritual of Death* for its lack of artistic skill.

Yasuoka Shōtarō says he is greatly impressed by the reality of the experience that Hayashi describes in *Ritual of Death*, but he adds that this is not the same as being impressed by its artistry.[22] Yoshiyuki Junnosuke wonders if Hayashi is not capitalizing on her wartime experience.[23] Nakagami Kenji, perhaps Hayashi's most severe critic, does not recognize her work as fiction at all.[24] Nakamura Mitsuo grants Hayashi some degree of fictionality in his statement that *Ritual of Death* is prenovelistic *(shōsetsu izen no shōsetsu).*[25] Ōoka Shōhei offers the most support with his praise that Hayashi is able to crystallize her A-bomb experience in fiction after the passage of thirty years. Yet he too first mentions the powerful nature of the story's subject matter: Hayashi's personal experience.[26]

Most of these critics believe that the strength of *Ritual of Death* lies in the fact that Hayashi is a victim of the bomb and this experience is what sustains the work. These critics then proceed to question the degree of literary completeness in the story. The tenor of these statements, not unlike much Japanese literary criticism, indicates that the quality of an author's work rests primarily on firsthand experience. Granted, it is impossible to read Hayashi's A-bomb works without being affected by the extraliterary fact that the author is a *hibakusha*. But Hayashi is not writing a personal testimonial in order to bring the reader to tears *(o-namida chōdai);* she is extending to her readers a fictional work regarding a matter of great personal concern.[27] Most critics focus their attention on Hayashi's own experience rather than the literary aspects of her writing, unsatisfying as this may be. Critics who go beyond Hayashi's eventful past will be noted throughout this examination of *Ritual of Death.*

The most conspicuous feature of *Ritual of Death* is Hayashi's use of time in her narration. In his study of atomic bomb literature, *Genbaku to kotoba: Hara Tamiki kara Hayashi Kyōko made* (The Atomic Bomb and Language: From Hara Tamiki to Hayashi Kyōko), Kuroko Kazuo notes that the difference between Hayashi and most other A-bomb writers is that "she skillfully incorporates into her works a consciousness of the thirty years that have passed since the bombing by creating descriptions in which past and present are intertwined."[28] Hayashi wrote *Ritual of Death* after three decades of accumulated silence. Yet the reader is made aware that, for the protagonist, this thirty-year period is anything but a void. In the years between the bombing and the narrative present, the protagonist has left her teenage years behind to marry and bear a child. The use of swift, intermittent flashes to the present, in a story about the bombing of Nagasaki indelibly set in the past, suggests that Hayashi does not view the past as divorced from the present.

Ritual of Death is replete with changes in time and perspective. Though the plot centers on a fourteen-year-old girl, the narration carries the leaden weight of the thirty years that follow the bombing. The forty-five-year-old narrator is versed in scientific facts about the incomprehensible force that struck her down in 1945 and brimming with personal details concerning the lives of less fortunate friends and teachers who suffered more intense physical pain. These facts and details, which could only be learned as an adult, well after the bombing, are interspersed within a tale told primarily by a narrator who describes the summer of her fourteenth year.

The story begins with a letter from American scientists who advise their former colleagues in Nagasaki to press for Japan's surrender. The narrator informs the reader: "It was impossible for me to read this letter calmly, for I was exposed to the atomic bomb in Nagasaki."[29] This "I" is a person older and wiser than the

"I" who, a few pages later, states: "On August 9th, I went to the factory in dark slacks and a short-sleeved blouse, with wooden clogs on my bare feet."[30] One can imagine the first "I," an adult, poring over scientific journals and artifacts related to the bomb, reinforcing her knowledge about nuclear energy. The second "I" is an innocent fourteen-year-old who faithfully reports to work unaware that, in fulfilling her obligation as a student laboring for her country, she would be the only one in her family to be hit by the bomb.

The opening scene, in which a wiser, experienced "I" bristles upon reading a letter sent by Americans before the bombing, sets a pattern that recurs as the story progresses. The older "I" is uncomfortable because it is she and the thousands of other Nagasaki denizens who are being discussed as the recipients of a "rain of atomic bombs" that "will increase manyfold in fury" barring surrender.[31] To mute the strong emotions this letter evokes, the narrator embarks on a tangential discussion of the cities targeted for the atomic bombing, the weather conditions that impeded visibility over certain cities, and the numbers of people killed at various points distant from ground zero. Each time a hint of emotion surfaces in the story it is smothered by a blanket of scientific facts.

The narration of *Ritual of Death* switches from the subjective experiences of *watakushi* ("I"), the child/woman narrator, to objective accounts of the bombing. Subjective moments generally involve the past, whereas objective moments concern the present. In discussing her debut, Hayashi says that she incorporates objective, verifiable data to avoid adhering too closely to her own experience.[32] These facts lend credibility to her memories as well, and the switches in viewpoint that they entail broaden the scope of Hayashi's story. The mixture of distant memories and contemporary facts enlarges the focus from a single, devastating moment in the past to a panorama of present realities.

The story continues with details about the layout of the munitions factory where the narrator was bombed. She describes the condition of her less fortunate classmates who worked elsewhere in the factory:

> Friends who worked in the Engineering Department, of which our section was a branch, became porcupines, filled with glass needles from the shattering of the huge windows that illuminated the work of drawing. After thirty years, glass splinters remain in their bodies and from time to time, they move. When the glass presses into the flesh, the pain is unbearable. An X-ray is taken to prepare for an operation, but by then, the splinter is no longer where it was. The doctor once quipped to a friend of mine, "This is your medal. Leave it in your body." It is easy to treat things lightly when one is not the victim.[33]

This vivid scene has compressed within it thirty years of agony. Hayashi's description of her classmate-turned-human-porcupine begins at the time of the bombing and ends with the medical treatment that is still necessary three decades after the bombing.

One of the ways in which Hayashi interjects the present into *Ritual of Death* is by citing newspaper articles. The first such article is dated October 10, 1970, and headlined "Monster Cartoons of Atomic Bomb Patients in Shōgakkan's *Second Grader's Monthly:* Middle School Student Criticizes Cruelty of Cartoons." As the headline indicates, a controversy arose when atomic bomb patients were drawn to resemble monsters. After giving further details about this incident, Hayashi makes a critical observation:

> The incident really did leave a deep impression on us. It was a taste of the cruelty of Time-equals-Oblivion. But the atomic bomb needs no sentimentality. Let them be, the cartoonists. Whether they draw monsters or clowns, they will stimulate someone to feel something about the bombing. Now, thirty years later, it has become difficult to portray the facts as they were.[34]

Citing the newspaper article accomplishes two things for Hayashi. First, the reader's attention is drawn away from the description, just two paragraphs earlier in the story, of the young girl freeing herself from the rubble after the bombing in 1945, to a specified day in 1970. Second, upon contemplating the article, Hayashi can make what will become a perennial point in her atomic bomb writing: "Time-equals-Oblivion." Although the idea of depicting atomic bomb victims as disfigured monsters is distasteful, for Hayashi these indelible portraits are less cruel than not remembering the victims and the bombing at all.

One or two hours after the bombing the young girl meets two uninjured women in the nearby mountains. Drawn to them because of their good health, she follows them to their home, which they soon discover is located near ground zero. Along the way the women urge the girl to eat part of a pumpkin they find in a field. The smell of the warm pumpkin nauseates her, and she vomits. This interlude into the past is broken when Hayashi makes the reader aware of the post-bomb future as she describes how food was irradiated by the bomb: "At this writing what strikes me as odd is the sweet potatoes that those women had bought at Michi-no-O. Instead of eating pumpkin à la radioactivity, we could have eaten those sweet potatoes."[35] The words "at this writing" *(kakitsuzurinagara)* are striking, for they clearly show that Hayashi is writing in the mid-1970s about events that took place in 1945.

Leaving the two women behind, the young girl goes to her school and then to her boarding house. Her mother, who has walked 25 kilometers searching for her daughter, reaches the boarding house three days after the bombing. At sunrise, mother and daughter start the long journey back to Isahaya. For the next two months the young girl is ill from the aftereffects of radiation exposure. The older narrator, versed with facts about leukemia, recalls her hair loss and the spots that formed on her arms and legs during those months. Hayashi writes of the fears with which she lives:

> If I had had a blood test then, the white blood cell count might have been as low as two or three thousand. A few years ago it was down to 3,600 when I was checked at the regular examination of bomb victims. I received a letter at that time indicating that I needed a closer examination. I feared death then more intensely than when I faced it so directly at age fourteen. By then I had a little son and prayed fervently, "I don't want to die now."[36]

In this passage Hayashi begins with what the narrator speculates her blood count might have been in October and November 1945, then sweeps forward to mention a blood count taken a few years prior to the narrative present. When this second count is taken the narrator is no longer a teenager; she is married and has a son. Older now and in a position of responsibility, her view of death has changed. As a teenager the idea of death was somehow romantic; as a *hibakusha* and a mother, death is nothing more than grim reality.

Near the end of the story the narrator remembers that a small sum of money was given as compensation to students who were required to work in factories during the war. The discussion turns to compensation for *hibakusha* who die. Hayashi describes the process for obtaining the 16,000 yen that is allotted for "special" *hibakusha* in the event of their death:

> To get the 16,000 yen after your death, someone has to fill out an application for the payment of funeral expenses, and take that, along with a medical certificate of death, a void resident card, a special atomic bomb victim health certificate and a seal to the proper authorities. I intend to leave a will saying, please buy flowers with the 16,000 yen. That's enough for eighty tulips, even in winter when they are 200 yen each. What a beautiful funeral that will be. If that is more than I deserve, radishes will do. Just awhile ago it would have been enough for eighty large ones, but while writing this, the price has gone up. Now it will buy only fifty-three radishes.[37]

This memorable passage succinctly reveals the narrator's anger, cynicism, and desires. It also contains the bitterness for which the author is noted.[38] Hayashi makes her displeasure at the absurd bureaucratic process known, but in a poignant and artistic way—with her wish for flowers. The present figures prominently in her discussion of the current market price of tulips and radishes. Even as she writes of her ideas for a funeral the prices increase.

Ritual of Death ends with the narrator recalling the memorial ceremony that was held in October 1945 for students and teachers who died as a result of the bombing. Hayashi describes the mixed emotions of the students attending the ceremonies: "Surviving students felt guilty to be there. The suppressed sobbing of mothers pierced our bodies."[39] The solemn ceremony cannot bring a sense of closure to the *hibakusha* present. At least one among them will continue to feel guilt and confusion about why she survived when so many others died. The last line of the story moves the reader away from the scene of the memorial ceremony to the narrator contemplating the conclusion of a film about the destruction wrought by the atomic bomb. Hayashi writes: "There is a beautiful line at the end of an American documentary film on the atomic bomb: . . . Thus, the destruction ended. . . . "[40] This ending, as ironic as the story's title, is powerful because it contains both Hayashi's hopeful wish—an end to the destruction—and her persistent fear that, for her, it can never end.[41]

Most critics privilege the factual content of *Ritual of Death* over the imaginative aspects of the story. Kuroko Kazuo, however, says that Hayashi "creates a unique flow of time" by consciously adding bits and pieces of information from the present to her story of the past.[42] In *Ritual of Death* it is clear that Hayashi possesses unusual powers of imagination to recall past experiences with great fidelity and reconfigure them in a nonlinear way. Within this story of the nuclear devastation of Nagasaki, Hayashi weaves together the prebomb past and postbomb future. These strands enable her to depict the mind of a fourteen-year-old during wartime and the consciousness of the fourteen-year-old who grows up, marries, and bears a child.

The thirty years that Hayashi intersperses between the bombing and the present are critical, for the author is questioning the bomb's meaning from a present in which, for many, the past is buried. The most powerful historical force that Hayashi has been subjected to lies in the past, across an abyss of time. To fill this abyss Hayashi includes contemporary facts and emotions. The present that Hayashi inserts into her story of the past bares the fact that the shadow of August Ninth is always with her. John Whittier Treat describes Ōta Yōko's writing about the bombing of Hiroshima as "one 'event' in a continuous process of dehumanization that resists being restricted to a single moment."[43] In her narratives Hayashi, too, illustrates that the atomic bombing extends beyond its historical moment. Placing the present alongside the past allows one to see many moments as one, showing the far-reaching consequences the bombing engendered.

By employing a narrative technique in which time is fragmented rather than linear, Hayashi makes the point that the catastrophic episode that occurred in Nagasaki is not simply an earth-shattering event that happened decades ago. Hayashi historicizes the present to illustrate the fact that although at first glance the present appears peaceful, this putative peace is maintained by a precarious balance of powers with nuclear forces far more destructive than the ones that struck Nagasaki and Hiroshima. Nakano Kōji writes that with each passing decade more *hibakusha* die and, concomitantly, the gap between those who experienced these wartime atrocities and those who did not grows wider.[44] Hayashi is keenly aware of this passage of time: references to time permeate her narrative.

The narrative method Hayashi employs in her cathartic debut, *Ritual of Death*, transforms the author's account of her experience as a bomb victim into a work of fiction. Hayashi's artistry in merging past and present throughout the narrative and her brilliant, restrained style with its distinctive low tone recreate the experience that lies within her still. Hayashi wrote *Ritual of Death* with the intention of capturing the atomic bombing of Nagasaki in its entirety.[45] Endō Shūsaku describes Hayashi's debut as cinematic and likens the changes in the story to the movement of film.[46] Hayashi achieves this effect by including numerous citations from extant texts to make the story as objective as possible. Shifts in point of view are made in order to keep the story from becoming too personal. Even the words Hayashi chooses to tell her story are free from ornamentation. Although these techniques are adopted to keep the work from being subjective, the cumulative effect results in a story that is intensely personal.

In "Shanhai to hachigatsu kokonoka," Hayashi writes that she believed the burden of August Ninth would be lightened once she finished *Ritual of Death*, but in fact it became more oppressive. After writing *Ritual of Death* she realized that there were many August Ninths: "My August Ninth was escaping from the demolished factory and going towards Mount Konpira on a single narrow path. It was just the August Ninth that I saw while fleeing via that single route. It was August Ninth, and it wasn't August Ninth."[47] In her subsequent writings on the atomic bomb Hayashi focuses her attention on the other August Ninths.

Less than two years after the publication of *Ritual of Death*, Hayashi began writing the twelve short stories that appear in *Giyaman biidoro*. In this collection of stories Hayashi underscores the differing experiences of Nagasaki *hibakusha.* The prose in *Giyaman biidoro,* restrained and polished, reflects Hayashi's growing confidence as a writer. Hayashi views these stories as small independent pieces that, pieced together, create a "mosaic pattern."[48] The author's comments suggest that this work is more consciously artistic than *Ritual of Death,* which was written to tell the facts of the bombing.

Though the collection tells of other August Ninths, each of the stories is narrated by a first-person voice, *watakushi,* unmistakably Hayashi's own. This narrator, a divorced woman who is both a *hibakusha* and a mother, is quietly present in all the stories. The stories are set either in Zushi, where the narrator lives with her son, or Nagasaki, where she returns twice: once before her old school is torn down, and again for the ceremonies commemorating the thirty-third anniversary of the bombing.

The critical reception of *Giyaman biidoro* was overwhelmingly positive. Nakano Kōji calls the collection Hayashi's best and most representative work.[49] Hirayama Mitsuo says that the stories secure Hayashi's position as a writer because of the conciseness of her prose and the absence of the sentimentality that marred *Ritual of Death.*[50] Kuroko Kazuo is impressed with Hayashi's ability to depict a wide range of differences in the way *hibakusha* regard their shared experience of being bombed.[51] Kawanishi Masaaki finds in *Giyaman biidoro* an artistic representation of the atomic bombing.[52] Kawanishi also notes the movement of time within the stories *(toki wa ugoite iru).*[53] In *Giyaman biidoro* the narrative present is from the summer of 1976 to the spring of 1977, but Hayashi characteristically moves backward to the time of the bombing and even before in stories where the narrator recalls her childhood in Shanghai. Nakano Kōji observes the temporal shifts in *Giyaman biidoro* as well: "This collection, which is centered around the experiences of Nagasaki *hibakusha,* firmly greets the present—thirty years after the bombing—and from this present, peers into a slumbering past, as if it were gazing at the bottom of a sea two fathoms deep."[54] As these two critics astutely point out, a marked feature of *Giyaman biidoro* is the melding of time.

"Akikan" (The Empty Can), the first story in the collection, features characters that reappear in other stories in *Giyaman biidoro.* Present are five women who meet in Nagasaki to visit their old school, soon to be demolished. Ōki is a single teacher, a *hibakusha,* who faces being transferred to a school on a remote island, where she worries she may not have access to medical treatment should she experience an atomic bomb illness. Noda is a *hibakusha* who is described as utterly dependent upon her husband. Hara is a *hibakusha* who still lives with her parents.

The narrator is a divorced *hibakusha* with one child. Nishida, a fashion designer, is the story's sole non-*hibakusha*. A sixth character, Kinuko, is absent because she requires surgery to remove glass fragments lodged in her body since the time of the bombing.

As the five women walk through the school trying to recall the location of their old classroom and the names of former teachers, they remember Kinuko bringing what they had assumed was an empty can to and from school after the bombing. As each recalls the empty can incident *(akikan jiken)*, Hayashi reveals the differences between the characters. Although each of the women remembers slightly different details about Kinuko carrying the ashes of her parents with her to school each day, the incident binds the women together as they collectively feel pain at the thought of Kinuko's anguish when her teacher requested that she no longer bring the can to school.

Glass fragments—what Kawanishi Masaaki identifies as the keyword in *Giyaman biidoro*—figure prominently in "The Empty Can."[55] The first mention of glass occurs as the narrator registers her surprise that the glass windows in the school have no missing pieces. The glass so properly in its place poses a striking contrast to the broken windows that remained unrepaired in the narrator's memories of her school after the bombing. Hayashi's focus on the undamaged glass pries the bombing from its resting place in the past. The second time glass is mentioned, it is in reference to the shards that pierced Kinuko's body during the bombing. Kinuko, now an elementary school teacher in her forties, feels a sharp twinge in her back after demonstrating a somersault to her students. She decides to go to the doctor even though she believes she is just feeling her age. The doctor's suspicion that there are glass fragments from the bombing in her body shocks Kinuko, who feels their presence for the first time after more than three decades have passed.

The story ends as the narrator remembers meeting Kinuko the year before the narrative present:

> Last year, when I had met her at K Temple, Kinuko hadn't mentioned her parents. She had said nothing about her past life or her present life. Perhaps the glass in her back had already begun to hurt around that time. Kinuko was to enter the hospital tomorrow. How many fragments of glass from thirty years ago would come out of Kinuko's back? What kind of a glow would those smooth white pearls of fat cast when they were brought out into the light?[56]

This last passage of the story, in which the narrator speculates about Kinuko's impending surgery, links the past to the present. Hayashi shows the cutting force the bombing has on its victims decades later.

Both Nakano Kōji and Kawanishi Masaaki remark that the glass-turned-pearls that remain in the bodies of *hibakusha* are real and symbolic. Kawanishi says the glass pearls are a splendid metaphor for the long years of pain the bomb has imposed on its victims.[57] Nakano calls the glass pearls an artistic expression showing the length of time that *hibakusha* have lived with the atomic bombing engraved in their minds (and bodies).[58] Throughout *Giyaman biidoro* glass appears as a recurring image representing the passage of time.

"Giyaman biidoro" (Cut Glass, Blown Glass), the story that gives the collection its title, takes place during winter in Nagasaki.[59] The narrator and Nishida are the only two characters present. The two women walk about Nagasaki in search of the glass for which the city is famous. Nishida, the fashion designer, is looking for a glass bowl. As they roam from one antique store to another the two women learn more about the history of glass art in Nagasaki. Soon the narrator desires a piece for herself. She is drawn to the corners and back rooms of the stores they visit. An air of mystery hovers over the story. No matter where they go they cannot find an unbroken piece of glass. This story makes few overt statements about the atomic bombing; instead, Hayashi uses the descriptions of fused and cracked glass to tell the horrors of August Ninth. The fused glass reminds the narrator of the skin of victims after the bombing; the cracked glass is likened to their damaged psyches.

The narrator finds a glass bowl with a hairline crack in it that reminds her of a French doll her sister cherished as a child. She recalls the time she played with the doll without her sister's permission and dropped it accidentally, cracking the doll's eyes. The bowl before her brings to mind the cracked doll eyes and the feeling of pity she experienced then for the first time. After this backward leap to the prebomb past, she realizes why she is simultaneously drawn and repelled by the cracked bowl: "While gazing at the wide crack in the bottom of the bowl my interest in the bowl cooled. . . . I realized anew the reality of the atomic bombing of Nagasaki on August 9, 1945. I was consciously trying to act like a tourist just passing through until I saw the glass before me."[60] Here Hayashi draws a parallel between the cracked glass and the fractured lives that *hibakusha* lead.

There can be no aesthetic distance for the narrator as she joins Nishida on a "touristy" glass-viewing excursion through Nagasaki. For a time she believes she is as free as Nishida, a non-*hibakusha*, to appraise the glass disinterestedly, behaving as a casual visitor to Nagasaki. But when she thinks about why it is so difficult to find any whole antique glass pieces after the atomic explosion, she keenly feels the brevity of her flight from August Ninth and the impossibility of ever completely removing herself from her past. "Giyaman biidoro" shows the firm hold that the bombing has on the lives of *hibakusha*.

"Kiroku" (A Chronicle) is a story about the life and death of Reiko Hachida, a classmate of the narrator's. In the narrative present, a gentleman who is compiling a book on students who were mobilized to work in factories in Nagasaki during the war asks the narrator for information about Reiko. His questions cause her to remember the aftermath of the bombing, when she was asked similar questions by Reiko's father about his daughter's whereabouts and welfare. When the narrator tells the book's author that she first learned of Reiko's death at the memorial service held for classmates and teachers at her high school in October 1945, he presses her for more details. She cannot recall much about Reiko, except that she was the daughter of a wealthy Nagasaki family that owned a grand piano and had plenty of food during the period of wartime austerity. She is reminded of her meeting with another classmate, Ōki, a year before the narrative present. Ōki tells her that the woman who brought a lunch box to school every day for a month after the bombing was Reiko's mother. Unable to accept her daughter's death, the woman came to the school daily hoping to see her daughter talking and laughing with her classmates.

In "Kiroku," Hayashi writes about the fears of *hibakusha* such as the narrator and Ōki. While talking to the gentleman about Reiko, the narrator worries that her memories are imprecise. Ōki is concerned about being assigned to teach outside of Nagasaki, where medical treatment for *hibakusha* might not be available, and about people's reaction if they learn that she is a *hibakusha*. The narrator reveals why she, the man standing on a ladder searching for a book to use in his forthcoming history of mobilized students, and Ōki are plagued by such fears:

> The present is August 9, 1945. For the man climbing the ladder August Ninth is the present. Neither the man nor I have taken one step past the day of the bombing. Even when I think I have taken a step forward, I realize that I'm still standing in August Ninth. It's the same for Ōki. . . . For her, living near the atomic bomb hospital obsessed with August Ninth and worried about an atomic bomb illness that may never develop is probably the way she survives. By disclosing her

pain to the public eye she confirms that she is alive, and that we *hibakusha* are connected to the path of life.[61]

Hayashi shows in this passage not only the fears that besiege *hibakusha* but the extensibility of August Ninth.

"Kiroku" ends as the gentleman questions whether he actually saw Reiko's coffin in a procession outside her house in 1945: "Did I really see it? Or was it a hallucination? Now that thirty years have passed I don't even remember anymore."[62] Hayashi depicts his memory as more illusory than real. The implication is that the atomic explosion, too, may have been just an illusion, since details of the event are so difficult to retrieve. In the story's last line the narrator answers the man squarely, dispelling any lingering confusion about the bombing and its casualties: "That person really did die."[63] This forceful conclusion is indicative of Hayashi's unwavering knowledge that the bombing did indeed take place and that its aftereffects, despite the inevitable obfuscation of human memory, had in no way diminished.

"No ni" (In the Fields), the final story in *Giyaman biidoro,* begins and ends with a description of the natural landscape that gives the story its symmetry and the collection its closure. The narrator, who has recently attended her thirty-third annual class reunion, meets her non-*hibakusha* classmate Nishida in Shinjuku to tell her about the reunion and show her a commemorative photograph. Nishida did not attend because she feels like an outsider in the presence of her *hibakusha* classmates. Hayashi's description of the photograph is unforgettable. The photo of the thirty middle-aged women was taken shortly after noon on the steps of a Buddhist temple. The camera's angle captures the women's contorted faces looking upward at the sky. The shadow of a tree branch distorted from the atomic blast is also reflected in the photo. After looking at the women's faces, etched by the passage of thirty-two years, Nishida returns the photograph to the narrator and tells her there is something strange about it. She looks at it carefully and agrees. Here Hayashi is showing the collapsed distance between the past and the present. The expression on the women's faces is not unlike the faces of victims after the explosion. The photograph might just as well have been taken at the time of the bombing.

In the course of the conversation the narrator tells Nishida that the brother of Sugino, a classmate who died during the bombing, attended the reunion in his sister's place. She recalls seeing Sugino's mother at the memorial service held at their school in October 1945. Sugino's mother's face bore such a look of bitterness that the narrator could not help but feel the woman's resentment that they were alive when her daughter was dead. Remembering her pain, she thinks: "Reiko's mother is burdened with a wound different from ours. But, like us she is crawling around August Ninth like a blind person, unable to escape."[64] In "No ni" Hayashi tells how the mother's pain is similar to and different from the narrator's pain and that of her surviving classmates. August Ninth confines them all.

Each of the twelve stories in *Giyaman biidoro* offers a glimpse of what Kuroko Kazuo calls the "fractured existence" of the *hibakusha*.[65] The lives of these *hibakusha* are splintered like the glass images that appear so often in the collection. The atomic explosion that ruptured the prebomb past from the postbomb future undermines every effort the *hibakusha* make to move forward. The weight of their experience may temporarily be lifted, but it always returns. The vignettes Hayashi paints in *Giyaman biidoro* confirm the differing experiences of *hibakusha* and the similarity of their bondage.

Naki ga gotoki, Hayashi's first novel-length atomic bomb work, is remarkable in that it contains almost no description of Nagasaki's destruction. Unlike *Ritual of Death* and *Giyaman biidoro,* both works in which Hayashi interweaves the story of the devastation of August Ninth with occurrences from the present, *Naki ga gotoki* is concerned largely with the present. This focus on the present in a work thematicizing a historical atrocity, together with Hayashi's employment of a bifurcated narrative and the woman narrator's expressed wish to be the *kataribe* for August Ninth, make *Naki ga gotoki* an important addition to Hayashi's writings about the atomic bombing.

Hayashi writes *Naki ga gotoki,* a story about the effects of nuclear warfare, by employing two narrative voices. Half of the work is related by an unnamed woman, called simply *onna,* the other half by an unnamed young girl designated by the first-person pronoun *watakushi.* The story begins as the woman, after a long absence, climbs up a steep slope leading to her childhood friend Haruko's home in Nagasaki. Haruko and her American husband Bob, a veterinarian, are hosting a dinner for a small group of friends on the eve of the atomic bomb ceremonies held in Nagasaki every year. Present are the woman, an elderly male physician, a middle-aged woman, and an older woman. Of the four guests, only the middle-aged woman is not a survivor of the atomic bombing. Missing from the gathering are Haruko's son Tōru and his friend Ichirō, the son of Haruko's childhood friend Hanako. While the guests await the arrival of the two young men, they discuss a variety of A-bomb-related issues in the manner of a "salon discussion."[66] The woman, reticent throughout the discussion, seems strangely detached. It is only through the voice of *watakushi* that the woman's character is fleshed out. This second narrative voice presents the childhood experiences of the woman, beginning with the months following the bombing. In this narrative sequence, the reader learns of the close friendship between the narrator, Hanako, and Haruko and how their lives are changed by the atomic bombing. Although the narrative present lasts just one day—August 8, 1979—Hayashi captures the years that have elapsed since the bombing by introducing a second narrative voice.

Naki ga gotoki received favorable reviews from critics when it appeared in one volume in 1981. Nakano Kōji calls the work a "coming of age" story *(seichō shōsetsu)* in which Hayashi offers a moving portrait of three young girls making the most of their lives after being directly and indirectly wounded by the bombing.[67] Oda Makoto praises the double narrative that permits Hayashi to relate more than just one point of view regarding the atomic bombing.[68] Akiyama Shun, too, remarks on the effectiveness of Hayashi's two parallel and complementary voices.[69] Matsumoto Ken'ichi believes that while Hayashi convincingly relates both the lives of the young women after the bombing in the voice of *watakushi* and the contemporary state of nuclear issues in the voice of *onna,* the link between the two narratives is weak at times.[70] The voices of the *onna* and *watakushi* narrators do not resonate as subtly as the voices of the paired narrators *boku* and *watakushi* or *boku* and *nezumi* in Murakami Haruki's narratives, but in *Naki ga gotoki* the reader knows from the first chapter that the two narrators *onna* and *watakushi* are one and the same, and by the end of the work the conflation cannot be disputed.[71] Matsumoto is also concerned that Hayashi does not provide vivid descriptions of the day of the bombing itself.[72] Initially this lack of detail does appear odd in a work categorized as an A-bomb piece. Oda Makoto responds to Matsumoto's criticism by arguing that Hayashi had already told the story of August 9, 1945, in *Ritual of Death.* Because Hayashi gives a comprehensive description of the day of the bombing in her debut as an atomic bomb writer, she is free in her subsequent works to move boldly past the actual bombing.

In the first chapter of *Naki ga gotoki,* as the woman walks to her childhood friend Haruko's home in Nagasaki after a long absence, she observes the city preparing for the atomic bomb ceremonies and reflects on the number of young people riding into the city on their motorbikes. The woman contrasts her inaction with the fervor exhibited by the young people. Hayashi describes her contemplating her own stance on the bombing: "The woman wishes to be the *kataribe* of August Ninth. She is a victim of the atomic bombing. Thus, the woman hopes to narrate August Ninth as faithfully as possible. For that reason she has repressed any superfluous emotions."[73] The woman has lived away from Nagasaki for over thirty years, returning occasionally to attend the commemoration ceremonies. The first time she returned to Nagasaki for the ceremonies was in 1963. At that time the woman was shocked by the festival atmosphere surrounding the event. Seeing the skies filled with fireworks and bags of cotton candy for sale, the woman feels the waning significance of the bombing *(kokonoka no fūka)*. As the years pass and the ceremony's name and sponsors change, the woman realizes that the idea of the bombing packaged in the ceremonies is different from *her* August Ninth, so she stops attending.

This first chapter does not mention the day of the bombing or the woman's experience as a victim, but Hayashi's unforgettable description of the woman walking slowly up the slope in the heat, stopping for water at a stranger's house along the way, evokes thoughts of dehydrated bomb victims seeking water and safety.[74] After giving moving details of the woman's arduous climb past homes with roofs still spotted with burns from the atomic blast, Hayashi places her in Haruko's home, where a discussion about nuclear-related issues ensues. As the group talks, the woman quietly observes. Certain topics remind her of events from the past. When she recalls these events, Hayashi uses the second narrative voice, that of *watakushi*. Unlike the narration of *onna*, the story of *watakushi* is personal, small in scale, dealing mainly with the lives of the narrator and her friends Haruko and Hanako. At the beginning of the young girl's story, Hayashi describes *watakushi*'s happy-go-lucky adventures with her friends after the war ends. The excitement of the teenagers is shown in passages describing the movies they saw, the stars they idolized, and the nylon stockings they desired. While Hayashi presents a rosy picture of the girls at the war's end, the first chapter concludes with the narrator remembering how she always had to wear long pants to hide the scars from the bombing.

As chapter two unfolds, she recalls increasingly darker memories. Hanako, who had aspirations of being a doctor, misses a critical examination because she is severely ill as a result of the bombing. The narrator remembers formless dreams about August Ninth that caused her to wet her bed. She describes the bombing's effect on her psyche: "The flash [I saw] on the Ninth flickers in every fold of my brain. Sometimes the flash burns my thoughts and perceptions and turns my memory pure white. Other times the light floods me and makes me as stupefied as I was the instant the bomb exploded."[75] The young girls, liberated from their mobilization work at the war's end, enjoy some experiences during their teenage years, but their happiness is eclipsed by the bomb.

After a lengthy reverie, midway through chapter three the narrative switches back to the woman. The adults are discussing the preparations for the next day's ceremonies. The middle-aged woman vents her anger about all the hustle and bustle. She says that every year the city becomes a madhouse as August Ninth approaches, and she does not see the necessity as it is now peaceful in Japan. The middle-aged woman goes on to state that the bombing was needed to end the war. Listening to these extreme statements, the narrator recalls a newspaper article dated July 2, 1976, in which a right-wing politician, faced with facts about the hazards of radiation and genetic defects, remarks: "Isn't there a way to exterminate *hibakusha?*"[76] The narrator, while horrified that a Diet member would utter such a preposterous question, is nonetheless forced to recognize the existence of such persons. The middle-aged woman's comments pale in comparison to those cited by the politician, but Hayashi shows that neither has any regard for *hibakusha*.

In chapter four, more texts are cited as Hayashi presents detailed facts about the bombing. The doctor quotes medical statistics about the rate of leukemia in *hibakusha*. Historical documents about war-damaged Nagasaki are used to verify the time and date of air raids. Many passages in *Naki ga gotoki* are studded with facts from verifiable sources. The reader is made aware, not only of the bombing of Nagasaki, but also the contamination of Three Mile Island, underwater atomic bomb testing at Bikini, and the nuclear warship *Mutsu* docked outside Nagasaki. Hayashi includes these sources for two reasons. First, they verify the true event upon which Hayashi's work is based. Second, one can surmise from these sources that atrocities tend to be repeated. In each recent example of continued nuclear presence lurks Hayashi's past referent: the bombing of Nagasaki.

Chapter four also contains a lengthy section concerning the health certificate the government issues to qualified survivors of the bombing. The woman regards the subsidized medical benefits as a mixed blessing. Life for *hibakusha* who manage to obtain a medical certificate is punctuated every six months by the physical examination to which they are entitled. Twice a year the worries of these *hibakusha* are compounded by the examination process and the excruciating waiting period they endure before they know if they are well. The woman resists this form of existence—marked by regular intervals of time—by refusing to apply for medical compensation. Slight as it is, her resistance to time is a form of rebellion. As she thinks about this, the woman also realizes that her wish to be Nagasaki's *kataribe* comes from the same impulse to resist time: "The reason that the woman decided to try to be a *kataribe* was because she wanted to prevent, if only a little, the weathering of August Ninth."[77] Here Hayashi clearly expresses the idea that telling the story of the bomb will slow its descent to oblivion.

The younger narrator continues her story in chapter five, but now it is the fall of 1950 and she and her friends are twenty years old. The girls have graduated from high school. Haruko and Hanako find work at a military post exchange near Nagasaki, and the narrator wonders if she should do the same. With the Korean War in full swing, the bases are bustling and opportunities for work are plentiful. The narrator contemplates leaving Nagasaki but worries about the consequences: "With each passing day our minds become heavy with August Ninth. What's strange is that after leaving our classmates and venturing off alone, we become conscious of August Ninth in everything. Leaving Nagasaki forces us to think of the Ninth and makes us uneasy."[78] Here the narrator reveals her double bind. In Nagasaki she must avoid personal questions because they will force her to talk about her experience during the bombing. To avoid this she thinks of leaving Nagasaki but knows that physical distance will not result in psychological remove since August Ninth has lodged itself within her.

In chapter six, the narrator reveals that in 1952 she leaves Nagasaki for Tokyo to get married. From Hanako's letters she learns that Haruko has quit her job and has begun living with an American named Bob. The bulk of this section is about the lives of Haruko and Bob. They have a child together, but Bob is sent back to America and then to Korea. In 1953 he deserts his ship to be with Haruko but is soon arrested. The narrator, now twenty-two years old, envies Haruko's good health. Of the three friends, Haruko is the best candidate for motherhood since, owing to a cold, she missed work on the day of the bombing, thereby suffering no exposure. The narrator and Hanako, on the other hand, are plagued with concerns about the effect of radiation on their offspring. For them having children would mean more reminders of August Ninth.

At this point in the novel, Haruko is cooking hamburger in anticipation of Tōru and Ichirō's arrival. The woman associates the smell with memories from the past:

> While they were talking the woman remembered the day Haruko taught her how to cook hamburger. The first time the woman had hamburger was when Haruko prepared it for her. It was during the time that Haruko lived in the town by the port. The woman had gagged when she first smelled the meat frying in the pan. The juices dripping from the ground meat resembled the sickening fumes of burning grass she smelled during her escape to Mount Konpira after the bomb-

ing. The woman took a bite and rested her chopsticks. After more than thirty years the woman found the same smell unsavory. More than the sense of smell or the cooking she felt the passage of time. In those years Tōru was born, Ichirō was born, and the woman gave birth to her son. Ichirō and the woman's son are known as second generation *hibakusha*. They possess certificates testifying that they are the children of *hibakusha*.[79]

In this single paragraph Hayashi presents the sweep of time that characterizes her atomic bomb writing. She begins with the present in Haruko's house, then recalls the visit to Haruko's house in the past when she was assailed by memories of the atomic bombing as Haruko fried meat. The intervening years between the distant past and the present are alluded to, as well, by the births of the sons. Hayashi uses the sense of smell, with its associations to memory, to link past and present. At the same time she merges the woman with the younger narrator. This remarkable passage conflates not only the past and present, but also the two narratives.

In the last four chapters the narratives continue to meld together as the two narrators become closer in age. The younger narrator begins to forget Haruko and Hanako as time passes. She is more concerned about staying healthy until her son turns fourteen, believing that after this age he can manage without her. The end of the work is filled with details of Hanako's slow, painful death. Unlike many *hibakusha* who died soon after being diagnosed with cancer, Hanako's disease lasts over thirty years and attests to the "persistence of August Ninth."[80] Hanako dies a few years prior to the narrative present. Another classmate who survived the bombing, Zoku, also dies. The woman begins to worry that she will be an ancient isolated survivor of the bombing *(genbaku kōrō)*.

The novel's final chapter is memorable because the narrator, who has remained largely undemonstrative, becomes emotional as she describes the birth of her son:

The day the woman gave birth cherry trees were in bloom in the hospital garden. There were also cherry blossoms around the pond visible from the second floor delivery room. The sky and the pond were awash with a light pink color. The air, too, was the color of cherry blossoms. It was twelve or thirteen minutes after 6 A.M. when the woman gave birth. At that hour during cherry blossom season it should have been dark. But, in the woman's memory, at the time she gave birth the inside and the outside of the hospital glittered with light and the color of cherry blossoms. That day and August Ninth were the only times in the woman's life that she was struck by the keen sensation of being alive. When she drank pure, cold mountain spring water out of an iron helmet after the bombing she wrapped her arms around her body and thought, "I'm alive."[81]

Hayashi spans decades in this single paragraph. The birth of her child and the day of the bombing are inextricably linked because both events confirm life for the woman.

Following the sentiment about the woman's child is a remark the narrator's husband makes to her before their marriage ended. After twenty years of marriage he says to the woman: "My marriage was nothing other than life with a *hibakusha*. If you intend to be a *kataribe*, you should talk about each day, leading to today, without distortion. You don't need the slightest embellishment—everyday is life as a *hibakusha*."[82] Remembering her husband's harsh words, the woman discovers that while she thought she was acting as a normal person would act when she left Nagasaki, married, and bore a son, all of her actions were predicated on the fact that she was a *hibakusha*. That is why she so desperately wanted a normal life. *Naki ga gotoki* ends with the woman's realization that there is no escape from August Ninth.

Naki ga gotoki is Hayashi's most comprehensive account of the life of survivors after the bombing. The protagonist tries to resist the effects of the bombing by refusing medical compensation and by leaving Nagasaki to start a family, but her resistance is thwarted by the dominant position the bomb occupies in her life. Her bitter experience leads her to resolve that she will be the *kataribe* for August Ninth. Hayashi's bifurcated narrative clearly shows that August Ninth is far more than the day of the bombing. The hell of August Ninth is still firmly lodged in the minds of her characters over thirty years later.

Hayashi's atomic bomb narratives reveal that August Ninth is always and everywhere present in the lives of *hibakusha*. What makes Hayashi continue to tell her stories is the forgetful present. By insistently incorporating a consciousness of the present in works that tell the story of the bombing, Hayashi resists time's destructive effect on human memory. Her bold leaps from past to present keep the bombing from a descent into oblivion.

NOTES

1. Nakano Kōji, "Kaisetsu," *Nihon genbaku bungaku zenshū*, vol. 3 (Tokyo: Horupu Shuppan, 1983), p. 411.

2. Hayashi Kyōko, "Shanhai to hachigatsu kokonoka," *Bunka no genzai: Chūshin to*

shūen, vol. 4, ed. Ōe Kenzaburō, Nakamura Yūjirō, and Yamaguchi Masao (Tokyo: Iwanami Shoten, 1981), p. 113.

3. Kyoko Selden's translation is titled *Ritual of Death.* A more literal rendering, "Festival Place," retains the irony of Hayashi's title. Though it does not sound as impressive, translating *"matsuri"* as "festival" conveys Hayashi's comparison of a city vibrating from the shock of an atomic bomb with the excitement of a *matsuri.* While the translation of the story's title may be questionable, Selden's translation of the work is competent and as moving as the original. Quotes from *Matsuri no ba* are therefore from Selden's translation.

4. Tsushima Yūko continues to write, but Nakagami Kenji died of liver cancer in the summer of 1992 at the age of forty-six.

5. Gotō Minako, also a Nagasaki *hibakusha,* wrote the atomic bomb story "Toki o hiku," which was nominated for the Akutagawa Prize in 1971. Five of the nine-member prize committee were unmoved by the story, however, so Higashi Mineo's "Okinawa no shōnen" was awarded the prize. At that time Gotō's atomic bomb theme was superseded by the intensely debated topic of Okinawa's restoration to Japan.

6. Kyoko Selden and Mark Selden, eds., *The Atomic Bomb: Voices from Hiroshima and Nagasaki* (New York: Sharpe, 1989), p. 249. Kyoko Selden uses the English word "chronicler" for *"kataribe,"* a rendering that fails to capture the historical significance of this archaic term. According to the *Kōjien,* 4th ed., ed. Shinmura Izuru (Tokyo: Iwanami Shoten, 1991), a *kataribe* is defined as an official in ancient court society responsible for orally transmitting national history. It is Hayashi's sense of mission that makes her continue telling the atomic bomb "story." Since no suitable English word has the connotations of *"kataribe,"* I use the Japanese term henceforth in this text.

7. See Robert J. Lifton, *Death in Life: Survivors of Hiroshima* (New York: Simon & Schuster, 1967), for a full account of survivor guilt.

8. Kuroko Kazuo, *Genbaku to kotoba: Hara Tamiki kara Hayashi Kyōko made* (Tokyo: San'ichi Shobō, 1983), p. 17.

9. Elizabeth Deeds Ermarth, *Sequel to History: Postmodernism and the Crisis of Representational Time* (Princeton: Princeton University Press, 1992), p. 20.

10. Ibid., p. 26.

11. John Bender and David E. Wellbery, eds., In *Chronotypes: The Construction of Time* (Stanford: Stanford University Press, 1991), Gayatri Chakravorty Spivak and other theorists from various disciplines cite the dearth of new studies on time.

12. Ermarth, *Sequel to History,* p. 28. This time is essentially an elaborately constructed means by which many people can say "now" simultaneously.

13. Julia Kristeva, "Women's Time" (Les temps des femmes, 1979), trans. Alice Jardine and Harry Blake, *Critical Theory Since 1965,* ed. Hazard Adams and Leroy Searle (Tallahassee: Florida State University Press, 1986), pp. 471–484.

14. Wesley A. Kort, *Modern Fiction and Human Time: A Study in Narrative and Belief* (Tampa: University of South Florida Press, 1985).

15. Ermarth, *Sequel to History,* p. 14.

16. Hayashi Kyōko, "Buji," in *Sangai no ie* (Tokyo: Shinchōsha, 1984), p. 138.

17. Hayashi was inspired by a motion made by one of her teachers, Okamoto Tadashi. Until his death in 1985, Okamoto, the former president of Kantō Gakuin Daigaku, spoke

monthly to Hayashi and several other women who belonged to a group called "Myōga no Kai" on the topic of art. Okamoto proposed that 1945 be made the first year of the nuclear era. See Hayashi Kyōko's essay "Genbaku yonjūninen ni," *Minshū Bungaku* 9 (1986):11–12.

18. Karatani Kōjin and Nakagami Kenji, "Sōsaku gappyō," *Gunzō* 2 (1982):288.

19. John Whittier Treat, "Hiroshima and the Place of the Narrator," *Journal of Asian Studies* 2 (1989):39.

20. Patricia Drechsel Tobin, *Time and the Novel: The Genealogical Imperative* (Princeton: Princeton University Press, 1978), pp. 41–42.

21. See comments from the *Gunzō* New Writer's Prize Committee in *Gunzō* 6 (1975): 16–22.

22. See Hirayama Mitsuo's summary of the critical reception of *Ritual of Death* in his essay "Hayashi Kyōko ron," *Kiyō* 43 (Yokohama: Kantō Daigakuin Daigaku Bungakubu, 1985), pp. 70–71.

23. Ibid.

24. Furuya Kenzō and Nakagami Kenji, "Shōsetsuka no kakugo," *Bungakukai* 5 (1977): 216–219.

25. Hirayama, "Hayashi Kyōko ron," p. 71.

26. Ibid.

27. In the introduction to his study of atomic bomb literature, Kuroko Kazuo reacts to Nakagami Kenji's view that A-bomb writing is nothing more than stories by victims *(higaisha no shōsetsu)* told to induce tears *(o-namida chōdai)*. See Kuroko, *Genbaku to kotoba*, pp. 13–19.

28. Ibid., p. 61.

29. Hayashi Kyōko, "Ritual of Death," transl. Kyoko Selden, in *Nuke-Rebuke: Writers and Artists Against Nuclear Energy and Weapons,* ed. Morty Skylar (Iowa City: Spirit That Moves Us Press, 1984), p. 21.

30. Ibid., p. 27.

31. Ibid., p. 21.

32. Hirayama, "Hayashi Kyōko ron," p. 73.

33. Hayashi, "Ritual of Death," p. 29.

34. Ibid., p. 34.

35. Ibid., p. 40.

36. Ibid., p. 53.

37. Ibid., pp. 54–55.

38. See Ōsato Kyōzaburō's essay *"Matsuri no ba:* kiroku to hihyō no buntai" for an analysis of the story in which he describes Hayashi's style as journalistic and critical rather than fictional; see *Kokubungaku: Kaishaku to Kanshō* 8 (1985):98–101.

39. Hayashi, "Ritual of Death," p. 57.

40. Ibid.

41. See "Shanhai to hachigatsu no kokonoka," p. 114, for Hayashi's description of her violent reaction to the ending of this documentary. She acknowledges that the physical destruction of buildings ended, but the destruction of *hibakusha* did not.

42. Kuroko, *Genbaku to kotoba*, p. 99.

43. Treat, "Hiroshima," p. 41.

44. Nakano, "Kaisetsu," p. 407.

45. Hayashi states this intention in a discussion of *Matsuri no ba* titled "Shōwa nijūnen hachigatsu kokonoka"; see *Bungakukai* 9 (1975):168.

46. Endō Shūsaku discusses the cinematic effects of *Matsuri no ba* with Minakami Tsutomu and Gotō Meisei in *Bungei* 11 (1975):264–273.

47. Hayashi, "Shanhai to hachigatsu kokonoka," p. 117.

48. Hayashi Kyōko, "Jisaku saiken: *Giyaman biidoro*," *Asahi Shinbun*, August 5, 1990, p. 11.

49. Nakano, "Kaisetsu," p. 410.

50. Hirayama, "Hayashi Kyōko ron," p. 75.

51. Kuroko, *Genbaku to kotoba*, p. 66.

52. Kawanishi Masaaki, "Hayashi Kyōko koron," in *Matsuri no ba/Giyaman biidoro* (Tokyo: Kōdansha Bungei Bunko, 1988), pp. 373–386.

53. Ibid., p. 373.

54. Nakano, "Kaisetsu," p. 411.

55. Kawanishi, "Hayashi Kyōko koron," p. 377.

56. Hayashi Kyōko, "Akikan" (The Empty Can, trans. Margaret Mitsutani), in *The Crazy Iris and Other Stories of the Atomic Aftermath*, ed. Ōe Kenzaburō (New York: Grove Press, 1985), p. 143.

57. Kawanishi, "Hayashi Kyōko koron," pp. 375–377.

58. Nakano, "Kaisetsu," p. 412.

59. In his précis of *Giyaman biidoro*, Hirayama Mitsuo states that glass is a noted product of Nagasaki. This special glass was first created in Nagasaki during the Edo period (1603–1868), when the art of cutting glass *(giyaman)* from Holland was combined with the art of blowing glass from Portugal *(biidoro)*. The production of this glass stopped in the Meiji period (1868–1912). See Hirayama, "Hayashi Kyōko ron," p. 75.

60. Hayashi Kyōko, "Giyaman biidoro," in *Giyaman biidoro* (Tokyo: Kōdansha, 1978), pp. 59, 65.

61. Hayashi Kyōko, "Kiroku," in *Giyaman biidoro*, pp. 166–167.

62. Ibid., p. 167.

63. Ibid.

64. Hayashi Kyōko, "No ni," in *Giyaman biidoro*, p. 245.

65. Kuroko, *Genbaku to kotoba*, p. 65.

66. Critic Tsukimura Toshiyuki divides *Naki ga gotoki* into two sections. One section comprises the author's memories; the other is a salon discussion *(saron dangi)* among the six adults gathered at Haruko and Bob's home. See the joint review of *Naki ga gotoki* in *Gunzō* 1 (1981):302–315.

67. Nakano, "Kaisetsu," p. 409.

68. Oda Makoto in a joint review of *Naki ga gotoki* with Matsumoto Ken'ichi and Mita Masahiro; see "Dokusho dokudan," *Bungei* 9 (1981):235–237.

69. Akiyama Shun, "Sōsaku gappyō," *Gunzō* 1 (1981):303–304.

70. Matsumoto, "Dokusho dokudan," p. 238.

71. See Murakami Haruki's *1973 nen no pinbōru* (Pinball, 1973, 1983; trans. 1985) and *Sekai no owari to haadoboirudo wandaarando* (Hard Boiled Wonderland and the End of the World, 1985; trans. 1991) for additional examples of narrative bifurcation.

72. Matsumoto, "Dokusho dokudan," p. 236.

73. Hayashi Kyōko, *Naki ga gotoki* (Tokyo: Kōdansha Bungei Bunko, 1989), p. 9.

74. See Lifton, *Death in Life,* for more detail about the significance of requests for water by the dying.

75. Hayashi, *Naki ga gotoki,* p. 45.

76. Ibid., p. 64.

77. Ibid., p. 77.

78. Ibid., p. 100.

79. Ibid., p. 146.

80. Ibid., p. 177.

81. Ibid., p. 211.

82. Ibid., p. 215.

4

DEMONS, TRANSNATIONAL SUBJECTS, AND THE FICTION OF OHBA MINAKO

Adrienne Hurley

Ohba Minako was born on November 11, 1930. Her family moved frequently when she was young, and she attended several schools, including Aichi Toyobashi Women's High School and Yamaguchi Iwakuni Women's High School. When she was fourteen, Ohba was sent to Hiroshima prefecture as part of the wartime student mobilization project, which involved daily manual labor and little rest. On August 6, Ohba and her fellow students witnessed the bombing of Hiroshima from where they were stationed in Nishijō. They were then sent to assist the bomb victims and participate in various relief efforts.

Ohba graduated from Tsuda Private University in 1955. In 1959, because of her husband's work, she moved to Sitka, Alaska, and spent the next eleven years in the United States. She won the prestigious Akutagawa Prize for her 1968 story "Three Crabs," and she continues to be a prolific writer. Some of Ohba's most popular and celebrated short stories are available in English translation, and her work is represented in numerous Japanese literary anthologies, including Yukiko Tanaka's *Unmapped Territories: New Women's Fiction from Japan* and Noriko Mizuta Lippit and Kyoko Iriye Selden's *Stories by Contemporary Japanese Women Writers*.

■

D rawing objects, ideas, and people together does not always constitute an integrationist gesture; it sometimes neutralizes differences or brings disparate forces into crisis. When different nationalities come into contact in Ohba Minako's fiction, all the trappings of national identity, as well as the various characters' foundational understandings of who they are and where they "come from," are brought into crisis, challenged, and in some cases dismantled beyond recognition. Karatani Kōjin has described a process of confrontation or contact based on inversions. This concept *(tenkō)* incorporates the idea of reversing or converting the status quo.[1] It could be argued that Karatani's model continues to invoke the relative positions of a center and a margin, even though he maintains that they are ever changing and subject to constant redefinition. But Ohba steps outside this ubiquitous (if protean) model of normative power relations, describing instead what can be read as feminist possibilities for a counterculture—or even alternative forms of community building—despite her seemingly apolitical prose.

Unlike many writers who deal with issues of nationality and identity in positivistic terms, Ohba does not attempt to create a transparent relationship between the "individual" and the "nation" that would leave the customary gaps and fissures unproblematized; nor does she rely on a monolithic or static view of the "nation."[2] Her fiction features characters who not only live outside of their native countries or reject their familiar surroundings, but who can call up magical forces and seek refuge in a realm in which the supernatural and the real coexist. Although her fiction most often addresses very individual responses to worldly and otherworldly events, it also opens up new possibilities for understanding the politics of transnational identities in our contemporary world.

Ohba's transnational subjects do not partake in the same kind of "transnational corporate culture" that Masao Miyoshi describes in "A Borderless World? From Colonialism to Transnationalism and the Decline of the Nation-State."[3] Rather, Ohba's characters seem to operate independently of our world of international politics and the logic of capitalism. When the marketplace does enter her stories, it tends to be in the form of the "primitive" small shop as opposed to the big multinational corporation. Both their longing for a sustainable local economy and, perhaps more important, an invocation of supernatural and psychic powers (which allows characters to live outside of dominant political and economic structures) enable Ohba's characters to resist or even bypass the very real hardships that the ever-increasing push for capital incurs, as well as to construct communities based on new kinds of relationships and affinities.

Alternative communities and relationships are central to an investigation of how nationality and transnationality are explored in Ohba's fiction. As the immigrants and their children, expatriates, deserters, and travelers who populate her stories recognize the ways that various national affiliations have hurt or hindered them, they seek out new alliances. But the very communication that engenders new communities in Ohba's works might more accurately be viewed as miscommunication, and the struggle to correct misunderstandings drives many of her plots. Even friendships emerge out of misunderstanding, and those who reject the limits and rules of their native communities and yearn for what they imagine to be better and more equitable possibilities abroad often overlook or misconstrue crucial differences when banding together with other expatriates. Her characters struggle to articulate feelings and experiences that are extremely difficult to communicate. And when their efforts at expressing themselves are not readily understood or accepted within one context, they find increasingly unique and sometimes violent ways to make themselves heard in another.

In the process of transgressing conventional community boundaries, individual characters, as I hope to show, must confront the colonization of their subjectivities by various dominant cultures. Deleuze and Guattari identify this problem in *Kafka: Toward a Minor Literature:*

> How many people today live in a language that is not their own? Or no longer, or not yet, even know their own and know poorly the major language they are forced to serve? This is the problem of immigrants, and especially of their children, the problem of minorities, the problem of a minor literature, but also a problem for all of us: how to tear a minor literature away from its own language, allowing it to challenge the language and making it follow a sober revolutionary path? How to become a nomad and an immigrant and a gypsy in relation to one's own language.[4]

By giving her characters opportunities to confront or oppose the "major language," Ohba helps break down conventional spatial and cultural boundaries, and she uses language in strange ways that often highlight what is otherwise repressed.

One venue Ohba uses to explore the limits and possibilities of alternative communication is the acquisition of foreign languages. But the bilingual character is not the only type in her fiction whose relationship to the dominant language is fraught with political tension. Sometimes her characters venture into supernatural realms where allegories for sexist, racist, and other forms of discrimination are played out indirectly. Here I wish to focus on two figures that appear frequently throughout Ohba's oeuvre: the immigrant (and her children) and the "witch" or demon woman.[5] Both of these figures (frequently embodied in the same character) provide exciting possibilities for resistance, charting creative ways to achieve some degree of agency even in the most adverse and unfair circumstances.

Ohba spent the better part of eleven years living in the United States, and several of her novels are set in rural Alaska, where she herself lived. *Garakuta hakubutsukan* (The Junk Museum), for example, is set in a small town that still shows signs of the Russian culture of a bygone era in Russian street names and Russian Orthodox churches. It is a town of so many immigrants, according to the local or "insider" narrator, that the people there see each other "simply as human beings," not as Japanese, Russian, or any other nationality.[6] The narrator goes on to claim that it is a place where nationality has "no meaning," and she prefaces one chapter by explaining that she will relate the story of a woman named Marya who lives in the "Dog House," instead of describing it as the story of a Russian woman living in the United States.[7] This very qualification belies her own inability to ignore national origin, and she unfailingly invokes nationality to identify and describe every character. No one is mentioned without her "home" country being invoked along with her.

Garakuta consists of three chapters, each of which features a different person and her or his immigrant experience. The first chapter, "Inu yashiki no onna" (The Dog House Woman), centers on Marya—a Russian woman who clings to a nostalgic ideal of the historical grandeur of her native culture but is unable to return. Marya calls her life story a "deserter's tale" and writes in her diary: "This is the tale of one deserter. It's nothing lofty like exile. I only came here to run away." The experiences and places from which she ran away, however, are disconnected from the "Russia" of her imagination (providing her with the opportunity to claim national pride and relate feelings of "homesickness" while still acknowledging her reasons for leaving).[8]

Marya laments the way "great" Russian literature has been translated, celebrating a nationally or ethnically specific "aesthetic" or "sensibility" that defies translation:

> Ahh, my precious Pushkin has been changed into such strange and crass words! What kind of translation is that? Those people truly mangle it all. When I go to a bookstore and read a translation of Chekhov or Pushkin, I begin to cry.[9]

There are moments, nevertheless, when she remembers that the "reality" of her own lived experience is far removed from her fantasy of a glorious national culture and expatriate's exaggerated sense of national identity—as when she tells another character an "African saying": "One has two options: to obey a country's customs or to run away from them."[10] Marya fled her homeland, only to "love" all the more an idealized and romanticized notion of Russia. Marya concludes that a person's freedom to choose a homeland provides the sole means of finding happiness. If she had happened to have been born in the country she was destined to love, she thinks she would have loved it without having wanted to live elsewhere —implying, of course, that Russia, despite her articulated yearnings for Russianness, was not her homeland of destiny. People who are not patriotic, according to Marya, are those who have not enjoyed the freedom to choose a country freely.[11]

Marya's closest friend is the subject of the second chapter, "Yorozu shūzenya no tsuma" (Mr. Fix-It's Wife), a Japanese immigrant named Aya, who, unlike Marya, tends to be ambivalent at best, but usually disdainful, toward her native country and its culture. The two women's friendship is built on experience rather than race, class, or cultural affinities. We observe Ohba's flair for finding humor in unlikely situations when the friendship begins after Marya's dog eats Aya's cat.[12] Aya's "American" husband grabs his rifle when he hears the news of the cat's death, ready to exercise "cowboy justice" and shoot Marya's dog, but Marya refuses to let him kill it. Eventually the two women sort through their disagreements, and their friendship develops.

Aya is revealed to be a clever and observant person, but other characters see her according to racialized gender stereotypes—as timid, simple, and subservient, always following Marya around. Ironically those who think the least of Aya are exposed to be the most simpleminded. Aya is constantly beleaguered by townspeople's questions about Japan and Japanese culture, as well as by their illinformed observations and thinly veiled Japan-bashing. Even when Aya attempts to disabuse them of their mistaken ideas, they walk away feeling that their racist assumptions about Japanese business practices or gender roles have been reconfirmed by a native "expert." Aya's frustration at the difficulty of answering such questions without either generalizing to the point of "giving them what they want"—a distinctly romanticized Other—or expending the energy required to explain complexities and details (in a second language) reveals one way in which miscommunication seems inevitable in *Garakuta*. The "multicultural" community in which Aya lives is not so ideal as the narrator claims, and Aya struggles to represent herself to the dominant or "major" community.

The discrepancy between people's perceptions of Aya and the Aya disclosed by the narrator to the reader is evident even before she leaves Japan. The "misfit,"

Aya, fails to communicate or be understood within two major cultures before building a new community with Marya. Both Aya and her American husband, Ross, were previously married, and both were subsequently abandoned.[13] Aya's first husband left her for another woman, and as a single mother in Japan with little in the way of community support, she felt alienated and betrayed. Aya's decision to marry Ross is portrayed as stemming from her wish to abandon the country she felt had abandoned her when she was at her most vulnerable. Ross enlisted in the military as a way to overcome his own feelings of betrayal after his first wife had left him. Instead of Vietnam, he was sent to Japan, where he met Aya, to whom he "was drawn" *(hikitsukerareta)*. Ohba uses the character meaning "to charm" or "to enchant" to express how Ross felt bewitched by Aya; this use of the passive also absolves him of any agency in the inauguration of their romance.[14] The narrator makes it clear that Ross sees Aya as simpleminded and naive in addition to enchanting. To some extent complicit in his fantasy, Aya never reveals to him that she is well educated: she pretends to be the simple and enchanting woman he has imagined her to be.[15] She and her daughter move to Alaska with Ross, where he runs a fix-it shop and makeshift junkyard.

Aya's daughter by her first marriage, Chizu (or Liz), is a particularly interesting character whose presence introduces the issue of second-generation identity and nationality.[16] Her field of experience is very different from that of her mother: she goes to a school where one in three students has divorced parents (her generation represents the first for which divorce is commonplace and not disgraceful), she grows up as part of a racial minority, and her native language, unlike that of her immigrant mother, is English.[17] Chizu encounters difficulty when she tries to understand her mother's feelings about "Japaneseness." This tension gets played out when Aya tracks down Chizu's biological father in Japan and arranges a meeting. (The only person to oppose the trip is Marya. Jealous that she cannot visit Russia and fearful of losing her best friend, Marya warns Aya not to go in fear that she might be lured back into Japanese culture and stay there forever.)

When Chizu meets her biological father, Takanobu, she qualifies their relationship and keeps him at a distance by calling him her "Japanese father." She rarely communicates with Takanobu directly, and Aya maintains this gulf by refraining from interpreting for Chizu and Takanobu. When the three of them go out to eat in Tokyo, it is a painfully evocative scene of awkwardness and disappointment. Although no one is satisfied with the encounter, Aya gains strength and confidence by confronting the man who abandoned her and her child. The reader learns much less about Chizu's experience of this encounter. Her voice is confined to predictable complaints about Japan being a wealthy country where everything is too expensive and unavailable to her. She encourages her mother—who, as Marya feared, is enjoying being back home in Japan—to return to Alaska.

Both Aya and Marya overcome their feelings of abandonment and dissatisfaction with conventional gender roles and go on to forge a close friendship and new community in Alaska. Alaska here—and throughout Ohba's oeuvre—is a space of new possibilities where Aya and Marya can build a new community so seemingly independent of their respective "homelands" that national identity seems subordinated to these remarkable characters' transnational identities. Lippit and Selden write that national identity is "superficial" in Ohba's works.[18] Although this seems to be the wish Ohba conveys in *Garakuta,* her narrator and other characters describe each other in terms of race, size, body type, hair color, ethnicity, and nation of origin. Although everyone in the novel wants to believe that nationality is meaningless, they cannot escape its grip even in small-town rural Alaska. The immigrant in *Garakuta* is caught in the interstices—somewhere between where she came from and where she is.

Garakuta hakubutsukan is merely one of many Ohba novels that describe transnational subjectivity in seemingly backward or cut-off spaces such as rural Alaska. But the experience of being both separate from a dominant culture and defined by that culture's major language is not limited to the discussion of nationality in Ohba's fiction. Even characters who remain within the boundaries of their homeland or for whom nationality is not problematized feel alienated, and they too construct alternative realities, often relying on mythic or supernatural ideals for inspiration. In these more fantastic stories, Ohba makes use of a wide variety of images, tropes, and even phrases from legends and classical Japanese literature.

Literary ancestry and cultural memory loom large in Ohba's fiction: in some novels, identity is explored specifically through these lineages. Ohba herself is well versed in classical Japanese literature and was urged by the late Enchi Fumiko to write a modern Japanese translation of *Ugetsu monogatari.*[19] Ohba's translation of the famous Edo collection of ghost stories is merely one example of her familiarity with a variety of literary traditions, and she uses mythic or literary figures in many of her more fantastic novels and stories. One of Ohba's stock characters is the *yama uba* or *yamamba,* an old demon woman or "witch" who lives in the mountains.[20] The subject of folklore, fantasy fiction, and even *Nō* plays, she represents part of a supernatural realm inhabited by ghosts, snake demons, fox spirits, other *oni* (demons), and eerie spirits. Many traditional *yamamba* tales share a similar skeletal plot: a young man gets lost in the mountains at night; an old woman appears; she chases him. In the classical *Nō* play *Yamamba*, the *yamamba* even conquers patriarchy by achieving enlightenment without having undergone a *henshin*, or sexual metamorphosis, into a male body (a standard formula).

Revising various Japanese, Chinese, and Western tropes of witchcraft, Ohba creates a new terrain on which familiar images collide or mingle with the new. Her representation of the supernatural is embedded in Japanese mythic and spiritual traditions, but it differs from those traditions in that an object of fear is transformed into a sympathetic subject—usually the protagonist. Ohba makes use of the patriarchal vocabularies of demonism and misogyny in her tales to convey the other side (or Other's side) of the story: that of the demon woman.

Although a feminist project or other political agenda is not claimed in Ohba's writing, her fiction is highly politicized in its rejection of traditional marriage practices, nationalized racisms and sexisms, and the arbitrary separation of certain modes of spiritual practice or expression, such as witchcraft, from the dominant culture and its sanctioned religions. Where do Ohba's women find the power to challenge these institutionalized practices? Inevitably there is a history somewhere that has been replaced, and the reclamation of this history gives Ohba's *yamamba* characters the power to be subversive and rebellious. At the same time, the actions of these women are never exclusively reclamative; therefore, they must also be read in terms of more immediate forces of oppression. Ohba's writing proposes many new ways to engage in counterhegemonic resistance, and each possibility she describes has roots in both historical narratives and contemporary society.[21]

Breaking down conventional spatial boundaries and creating new ones, Ohba transports the reader into a space where the supernatural and natural coexist. The border between the material and the abstract or spiritual in Ohba's fiction is very porous, and women with supernatural attributes emerge in even the most unremarkable circumstances. As Yukiko Tanaka, the translator of one of Ohba's short stories, "Candle Fish," comments, Ohba uses the *yamamba* as "the embodiment of all women who defy the constricting rules of society."[22] Ohba's fiction creates spaces for "ordinary" housewives to become "extraordinary" *yamamba*.

Rarely do Ohba's women strive to (or even bother to) conform to masculinist or heterosexist ideals of feminine beauty or behavior. Ohba recasts prescribed and proscribed models of "feminine behavior" by re-presenting what was dangerous or evil in prior literature as considerate or virtuous in her stories. In classical *yamamba* tales, for example, mind reading was coded as demonic. Old women would recite their victims' thoughts before attacking. Ohba's resurrected *yamamba* use the same knowledge both to articulate anger and to respect the thoughts and feelings of others. But the *yamamba* who strives to respond to the desires of others is nonetheless subject to other interpretations; confused by the constant noise of other people's thoughts, she is burdened with excessive knowledge, always knowing that her efforts are insufficient. In this case, the *yamamba*'s struggle is emblematic of the difficulty women encounter when trying to represent their experiences within a patriarchal code—the dominant language—that is designed to exclude them and deny the very reality of their lived experience.[23]

In *Onna no danseiron* (A Woman's Theory of Men), Ohba comments on women in her fiction, noting that her protagonists rarely are married or, if they are, they are not thoroughly or happily participating in married life. She asserts that the "collapse of the household" *(katei no hōkai)* readers notice in her fiction is linked to her intent to examine the "expression of individual consciousness."[24] Ohba's premise is that a woman's individual consciousness cannot be expressed within the confines of a traditional marriage. As a solution, she constructs *yamamba*, women who can speak and act more freely, in her fiction. Ohba expands her discussion to include issues of race, class, and national identity, focusing on similarities between two very different examples of ongoing oppression:

> Men are afraid of women for the same reason that whites are afraid of blacks. Histories of slavery and oppression have been advanced through a social rhetoric that defines men and whites as better than women and blacks. Women were to comfort men. We have been made to believe that men are really better than women, and this has hurt us more than anything else.[25]

The commonality Ohba posits, although it lumps together two distinctly different examples, aspires to be a strong political statement. The indignation and revolutionary spirit that enable women in her fiction to live amazing lives are inextricably linked to specific experiences of oppression or misfortune. It could be argued that, rather than writing "stories," with clear beginnings and endings, Ohba writes "people," whose fictional experiences of oppression are the story.

In an afterword she wrote for an anthology that included many of her short stories, Ohba emphasizes the importance of lived experience and communion with the world to her creative process and product:

> When I think about it, it seems that, after "Three Crabs," every work I've written has been a result of the power of people I have encountered along the way as

opposed to my own power, and I do not know from whence it comes—whether
or not it is a mysterious power cast on me—but it is with such a power that I have
come to write.[26]

This portrait of a possessed woman can describe her fictional counterparts as
well. The *yamamba* and other magical women who lash out against injustice find
their power in unlikely ways and places, as is the case in "Sanbashi nite" (By the
Pier), in which the practices of *noroi* (cursing) and hammering nails in *noromaningyō* (cursing dolls) serve as allegories of women's resistance and anger.[27] Similar to a voodoo doll, the *noromaningyō* can be used to inflict pain on another
person's body. In the opening passage of "By the Pier," we see how one woman
redresses injustice:

> "Do you know what times are the happiest for me?" asked the red-haired woman.
> "They're when I curse the person I hate. In the dead of night, I'll wear a sheer white
> kimono and climb the cemetery hill barefoot, running so quickly—like I'm flying
> —that my diaphanous kimono never touches the ground. Since it's a very, very
> old cemetery, here and there the earth has sunk and caved in, and there are shards
> of broken bottle glass, crushed Coca Cola cans, as well as things that stick into the
> soles of your feet. Now, since the skin on the soles of my feet is thick and hard, I
> rarely prick or wound it enough to draw blood."[28]

This short story opens with a confession of hatred by a clearly unconventional
woman. Like Marya in *Garakuta* and many other strong-willed women who
appear throughout Ohba's writings, this character has red hair. For a seasoned
Ohba reader, familiar with her system of signs that, like a foreign language, can
be learned, this opening monologue establishes the red-haired woman as one of
Ohba's subversives who fight back with creative vengeance. The red-haired
woman continues describing her cemetery ritual:

> As I pass through the wooded side of the cemetery, I chant that woman's name
> over and over so fast that I nearly bite my tongue.[29]

She reveals here that the object of her rage is another woman. Chanting a victim's
name or writing the name on the doll itself helps the red-haired woman establish
the identity of the victim. This can also be achieved with a lock of hair.

The purgative moment in the ritual is violent. After falling down in a fresh grave and running through the cemetery as if she were in a trance, the red-haired woman reaches her ultimate destination:

> After I reach the top of the hill, I nail the cursing doll to a big plum tree with a three-inch nail. And then I hammer more nails into the white forehead of that black-haired woman. Then, the tip of her nose, her teeth, her eyelids—and blood gushes out. Then her two breasts, her navel, then I wonder where I should stab her next.[30]

Violence—albeit displaced—provides an effective means of releasing anger and punishment. Like the oppressed and colonized "native" described by Frantz Fanon, the red-haired woman can finally feel her power in the bloody torture of her (perceived) oppressor.[31] Fanon's native, like Ohba's demon woman, reacts violently in proportion to the violence—or sometimes symbolic violence—he or she has suffered, and the native hopes to supplant the colonizer and occupy the colonizer's position. (The revolutionary aspirations in this case do not extend to challenging the presence of differential power relations.) Ohba's red-haired women choose methods of retaliatory counterviolence, such as cursing, for similar purposes. But as "Sanbashi nite" progresses we learn that she has misidentified her greatest enemy by cursing the "other woman" and not the man whose infidelity proves the catalyst for her intense anger—a vestige of the patriarchal invention that makes it easier for women to see other women as the enemy in order to maintain male dominance. As the red-haired woman continues to tell her story (to an increasingly disgusted and nauseated woman by the pier), we learn more about her "victim":

> That woman had long jet-black hair like shiny silk threads. Hey now, you don't need to get all excited. It wasn't at all like your dull brownish hair. And she didn't section it off into three cords to braid either. No matter what time it was, she left her hair down, long over both shoulders. That hair clung to him, and he gasped for breath to explain. During that time, he always gasped like a goldfish, with his eyeballs bulging out. . . . So, you see, every night, under the moonlight, I see the same hateful vision. Are you all right? Are you feeling sick? They'd haul me off to prison if I really did any of that to her real body anyway. Right? That's how it goes . . . in this world of ours. But no one is going to complain about my moonlit nights of wetting my lips and hateful dreaming. I plunge the three-inch nail into the plum tree. When I stick the long nails into the white skin, it sounds like breaking bones.

Like pinning a pocket in place before sewing it up on the machine, I stick tons of pins all around her mouth. Those lips that stuck to him like gnarled leeches will make her crawl in agony.[32]

With careful attention to detail and ritual in performance, the red-haired woman exorcises her rage. She mentions the figure of her pathetic husband searching for the best lies and the hair of the "other woman." But rather than narrating a tale of betrayal, she describes what she does: how she fights back.

To accommodate such angry and powerful women, Ohba often maps out new countries and provides them with cultural histories. Although many proper names in her work have the trappings of realism, upon closer examination one finds that slight differences reveal a "virtual realism." That is to say, a word might be altered to disarticulate it from its ordinary referent. Ohba's playful use of familiar and unfamiliar proper names is particularly evident in "Yureitachi no fukkatsusai" (The Ghosts' Easter), in which characters refer to places that are almost real—such as "Latin Ameriya" *(raten ameriya)* and "Anglo Ameriya" *(anguro ameriya).*[33] This unstable terrain, as well as the similarly fantastic worlds in other stories, serves as a "home" for a variety of characters, many of whom are expatriates like Marya and Aya in *Garakuta.* Ohba's alternative "realities" can be in the form of other nations, supernatural realms, or sometimes both, and demons and spirits can interact with "real" people. Women with spiritual or psychic abilities figure most prominently throughout Ohba's work, and they too are associated with a variety of "real" and "unreal" nationalities. National identity is subordinated to women's connections to other women, however, whether they are "from" Japan or the United States. Like the women in *Garakuta,* the main characters in "Candle Fish," which is available in English translation as part of Yukiko Tanaka's *Unmapped Territories,* become great friends in rural Alaska. Long after the narrator of "Candle Fish" returns to Japan, she has visions of her friend:

There is a woman who comes to me on sleepless nights, when I lie awake in bed imagining things. I call her Tsukiko, the daughter of the moon, since she wears a robe that changes colors like the moon. . . . Sometimes when I can't sleep I am transformed into a yamamba, the old witch of the mountain. It is then that Tsukiko comes to me. . . . And I'd rather call her Tsukiko than Olga.[34]

This narrator engages in the performative act par excellence: she renames her obsession, relying on magic language to convey her desire. The homoeroticism in this story provides yet another avenue for forming community, and we are left feeling that the narrator is separated from the one person with whom she was able to communicate. When "Tsukiko" visits the narrator's dreams, they speak in a special language in which "neither the names we were given at our birth, nor our nationalities, nor the language we grew up speaking matters."[35] In Ohba's writing, women's bonds to other women can be both liberating and romantic, but only if women develop the capacity to discard traditional gender roles and explore new ways of engaging with each other.

Ohba Minako was able to address the strangling power of traditional gender roles in greater detail after she was approached by the Asahi newspaper with the idea of reconstructing the diary of Tsuda Umeko.[36] Tsuda was one of the first five Japanese female foreign exchange students to the United States over a century ago; she went to the United States at the age of seven and did not return to Japan for eleven years (the same number of years Ohba spent in the United States years later). Tsuda serves as yet another discursive vehicle for exploring cultural exchange and national identity, but one of the most interesting issues that Ohba teases out in *Tsuda Umeko* is the impact of prescribed gender roles on individual lives. Marriage, for example, was a "big problem" for Tsuda.[37] She had not met many Japanese men (international or interracial marriage was considered impossible), nor was she prepared to give up her autonomy to become someone else's wife.[38] This gives Ohba an opportunity to engage in a sustained discussion of turn-of-the-century normative heterosexual relationships in the United States and Japan through the voice of a young woman who wants to forgo the many constrictions that society has in store for her.

The difficulties that Tsuda experienced as she tried to imagine herself fitting into the strictly defined role of a Meiji-period wife are not unlike the challenges other women face in Ohba's fiction. When only a few unsatisfactory possibilities are available or when their lives are threatened, Ohba's characters develop radical ways to resist—such as leaving their nation of origin or practicing witchcraft. When women like the narrator of "Candle Fish" do not transform their situations through active means, they are left to dream about the lives they wish they could enjoy. Ohba's insistence that we recognize oppression—even if only in subversive dreams—raises questions that perhaps anticipate the work of younger writers (such as Uchida Shungicu, who grapples with the trauma of childhood sexual abuse and its long-lasting effects) who are taking on the personal in increasingly direct and powerful ways. The extreme difficulty facing those who attempt to articulate and communicate very personal experiences of oppression lends itself to allegorical and other indirect styles of expression, not only because there are often no words to express these experiences, but also because of the fear that few people will extend themselves to hear such stories.

NOTES

Jim Fujii's detailed criticism contributed to this essay in innumerable ways. I also benefited from the comments of two anonymous readers and the insights of Dana Bryon-Staub, Wilson Chen, and Jennifer Robertson. Any mistakes and misinterpretations, of course, are entirely my own.

1. See, for example, Karatani's *Origins of Japanese Literature,* trans., Brett de Bary (Durham, N.C.: Duke University Press, 1993).

2. As Homi Bhabha reminds us in his introduction to *Nation and Narration* (New York: Routledge, 1991), pp. 1–3, although it is often invoked as something timeless, a nation is just as subject to temporal limits as those who live in it.

3. Masao Miyoshi, "A Borderless World? From Colonialism to Transnationalism and the Decline of the Nation-State," *Critical Inquiry* 19(4) (Summer 1993):726–751.

4. Gilles Deleuze and Félix Guattari, *Kafka: Toward a Minor Literature,* trans. Dana Polan (Minneapolis: University of Minnesota Press, 1986), p. 19. Despite her canonization and inclusion in many anthologies, Ohba's fiction can be read as a "minor literature." It is helpful to remember Deleuze and Guattari's three features of a minor literature (deterritorialization of language, political import, and collective value) when considering the feminist possibilities for a counterculture that emerge in Ohba's seemingly apolitical prose.

5. These categories are fluid and there are many variations. It is also common to find one character who embodies both the immigrant and the demon.

6. Ohba Minako, *Garakuta hakubutsukan* (Tokyo: Bungei shunjū, 1988), p. 21. This translation and all others, unless otherwise indicated, are my own. Out of respect for the author, I am spelling her name with the romanization that she prefers, as opposed to the conventional spelling (Ōba). The practice of choosing how one's name is romanized is not uncommon—the contemporary novelist and *manga* author Uchida Shungicu uses a *"c"* instead of the conventional *"k"* in her name.

7. Ibid.

8. Ibid., p. 30.

9. Ibid., p. 16.

10. Ibid., p. 44.

11. Ibid., p. 124.

12. Ibid., p. 12.

13. Ibid., p. 92.

14. Ibid., p. 93.

15. Ibid., p. 94.

16. Chizu/Liz was a toddler when Aya moved to Alaska.

17. Ohba, *Garakuta,* p. 108

18. Noriko Mizuta Lippit and Kyoko Iriye Selden, *Stories by Contemporary Japanese Women Writers* (New York: Sharpe, 1990), p. 218.

19. In the preface to *Ohba Minako no Ugetsu monogatari* (Tokyo: Shūeisha, 1987), p. 4, Ohba recalls that she was summoned to Enchi Fumiko's hospital bed where Enchi, grabbing the younger writer's hands, entreated Ohba to study *Ugetsu*, a "truly fine work."

20. Baba Akiko, *Ōhime kangae: hakumei no erosu* (Tokyo: Daiwa shoten, 1972), p. 29. Baba does not use the word "witch," and I use it cautiously to avoid conflating distinct images, traditions, and practices.

21. Miura Masashi notes in Ohba's fiction the frequent occurrence of dual or multivalenced representations, such as the use of animals to allegorize humans or the conflation of opposite phenomena. He contends that rather than using opposites, such as dark and light or alive and dead, Ohba reveals their similarities by mixing them together. When an object or character gets cast as another, he says, it creates a "double image" as opposed to erasing one with the other. See *Shōsetsu to iu shokuminchi* (Tokyo: Fukubu shoten, 1991), pp. 186–187.

22. Yukiko Tanaka, ed., *Unmapped Territories: New Women's Fiction from Japan* (Seattle: Women in Translation, 1991), pp. xii–xiii.

23. Uchida Shungicu, in her autobiographical novels *Father Fucker* and *Atashi ga umi ni kaeru made*, takes this one step further by addressing the trauma of prolonged and repeated sexual abuse. These novels describe instances of severe abuse, as well as the young protagonist's attempts to escape from the perpetrator (her stepfather).

24. Ohba Minako, *Onna no danseiron* (Tokyo: Chūokōronsha, 1982), p. 23.

25. Ibid., p. 48.

26. *Shōwa bungaku zenshū*, vol. 19 (Tokyo: Shōgakkan, 1987), p. 1008.

27. The Edo-period doll maker Noroma Kambeiei may have been the first to use dolls in this way.

28. Ohba Minako, "Sanbashi nite," *Ohba Minako shū* (Tokyo: Kawaide shoten, 1972), p. 137.

29. Ibid., p. 137.

30. Ibid., p. 138.

31. This is discussed at length in the chapter "Concerning Violence" in Fanon's *The Wretched of the Earth* (New York: Grove Press, 1963).

32. Ohba, "Sanbashi nite," p. 188.

33. Ohba Minako, "Yureitachi no fukkatsusai," *Chikuma gendai bungaku taikei*, vol. 91 (Tokyo: Chikuma, 1978).

34. Ohba Minako, "Candle Fish," in *Unmapped Territories: New Women's Fiction from Japan*, ed. and trans. Yukiko Tanaka (Seattle: Women in Translation, 1991), pp. 18–21.

35. Ibid., p. 21.

36. Ohba Minako, *Tsuda Umeko* (Tokyo: Asahi, 1990). Asahi approached her with this project in 1986.

37. Ibid., p. 69.

38. Ohba discusses comparative marriage practices at length in *Onna no danseiron*.

5

DOUBLE VISION: DIVIDED NARRATIVE FOCUS IN TAKAHASHI TAKAKO'S *YOSŌI SEYO, WAGA TAMASHII YO*

Mark Williams

Takahashi Takako was born in Kyoto in 1932. She graduated from the Department of French Literature at Kyoto University in 1954 and, in the same year, married fellow author Takahashi Kazumi. She received an M.A. in French Literature in 1958 and, by the time of her withdrawal from literary circles in the mid-1980s, she had established a reputation as a writer, not only of carefully constructed psychological novels, but also a series of intriguing short stories that owe much to the fantastic tradition in Japanese literature.

The psychological category includes such acclaimed novels as *Sora no hate made* (To the Farthest Reaches of the Sky, 1973), *Yūwakusha* (The Temptress, 1976), *Yosōi seyo, waga tamashii yo* (Gird Up Thyself, O My Soul, 1982), and *Ikari no ko* (Child of Wrath, 1985). It was with *Sora no hate made*, a dramatic portrayal of a woman struggling to come to terms with the forces of evil she discerns within, that Takahashi emerged to public prominence. Conferral of the prestigious Tamura Toshiko Prize secured her literary reputation, and in the decade that ensued there followed a series of novels in which Takahashi consistently depicted the drama of individuals brought face to face with the voice of their unconscious.

It may be in the full-length novels that Takahashi's genius for portraying the drama of the soul is best appreciated. But these were accompanied by a series of short stories—epitomized by "Sōjikei" (Congruent Figures, 1971; trans. 1991), "Seihō no kuni" (The Country to the West, 1972), and "Ningyō no ai" (Doll Love, 1976; trans. 1982)—in which the author explored the image of individuals confronted by their double, or alter ego. The image of the unfathomable power of the unconscious cultivated in these stories attracted considerable critical attention at the time of their publication and prepares the reader for the extended consideration of human psychology to be found in the full-length novels.

Throughout the early 1980s, Takahashi wrote repeatedly of the tension she discerned between her chosen profession as author and the call of the Catholic faith into which she had been baptized in 1975. Eventually, in 1986, she went on public record announcing her retirement from all further literary activity and her determination to devote all her future energies to the establishment in Japan of the Carmelite order of nuns in which she had increasingly sought refuge in Paris.

■

Appended to the end of the *nenpu* (bibliography of major literary works) provided for the novelist Takahashi Takako (b. 1932) in the recently published *Shōwa bungaku zenshū* is a cursory statement, penned by the author herself, in which she indicates her intention to refrain from all further literary activity and devote herself entirely to "a life of prayer and meditation."[1] With this and other statements of the time, Takahashi served notice to the Japanese literary community, not only of her desire to refrain from all creative writing in the future, but also to distance herself from all discussion of her not inconsiderable literary production to date. The loss was keenly felt in literary circles in Japan.[2] At the same time, however, Takahashi's retreat from the limelight provided the impetus for several critics, most of them Japanese, to attempt to place the author's literary legacy into clearer perspective.[3]

Reevaluation was long overdue. As Livia Monnet has pointed out, critical discussion of Takahashi's art to that date had tended to focus, almost exclusively, on the author's apparently insatiable fascination with the negative side of human nature and, in so doing, to have overlooked the obvious: "the interdependence of [Takahashi's] life and art."[4] As Monnet is the first to acknowledge, the call here is not for "a biographical reading of Takahashi's literary output in the (now discredited, albeit still influential) *sakkaron* manner."[5] Rather, Monnet is here advocating a reading of Takahashi's works that, while questioning "the sociocultural determinants of Takahashi's identity," nevertheless maintains the focus on the narrative techniques evidenced in the texts themselves.[6]

This essay applies such criteria to *Yosōi seyo, waga tamashii yo* (Gird Up Thyself, O My Soul, 1982)—the novel that, in conjunction with the author's final work of fiction, *Ikari no ko* (Child of Wrath, 1985), has secured Takahashi's reputation in Japanese literary circles. Before turning to the text itself, however, let us place the novel in its literary context.

EMERGENCE OF A SPLINTERED PERSPECTIVE

While acknowledging the role exercised by the various "sociocultural determinants" in shaping the narrative perspective evidenced in a text, we must avoid any reading that seeks to privilege these forces as unidirectional influences and views the text itself as a reflection of some abstract authorial philosophy. As James Fujii has pointed out in his increasingly influential study of the position of the subject in what he describes as the "modern Japanese prose narrative":

> A text is best conceived not as the simple expression of a given person's thoughts, ideas and views; more compellingly, it is the product of a multitude of historically prior events (genre conventions, specific earlier texts, the absence of certain texts) and contemporaneous events, both narrative and other.[7]

His caveat would appear particularly applicable when considering the literary texts of an author like Takahashi. Given the recent advances with regard to critical understanding of the significance of "confession" in twentieth-century Japanese literature, it is surprising to note the extent to which Takahashi's critics of the time chose to read her earlier works as reflections of her personal spiritual journey. Seizing upon the reality of the author's public affirmation of the Catholic faith through baptism in 1975 and the increasingly protracted periods she subsequently spent in silent meditation both in France and in Japan, such critics proceeded to read Catholic "influences" into each of Takahashi's novels as they appeared off the press. To some extent, these attempts were encouraged, paradoxically, by the author's frequent and, on occasion, vehement denials of all connection between her literature and her faith.[8] And fortunately, these commentators have, on the whole, refrained from mining Takahashi's works in search of autobiographical detail drawn from her own life. In the tendency to posit the existence of a prototypical Takahashi heroine—a composite of the protagonists of the novels that comprise her oeuvre who comes to be portrayed in an increasingly optimistic light —they have, nevertheless, reinforced the impression of these works as the immediate product of the author's own journey toward spiritual renewal. Not only has the distinction between the various novels as discrete narratives been unjustifiably eroded, but the whole corpus has come to be viewed as an exposé, as complete as possible, of the author's conscious self, presented through the voice of what appears as an enslaved narrator, often barely distinguishable from that of the author herself.

Much less rigorously addressed—and of much greater significance to critical discussions of Takahashi's art—is the extent to which the author's novels conform to, and differ from, prevailing narrative trends in postwar Japanese fiction. While this is no place for extended consideration of developments within the postwar prose narrative form—and while acknowledging the need for greater critical discussion of the author-narrator-protagonist paradigm following the demise of the all-consuming identification with their creations by many authors of the prewar *shishōsetsu* tradition—a brief discussion should help to locate Takahashi closer to the postwar literary mainstream than is often acknowledged.

In a series of articles written around the time of her emergence on the literary scene in the early 1970s, Takahashi placed herself on record as wishing to distance herself from the *shishōsetsu* tradition, which she saw as excessively narrow in its concerns.[9] For Takahashi and others of her generation raised during the upheaval of the Pacific War and the subsequent Allied Occupation of Japan, the need was keenly felt for the establishment of a new narrative perspective—one better suited to the authors' identities, both as survivors of the years of turmoil and as observers of a society hell-bent upon rescuing a sense of pride from the ruins, both physical and metaphysical, confronting them. In the immediate aftermath of the events of 1945, the catalyst for this search was often, quite literally, the need to "endure" the rigors of daily existence that, even if they were spared the physical horrors of war, still represented an all-consuming challenge. It was to this end that many sought literary inspiration in Marxist ideology or in the existential philosophy of Camus and Sartre.[10]

For Takahashi and others whose rise to literary prominence would coincide with the increased economic confidence of the nation as a whole in the ensuing decades, however, the more pressing challenge was that of coming to terms with the feelings of ambivalence occasioned by consideration of their own personal contribution to the task of nation building so assiduously and conspicuously pursued by their peers in the economic sector. Dismissive of what they viewed as the inability of their forebears in the prewar *shishōsetsu* tradition to acknowledge a greater complexity to the process of recording individual experience by "delving beyond the level of the psyche" in their portrayals of human nature,[11] many turned to study of the Western psychoanalytic critical tradition in support of their goals. At the same time, convinced of the need to exercise a greater degree of objectivity in the positioning of the narrators on whom their fictions depended than had been evidenced by the *sengoha* authors, a considerable number of them found themselves increasingly drawn to question the reliability of the perspective offered by their own narrators. The result was a series of texts in which the hitherto privileged position of the narrator was seemingly wilfully undermined by the presence of an alternative perspective on characters and events—a perspective that, by definition, cast doubt on previously inviolable visions of "truth" and "reality."

The fiction to emerge from this reevaluation has been categorized by Van C. Gessel as "a literature of dual perspectives."[12] Portraying "a good portion of the fiction written in Japan since its defeat in World War II" as attempts to "attack . . . and crush . . . the strong, confident literary self that stood at the center of prewar Japanese fiction," Gessel defines the resulting texts in the following terms:

> Like the picaresque fiction produced in postwar Germany, these Japanese works involve an expanded, often splintered range of perspective and point of view; questioning of the narrator's reliability and authority to speak by his own alter ego; and a new, invigorating dosage of irony. These stories are told both in the voice of the narrator, who relates his personal experience in much the same manner as the creators of *shishōsetsu* (I-novels) who dominated the realm of fiction before the war, and in the voice of the narrator's *doppelgänger*—his "spirit double"—who infuses the text with a critical commentary or provides an ironic view of the narrated events.[13]

Gessel's portrayal of the fiction of the generation of postwar writers could have been written with the novelist Takahashi firmly in mind. Convinced that "the Japanese have traditionally sought to avoid over-close scrutiny of the inner being,"[14] here is an author whose narratives were born of a determination to penetrate beyond the world of appearance and to explore, through her art, what she frequently portrayed as unfathomable human impulses. In pursuit of these ends, such a "splintered" perspective was highly appropriate. Without such an alternative—without the "critical commentary" entrusted to "the voice of the narrator's *doppelgänger*"—the portrayal of individual protagonists struggling to come to terms with a deeper level of their being would inevitably lack for objectivity and the depiction of their journeys toward greater self-awareness would, of necessity, be deprived of psychological verisimilitude.

For Takahashi, such attention to the inner being was no mere intellectual exercise. In hinting at a greater complexity to her protagonists than is initially acknowledged, the author was constantly at pains to draw attention to the role exercised by the unconscious in the formulation of the composite individual. A brief glance at the *nenpu* cited earlier, for example, reveals a series of critical essays whose titles appear designed to draw attention to this focus on the realm of the unconscious in the development of her fictional worlds.[15] To be sure, one must avoid the temptation to give more weight to such theoretical pronouncements than to the texts themselves. But as even the most cursory glance at these essays reveals, the desire to explore the "often demonic forces that underlie [the world of appearances] at the level of the unconscious"[16] was born of a vision of "a duality within the individual"[17] for which the splintered narrative perspective would appear ideally suited.

The result, in Takahashi's fictional world, is a series of novels in which the protagonists pursue a remorseless quest: a search for greater understanding, not merely of the motivating force behind their impulsive behavior, but, by extension, of the relationship between the conscious persona they have presented to society and their unconscious being in which such actions are rooted. Troubled by the malice they discern in themselves and obliged to acknowledge their powerlessness to exercise control over this realm increasingly dismissed as "unfathomable," they find themselves in direct confrontation with a doppelgänger, their own double whose very existence they struggle, in vain, to deny.

As Takahashi herself suggests in an early essay on the subject, the initial impetus for her interest in the subject may have been the discovery of "a plethora of works in the West focusing on the self and the other self, the two invariably established as *opposing poles of a binary tension*."[18] When viewed in the light of the thesis concerning the discovery of "interiority" advanced by the critic Karatani Kōjin, however, the trait can equally be viewed as a logical extension of the move toward "interiority" that Karatani cites as a dominant trend in the twentieth-century Japanese literary tradition, a trend he traces back to the turn of the century.[19] Karatani attributes the "discovery of interiority" to Kunikida Doppo and other authors of the late Meiji era traditionally categorized as precursors of the naturalist tradition in Japan. But as Karatani is at pains to emphasize, the discovery was to have far-reaching implications: the vision of an alternative self, of another "self . . . severed from the self," a significant and recurrent motif in the subsequent prose narrative tradition in Japan. For as he acknowledges:

> The illusion that there is something like a "true self" has taken deep root. It is an illusion that is established when writing has come to be seen as derivative and that voice which is most immediate to the self, and which consititutes self-consciousness, is privileged. The psychological person, who begins and ends in interiority, has come into existence.[20]

To Karatani, the tendency to privilege "that voice which is most immediate to the self" provided a significant impetus to those authors of the subsequent *shishōsetsu* tradition in their search for closer identification with their fictional constructs. As suggested by my depiction of Takahashi as an author determined to give literary expression to the sense of the "self . . . severed from the self" through focus upon individual protagonists struggling to come to terms with the existence of their own perceived double, however, the search for "interiority" can here be seen continued, with renewed intensity, into the postwar era. True to Karatani's prediction, 'true self' " had indeed taken deep root. And there is a marked tendency, especially in the earlier Takahashi texts, for protagonists to view this alter ego not merely as "another self" *(mō hitori no watashi)* but as approximating their "true self" *(hontō no watashi / hontō no jibun).*[21]

At this stage in Takahashi's career, depictions of the "severed self" invariably assume a concrete guise: the "other me walking about out there" specifically perceived as a distinct physical entity.[22] The portrayals are hardly surprising: these works with which she established her literary reputation were, after all, written in the immediate aftermath of the death of her husband, Kazumi (1939–1971), himself an intellectually charismatic author to whom Takahashi Takako had appeared content, during his lifetime, to afford center stage. The effect of Kazumi's untimely death on the young Takako is hard to exaggerate. Cast suddenly into the limelight, Takako's public response to personal tragedy was to assert her desire to carry on her late husband's work. Indeed, she declared her determination to "suppress consciousness of her own femininity and to devote her efforts to securing recognition as a member of the male species."[23] In the years that followed, the issue of gender, always important to Takahashi, came to assume increased significance. The desire to break free from the traditional constraints of gender-specific roles constitutes a constant refrain among the various female protagonists in the narratives of the time. Troubled by the apparently inescapable presence of the divided self, these protagonists struggle with a seemingly insoluble conundrum: unable to accept their gender as women, they are nevertheless denied acceptance by the masculine world. With time, however, the concept was refined. Ultimately the vision of the individual trapped by an insurmountable gender divide gives way to a vision of greater complexity: the composite, individuated being.

Again one must resist the temptation to attribute this changing perspective to a series of external influences—to a range of "sociological determinants." The neat conclusion that this reassessment was an inevitable consequence of the influences—of Kazumi, of Christianity, of Jungian psychology—to which the author makes most frequent reference in her critical essays is of most benefit to the critic when considered in the light of Fujii's call to replace "the notion of 'influence,' which suffers from the problem of privileging the person or work 'influenced,' " with a view of "narrative as productive—creating something new from the collision of differences."[24] Fujii's distinction is instructive. The view of Takahashi's art as indeed born of such a "collision," most notably the clash of gender differences, is very revealing. In seeking a literary appraisal of Takahashi's art, therefore, it is to those narratives that contribute most toward reconciliation of such distinctions that our attention is most profitably addressed. Viewed in this light, it is to the more recent Takahashi texts in general—and to *Yosōi seyo, waga tamashii yo* in particular—that the critic is drawn. With this in mind, let us shift the focus of this discussion to the novel in which the divided narrative perspective is most consistently deployed.

DIVIDED VOICE IN *YOSŌI SEYO, WAGA TAMASHII YO*

Born of the author's repeated visits to Paris following the death of Kazumi, the novel *Yosōi seyo, waga tamashii yo* represents fertile ground for the critic intent on analyzing the splintered narrative perspective evidenced in postwar Japanese fiction—and the focus on the doppelgänger that will, by definition, ensue. A brief synopsis of the work should suffice to highlight the extent to which the author avails herself of this alternative perspective to hint at a greater depth to her protagonist.

The plot itself is relatively uncomplicated. The determination to parody the prewar *shishōsetsu* form, with its relentless authorial identification with a single protagonist, is immediately evidenced in the choice, as protagonist, of Yamakawa Namiko. Namiko is a Catholic composer who finds herself repeatedly drawn back to Paris as the place where, through confrontation with herself naked and alone, she feels best equipped to answer fundamental questions concerning her own identity. In Paris Namiko finds herself entangled in a series of complex relationships, all of which heighten her understanding of human nature, less through a probing of the other's psyche, more through the manner in which such relationships enable Namiko to confront her own inner being.

First to exercise such an influence on Namiko following her arrival in France is Olivier, the "nihilistic realist" with whom she becomes acquainted as an indirect result of her decision to practice the pipe organ. With their acquaintance limited to a few casual exchanges in a coffee shop following Namiko's regular practice sessions, Olivier's invitation to join him for a weekend in Normandy may take Namiko by surprise. But far more surprising for Namiko—and more reminiscent of the "unfathomable" impulses to which Takahashi's protagonists had consistently succumbed—is her instinctive decision to accept the invitation. In so doing—in agreeing to become more deeply embroiled with Olivier than her own sense of logic would appear to condone—Namiko is clearly portrayed as responding, not so much at the level of conscious rationale, but as a result of a prompting born of the unconscious that she finds herself unable, or unwilling, to resist. Even after their arrival in Normandy, the motivation behind Olivier's invitation and Namiko's acceptance remains shrouded in mystery—the more so following the arrival of Isabel, the other woman caught up in Olivier's search for fulfillment. That Isabel's appearance is part of some premeditated design on Olivier's part is openly acknowledged at the narrative level. The full significance of the triangular relationship that is thereby established remains, however, unclear. The extent of the influence these two companions will ultimately exercise on Namiko's journey toward increased self-awareness is as yet unresolved.

Following her return to Paris, Namiko continues to immerse herself with renewed determination in the weekly round of practice sessions on the pipe organ. The more practical concerns to which she had earlier devoted so much of her time are increasingly dismissed as of diminished significance. The search for a room to serve as a base during her stay in Paris, initially so high on her list of priorities, is now aborted: the need for physical stability has been rendered subservient, it seems, to her growing recognition of the paramountcy of spiritual security. Instead—once more in response to an unfathomable impulse—Namiko takes off again, this time in midwinter, to a convent deep in the snow-clad mountains on the Swiss-French border. For Namiko the only conscious connection with this place is the address, scribbled on the piece of paper she rediscovers in her bag, which had been given to her, entirely unsolicited, by a young woman awaiting her turn to practice on the pipe organ. Despite the tenuous nature of this link, the narrative portrays a Namiko drawn to visit the convent by an impulse she is powerless to resist. The depictions of Namiko penetrating ever deeper into the heart of the mountains are increasingly juxtaposed onto portrayals of the journey toward confrontation with a deeper level of her own being.

The convent provides the backdrop for the denouement of the novel. It is the priest whose acquaintance she makes there, however, who represents the conduit by which Namiko is enabled, slowly but surely, to achieve increasingly conscious recognition of elements of her unconscious being. The more Namiko confides in the priest, the more he is entrusted with the narrative role of providing an exegesis—and, in so doing, of elucidating the relationship, already depicted as integral to the novel, between the Namiko who arrives in France in search of renewal and the Namiko who leaves the convent, for whom renewal has come to assume a new, and entirely unexpected, significance. Apprised by the priest that the process upon which she was engaged was one of rebirth, "no less than your former self dying minute by minute and a new person rising up within you to replace it,"[25] Namiko's instinctive response is to resist. She is concerned by the ramifications of such an assessment for her future life in Paris. The more she gives herself over to "the sound of silence welling up . . . from the depths of her being" (p. 322), however, the more she finds herself incapable of resistance, increasingly convinced of the need to recognize the complexity incorporated within this realm. The Namiko who emerges from the convent, therefore, has traveled a long way toward acknowledgment of the role exercised by the unconscious in formulating the composite individual. Her instinctive decision, at the conclusion of the novel, following a further visit to the convent, to board a train bound, not for Paris where she was ostensibly headed, but traveling in the opposite direction toward Marseilles, may appear every bit as rash and impulsive as the decision to accompany Olivier to Normandy. Viewed in light of the development evinced by her journey toward heightened self-awareness, however, the decision comes to be portrayed, rather, as a logical submission to a prompting that, however unfathomable, is clearly identified by the protagonist as emanating from her own inner being.

For those intent on locating the "events" of the novel in Takahashi's personal experience, spiritual if not necessarily physical, during her stays in France, the task would appear relatively easy. From the outset the narrative draws overt attention to Namiko's role as a literary double: the parallels with Takahashi's own journey are highlighted by publication, almost simultaneously, of a series of essays recounting the author's experiences in France and actively encouraged by the portrayal of a protagonist increasingly drawn to the greater freedom that Paris appears to offer and drifting inexorably toward the world embodied by the convent.[26]

Viewed in this light, the author's identification with her female protagonist could hardly appear more complete. The consequent temptation to read the novel as a fictional depiction of the author's own soul searching has been epitomized by one critic as representative of "the balance sheet of the author's own soul."[27] To categorize the novel in this way, however, is to ignore the extent to which the work exists, rather, as a parody of the self-referential narrative and to overlook the presence of the splintered narrative perspective that, as outlined earlier, is so integral to the text. To be sure, throughout the novel it is possible to discern Namiko's perspective on the situations in which she finds herself. But there is another perspective at work here: another narrative voice beneath the surface which keeps reminding the reader that, for all the apparent purposelessness of Namiko's life in Paris (she is, after all, drifting from one practice session on the pipe organ to the next, from one unfulfilling relationship to another), there is an additional significance to her journey. Without this added perspective, portrayal of Namiko as a young woman who, having escaped from Paris in total despair, is ultimately rescued through confrontation with a being of a higher dimension might indeed appear justified. Without the additional commentary provided by this alternative voice, patience might indeed run thin for a protagonist seemingly oblivious to the need for a firm grasp on the reality of her situation. In practice, however, it is at this point that the alternative perspective—that volunteered by the narrator's "spirit double"—assumes prominence, reassuring both Namiko and the reader that the former is not simply drifting aimlessly, but engaged on a search of profound significance, and that her efforts will not prove fruitless. The object of her quest may remain shrouded in ambiguity, not least for the protagonist herself. It is on this additional voice, however, that the image of Namiko struggling to reconcile herself—both to her gender and to the sense of "the self . . . severed from [her] self" is premised.

During the course of the novel, these two voices are gradually reconciled. The exact nature of this narrative device is reflected in Namiko's increasing ability to acknowledge this other voice specifically—and respond to it positively. The development is clearly evidenced by comparison of the two impulsive decisions made by Namiko. In the depiction of the protagonist agreeing to accompany Olivier to Normandy in the early stages of the novel, therefore, the narrative rests squarely on the workings of the mind of Namiko herself. Its inability to provide any logical justification for her spontaneous acceptance results in a lack of verisimilitude that leads Monnet to dismiss the episode as "a rather ludicrous elopement."[28] Such a charge would sit much less easily on the portrayal of Namiko, at the very end of the novel, boarding the first train, regardless of its destination, that approaches the platform on which she is standing. In one sense this decision appears to be equally impetuous, equally devoid of rationale. But because of this alternative narrative voice, by now clearly acknowledged, the decision is justified as a logical progression in Namiko's effort to reconcile herself to herself—to come to terms with her own divided self as a woman.

But how is this effect achieved? To what is the reconciling of the conflicting narrative voices to be attributed? And to what extent does the narrative depend on the increased objectivity provided by this alternative perspective for its overall effect? The rest of this essay considers these questions—and, more specifically, the process whereby Namiko comes increasingly to respond in a positive manner to this other voice.

TOWARD RECONCILIATION

In seeking to identify the manner by which the reconciliation of the narrative voices is effected within the novel *Yosōi seyo, waga tamashii yo*, the critic is inevitably drawn to those instances, increasingly pronounced, in which, the reader is on the verge of identifying with the perspective of the protagonist only to find the text subverting this identification by drawing attention to its own splintered vantage point. This it achieves, not by introducing a separate locus of perspective, but by confronting Namiko with her own shadow being, whether in the form of the protagonist's persistent visions of her own doppelgänger or identification with one of the other characters, each of whom ultimately serves as an expression of the protagonist's alter ego. In the early stages of the novel, this "other self" tends to appear in concrete guise—in the form of Namiko's instant identification with several of the women with whom her path crosses, if only for an instant. As she wanders the streets of Paris in a determined effort to penetrate behind the daunting facade she discerns in the dilapidated old buildings, for example, this alternative self is clearly perceived in a woman, a complete stranger to Namiko, who had stood next to her in the crowd listening to an impromptu concert in the Place de la Madeleine:

> Namiko passed on and continued walking around the square. As she did so, she felt as though she were somehow leaving herself behind. She was much younger than that woman and there were no obvious external similarities; and yet that woman and Namiko herself were the same woman, if only for a moment. She was totally unable to explain that feeling, but that was how she felt. This was no mere figure of speech: these were two distinct manifestations of the same woman. [p. 20]

Inevitably such experiences—and this is by no means an isolated incident—are disconcerting to Namiko. For all this, however, and painful though the lesson may be, such identification with those around her—and the perception of interdependence that is the inevitable corollary of such feelings of affinity—nevertheless represents a significant development: the portrayal of the protagonist gradually awakening to the need to view herself, not as existing in a vacuum, but in the context of her surroundings, an important if early milestone on her journey.

From this point on, Namiko becomes engrossed in her search—her desire to assuage the discomfort she continues to feel as a result of her womanhood and, in so doing, to locate a greater sense of fulfillment in her own existence symbolized, at the narrative level, by her quest for suitable accommodation in Paris. Understandably her first steps in this direction are tentative. But even if she is as yet unable to answer her own question, "What exactly am I looking for?" (p. 28), the narrative is at pains to portray Namiko as acutely aware of some quality missing from her life. The more she scans the pages of the newspaper in search of a room, therefore, the more the narrative draws attention to the half-hearted nature of her quest through implicit comparison with the Swedish youth who, like Namiko, is seeking a permanent base in Paris. Compared to the Swede, determined to move out of the hotel at the earliest possible opportunity, Namiko evidences a distinct lack of urgency. To be sure, Namiko's nonchalance is attributed, in part at least, to her more favorable financial circumstances. The distinction is not limited to practical considerations, however. As a direct result of the frequent intervention of the alternative narrative perspective, the symbolic nature of Namiko's search is increasingly highlighted by the text. The physical search may consequently be aborted after a few tentative approaches. But it has been established that the room for which Namiko has been seeking is, in fact, within her. And the need for some form of resolution to her quest for spiritual as opposed to physical security has been duly emphasized.

With Namiko now convinced of the futility of her physical search, the remainder of the novel focuses on the portrayal of a protagonist intent on probing her own inner being and, specifically, seeking resolution of the conflicting forces she has come to see at work there. The shifting emphasis is clearly evidenced in her analysis of her tastes in music during the course of the conversation with the last landlord she meets before abandoning her physical search:

> I like Wagner, for example, but only his modern works in which certain holy and devilish qualities are combined into a state of chaotic darkness. . . . How can I describe it? Music which incorporates an element designed to arouse a sense of fear at the very core of the human being. [p. 69]

For Namiko, the two opposing forces she senses within herself represent a clear source of tension—a conflict that, on the one hand, facilitates her understanding of human illogicality but, on the other, constitutes the major obstacle to self-understanding. Her reaction, on learning from the hotel proprietor of the Red Army hijacking of the Japanese DC-8 at Dacca airport, is thus significant: her acknowledgment of the "primordial" sentiments by which the passengers and hijackers must be linked evinces a burgeoning desire to fathom human behavior in all its extremes:

> More than one hundred "civilized" people were locked up in a plane with a handful of "primitive" people. But, right now, the "civilized" people, too, had no doubt been reduced to basic, primordial feelings through fear, uncertainty and anger. In the final resort, we all fall short. [p. 97]

Namiko's concern with man's inhumanity to man is deep-rooted, and the ensuing narrative sets great store on the portrayal of a protagonist drawn to consideration of a series of indices of inhuman behavior—from the torture machines that Namiko had seen exhibited in Belgium to the aggression of Hitler to the bombings of Hiroshima and Nagasaki. Taken out of context, such references may indeed lead to the impression of a protagonist possessed of a morbid fascination with the forces of evil per se. To offer such a conclusion, however, is to reckon without the alternative perspective that permeates the narrative—at precisely those moments when Namiko gives vent to the greatest doubts about human nature.

Namiko reads of the Red Army hijacking, for example, just as she is leaving the hotel in search of a music score. Too caught up in her own small world to worry unduly about the latest development on the world stage, Namiko puts the article to one side. Instead she heads for the music store where she hopes to acquire a copy of the melody that has intrigued her ever since she overheard it in the Place de la Madeleine. The timing of the decision to continue her personal search uninterrupted by mundane concerns about the hijacking drama has been carefully considered. For it is as a direct result of this visit that Namiko learns of the possibility of renting time on the pipe organ in the crypt of the cathedral of St. Sulpice.

For Namiko, a talented musician, the joy she experiences with this discovery is intense. As a result of the juxtaposition of the alternative narrative perspective at this point, however, the development is portrayed equally as an important step on Namiko's journey of self-discovery. As this voice consistently reiterates, in practicing the pipe organ Namiko is overwhelmed by a sense of having gained access to a deeper level of her being: the correspondence between the voice of the organ and the voice of her "other self" is immediately cited as an important reason for her delight on learning of this unexpected opportunity. Thereafter, in the depiction of Namiko arriving at the church the following Saturday, the force of the symbol is enhanced by focus on the organ's physical location in the depths of the church. The protagonist's thoughts as she descends ever deeper toward the crypt represent an early example of this juxtaposition:

> As Namiko descended the stairs behind [the attendant], she was assailed by a continuous sense of uncertainty. But such uncertainty also comprised a sense of joy which twinkled like gold-dust. She was aware of herself penetrating rapidly into the heart of this town—in a way that had eluded her for so long. [p. 114]

Clearly this passage underlines the heightened understanding of Paris achieved by Namiko as a result of her newfound freedom to explore. At the same time, however, there is a depth to this portrayal—a suggestion of the protagonist caught up in the process of rebirth—that will have major repercussions on the remaining narrative. The depiction of Namiko descending into the silent darkness of the crypt is presented as an uneasy moment of truth for the protagonist. Equally, however, this portrayal and the lengthy focus on Namiko's emotional turmoil that ensues draw attention to the alternative narrative focus—to Namiko's descent toward confrontation with her own unadorned being. Significantly in this regard, her fear of the unknown dissipates almost as soon as her fingers touch the keyboard. The subsequent depiction of Namiko's response to the "life-force" she senses emanating from the keys is couched in the language of regeneration:

> She decided to practice the manual part only and began to play. As she did so, a strong life-force arose within her. It was a vague feeling and she was unable to ascertain whether it stemmed from the keys or from within herself. But it seemed to emanate from some large, unfathomable depths. As she pressed the keys, she heard, not sounds, but breaths—and each small breath seemed to merge into one large breath. She knew plenty of beautiful pieces for the piano, for other instruments or for voice, but the beauty of this was somehow different and could probably never be reproduced on the piano. There was something behind the piece giving life to it: it was as though this background force was the inner being of this instrument—and of Namiko herself. It also seemed to represent the depths of this vast, stone building. . . . It was some inexplicable force—something that could only be described in this way. [p. 118]

Namiko's impulse to resist this inexplicable force is suggested by the profound sense of relief she experiences upon reemergence into the outside world. At the same time, however, by the end of this first practice session, she has come to "recognize in this darkness, the existence of some power more real than any visible object" (p. 123). There is a reality to the sensation of regeneration she has just experienced—and an acceptance of this as an integral part of her process of individuation—that accounts for the sense of anticipation with which she awaits the next practice session.

From this moment on, the regular practice sessions lend a semblance of order to Namiko's weekly routine. Significantly, however, far from a narrative focus on a protagonist increasingly drawn to introspection through this experience, it is at this point that Namiko becomes embroiled in the relationships—with Olivier and subsequently with Isabel—that will lead to increasing acknowledgment of the role exercised by others in the process of self-discovery. It is at this stage that, in addition to the double she has already confronted within her own being, Namiko comes face to face with a different dimension of her "other self"—in the form of a succession of acquaintances who confirm her belief in the shared experience of all humans.

As one might anticipate from this discussion of the text as possessed of a more complex narrative perspective than initially suggested, depiction of the protagonist as a link in the chain of humankind is to be found juxtaposed with the portrayal of Namiko oblivious to concerns outside her own restricted world. At the very moment the narrative appears to be drawing attention to Namiko's lack of concern for the fate of those caught up in the hijacking incident, for example, this alternative voice intervenes, suggesting a very real sense of empathy with the worlds of those around her. Again, it is to music that this realization is attributed:

> When composing . . . , [Namiko] was aware not only of her own feelings, but those of countless other, distant people, unknown to her—and these, too, were incorporated into her composition. [p. 97]

The narratorial aside is offered just before Namiko's first encounter with the pipe organ in St. Sulpice—and provides a valuable insight into her subsequent ability to find solace in these sessions as she struggles to discover a modus vivendi in Paris. On the one hand, this alternative perspective reinforces the image of the protagonist attuned to "her own feelings" on these occasions; on the other, in highlighting Namiko's awareness of the shared nature of human experience, the comment foreshadows the role that will subsequently come to be exercised by others on the protagonist's journey of self-discovery.

In the ensuing narrative portrayal of Namiko practicing alone in the crypt of the church, therefore, the ability of music to effect a link between the protagonist and the rest of humanity—and the role of the pipe organ as a conduit in this process—is nowhere explicitly presented as Namiko's primary concern. As a result of the focus on the spiritual effect these sessions exert on the protagonist, however, the development is clearly anticipated. And the dream Namiko experiences shortly after embarking on this routine reinforces the impression of her heightened identification with the world beyond her own microcosm:

> Kneeling down in the charred remains of her life, someone was crying. But the cry emanated from the very depths of her being so that the tears were not immediately evident to those who passed by. That person was herself and, at the same time, it was everyone else. At that moment, that person merged into someone beyond the contours of her own being, developing into a nameless everybody. [p. 131]

The Namiko who awakes from this dream has in no way been disabused of her determination to confront the double she has come to perceive within herself. As a result of the additional focus on the protagonist's newfound awareness of the potential for enhanced consciousness of the self through interaction with others, however, the stage has been set for the introduction of the various characters who will provide an additional perspective on subsequent developments. In the pages immediately following this dream, therefore, Namiko makes the acquaintance of Olivier and, in rapid succession, the "nameless man" she keeps confronting in the hotel. The function of both as narrative doubles is immediately intimated—in the depiction of Namiko's response to the footsteps she hears climbing the hotel stairway as she lies in bed:

> [As she listened], she felt as though she herself had expanded to the size of the hotel and that someone was climbing up from the very depths of her being. Engrossed in listening to this, she felt as though she both hoped and feared that those steps would lead to her. She had become a vast, passive being. [p. 153]

As a "vast, passive being," Namiko is here portrayed as an individual receptive to the lessons to be gleaned from the various figures with whom her destiny is now linked. From this moment on, the emphasis is on Namiko's willingness to acknowledge the additional function of the relationships she is forging in Paris and, increasingly, to view as incomplete the persona she has presented in public to date. Again, the reevaluation is by no means painless. But the more Namiko is portrayed in terms of her relationship with both Olivier and Isabel, the more the narrative focuses on the contribution of those around her in this process of self-reassessment. During the course of a conversation with Isabel shortly after this incident, for example,

> Namiko found herself thinking of herself. From within the self she knew so well, she discovered an unknown self—she continued to discover an unknown self. That was the sum total of her being. [p. 181]

The vision of Namiko embarked on a journey has been established. And this is subsequently complemented at the textual level by a fluidity of location of the events themselves—as the narrated locale shifts rapidly from Paris to Normandy and then to a series of visits to the mountain convent. It is during the first of these journeys that the full extent of the roles to be exercised by Olivier and Isabel as narrative doubles is most comprehensively explored. For all her lack of interest in becoming embroiled in a physical relationship with Olivier, the prospect of confronting the "vast expanse" of open sea possesses considerable appeal for the "searching" protagonist—and it is at this level that the decision to accept Olivier's invitation is supported by the text. And indeed it is to the sea that Namiko heads immediately on arrival in Normandy. But once there she is confronted, not by the traditional seascape she had envisaged, but by the endless void of mud to which that particular stretch of coastline was reduced at low tide. The scene is one of complete desolation:

> As [Namiko] stepped outside the car, she was assailed by a cool sea breeze that blew straight at her. The cloudy sky was a checkerboard of black and white and stretched out over the sea to the horizon. The sea itself was a vast expanse of dark mud and the film of water that appeared to be visible in the distance was possibly no more than a figment of her imagination. A naked sea, an exposed sea, a sea deprived of its very essence, a barren sea. All that stood out was the occasional cluster of seaweed, darker than the muddy surrounds. . . .
>
> The wind began to blow with renewed intensity showing no signs of dissipating. Namiko felt chilled to the bone. But she had no desire to leave this place. The black mud, the twilight sky, the cruel wind, . . . yes, this great void. She had finally arrived at the place she had determined to visit for all those years. [pp. 221, 222–223]

Once more the narrative timing of this section is highly significant. At the time, Namiko is standing alone, preparing herself to return to Olivier and an uncertain future. The more the narrative dwells on the bleakness of her physical surroundings, however, the more the portrayal is juxtaposed with the depiction of Namiko thereby enabled to acknowledge the complexity of her own being. Through confrontation with this barren expanse of mud, she is again alerted to a greater depth to her being: her reaction to the desolate seascape is overtly reminiscent of her response to the strains of the pipe organ. Thus the depiction serves a clear proleptic function: that of presaging the arrival on the scene of Isabel, the person best equipped to nurture Namiko's conscious awareness of this process. To Namiko, at least, Isabel's appearance in Normandy is totally unheralded, and she instinctively blames Olivier for having manipulated her into a complex web of relationships. At the one level, therefore, the two women give vent to the sense of jealousy and rivalry that the other has come to embody in conventional terms. For all the underlying confrontation, however, the narrative provides an additional perspective on the situation. And it is the consequent establishment of Isabel, not as rival, but as the spiritual side of Namiko's being that accounts for the sense of optimism that permeates the ensuing narrative.

The sense of renewed optimism that envelops the text from this moment on is indeed marked. In fact, it stands in complete contrast to the uncertainty and tension that Isabel's arrival should engender. On the one hand, the relationship between the two women is epitomized by mutual caution; on the other hand, however, there is an alternative voice informing the narrative—a voice that intrudes increasingly in the pages that follow to give expression to the thoughts and feelings which neither Namiko nor Isabel is in a position to countenance at the conscious level. The result is a subversion of the depiction of the two as simply immersed in bitter rivalry and a growing suggestion that they are engaged in a symbiotic relationship, one in which the two come increasingly to appear as a "self . . . severed from the self."

Such an assessment may go a long way toward accounting for the unease that Isabel's presence induces in Namiko. Equally significant, however, is the progress, in terms of Namiko's self-awareness, that is effected by Isabel at this point. In contrast to the tentative young woman who is troubled by the vision of human nature she sees engendered in Olivier when the two are alone, the protagonist who stands looking out to sea with Isabel appears confident. As a rhetorical device, the depiction of the two women reciting the Lord's Prayer as they gaze out over the barren expanse may appear somewhat contrived. But this in no way detracts from the subsequent image of Namiko brought to a heightened awareness of the direction in which her search is leading her through exposure to the "other self" identified here with Isabel more overtly than on any previous occasion. Again, the development is embodied in the narrative portrayal of the ocean that confronts Namiko as she is left alone:

A swath of cloud engulfed the entire scene, the vast expanse of black mud eventually disappearing into the mist. Walking along the same breakwater that Isabel had earlier explored, Namiko felt as though she were enveloped in a current of damp air, her face constantly assailed by drops of mist. Here and there were the clusters of seaweed, standing out as darker patches of mud, but they too appeared faint as though veiled from sight. *But this was very different from the spectacle that she had witnessed at low tide on her arrival the previous day.* Compared with the intensity of that barren void, this scene, while equally barren, was far more bleak and disturbing. [p. 152; my emphasis]

In physical terms, the seascape before Namiko's eyes at this point is no different from the one that greeted her the previous evening. Even the barren nature of the present scene cannot obliterate the fact that this is the same sea to which she had always been attracted. As the narrative is quick to establish, however, "this was very different from the spectacle that she had witnessed at low tide on her arrival the previous day." As a result of her interaction with others, Isabel in particular, Namiko is here discovering an entirely new landscape—one resident deep within her being.

Again, it was the critic Karatani who cited the "discovery of landscape" as a result of an altered perspective on the mundane as a distinctive trend in modern Japanese literature. Karatani sees a process of "inversion" *(tenkō)* at work here: that which had been viewed as mundane comes to assume an entirely new meaning. He argues:

> Landscape . . . is not so much that which is outside. A change in our way of perceiving things was necessary in order for landscape to emerge, and this required a kind of reversal. . . .
>
> It is only within the "inner man," who appears to be so indifferent to his external surroundings, that landscape is discovered. It is perceived by those who do not look "outside."[29]

For Karatani there is a distinct "link between landscape and an introverted solitary situation,"[30] and it is in these terms that the change effected in the portrayal of Namiko during the course of her stay in Normandy is best encapsulated. As she stares at the barren sea, Namiko becomes increasingly indifferent to her external surroundings. But it is precisely with her recognition that there is nothing of significance in this external scene that the requisite "change of perspective" takes place and she comes to acknowledge the alternative "landscape" within her. The narrative function of the Normandy trip has now been served, and Namiko leaves imbued with a new optimism born of interaction with her alter ego in the person of Isabel. She is now prepared for the journey that will take her to a more conscious recognition of the source of the optimism she has seen embodied in Isabel: the visit to the Catholic convent hidden in the depths of the French Alps.

In terms of plot, the decision to embark on this journey can certainly be viewed as a plea for breathing space—for the chance to assess the repercussions of her aborted relationship with Olivier and the extent of Isabel's contribution to her self-understanding. At the same time, however, the trip is a logical culmination to the narrative to date and symbolizes the unknown territory she must chart—and the depths to which she must penetrate—before any real acquaintance with this inner landscape is possible. The process of "descending into the recesses of her being" (p. 282), initially attributed to the pipe organ and subsequently to contemplation of the desolate Normandy coastline, now reaches a new level of intensity as the taxi transports her further into the mountains: to the chapel, recurring index of rebirth in Takahashi's literature. Juxtaposed with the portrayal of Namiko arriving at the chapel still wary of the consequences of this latest "impulsive" journey, therefore, is an additional perspective: this experience gives her a new understanding of events that she would once have dismissed as unfathomable:

> She felt as though listening to the sound of silence within her, and sat down on the straw mat. As she did so, she felt as though she heard another sound—though, this time, it emanated from a deeper part of her being and she herself had passed through to that realm. She had passed through the shallow part of her being in which the traces of the earlier sense of emptiness still lingered and was bathed in the sparks which rushed out from the depths of her inner being to meet her. [p. 322]

By this stage Namiko is prepared, both spiritually and psychologically, to meet the priest in whom she will confide during her stay—and, in particular, to accept his interpretation of the search upon which she had been engaged ever since her arrival in France:

> "You must always be in possession of your own room. . . . Wherever you are, all you need to do is to remain in that room. You know what kind of room I am talking about, don't you?"
> "By 'that room,' you mean to be alone, alone with a certain 'man,' don't you?"
> "All you have to do is to make sure that you take that 'inner room' with you wherever you go."
> "So I should wait for 'that man' to visit me in that room?"
> "He will be with you twenty-four hours a day. In other words, he is by your side, always." [pp. 324–325]

Had Namiko been confronted with this conclusion any earlier, it would have remained an abstract philosophical notion. As it is, however, the words represent a source of reassurance that her journey involves, not a descent into a dark, endless tunnel of burgeoning self-doubt, but an ascent to an unprecedented level of self-confidence. The sense of optimism, previously only hinted at in the narrative contributions of the various facets of the double Namiko encounters along the way, is now finally evidenced by the protagonist herself. It finds concrete expression in her reassessment of the being she had always sensed beside her when playing the pipe organ. In a letter to Yukio, her friend from Japan, she confides:

> Since the New Year, I have been able to borrow another pipe-organ, and I now practice four to five hours every day. Given your love of music and of my own compositions, you might just be able to understand the feeling; but over the past couple of months, when playing pieces composed by someone else, I feel as though someone apart from me is playing. Thereafter, as I distance myself from that piece, I gradually realize that it is a piece I composed. In the past, I have often felt, when composing, that it was someone beside myself who was so doing. But this current feeling is totally different. Whereas previously with the piano I used to create a powerful darkness penetrated only by a dim light, I now feel that, with the pipe-organ, I am climbing to the source of that light. . . . That's the kind of piece I will compose for the pipe-organ in future. They will no longer represent "art." They transcend art, proceeding to a higher dimension. [p. 334]

Namiko's desire to reconcile herself with this "someone apart from me" is now absolute. Her willingness to contemplate a new interpretation of decisions that earlier she would have attributed to her impulsive nature is now explicitly linked to her newfound confidence. Without this image of the protagonist induced to face the future with optimism as a result of confrontation with this latest, and most explicit, "spirit double," Namiko's decision to leave the convent for an unpredictable future in Paris would lack authenticity. Her abrupt change of mind when confronted with the Marseilles train at the local station would indeed be open to the charge of an overhasty response to an inexplicable impulse. As a result of the increasingly prominent presence of this alternative voice within the narrative, however, this latest turn of events does not lack the ring of authenticity. The image of Namiko convinced that she can continue her search regardless of her physical whereabouts is a far cry indeed from the tentative and lonely woman who had arrived in France less than a year ago.

THE CREATION OF "SOMETHING NEW"

The tendency to infuse the narrative with a splintered perspective is by no means unique to Takahashi. In keeping with a whole generation of postwar Japanese authors whose childhood experience of the Pacific War had crushed their self-belief and whose exposure to the all-pervasive legacy of the prewar *shishōsetsu* tradition had led them to question the integrity and reliability of their own narrators, Takahashi was increasingly drawn to deployment of alternative perspectives on her material. This aspect of her art, however, has rarely elicited mainstream critical acclaim.

To some extent, this muted response may be seen as an inevitable corollary of Takahashi's decision, reached shortly after completion of *Yosōi seyo, waga tamashii yo*, to renounce all ties with the literary world: critics, consciously or not, appear to have accepted the author's widely cited conviction that, by the early 1980s, her "powers of imagination and recollection had ceased to function."[31] As evidenced by the alternative "voice" that permeates this work, however, critics' claims that the novel lacks narrative complexity—simply representing the "balance sheet of the author's own soul"—do scant justice to the role exercised by the "expanded . . . point of view" evinced in the text. There is a degree of complicity here: a questioning of the seemingly unambiguous and unified narrative focus as a result of which the text succeeds in undermining the perspective, initially portrayed as all-embracing, that is presented in the guise of the protagonist's instinctive response to events. Through the increasingly prominent insinuation of the voice of Namiko's "spirit double," initial assumptions are indeed challenged. And as the various voices are gradually juxtaposed, so the depiction of a protagonist willing and able to accept these voices, not as belonging to some unrelated "other," but as integral to her own composite being, is enhanced. To the end, no attempt is made to deny the distinctive nature of these various viewpoints. Instead, as a result of the concerted challenge on the privileged position ostensibly afforded the "enslaved" narrator at the outset of the novel, it is on the basis of such distinctions that the portrayal of Namiko, the individual who ultimately comes to confront the future with renewed optimism, is founded. "Something new" has indeed been created from "the collision of . . . differences."

NOTES

1. *Shōwa bungaku zenshū* (Collected works of Shōwa literature), vol. 30 (Tokyo: Shōgakkan, 1988), p. 1010.

2. I myself attended a meeting in April 1988 at which several prominent authors (including Endō Shūsaku and Kaga Otohiko), while obviously respecting Takahashi's decision, were seeking to convince her of the loss to the literary world that her retirement entailed.

3. Most significant in this regard are Yonaha Keiko, "Takahashi Takako-ron" (A study of the literature of Takahashi Takako), in *Gendai joryū sakka-ron* (A study of contemporary women writers) (Tokyo: Shinmisha, 1986), and Sunami Toshiko, *Takahashi Takako-ron* (Tokyo: Ōfūsha, 1992).

4. Livia Monnet, "'Child of Wrath': The Literature of Takahashi Takako," *Transactions of the Asiatic Society of Japan* (4th series) 5 (1990):88–89.

5. Ibid, p. 89.

6. Ibid.

7. James Fujii, *Complicit Fictions: The Subject in the Modern Japanese Prose Narrative* (Berkeley: University of California Press, 1993), pp. 23–24.

8. See, for example, *Ningen no naka no X* (The "X" within the individual) (Tokyo: Chūō Kōronsha, 1978).

9. See, for example, "Kyokō jisatsu to chinōhan jisatsu" (Suicide as fallacy and as intellectual offense), *Bungakkai* 2 (1971), and "Watashi to 'watashi' no kankei" (The relationship between myself and "the self"), *Waseda bungaku* 1 (1975).

10. Here I am referring specifically to the group of writers usually described as *sengoha* (postwar). It was one of their number, Shiina Rinzō, in particular, who so consistently evoked the need to "endure" *(taeru)* the current reality amid the ruins of Japan in the immediate aftermath of the Pacific War.

11. This characterization of the *shishōsetsu* appears in *Ningen no naka no X,* p. 161.

12. Van C. Gessel, "The Voice of the Doppelgänger," *Japan Quarterly* (April–June 1991):199.

13. Ibid.

14. "Ningen to wa" (What is man?), in *Reiteki na shuppatsu* (A spiritual departure) (Tokyo: Joshi Paolo-kai, 1985), p. 13.

15. Such titles include "Doppelgengeru-kō" (Some thoughts on the concept of the doppelgänger), 1974; "Senzai sekai e no gyakkō" (Regression to the subliminal world), 1977; and "Muishiki o horu" (Plumbing the unconscious), 1980. See also several of the studies incorporated into Takahashi's two recent collections of critical essays, *Reiteki na shuppatsu* and *Kami no tobihi* (Divine sparks) (Tokyo: Joshi Paolo-kai, 1986).

16. *Ningen no naka no X,* p. 161.

17. "Doppelgengeru-kō," *Bungakkai* 28(4) (1974):15.

18. Ibid.; my emphasis.

19. See the series of seminal articles published by Karatani between 1978 and 1980 translated as *Origins of Modern Japanese Literature* by Brett de Bary (Durham: Duke University Press, 1993).

20. Ibid., p. 69.

21. Portrayal of protagonists troubled by perception of a doppelgänger as their "true self" lies at the heart of the early novella *Seihō no kuni* (The country to the west, 1972) and the novel *Sora no hate made* (To the farthest reaches of the sky, 1973).

22. This example is taken from *Seihō no kuni,* in *Chikuma Gendai Bungaku Taikei* 97 (Tokyo: Chikuma shobō, 1978), p. 161. *Sora no hate made* is replete with similar examples of characters troubled by thoughts of a physical double.

23. "Kuruu" (Madness), in *Kōza onna 2: onna no sei* (Tokyo: Chikuma shobō, 1973), p. 147.

24. Fujii, *Complicit Fictions,* p. 23.

25. *Yosōi seyo, waga tamashii yo* (Tokyo: Shinchōsha, 1982), p. 305. All subsequent references to the novel are drawn from this edition and cited, as page number only, in parentheses in the text. All translations are my own.

26. See Takahashi Takako and Inoue Yōji, "Pari-Tokyo ōfuku shokan" (Letters between Paris and Tokyo), serialized in *Akebono* (Jan.–Dec. 1982). Takahashi continued to publish monthly installments, born of her experiences in Paris in the journal *Akebono* throughout 1983 and 1984. They were subsequently edited and published as *Reiteki na shuppatsu.*

27. Oketani Hideaki, in Kaga Otohiko et al., "Dokusho teidan: *Yosōi seyo, waga tamashii yo*," *Bungei* 22(1) (1983):328.

28. Monnet, "Child of Wrath," p. 108.

29. Karatani, *Origins of Modern Japanese Literature,* pp. 24–25.

30. Ibid., p. 25.

31. "Kokoro no naka no itten" (A single point within the heart), in *Reiteki na shuppatsu,* p. 37. It is this line of argument that is adopted by Oketani in Kaga et al., "Dokusho teidan."

6

IN THE TRAP OF WORDS: NAKAGAMI KENJI
AND THE MAKING OF DEGENERATE FICTIONS

Eve Zimmerman

Nakagami Kenji was born on August 2, 1946, in Shingū, a small city in Wakayama prefecture, bordered on one side by the sea and on the other by mountain forest. Kasuga-chō, the site of Nakagami's birth, lies within the boundaries of Shingū's outcaste *(burakumin)* neighborhood. Nakagami would later use the word *"roji,"* or alleyway, to describe the twisting, narrow streets of the outcaste community and set much of his fiction there.

Nakagami often spoke of his family as a matriarchy: he was an illegitimate child raised in a group of half-siblings from his mother's two marriages. (The second husband, a successful contractor, raised Kenji.) His real father was a small-time gambler and businessman with whom he had little contact. Nakagami's brothers and sisters never learned to read or write, but the egalitarian tenets of the postwar constitution prompted many *burakumin* to take advantage of their legal right to education: Nakagami was sent to school. In a 1989 interview, he described his education:

> I was one of the first in my neighborhood to get an education. If Japan hadn't been defeated in the war, I wouldn't have become what I am today. I was one of the first to "get letters." It was like being the first person to speak. I remember it as a child; people thought that I was very bright because I could read my own name.

In 1965, Nakagami graduated from the local high school and migrated to Tokyo, where he spent his days listening to jazz. In 1966, he began publishing poetry and short fiction in small magazines and became active in left-wing groups. His 1970 marriage to Nakagami Kasumi (an established writer of mystery novels under the name Kiwa Kyō) coincided with a brief period when he worked in ground services at Haneda Airport. Their first of three children, a daughter, was born a year later.

Nakagami's novella about a young man growing up in Shingū, *Misaki* (The Cape), won the 1976 Akutagawa Prize for fiction. *Karekinada* (The Straits of Kareki, 1977), a reexamination of the themes of *Misaki*, won two literary prizes. *Sennen no Yūraku* (A Thousand Years of Pleasure), a mythical treatment of semidivine outcastes, appeared in 1982; 1984 saw the publication of both *Chi no Hate Shijō no Toki* (The Sublime Time at the Ends of the Earth), a long work detailing the destruction of the *roji*, and *Kumano-shū* (A Kumano Collection), a set of upside-down mythic tales. In the late 1980s and 1990s Nakagami continued his voluminous output with *Jūryoku no Miyako* (City of Gravity), *Kiseki* (Miracles), *Sanka* (The Hymn), *Keibetsu* (Scorn), and *Izoku* (The Tribe), among others, when he was diagnosed with kidney cancer. By August 12, 1992, he was dead. On a sweltering August afternoon, a crowded memorial service was held in Tokyo. Karatani Kōjin spoke about the man he had known for twenty-five years:

> Nakagami's books made a strong impression and so did he. Even those who don't read—who, bluntly speaking, are illiterate—were left with a lasting impression. This was surprising. Nakagami was a more intellectual writer than most; in fact I don't know any writer who was more of an intellectual. But I also don't know any writer who made such a deep impression on people just for being who he was. Nakagami has died and I have lost my sense of gravity.

■

n an essay entitled "Monogatari no Keifu: Danshō" (Notes on the Genealogy of the Prose Narrative, 1979), Nakagami Kenji spins a news event into a parable. A robber bursts into a bank in Osaka brandishing a gun and takes the customers hostage. After shooting two people, the man is taken captive. The position of the man surrounded by his captors, Nakagami writes, is equivalent to the position of the Japanese writer who is surrounded by the law/system *(hō/seido)* of Japanese culture. The writer who takes action will be sacrificed by those who make up the circle. And when his crime is broadcast over the media, the circle is broadened to encompass the island of Japan.[1]

In fiction as in life, Nakagami betrays a fascination with the young male drifter whose violent urges escalate as the circle closes in around him. Through acts of assault, rape, incest, and murder, Nakagami's protagonists issue a series of challenges to the established order. Yet every brutal shock seems to echo the deeper rythms of the *hō/seido* (law/system), rhythms that require an ongoing cycle of transgression, violence and retribution—often in the form of death. The death-directed arc of his protagonists' stories reveals the extent to which Nakagami revels in contradictions. The upstart rises in an eternal gesture of rebellion, but the arms of the circle render this action null and void. In its static nature, the figure of the trapped rebel is mythic, its roots buried in the sacred time *(in illo tempore)* before the history of the world began.[2] To Nakagami, this is the source of its appeal and its fundamental weakness. Myths are stories, the repetition of which fulfills a human need for order and for pleasure, but they can prove binding, even murderous, in the wrong hands. In Nakagami's case in particular, Japanese cultural myths demand examination because they contain clues to the denigration of his people.

In more simple terms, the trapped robber speaks directly to Nakagami's personal dilemma of belonging to a despised class of outcastes *(burakumin)* who are still the target of discrimination in modern-day Japan.[3] Like the robber in the circle, the *burakumin* is both a sacrificial victim and a blank slate upon which majority Japanese project their horror and fears. *Sabetsu,* or discrimination against the *burakumin,* is a constant theme of Nakagami's fictional and critical works. But rather than engage in a static critique of oppressive practices, Nakagami states: "I want to turn the clock back to the beginning and write books in which both victim and victimizer are beautiful."[4]

In *Sennen no Yūraku* (A Thousand Years of Pleasure, 1982), a series of linked stories about six young *burakumin* men, Nakagami's exploration of discrimination *(sabetsu)* begins with an examination of words themselves. Oryū no Oba, the old midwife of the community and the consciousness through which the tale is filtered, tells a story about the young men of the *roji* and the Fire Festival. It is February, and the young men have been preparing for the festival by undergoing ritual purification, fasting, and sexual abstinence. As they prepare to climb the mountain carrying burning torches, Oryū witnesses the following:

> Oryū no Oba felt a stab of pain when she witnessed the excitement of the young men at festival time. One, who was preparing to ascend the mountain with a torch during the Fire Festival, had inadvertently wrapped the sacred rope around his waist not two but four times, and because he was an untouchable, the number four evoked both death and four-legged creatures. Oryū first felt sad, then angry and disappointed when the others stumbled into the trap of words, angrily yelling at their friend, "No good! Do it again!"[5]

The young man's transgression hinges upon a complicated web of numbers and words. Of the many names used to refer to the *burakumin,* perhaps the word *"yotsu"* has the greatest weight. *"Yotsu"* means "four," but it also denotes four-footed creatures and is used derogatively to describe the *burakumin,* whose traditional occupations of cattle slaughtering and leatherworking brought them into close contact with animals. Yet the word *"yotsu"* has an even more ominous meaning: when *"yotsu"* is given its alternative reading, *"shi,"* it becomes a homonym for death. By invoking the number four, the defilement incurred by a mention of four-legged creatures is made doubly potent by the suggestion of death.[6]

The preceding passage is only one example of the "trap of words" that holds both the majority and the outcastes firmly in its grip. Oryū's sadness stems from the fact that the victims of *sabetsu* (discrimination) are themselves willing to be ruled by a semiotic order that places them at the very bottom of a social and symbolic hierarchy. This hierarchy not only reveals itself in single words; it has also shaped what Nakagami calls the *monogatari,* or tale. In a 1989 interview, Nakagami discussed his strategy when confronted with stories that seem ubiquitous:

> You can't resist the *monogatari* [tale] either. It's impossible. . . . Take the story of Cain and Abel. It pops up in both fiction and life. When you write about the relationship between brothers, you bump up against the story of Cain and Abel again and again. What can you do about this? Well, there's a basic shape to every story —an archetypal pattern or *genkei.* The *"gen"* of *"genkei"* signifies that it might be an old shape, but it is still one that exists in the present. . . . So because it's impos-

sible to overturn these *monogatari,* you have to work closely with them, shift them a little, try to dismantle them. That's the only thing you can do.[7]

In his description of the challenges posed by the *monogatari,* Nakagami once again reverts to figures to make his point. Despite his pessimistic assessment of the room to maneuver, however, Nakagami directed his considerable energies to carving out spaces between the archetypes. He took particular interest in the materials of Kumano (the old name for Wakayama prefecture), for example, an area known for its three sacred shrines, its identification with the creation myth of Izanami and the country of the dead, and its numerous myths, legends, and historical accounts, both native and imported. This essay focuses on a few of the *genkei,* or archetypes, that consumed Nakagami throughout his writing life— the tainted and thus sacred blood of the *burakumin,* the enmity between brothers, the return of the exiled father—and considers the tenuous balance that Nakagami struck with such archetypes as he examined and reexamined the "trap of words."

Sennen no Yūraku is a series of linked stories about six young men of the Nakamoto clan, outcastes of the *roji* (alleyways) of Shingū, the quarters of the *burakumin,* who are born with marks of divinity only to transgress and die young. The first of these is Hanzō, a beautiful young man who sleeps with every woman in the *roji* and is eventually cut down by a jealous husband. Five Nakamotos follow Hanzō, each with his own mark of divinity (Fumihiko is covered with hair at birth; Miyoshi sports the tattoo of a dragon on his back) and each one dying an early death at his own hands or the hands of others. The narrative of *Sennen* is filtered through the mind of an old midwife, Oryū no Oba, whose tale has a ragged quality and is filled with repetitions, circumlocutions, and anecdotes. As the critic Yomota Inuhiko once observed, *Sennen* reads as if it should be spoken aloud.[8]

The explanation for the early death of each Nakamoto is as simple as the blood that flows through their bodies: sacred but stemming from an impure source, this potent combination of opposites can only support life for a short time. In fact the narrative of *Sennen no Yūraku* flows in and around a central paradox—that the blood of the Nakamotos is sacred *because* it is thoroughly impure ("jibun no naka ni nagareru sono yodonda, iya sore yue ni kiyoraka na chi").[9] The power of a paradox lies in its ability to upset the categories by which we organize our world. As Rosalie Colie has noted: "Redirecting thoughtful attention to the faulty or limited structures of thought, paradoxes play back and forth across terminal and categorical boundaries. . . . The paradox is at once its own object turning endlessly in and upon itself."[10]

Cultural anthropologist Barbara Babcock locates the source of paradox in the negativity of religious symbolic systems that are based on the moral injunction "thou shalt not."[11] In this view, paradox is a response to a landscape envisioned by the moralizing eye. In the case of Hanzō, the first Nakamoto, whose life is a stream of transgressions and reversals, however, the moral dimension seems irrelevant. Hanzō is punished for certain things and not for others; he learns nothing from his crimes. Rather, in the rise and fall of the antihero, traditional categories lose their weight. In place of a double negative, paradox in *Sennen no Yūraku* opens up a field of play that would not otherwise be possible—what Victor Turner calls a "realm of pure possibility."[12] The untouchable is a god; night equals day; the lotus pond of paradise lies concealed beneath the sewers of the *roji*. Paradox makes every category interchangeable and rational ordering of the world impossible.

Within this "realm of possibility," Nakagami dismisses the anthropocentric bent of the novel of transgression (*Crime and Punishment*, for example), negating concepts of individual free will or responsibility, which he always considered illusory. Although Miyoshi, the thief, commits murder, Oryū no Oba claims that he is innocent; and when Miyoshi tells Oryū that he wants to settle down and reform, she nearly tells him that "this world is no more than a fretful dream; no matter how free we believe ourselves to be, our actions do not matter—we are all dancing on the Buddha's palm" (*Sennen*, p. 60). Oryū no Oba has learned the lessons of Buddhism well, yet she chafes at the early deaths of the Nakamoto men. The birth of innocent beings who are put in this world only to die young contradicts her belief in the benevolence of the Buddha. The deaths of the Nakamotos lead Oryū beyond familiar questions of transgression and retribution into the equally fundamental contradictions that stem from the animal nature of human beings and the origins of life itself. While lifting so many babies into the world, Oryū has discovered that there is no difference between human life and other forms of life. Life is merely larvae swarming over the surface of a puddle (*Sennen*, p. 61). She takes this revelation one step further:

Even as Oryū no Oba sponged off the blood, cut the cord, and checked to see if the infant was healthy, she knew that a newborn only became a baby when the parent or relative claimed it as their own. A newborn who merely popped its head out of the womb for an instant and then returned to the darkness couldn't make itself into anyone's child and Oryū mourned because she felt these little helpless souls pressing in upon her. [*Sennen*, p. 89]

Oryū is left with a quandary: if the newborn is not fully human, if it must wait to be claimed, why must the Nakamotos who are innocent at birth die so soon? Why is their blood tainted?

In *Edo to Aku* (The Edo Period and Evil, 1991), Noguchi Takehiko points to a similar absence of moral explanation for retribution and punishment in the opening chapters of the *Hakkenden* (The Tale of Eight Dogs, 1814–1841) by Takizawa Bakin. Rather than construct a social mechanism of transgression and retribution, Bakin approached the problem through animism, invoking the idea that "grasses, trees, and animals all come from the same root."[13] Noguchi asks: Was not the death of the wicked Funamushi a form of evil itself? Yet he concludes that in a nonanthropocentric universe, Funamushi is merely suffering the same fate as her namesake, the *funamushi,* or sea louse, of nature—to be stomped to death underfoot. One's name signifies one's destiny.[14]

In the absence of any transcendental notion of transgression and retribution, the fate of the Nakamotos ("origin of the middle"), too, can be traced to their name, which plays with the notion of "within" or "the middle." The paradox of the blood—that it is only sacred because it is impure—is an endless, self-referential riddle that perpetuates itself within the bodies of the Nakamotos. The Nakamotos straddle the categories of pure/impure, sacred/profane, male/female, high/low. Hanzō, for instance, manifests both the male and the female within himself. Dabbing his body with white powder, he is both pursuer and pursued, embracer and embraced, giver and receiver of pleasure. Hanzō becomes sexual union itself, which eventually collapses into autosexuality. (In the end, Hanzō is in love with himself.) Fumihiko, on the other hand, treads the boundary between the human and the animal; he is covered with hair at birth, and he alone can see the mythical bird-monster, the *tengu.*

Although the Nakamotos exist "betwixt and between,"[15] and thus counteract *sabetsu,* they are also mythic beings who are born to begin their journey back into death, safe from the ragged currents of history, their only task to live out the time that has been allotted to them. Because their bloodline washes out differences and reduces six men to one, it has what Norma Field calls the "logic of identity," which she contrasts with the "logic of resemblance," the main element of fiction. She writes: "Indeed it is the logic of resemblance that allows fiction to distinguish itself from myth, which is governed by the logic of identity, whereby, for example, a deity known for destructive furor in one region turns out to be a beneficent deity in another."[16]

The logic of identity is evident in Nakagami's veiled references to a group of traditional legends, the *kishu-ryūri-tan* ("of the noble exile"). Ethnologist Origuchi Shinobu describes *kishu-ryūri-tan* as "tales about frail and delicate creatures, exalted beings resembling the offspring of gods, who wander from land to land."[17] In an attempt to penetrate the mystery of the Nakamotos, Oryū no Oba reads the *kishu-ryūri-tan* pattern into their beautiful faces, imagining that they are descendants of the defeated exiles of the Heike clan or noble wanderers who were seduced by the pleasures of music and wine and ceased their travels. When Nakagami links the Nakamotos to the *kishu-ryūri-tan* myth, he not only practices symbolic inversion but suggests that all *burakumin* share the Nakamotos' mysterious origins. Yet he means to do more. By making the Nakamotos into "noble exiles" and placing them at the top of the hierarchy, Nakagami implicity equates them with the emperor of Japan, whose origins are similarly shrouded in the mists of time. During the 1989 interview, Nakagami equated the *burakumin* and the emperor, stating that neither of them could be said to have an *ie* or family line that can be traced back through history. Instead their origins lie in myth. For this reason Nakagami considered them to be two sides of the same coin *(ura/omote)* and, at the same time, sacred outcastes.[18] Here we see Nakagami using the "logic of identity" in life.

On the one hand, such a suggestion is radically subversive: by equating the high and the low, Nakagami suggests that such categories are interchangeable and thus illusory. On the other hand, he is courting danger: by giving the *burakumin* and the emperor a similar mythic (and possibly divine) origin, Nakagami runs the risk of stripping his people of their unique history, a tale of suffering under the hands of the majority after settling in the castle town of Shingū in the Tokugawa period. In *The Sense of an Ending*, Frank Kermode presents his own distinction between myth and fiction. Here he discusses the dangers of blurring the lines between myth and fiction in a discussion of Nazism:

> We have to distinguish between myth and fiction. Fictions can degenerate into myths whenever they are not consciously held to be fictive. In this sense anti-Semitism is a degenerate fiction, a myth, and Lear is a fiction. Myth operates within the diagrams of ritual . . . it is a sequence of radically unchangeable gestures. Fictions are for finding things out and they change as the needs of sense-making change.[19]

Kermode's discussion illuminates the debate that is currently being waged in Japan on the political ramifications of Nakagami's work in the wake of his early death. When Japanese critics, such as Karatani Kōjin and Yomota Inuhiko, phrase their debate in terms of whether Nakagami leaned toward right-wing or left-wing politics,[20] they do so because the work itself raises serious questions: it is revolutionary, demanding an end to arbitrary discrimination; at the same time, it is reactionary, assigning a mythic status to both *burakumin* and emperor.

How does one read a body of work that sets up such contradictions? Indeed, at times *Sennen no Yūraku* seems to be weighted down by the ritualistic gesture. Oryū no Oba, for example, laments both the inevitablity of the Nakamotos' deaths and the fact that she can do nothing to manipulate the material she has been given. She reveals that the Nakamotos dwell in a realm that barely touches this world, a mythic realm floating above and beyond the random site of fiction. Oryū contemplates the death of Tatsuo, another Nakamoto:

> Oryū mused. If you write your own story, you can put down the pen if things are getting ahead of themselves or if you're telling the tale, you can pause and then come back to the theme. . . . But those strategies won't work if the tale has been set down in the far-away country of the Buddha, Oryū realized, and she choked on her tears. [*Sennen,* p. 227]

In this passage, Oryū no Oba participates in the construction of what Kermode calls a "degenerate fiction"—a fiction that is not conscious of itself as such. Although she admits of the possibility of creating open-ended fictions (writing your own story), in the case of the Nakamotos, the tale has the weight of religious dogma as a "story set down in the far-away country of the Buddha."

At the moment when the predetermined tale seems unbearably constricting, however, Nakagami opens the door to other possibilities. As we have seen, the beautiful Hanzō moves slowly down his predetermined path, laying the stones of his own death. At the same time, however, he evinces fascination for a bush warbler *(uguisu)* that is given to him by one of his lovers, a widow who lives outside the *roji.* The bird, named Tenko, "drum from heaven," has been kept in a cage to train its beautiful voice. The name Tenko sparks many intertextual associations —above all the *Nō* play by Zeami (1363–1443). In this play, a drum falls from heaven into the hands of a boy named Tenko, who plays it beautifully. When word of the drum spreads, it is taken away from the boy and presented to the emperor. The boy subsequently drowns and the drum falls mute.[21] As in the *Nō* play, Tenko offers Hanzō the gift of sound and with it the possibility of making up his own stories instead of passively following the bloodline back into death.

Tenko, the bird, belongs to the world of resemblances: it is a highly weighted cultural commodity whose value is measured in money and prestige. Even more important, when Hanzō takes the bird he too enters the world of resemblances and like the bird becomes a commodity to be bought and sold. Hanzō discovers this when he comes to borrow money from the widow and stays to participate in a night of sadomasochistic play with the widow and another man. The next morning the man discovers that Hanzō is from the *roji*, and he speaks to him condescendingly: "Oh, you're from Nagayama. . . . You're pretty good-looking" (*Sennen*, p. 30). Like the caged bird, Hanzō realizes that the body of the beautiful untouchable is an exotic novelty, and this realization is accompanied by feelings of disgust. At this moment Hanzō is thrust out of his mythic cocoon into the world of resemblances where one thing—in this case, money—can stand for something else. The shock is too great, and Hanzō slashes his own beautiful face.

Like the other Nakamotos, Hanzō lives out the story set down in the country of the Buddha. Yet his desire for the bush warbler introduces a note of uneasiness into an otherwise seamless mythic construction. Desire itself belongs to the logic of resemblance because it is born of incompleteness; when it attains its object, it ceases to be. Hanzō's desire momentarily halts his progress down the path to death and the point of origin. It temporarily leads the narrative away from the sterility of mere repetition because it teaches the Nakamotos about the possibilities of invention and the cruelties inherent in such actions.

Rather than cancel each other out, the mythic and the fictional enter into a complementary relationship in *Sennen no Yūraku*. At the moment the narrative settles down into the mythic logic of identity, the balance tips back toward the fictional. Mythic and fictional thus become intertwined and defined in concert with one another. And it is often the recognition of fiction that sparks the recognition of the myth. In the following passage Oryū recalls the story that Fumihiko, the visionary, told her about meeting his lover in the mountains:

> Later Oryū felt that the story Fumihiko had told her about meeting the woman was lustful enough for a Nakamoto and yet at the same time had delicacy. . . . *But she also felt that he might be making it up.* Fumihiko and the woman were a noble and a prostitute from a thousand years ago and Oryū no Oba had been listening to their tale all that time. [*Sennen*, p. 101; emphasis added]

This passage illuminates Nakagami's treatment of myth and fiction in *Sennen no Yūraku*. At first we are presented with the possibility that Fumihiko is simply inventing his tale; this is fiction in the sense of Kermode. But Oryū no Oba then falls back into the mythic prototype and the logic of identity: Fumihiko and his lover *are* the couple of a thousand years ago and Oryū *is* the audience; this is myth in the sense of Field. In the slippage between the two poles, even Oryū no Oba, the seemingly omniscient narrator, becomes confused. Yet Nakagami purposefully exploits such tensions. By embracing the mythic, he dismisses the possibility of the pure fiction that is conscious of itself as such. At the same time, by injecting a fictional note into the mythic construct, he also denies the reader the comforting possibility of belief. Rather than create cautionary tales about the pitfalls of the mythic or address a concrete political agenda through his work, Nakagami is a trickster whose goal is to ensure that the ground beneath our feet remains slippery. He taunts the reader with riddles: perhaps Fumihiko and his lover are the original couple; perhaps they are frauds; perhaps we are not in a myth at all but merely in a realm that aspires to a mythic state of immutability.

Sennen no Yūraku explores the myth of the sacred but tainted blood and thus stirs up controversial issues surrounding ethnicity and social hierarchies. *Karekinada* (The Straits of Kareki, 1977), however, a realistic portrayal of the early life of a young laborer named Akiyuki, reads like a *shishōsetsu* or "I-novel"—a form that by adhering closely to the perceptions of its central subject tempts the reader into blurring the boundaries between fiction and autobiography.[22] Yet even here Nakagami saturates realism with the mythic and by doing so suggests that the "authentic" experience of the pseudo-autobiographical *shishōsetsu* draws its shape from predetermined archetypes.[23]

As Karatani Kōjin has pointed out, *Karekinada* traces the archetype *(genkei)* of enemy brothers: the story of Cain and Abel that Nakagami continually "bumped into" when he was writing about the relation between brothers.[24] Indeed, the central event of *Karekinada* is a fratricide; Akiyuki murders his younger half-brother, Hideo, who shares a father with him. During childhood the brothers confront each other, and Akiyuki senses Hideo's eyes taunting him for being the illegitimate son. Eventually the tension between the brothers erupts during the Festival of the Dead in August: during a fight on the riverbanks, Akiyuki smashes Hideo's skull as their respective families pay tribute to their dead.

Clearly the murder of Hideo allows Akiyuki to sweep away rivals and create a direct link to his natural father, Hamamura Ryūzō; with Hideo gone, Akiyuki becomes Hamamura's heir (although Hamamura has another younger legitimate son). Viewed in this light, the emnity between brothers is the surface manifestation of a deeper movement in which the son, Akiyuki, discovers and then defines himself in opposition to the father. This movement begins in the novellas *Kataku* (The Burning House, 1975) and *Misaki* (The Cape, 1976), continues through *Karekinada,* and culminates in *Chi no Hate Shijō no Toki* (The Sublime Time at the Ends of the Earth, 1983) with the suicide of Hamamura Ryūzō.[25] But in addition to such oedipal dimensions, the murder of Hideo speaks to a formal problem of the narrative: the specter of repetition that haunts the lives of the characters. Another story lies buried beneath the conflict between Akiyuki and Hideo, a story that is only revealed through the distorting lens of memory. As a child, Akiyuki had an elder half-brother named Ikuo who was the son of Akiyuki's mother, Fusa, by her first husband. After her first husband died, Fusa had a brief affair with Akiyuki's natural father, Hamamura Ryūzō, which resulted in Akiyuki's birth. When that relationship ended, Fusa remarried and moved in with her new husband, leaving behind her older children but taking Akiyuki with her. This enraged Ikuo, who often appeared at the new house drunk, waving a knife and threatening to kill Akiyuki and his mother. Although this brother committed suicide at the age of twenty-four, his presence continues to haunt Akiyuki's waking moments:

> Akiyuki remembered. His older brother had come down this street with a knife meaning to stab them. . . . In a drunken blur Ikuo had walked down this street plannning to murder his mother and Akiyuki, his younger brother. Plunging the knife into the tatami, he screamed, "I'm going to kill you!"
>
> Akiyuki replayed the scene over and over again in his mind. At twenty, at twenty-four, now at twenty-six, he kept thinking that he had gotten Ikuo's life because there was only room for one of them.[26]

In light of Ikuo's agression against Akiyuki, Akiyuki's murder of Hideo becomes merely a reenactment of the earlier pattern, which in turn conforms to a set prototype of fraternal conflict. Through the story of Akiyuki and Hideo, Nakagami touches upon the problem of the archetype, forcing the reader to recognize the lack of spontaneity involved in telling the tale.[27] Through repetition, Nakagami subtly leads us back into the mythic archetype that unfolds *in illo tempore,* the sacred time when humanity participated in a divine order. Paradoxically the story of Akiyuki and Hideo assumes dramatic proportions because it is not unique. Its strength lies in its ability to duplicate the archetype, to represent itself as the story of all enemy brothers.[28]

While revitalizing the mythic, repetition also sets the stage for transformation

—for permutations and digressions from the original tale. In *Reading for Plot,* Peter Brooks contends that all narrative is based on repetition,[29] as in the detective story when the detective retraces the steps of the murderer, and that repetition is essential to narrative because it "may in fact work as a 'binding,' a binding of textual energies that allows them to be mastered by putting them into serviceable form."[30] In this psychoanalytic interpretation, repetition becomes a means to overcome a painful subject or event.

In *Karekinada,* the review of painful memories is not sufficient to transform Akiyuki; it is only when he acts that such memories become cathartic. When Akiyuki smashes Hideo's head with a rock, he becomes his elder brother, Ikuo:

> Suddenly Akiyuki realized it. His body shook. He was exactly like Ikuo who had died at the age of twenty-four when Akiyuki was only twelve. In place of Ikuo, Akiyuki had killed Akiyuki. [*Karekinada,* p. 264]

At the same time, the murder creates an essential difference between them: whereas Ikuo directed his rage inward and killed himself, Akiyuki directs his outward and kills his brother. Through this transformation, Ikuo's hold upon Akiyuki is broken, and the logic of identity proves to be liberating.

By doubling the mythic archetype back upon itself and using it as a tool of liberation, Nakagami finds a solution to the dilemma of repetition and the problem of the archetype *(genkei).* Through the fluid identities of Akiyuki, Ikuo, and Hideo, Nakagami has managed to shift and transform the narratives that bind us. Moreover, through the manipulation of mythic archetypes Nakagami has written a *shishōsetsu* that has no authoritative consciousness: it is a pseudo-autobiography that lacks a center.

The murder of Hideo graphically illustrates the ways in which Nakagami subsumes the autonomous subject in the mythic. Not only does the murder erase Ikuo's presence from Akiyuki's life and allow transformations that move the narrative forward, but it also takes the narrative to an elegiac level in which the histories of individuals are subsumed in the contours of the land itself. In the following passage Akiyuki retaliates against Hideo, who jumped him on the dark riverbank after Akiyuki had issued a challenge to their father:

> Akiyuki looked down at Hideo who was pinned beneath him. Hideo's eyes were on him. That set him off. Aiming at the eyes, Akiyuki curled up his fist, coiled his arm and began punching. Something tore open inside Akiyuki with the painful

impact of his fist on Hideo's face. . . . His body felt hot, flames engulfing him. Hideo struggled to get out of the way but Akiyuki held him down, picked up a wet rock from the riverbank and bashed in his head. He would kill him.

Blood streamed from Hideo's nostrils. His shirt was stained black with it. Letting out a scream, Hideo covered his face with his hands trying to ward off the blows. This Hideo was different from the one he had met in town, the one who ten minutes before had been staring vacantly at Akiyuki and then rushed at him suddenly yelling, "How dare you talk to my father that way!" . . .

There was blood everywhere. But in the darkness he couldn't distinguish between the dark water of the river and Hideo's blood. A flower floating in the swollen waters of the river appeared in Akiyuki's field of vision. . . .

Something that could either have been Hideo's blood or the water of the river made little waves as it lapped between the spaces in the rocks. It flowed black all the way to the sea. To the sea in the distance that covered Arima, this region, and the straits of Kareki. "Run!" yelled Tōru.

"Where to?" said Akiyuki.

Akiyuki looked at Hideo. Lying there with blood streaming down and his body convulsing, he didn't look like Hideo. He was somebody without a name. [*Karekinada*, pp. 259–260]

The passage begins with a realistic treatment of the cause of the fight between the two brothers: Hideo's eyes, which are filled with scorn; yet soon, like the river that flows to the sea, the narrative leaves behind the particulars of the conflict between Akiyuki and Hideo, carrying us into a panoramic landscape in which Hideo's body becomes a nameless mass that is no different from a tree or stone, his blood mingling with the river as it flows down past Arima into the Straits of Kareki. The archetype of Cain and Abel itself seems rooted in the land, a feature as natural as any other, and Hideo becomes a sacrificial victim to *Karekinada* itself.

Through the murder of Hideo, Nakagami once again brings the narrative to the edge of the mythical, where the subject shrinks in the face of the external. By doing so, he challenges the conventions of the *shishōsetsu* in which the subject, tortured though he or she may be, is central to the construction of narrative. Here Nakagami suggests that landscape is as powerful a force as consciousness—that Akiyuki and his people are the puppets of forces beyond their control. The very forms of the landscape—a metaphor for the predetermined shape of narrative itself—render the human subject nameless and faceless, like Hideo's body.

Hidaka Shōji has written: "The novelistic language of *Karekinada* makes the

landscape into a metaphor for Akiyuki's internal life."³¹ Yet in fact Nakagami
attempts the reverse: to divest the text of all metaphor and make Akiyuki into an
open system through which the world flows and recedes. In a lyrical rendition of
Akiyuki's work as a laborer in the mountains, Nakagami breaks through Akiyuki's
tortured deliberations about himself (in which he attempts to read himself through
the tangled, metaphoric relations of the family) and suspends him in a realm of
pure sensation:

> The sun penetrated Akiyuki as if he were a tree in the landscape. The wind caressed
> him as it did the blades of grass. While working Akiyuki understood that he
> became an object that couldn't think about or know itself, couldn't see or reply,
> couldn't listen to music. . . . Akiyuki was no longer Akiyuki but rather the love
> that he felt towards the sky, the sun in the sky, the mountains warmed by the sun,
> the houses, the illuminated leaves, the earth, stones, each detail of the landscape
> around him. He was each and every thing. To Akiyuki working as a laborer, the
> sun-soaked landscape was like music. Even the sounds of the cicadas which until
> just a moment ago had sounded like the Buddhist chants *namu-amida-butsu* or
> *namu-myō-hō-renge-kyō* had now become the breath of the mountain. Akiyuki *was*
> breath. . . . [*Karekinada*, p. 123]

Here landscape does not serve as a window into Akiyuki's interior life; rather,
it creates Akiyuki and brings him to a state of ecstasy. Nakagami does not dispense
with Akiyuki altogether, nor does he jettison the trappings of realism, but he continues to test the boundaries of the self by placing Akiyuki in figurative, mythic
landscapes. After Hideo's murder, for example, Akiyuki travels up into the mountains and describes the features of the land that are spread out before him, placing
each one in its mythic context.³² In the recitation of the names, Nakagami creates
a mandala: a map of space out of words like the ones that the faithful in the Muro-
machi period would worship in lieu of traveling to the three sacred sites of
Kumano. Akiyuki's gesture is also reminiscent of the *kunimi* ritual of Manyōshū
poetry, in which the ruler would climb to the top of a mountain and assert his
control over his domain by describing it in poetic tones. By setting up such reverberations in his texts, Nakagami suggests that the contours of Kumano are as much
a product of myth as they are an external space:

> From that region if you went by sea you'd reach Osaka, over the mountains Nara.
> A chain of mountains, people living at the foot of them, and a town had been estab-

lished long ago at the southeastern end of Kii Peninsula with its population of about 400,000 people. . . . From olden times, it was said that *hana no iwaya,* the large rock that honored Izanami no Mikoto who died giving birth to the fire god, looked like a vagina from the sea. It was also the place where the pilgrims to the three sacred sites of Kumano stayed. . . . [*Karekinada,* p. 262]

and

The whole area was the same: mountains stretching on to Koya, Nara, and Ise; mountains upon mountains piled on one another and then in the little breaks, a little piece of land or the sea. This was Kumano. In every region the sun beat down, strong winds blew, and the typhoons came each summer. There were many fires and many murders. From long ago Kumano was a place of legends. [*Karekinada,* p. 157]

Landscape as a mythic construction is perhaps best represented in the figure of Akiyuki's natural father, Hamamura Ryūzō, an unsavory drifter who appeared in the *roji* after the war, impregnated three women, and set fires in the employ of a developer named Arikura. Hamamura originally came from Arima, but when Akiyuki probes into his background, he finds out little about his father except that he came from peasant stock. In spite of Akiyuki's mother's attempts to separate him from his father, Hamamura makes direct contact with Akiyuki after many years and eventually offers him a position in a lumber business he has built up through shady moneylending practices. Despite his lowly origins, Hamamura Ryūzō claims that he is a descendant of Hamamura Magoichi, a nearly mythical warrior who fought against Oda Nobunaga in the wars of the sixteenth century.[33] According to legend, Magoichi was defeated in battle and then fled into the mountains with one wounded leg and a missing eye, eventually descending to Arima by the sea to establish "the last paradise" *(saigo no rakuen)*.[34] To assert his claim, Akiyuki's father has erected a monument to his supposed ancestor at a temple in Arima that has a sweeping view of the surrounding area.

As he grows up, Akiyuki's reaction to his mysterious father is ambivalent. At first he despises Hamamura Ryūzō and, in an effort to deny the authority of the father, he sleeps with a half-sister, Satoko (another illegitimate child of Hamamura Ryūzō), and then confronts his father with the news of this incest. Early in the narrative, he dreams that his father is dying,[35] and on the night he murders Hideo, Akiyuki confronts his father with the many crimes that the father has committed against the people in order to enrich himself.[36] Akiyuki's resentment of his father is softened, however, by intense curiosity. He travels to the monument to Magoichi and is fascinated by the stone, which he sees as a symbol of his father's quest for eternal life and his ever-present phallus. (The lingam that dominates the landscape is obviously a response to the vagina-shaped rock, *hana no iwaya*.) Through Magoichi, Hamamura has recreated himself as a mythic *kishu-ryūri-tan* figure: he, like Magoichi, returned from war to claim a place in Kumano, an achievement for a man the people have always called "Horse's Bone" and "King of Flies."

As Magoichi provides the means for Hamamura to recreate himself in the image of the noble exile, so too does Magoichi become a vehicle for Akiyuki's own self-creation. As Peter Brooks observes in a discussion of Julien Sorel of *The Red and the Black*, the mysterious father offers one the chance to become "something that one isn't by birth."[37] In this case, through the mysterious grandfather, Akiyuki will claim a genealogy that will erase his bastard status and place him in a long line of noble fighters. Akiyuki imagines:

> I wish he'd yell at me, knock me down, he thought. Then he'd be Hamamura's child, he would suffer from the same madness as his father, and believe in the false story that he had a grandfather, a great-grandfather, and an ancestor named Magoichi. It would solve the riddle that was half of himself. He would be free. [*Karekinada*, p. 187]

In this passage, Akiyuki stands outside the degenerate fiction, separated from his father and grandfather by the thin veil of belief. Akiyuki realizes that the story of Magoichi is madness, but it is perhaps his only means to escape the coordinates of his present existence—"to solve the riddle that was half of himself." Again Nakagami's use of the mythic falls in between the distinct categories of myth and fiction set up by Kermode; rather than functioning as a past-directed, ritualistic mode, the mythic becomes the source of self-invention in the present.

Despite the temptations posed by the myth of Magoichi, Akiyuki maintains an ambivalent stance toward his father and his monument. Like Hanzō, Akiyuki keeps a foothold in the world of resemblances. Yet it is typical that Akiyuki fluctuates, at times viewing the landscape through the eyes of his father, at other times seeing the landscape as a degenerate fiction. Two passages from *Karekinada* illustrate the poles of belief and skepticism:

The mountains were the kind that appeared in fairytales. Even the *mikan* fields, which stretched toward the foot of the mountains across from the temple with the monument, looked false. These mountains, these fields, were nothing more than stories fabricated in the mad brain of Hamamura Ryūzō, the King of Flies, the man with the big body and the snake eyes. The tomb of the goddess Izanami who died giving birth to the fire god was only five minutes from here by car. This was the mythic country of the dead. All around him. And it was here that Hamamura had built his monument. [*Karekinada*, p. 161]

Akiyuki brooded. As Hamamura's son and the descendant of a dead man, Akiyuki gazed out on the landscape where the wind blew, the leaves were stirring and the sun was shining. Maybe he, too, was a dead man. Maybe Kumano really was the land of the dead. . . . [*Karekinada*, p. 242]

In the first passage Akiyuki functions as an observer whose distance from the landscape allows him to view it as a fundamentally false construction: the illusion of a mad brain. Akiyuki stands outside of his father's fabulous construction looking in, briefly trying on his father's vision when he states that Kumano is "the mythic country of the dead." In the second passage, Akiyuki's embraces and experiments with his father's genealogy, creating degenerate fictions around the notion of a self (Akiyuki is the dead Magoichi) and turning the world upside down (the land of the dead exists here and now).

Akiyuki's tentative stance, however, suggests that he recognizes the presence of degenerate fictions which suppress their origins as such. Implicit in Akiyuki's ambivalence is a warning: myths provide necessary explanations, but one must weigh them carefully, remain skeptical, in order to survive. This is made clear in *Chi no Hate Shijō no Toki* when Hamamura Ryūzō's belief in his own monstrous fiction leads to self-annihilation whereas Akiyuki, who periodically remembers that he is living a self-made fiction, survives.

The importance of skepticism is reiterated in *Karekinada* when Akiyuki examines the myth of Magoichi dispassionately and suspects that it may contain a grain of historical truth. Gazing out over the landscape, Akiyuki concludes that, like Magoichi, the *burakumin* must have crossed the mountains into Hongū and then followed the river to the sea.[38] Similarly, in *Kishū: Ki no Kuni Ne no Kuni* (Kishu: Land of Trees, Land of Roots), a nonfictional account of a journey he took around the Kii Peninsula, Nakagami discusses the relationship between history and myth: in the *kishu-ryūri-tan* myth he detects the origins of the *burakumin*—exiles who were unsettled by war or unrest and forced to wander far from home.[39]

When Nakagami scans myth to extract the grains of history, he is quick to condemn it as well. His distrust of the mythic and of the ways people transform history into myth leads back into his experiences of *sabetsu* or discrimination. In *Kishū: Ki no Kuni Ne no Kuni,* Nakagami discusses the darker side of the *kishu-ryūri-tan* myth: the noble exiles, forced to wander in disguise, are the equivalent of the *burakumin,* who must hide their origins when they venture into majority society. As an example, Nakagami points to a Meiji-era politician named Hoshi Tōru, whose biography is shrouded in mystery. Visiting a temple in Arima, Nakagami believes that Hoshi Tōru switched identities with a local boy named Iroku in order to escape the stigma of being *burakumin* and then posed as the son of a Tokyo samurai. It is this connection to discrimination that gives teeth to the *kishu-ryūri-tan* myth and makes the mythic an instrument of oppression.[40] Nakagami explains:

> It would be possible to clear up the issue of whether the dead Iroku was actually Hoshi Tōru. But what is harder to resolve is why the biographers have conflicting versions. . . . In Arima, I learned of Magoichi and now I hear about Hoshi Tōru and I feel that I am witnessing the construction of oral legends and the evolution of the *kishu-ryūri-tan* [noble exile] myth. This is the way that the people invent *monogatari* [tales].
>
> Yet if Iroku turns out to be Hoshi Tōru, the situation becomes grave. If the invented *monogatari* [tale] is read in the context of *sabetsu* [discrimination], as in the story I heard in Arima, then it is no longer a pleasant construction but becomes "a story that explodes in blood" *(chi no deru monogatari).*
>
> The "story that explodes in blood" is the story of our efforts to remove the outcaste stigma from ourselves and our children. *Sabetsu* [discrimination] kills. . . . *Sabetsu* springs up spontaneously, it's easy to practice, but once the stigma is there, it's hard to erase—that's the structure of Japan. [*Kishū: Ki no Kuni Ne no Kuni,* pp. 148–149]

It is Nakagami's penchant to peel back the familiar shapes of the mythic and expose the history underneath that saves his work from being merely a nostalgic revisiting of myth. In the tales of discrimination, Nakagami traces the outlines of the circle that make up the *hō/seido,* the law/system, of Japanese culture. Viewed in this light, Akiyuki's ambivalence makes sense: through Akiyuki's self-conscious knowledge of his father's lie, Nakagami portrays the perils of the mythic construct while at the same time suggesting that it is also the source of self-invention, of fantasy, of storytelling itself.

Nakagami was not completely free of the lure of the mythic himself—as in *Sennen no Yūraku,* when he is clearly tempted by the divinity of the Nakamotos. Perhaps by playing with the mythic archetype and the problem of belief, Nakagami hoped to find a place of perfect rest, a place where one could dwell at peace with words, a place beyond time, history, and the problem of identity. Yet at the same time, he realized that such a wish was a utopian fantasy: one could never recapture the point of origin. In the 1989 interview, he discussed his temptations:

> Storytelling has its basic rhythms. When you enter into this fixed rhythm you feel tremendous pleasure. It's like life in the *roji.* You wake up, go to work, come home, make love, drink, and go to sleep. Nothing could be happier. There's perfect pleasure in the *monogatari* [mythic tale]. If you leave everything up to the *monogatari,* it will carry you through. But then you don't make any progress. You are left powerless. Once you wake up, though, it's incredibly painful. . . .[41]

The pain upon waking is dramatically illustrated in a passage from *Sennen no Yūraku* in which Hanzō waits anxiously for news of his newborn child. Aware of the strange blood of the Nakamoto clan and his own peculiar destiny, Hanzō is obsessed with the possibility that his child will be born with a deformity, as was his uncle Gen, who has a misshapen hand. When Oryū no Oba emerges and informs Hanzō that his baby girl is a "little Buddha," Hanzō assumes that Oryū is using a euphemism to inform him that his child is not whole. But Oyrū no Oba chides him for his reaction: "Don't say such arrogant things when you don't have enough faith" (*Sennen,* p. 10).

Hanzō's reaction reveals him to be the typical Nakagami protagonist. Trapped within a mythic narrative in which he is destined to return to the divine order that gave birth to him, Hanzō assumes that his child will be similarly marked. Yet his lack of faith in the fictions in which he dwells means that he has forfeited his position. Unlike Oryū, who believes that the perfection of the Buddha and the deformity of the outcaste are identical marks of divinity, Hanzō recognizes such equivalences as degenerate fictions. In his mouth, the words of the faithful merely sound mocking

This is the problem of Nakagami's narratives in general: the characters never have enough faith. Confronted with evidence of an imperfect logic of identity, they can neither revel in the purely fictional nor return to the womb of belief. Myth and fiction have run together, muddying the current in the process. Nakagami's protagonists are trapped "betwixt and between"; they depend on the mythic archetype *(genkei)* because it is the source of all stories, the explanation of origins. But as in the case of Hanzō, whose strange blood draws him to his fate, it is also an instrument of *sabetsu* and death.

NOTES

1. Nakagami Kenji, "Monogatari no Keifu: Danshō," in Karatani Kōjin and Nakagami Kenji, *Kobayashi Hideo o Koete* (Beyond Kobayashi Hideo) (Tokyo: Kawade Shoboshinsha, 1979), p. 150.

2. For a discussion of various dimensions of myth see Mircea Eliade, *The Myth of the Eternal Return,* trans. Willard R. Trask (Princeton: Princeton University Press, 1954), pp. 3–48.

3. The *burakumin* are members of a group of outcastes whose low status was traditionally linked to the "unclean tasks" they performed—leatherworker, shoemaker, undertaker, butcher—and who occupy the bottom rungs of Japanese society both literally and figuratively. Majority Japanese sometimes contend that the *burakumin* have strange features and sexual habits, blood that will pollute upon contact, and even different racial origins from other Japanese. Since the Edo period, prohibitions against intermarriage between outsiders and members of the group have been especially strong. See George De Vos and Hirsohi Wagatsuma's classic study in English, *Japan's Invisible Race* (Berkeley: University of California Press, 1966), or Ian Neary, *Political Protest and Social Control in Pre-War Japan: The Origins of Burakumin Liberation* (Atlantic Highlands, N.J.: Humanities Press, 1989).

4. Personal interview with Nakagami Kenji, January 1989.

5. Nakagami Kenji, *Sennen no Yūraku* (A thousand years of pleasure) (Tokyo: Kawade Shobōshinsha, 1982), p. 96.

6. For a discussion of the number four and other numbers in *Sennen no Yūraku* see Suga Hidemi, "Gūsū to Kisū—*Sennen no Yūraku* o Yomu" (Even numbers and odd numbers—a reading of *Sennen no Yūraku*), *Shunkan Dokushojin* (September 1982):95.

7. Personal interview with Nakagami Kenji, January 1989.

8. Yomota Inuhiko, *Kishu to Tensei* (Exile and rebirth) (Tokyo: Shinchōsha, 1987), p. 52.

9. Nakagami, *Sennen no Yūraku,* p. 18.

10. Rosalie Colie, *Paradoxica Epidemica: The Renaissance Tradition of Paradox* (Princeton: Princeton University Press, 1966), pp. 7–8.

11. Barbara Babcock, ed., *The Reversible World: Symbolic Inversion in Art and Society* (Ithaca: Cornell University Press, 1978), p. 18.

12. Victor Turner, *The Ritual Process* (Chicago: University of Chicago Press, 1969), p. 95.

13. Noguchi Takehiko, *Edo to Aku* (The Edo period and evil) (Tokyo: Kadokawa Shoten, 1991), p. 41.

14. Ibid., p. 43.

15. The phrase comes from Victor Turner, "Betwixt and Between: The Liminal Period in Rites of Passage," in *The Forest of Symbols* (Ithaca: Cornell University Press, 1967), p. 106.

16. Norma Field, *The Splendor of Longing in the Tale of Genji* (Princeton: Princeton University Press, 1987), p. 25.

17. Origuchi Shinobu as quoted in Field, *Splendor of Longing*, p. 33. Perhaps the best-known example is Prince Genji's banishment to Suma in the *Tale of Genji*.

18. Personal interview with Nakagami Kenji, January 1989.

19. Frank Kermode, *The Sense of an Ending* (London: Oxford University Press, 1966), p. 38.

20. Watanabe Naomi, Karatani Kōjin, Suga Hidemi, Yomota Inuhiko, and Eve Zimmerman, "Sennen no Bungaku" (Writing for the millennium), *Bungakukai* 47 (October 1993):138–168.

21. For a synopsis in English see P. G. O'Neill, *A Guide to Nō* (Tokyo: Hinoki Shoten, 1953), pp. 188–189.

22. For a discussion of the implications of the *shishōsetsu* form see Edward Fowler, *The Rhetoric of Confession* (Berkeley: University of California Press, 1988), pp. 3–27.

23. In his introduction to the new edition of *Chi no Hate Shijō no Toki* (The sublime time at the ends of the earth, 1983) Karatani Kōjin has written that the works which feature the protagonist, Akiyuki, are unique because they question the concept of a self (p. 605).

24. Ibid.

25. Karatani Kōjin does not believe that the oedipal conflict is central to *Karekinada* (or the other works in which Akiyuki figures as a protagonist); the fact that Hamamura commits suicide indicates this was an "empty vein" for Nakagami; see Karatani, "Introduction," p. 607. Hidaka Shōji too denies the oedipal implications of the battle between Hamamura and Akiyuki; see Hidaka Shōji, "*Karekinada* Kara *Chi no Hate* e" (From *Karekinada* to *Chi no Hate*), *Kokubungaku* 36(14) (December 1991):69–77. Indeed the oedipal conflict is weakened by Hamamura's own anarchistic nature and by Akiyuki's tendency to mythologize his father rather than openly confront him.

26. Nakagami Kenji, *Karekinada* (Straits of Kareki) (Tokyo: Kawade Shoboshinsha, 1977), p. 61.

27. Among Japanese critics, Yomota Inuhiko is particularly interested in the problem of repetition in Nakagami's work. He argues that Nakagami's work is circular and that the only chance for the characters to move forward is to descend into perverse imitations of the stories that have shaped them. See Yomota Inuhiko, *Kishu to Tensei* (Tokyo: Shinchōsha, 1987), p. 156.

28. In discussing primitive belief systems Mircea Eliade writes: "An object or act becomes real only insofar as it imitates or repeats an archetype. Thus reality is acquired solely through repetition or participation." See Eliade, *Myth of the Eternal Return*, p. 34.

29. Peter Brooks, *Reading for Plot* (Cambridge, Mass.: Harvard University Press, 1984), p. 97.

30. Ibid., p. 101.

31. Hidaka, "*Karekinada* Kara *Chi no Hate* e," p. 71.

32. Nakagami, *Karekinada,* p. 262.

33. Nakagami Kenji, *Kishū: Ki no Kuni Ne no Kuni* (Kishū: Land of trees, land of roots) (Tokyo: Kadokawa, 1986), pp. 143–153. The chapter on Arima describes the Magoichi legend.

34. Nakagami, *Karekinada,* p. 161.

35. Ibid., p. 14.

36. Ibid., p. 255.

37. Brooks, *Reading for Plot,* p. 84.

38. Nakagami, *Karekinada,* pp. 242 and 255.

39. Nakagami, *Kishū,* pp. 146–148.

40. Ibid., pp. 148–149.

41. Personal interview with Nakagami Kenji, January 1989.

7

(RE)CANONIZING KURAHASHI YUMIKO: TOWARD ALTERNATIVE PERSPECTIVES FOR "MODERN" "JAPANESE" "LITERATURE"

Atsuko Sakaki

Kurahashi Yumiko was born in Kōchi, Japan, in 1935, the eldest daughter of a dentist and his wife. Having spent a year as a college student in Japanese literature in Kyoto, she moved to Tokyo primarily to obtain a dental hygienist's certificate. Then she began to major in French at Meiji University, which then offered courses by such leading literati as Nakamura Mitsuo, Hirano Ken, and Yoshida Ken'ichi. She devoted herself to reading Camus, Kafka, Rimbaud, Valéry, Blanchot, and other contemporary writers.

Without joining any group of writers-to-be, she completed her first work, "Zatsujin bokumetsu shūkan" (Week for Extermination of Mongrels),[1] in 1959. Nominated for the Meiji University President's Prize, the story was nevertheless banned by the university newspaper for its satirical look at the New Left movement. This ambiguous literary debut was followed by publication of the much proclaimed and yet controversial short stories "Parutai" (Partei)[2] and "Natsu no owari" (The End of Summer)[3] in 1960, both of which were shortlisted for the Akutagawa Prize.

The discrepancy between positive and negative readings of her work reached its apogee when she was accused by the critic Etō Jun of plagiarism in her first novel—or antinovel, to be precise—*Kurai tabi* (Blue

Journey, 1961). This, however, did not put a stop to her literary career. Instead she continued to produce experimental narratives: *Sei shōjo* (Divine Maiden, 1965), *Sumiyakisuto Kyū no bōken* (The Adventures of Sumiyakist Q, 1969), and the ongoing saga beginning with *Yume no ukihashi* (The Floating Bridge of Dreams, 1970) and including *Shiro no naka no shiro* (Castle within the Castle, 1980), *Shunposhion* (Symposium, 1985), *Popoi* (1987), *Kōkan* (Pleasure Exchange, 1989), *Yume no kayoiji* (The Passage of Dreams, 1989), and *Gensō kaiga-kan* (Museum of Fantastic Pictures, 1991).

■

There was no one in him; behind his face (which even through the bad paintings of those times resembles no other) and his words, which were copious, fantastic and stormy, there was only a bit of coldness, a dream dreamt by no one.

— Jorge Luis Borges, "Everything and Nothing"

The fact is that every writer creates his own precursors. His work modifies our conception of the past, as it will modify the future. In this correlation the identity or plurality of the men involved is unimportant.

— Jorge Luis Borges, "Kafka and His Precursors"

Cervantes takes pleasure in confusing the objective and the subjective, the world of the reader and the world of the book.

— Jorge Luis Borges, "Partial Magic in the Quixote"

In 1833, Carlyle observed that the history of the universe is an infinite sacred book that all men write and read and try to understand, and in which they are also written.

— Jorge Luis Borges, "Partial Magic in the Quixote"

■

"CONTINGENCIES OF VALUE": KURAHASHI AND *BUNDAN*

That Ōe Kenzaburō was awarded the 1994 Nobel Prize for literature invites us to reconsider what should represent modern Japanese literature in the world. In *Nihon kindai bungaku no kigen* (Origins of Modern Japanese Literature), Karatani Kōjin has succeeded in denaturalizing the concepts of the "modern," the "Japanese," and "literature" by foregrounding several examples of "doxa," borrowing Roland Barthes' terminology, with which certain works have been canonized as representing modern Japanese literature.[4] Here I want to look at the same coin from the reverse side—that is, to delineate canonicity of modern Japanese literature by examining a decanonized author: Kurahashi Yumiko. This way, the domain of modern Japanese literature should be defined not only by what it contains, but also by what it unduly excludes. The following examination of her texts and the context in which she has produced them will show how central she would have been to contemporary literary studies had she written in a European language. Indeed, the issues she raises about textuality, themes, and narration have all been explored by canonical postmodern authors and critics in Euro-America. It is not that Kurahashi deserves decanonization, but that the Japanese literary establishment should be marginalized in worldwide literary studies.

Decanonized as she may be, Kurahashi has not remained in obscurity. She has attracted a number of readers in Japan as well as in other countries. Her novels, short stories, and essays have been made available in the market in Japan by major presses such as Shinchōsha, Kōdansha, and Fukutake shoten, first in hardcover and then, almost invariably, in paperbacks. Her fiction to 1971 has been collected in *Kurahashi Yumiko zen sakuhin* (Complete Works of Kurahashi Yumiko) and her work has been included in nine anthologies of contemporary Japanese literature. This suggests that her work should be considered "serious" and that it is marketable.

I do not mean to suggest that Kurahashi has been completely neglected by all major literary critics. She has received various literary awards, among them the *Meiji daigaku gakuchō shō* (Meiji University President's Prize) in 1960, *Joryū bungaku shō* (Women's Literature Prize) in 1961, *Tamura Toshiko shō* (Tamura Toshiko Prize) in 1963, and *Izumi Kyōka shō* (Izumi Kyōka Prize) in 1987.[5] She was even nominated twice, though unsuccessfully, for the Akutagawa Prize, the most prestigious literary award for new fiction writers in Japan.[6] Nevertheless, only one book of criticism and two special issues of periodicals concerning Kurahashi's works have been published in Japan. To discover the reasons for this critical neglect in Japan, as well as provide some information regarding Kurahashi, who remains relatively unknown in North America, let us examine the context in which she emerged as a fiction writer.

For those readers who approach authors as a prelude to understanding their oeuvre, it might be interesting to learn that Kurahashi Yumiko's biographical data coincide with Ōe's to a considerable degree. Both were born in Shikoku in 1935 and thus have shared presumably similar natural and social environments. Both moved to Tokyo to major in French at colleges, and both loved to read Jean-Paul Sartre.[7] Both had their talent acknowledged by the same literary critic, Hirano Ken, and both made successful debuts in the literary establishment when still university students.[8] Similarities, however, end here. From now on, I will summarize only the process in which Kurahashi contended with critics from the literary establishment, rather than comparing her career with Ōe's, which is already well explained elsewhere.

While enthusiastically supported by certain critics and the mass media, Kurahashi's earlier works were also vehemently criticized by other well-known literary critics who valorized romantic or realistic views of literature. An animated debate about the value of her work continued in the *bundan* or literary establishment of Japan.[9] A notable example of this quarrel is a lengthy debate between Kurahashi herself and the literary critic Etō Jun in which Ōe Kenzaburō has sided with Etō. This debate has developed into the "*Kurai tabi* ronsō" (dispute over *Blue Journey*) and has involved critics such as Okuno Takeo on Kurahashi's side and Shirai Kōji (the Japanese translator of Sartre's *La Nausée*) on Etō's.

These debates have been largely concerned with the propriety of Kurahashi's ideas regarding novel themes, the writer's role, and the methodologies involved in writing novels. Kurahashi's opponents contend that she employs abstract or artificial words that lack correspondence to concrete objects in the real world, to inner reality, and to her own life.[10] Moreover, they claim that her fictional topics are amoral and lacking in serious commitment to the betterment of society. Finally, they suggest that Kurahashi is a plagiarist and has not developed her own independent fictional content or form. These objections illustrate the values of many modern Japanese critics: they stress mimetic representation *(shajitsu-sei)*, morality *(dōtoku-sei)*, and originality *(dokusōsei)*—notions that Euro-American literary studies have problematized.

Kurahashi has vigorously defended herself against these charges by publishing critical replies to her opponents, refuting condemnations in newspapers and

periodicals, and adding expository postscripts to her works when they were repub-
lished in *Kurahashi Yumiko zen sakuhin*. It is evident in these writings, most of
which are collected in four volumes of essays to date, that her writing itself challenges the very criteria by which she is judged, rather than attempting and failing to fulfill them. Most of Kurahashi's critical essays seem to have been written
in order to refute attacks by Japanese critics. She rarely comments upon her narrative strategies, for instance, to which little critical attention has been devoted,
instead devoting attention to her views of literature, compositional methods,
and thematic concerns, which have been of interest to critics. Kurahashi's silence
regarding the narrational aspects of her fiction should thus be considered a strate-
gic one. As we shall see, Kurahashi's narrative methodologies are in fact explicitly
linked to thematic and compositional concerns.

Kurahashi's view of thematics is directly opposed to that of her critics. She is
opposed to romantic poetics, which exalts the author's self-projection into his or
her works, and to nineteenth-century realism, which values mimetic representations of "reality" in the actual world. In an essay called "Shōsetsu no meiro to hiteisei" (The Labyrinth and Negativity of Fiction, 1966) Kurahashi maintains that she
does not wish to write novels to "report facts," including her own "experiences
or life."[11] The fact that Kurahashi's works do not deal thematically with her own
life, then, is not a failure of her project. It is an expected consequence of her philosophy that words do not correspond to objects in the actual world. In the same
essay and elsewhere, Kurahashi declares that she does not use words as "tools for
communication" but writes novels and stories with poetic words that are, rather,
"an objective in themselves."[12] In other words, she believes in the autonomy of
words in prose as well as in poetry. Thus it is irrelevant that Nakamura Mitsuo
criticizes Kurahashi for transgressing the discipline of prose, which he sees as
intended to explain things, and that she instead writes "poems of ideas."[13] Kurahashi finds the distinction between "words of 'poetry' " and "words of 'prose' "
"problematic."[14] As Kurahashi repeatedly maintains, the content—the "what to
write" of the novel—is not her primary concern but is subject to the "style," or
"how to write." In her view the novel is "an art in which 'what to write' always
depends on 'how to write,' or the 'style,' "[15] just as poetry is taken for granted to
be such an art.[16]

Some critics have condemned Kurahashi's works as "fakes" and criticized her
for lack of originality. They frown at her habit of explicitly naming, or drawing
obvious parallels with, other texts, assuming that Kurahashi's work is too intellectually barren to warrant serious research. In response to such condemnation,

Kurahashi has made frequent and extensive statements about her art of pastiche (as opposed to forgery). Kurahashi does not intend to develop her own "original style" but concerns herself instead with the elaborate use of rhetoric and the imaginative manipulation of established compositional forms. She claims in "Miko to hiirō" (The Sybil and the Hero, 1965) that "the respect [a writer pays to another writer] is shown only in the way [the precursor's ideas] are stolen": "the pride of a writer lies in cleverly stealing, the honor of a writer, in being stolen from."[17] Kurahashi compares the whole process of copying to "alchemy," emphasizing the complexity of this activity, unlike the simple acts of "pouring material into a mold" and "manufacturing on the spot."

> A painter does not draw an apple because he or she wants to eat it, but because he or she obtains a vision of the invisible world through the apple and is driven to creation. In addition, the royal road to this world is nothing but a series of styles discovered by preceding masters.[18]

Such a method, comparable to "alchemy," "a secret charm," or "the royal road," should not be labeled pejoratively as "plagiarism." Indeed, Kurahashi calls it "pastiche" (given in French by Kurahashi) of "forerunners' 'styles'" in her essay "Hihyō no kanashisa: Etō Jun san ni" (The Misery of Criticism: To Mr. Etō Jun, 1961).[19] Unlike plagiarism, which presupposes and values "originality," pastiche indicates the conscious display of echoes of anterior texts in a particular text— that is, a demonstration of intertextuality.

To defend her art of pastiche, Kurahashi mentions many writers from European and East Asian traditions who use the method. Thus she writes in "Rorensu Dareru to watashi" (Lawrence Durrell and I, 1964): "Surely, as Durrell himself admits, his style consists of stolen objects from many writers; thus, his style is beautiful."[20] Similarly, she comments on Matsuo Bashō in "Hiraizumi de kanjiru 'eien' to 'haikyo'" ("Immortality" and "Ruins" Perceived at Hiraizumi, 1963): "In *The Narrow Road Down to the North*, . . . the reality of a travel document is unhesitatingly distorted for the sake of poetic reality. In short, *The Narrow Road* is not a mere travel account, but a faint trace of Bashō's imagination inspired by others' styles."[21] It is easy to compare Kurahashi with other writers of the same inclination: Fujiwara no Teika, who established the method of *honkadori* or allusive variation in *waka;* Zeami, who wove poetic allusions into *Nō* texts in medieval Japan; and Mori Ōgai, Akutagawa Ryūnosuke, and Tanizaki Jun'ichirō, all of whom used motifs from ancient literature in narratives with modern settings.

VISIONS OF NEGATIVITY: "ANTIWORLD"
AND PERFORMATIVE FEMININITY

I wish now to return to the thematic issues discussed in her essays. First I want
to examine her theory of *han-sekai* (antiworld) that she wishes to construct in her
novels. Next I will explicate the analogies she draws between the antiworld and
the socially subordinate position of females, between the act of novel writing
and the act of secretion from female bodies, between the nothingness behind
fiction and the void of the womb inside female bodies, and, finally, between the
performativity of fiction and the masquerade of femininity itself.

In "The Labyrinth and Negativity of Fiction," Kurahashi defines fiction as a
form of the antiworld—"the world that is not this [actual] world," "the labyrinth
of 'imaginary space' "—which is given by Kurahashi as an initial hypothesis or
"axiom, to use a term from mathematics." Characters in the antiworld are "variables" rather than "human beings" and are thus "represented by signs such as K,
L, S, M." The antiworld is governed by "a logic of 'dreams' " or "nightmares."
"Leaps and twists which are inherent to dreams transform this world into a
grotesque 'form.' "[22] Thus the relationship between the antiworld and the "real"
world is clarified. The former is not a faithful representation of the latter; it is a
deformed version of the latter, and thus subject to it.

Kurahashi's antiworld is thus analogous to the female position in a patriarchal
society. In "Watashi no 'dai-san no sei' " (My "Third Sex," 1960), she maintains,
again using mathematical terms:

> This world has the sign of sex. Just as we forget that the numbers we deal with in
> our daily life have a positive [plus] sign, so we forget the sexual sign, the male sign,
> which exists in this world. Women are shut in the world of the negative [minus]
> sign, or the antiworld in the [actual] world, so to speak. In short, this [actual] world
> belongs to men. In it, women are regarded as nothing but those who have the other
> sex of female, as opposed to male. As Beauvoir points out, women belong to the
> category of "the Other."[23]

Kurahashi does not try, however, to usurp the male power in the "real" world.
Toward the end of the same essay, she claims: "But rather, the position of women,
projecting out into the reverse side of this world, provides them with a splendid
viewpoint from which to objectivize the men's world."[24] She attempts to take
advantage of the subordinate position females are given and to objectivize the

order, norm, natural law, or "doxa," which has been presupposed and taken for granted by a patriarchal world. Through this strategy she suggests the fictional, suppositional nature of the "real" world. The analogy between the novel as an anti-world and the subordinate social position of women is a recurrent theme in Kurahashi's work: the world of the novel is a metaphor for woman; woman is a metaphor for the world of the novel.

Kurahashi also draws an analogy between the act of novel writing and female secretion. In the following excerpt from an essay, "Yōjo de aru koto" (Being a Witch, 1965), she alludes to the anatomical observation that in a woman there is an empty space—the womb—while at the same time cleverly fictionalizing this anatomy:

> An old woman who has had a hysterectomy appears in *Komachi hensō,* the latest work of Ms. Enchi Fumiko. In fact, it seems to me this monstrous woman indicates the true nature of a woman who writes novels. Such a woman who writes novels does not have her womb by nature, so to speak, but, instead, an empty darkness that secretes words.[25]

Further, in "Dokuyaku to shite no bungaku" (Literature as Poison, 1967), Kurahashi maintains that "it is not an 'activity' but a secretion for women to write."[26] The metaphor of secretion describes the nature of Kurahashi's fiction. In contrast to stories and novels that present the actions of the characters—clarifying the "five Ws": when, where, who, what, why—her ideal fiction creates "a building in air" where, "at an unknown time, in a nonexistent place, someone who is nobody, without any reason, tries to do something, but eventually does not do anything."[27] In short, nothing happens in Kurahashi's ideal fiction, just as in feminine life.

Kurahashi's fiction does not impose any manifesto onto the "real" world; it instead suggests the nothingness it contains—just as women have a womb inside them, instead of a penis sticking out. Thus her fictions are comparable to female physiology, as expressed in this excerpt from "Yōjo de aru koto":

> What on earth can modern novelists give their readers? Even if I offer too general an answer of "an imaginative world," the passage to lead readers into this world is a "labyrinth," like bitterness itself, and what lies beyond it is not a brilliant "kingdom," but only "death" and "nothingness."[28]

Such nothingness in fiction relates not only to the presence of the womb but also to an acknowledgment of personal inner emptiness, made by Kurahashi in another essay, "Aru hakaiteki na musō" (A Destructive Dream, 1963): "I am tired of [pretending to love somebody], when inside myself extends an empty darkness which is probably large enough to accommodate the galactic system. However, I do not intend to fill it up with love, religion, or marital life."[29]

Kurahashi is conscious of the emptiness of her "self" as well as that of her fiction. It is thus no wonder that she does not write autobiographical novels, since she does not consider that she has any essential self to be expressed. Kurahashi maintains in "Nichiroku" (Diary, 1965) that she does "not have 'a real face' to be revealed by peeling off the skin."[30] Such emptiness enables both fiction and the "self" to be performative; they can perform any role they are assigned. Thus Kurahashi's fiction becomes pastiche and her "self" displays a variety of attributes. In "*Kurai tabi* no sakusha kara anata ni," Kurahashi maintains: "My novels are like an onion with one layer of pastiche after another. If you peel them infinitely, you will find nothing inside them."[31] This sarcastic reference to the unoriginal nature of her fiction parallels her ideas of the female self, a self that is not constative but performative. These ideas are expressed in "Watashi no 'daisan no sei' ":

> The women accept being women, and write as women, just as Genet accepted his
> status as a thief. [Genet] was petrified as a complete "other," or *objet,* and tried to
> succeed in reachieving his freedom both by making the choice "I am going to be
> a thief. I have decided to become the 'I' which crimes have made me into," and
> by his creation of literature.[32]

Instead of rejecting the roles assigned by the "real" world and fighting for the subjective and substantive self that men have, Kurahashi decides to play the role of woman and create the "other" world of fiction.

To sum up: reality, selves with stable identities, natural law, truth, and originality do not exist in Kurahashi's view. Instead the world consists of a series of perceived images, preexisting attributes that are ascribed to subjects in a multilayered manner, culturally constructed norms, and intertextualities. Since there is no pure, true, or stable reality, self, nature, truth, or origin, it is impossible to achieve the kind of representation praised by the mainstream critics. Rather, the novel is fiction and demonstrates the fictionality of all anthropocentric views of the world within discourse. Every verbal notion is culturally encoded and thus evaluated within ideology. The issue in Kurahashi's works is no longer a search for the authentic representation of truth, but a conscious manipulation of discursive perceptions.

Kurahashi's views of the world and literature are visible, not only in her manifestos regarding compositional methodology, but also in her fictional practice. Her themes involve the "unrealistic" world (which she calls the antiworld), "unidentifiable" subjects who perform diverse roles depending on their contexts, "abnormal" relationships such as transgressions of sexual norms, and an interest in "unnatural" phenomena that cannot be explained by modern Western science. Persons, places, and situations in Kurahashi's work are not "unique" but reminiscent of other things and selves—in other words, they are not themselves but rather traces of others.

RECONFIGURATION OF SEXUAL RELATIONS

Kurahashi explores the transgression of norms most extensively in her writings that combine sexual relationships with questions of medical and juridical legitimacy. She presents subversions of the sexual norm considered to be "natural" and "legitimate" in the modern West and Japan: that two living human beings should have a heterosexual, monogamous, and exogamous sexual relationship. Kurahashi challenges the norm of binary divisions of gender by the motif of masturbation; demarcation between life and death by necrophilia; anthropocentricity by the theme of bestiality; heterosexuality by homo- and bisexuality; exogamy by incest; and monogamy by polyandry.

The motif of masturbation recurs in works such as *Kurai tabi* (1961), a novel that questions the demarcation between the self and other that "natural" sexual relationships presuppose. In the act of masturbation, the self and other are merely roles to be performed by the same subject. Seen from the opposite perspective, masturbation dissolves the substantial identity of the self, by making him/her play a divided role.

Sexual intercourse is not restricted to living creatures in Kurahashi's world. In *Yume no kayoiji* (The Passage of Dreams, 1989)—a collection of short stories most of which feature the same heroine, Keiko—Kurahashi explores the motif of physical intercourse enjoyed by living human beings and spirits of the dead.[33] Keiko, as well as other women in the collection, is capable of seeing and having intercourse with people who come from Hades to this world through the passage of dreams. The dead sexual partners of Keiko include historical Japanese poets— such as Fujiwara no Teika, Saigyō, and Nishiwaki Junzaburō—whom Kurahashi admires for their intertextual poetics and practices.

In Kurahashi's novel *Popoi* (1987), a decapitated man's head is kept alive by futuristic artificial life support technology, and, within his own consciousness, he falls in love with the female narrator, Mai. His brain even "ejaculates" when he sees Mai's naked body. The motif of beheading appears in Kurahashi's earlier short story "Rinne" (Reincarnation, 1962), in which the female narrator, who is simultaneously the illegitimate daughter and mistress of Stalin, is beheaded and her brain inserted into a boy's head. Her consciousness still longs for her male lover in her former life, whom s/he can see constantly. Such examples suggest the arbitrariness of the medical distinction between life and death.

Another way of subverting sexual norms in Kurahashi's works is robotic sex. In her science fiction story "Gōsei bijo" (Robotic Beauties, 1961), the longtime husband of the heroine Michiko turns out to be a robot operated by electricity. At the beginning of the story, Michiko buys a "robotic beauty" as a housemaid, following the fashion of the day, and names "her" Eriko, believing that "she" is not human. The increasing intimacy between her husband and Eriko makes Michiko jealous to a point at which she "kills" Eriko, only to find that the "robotic beauty" is, in fact, a human being sold at the department store. Conversely the husband, who is shocked by Eriko's death and commits "suicide" by becoming overcharged with electricity, is proved to be a robot. In the disguise of a nonsensical story, "Gōsei bijo" suggests uncertainty regarding the definition of "humanity."

If the border between life and death can be transgressed, so too can the distinction between human and inhuman. Thus the theme of bestiality is explored extensively in "Koibito dōshi" (We are Lovers, 1963), which is narrated by a female black cat, Mika. Mika's keeper, K (a man), is engaged to L (a woman), who keeps a male white cat, Yanni. Although Mika and Yanni are interested in each other, both of them are also involved with their keepers. Yanni is overcome with joy when L squeezes him between her breasts. Mika has oral sex with K and makes him ejaculate by fellatio. One might wonder, as Kurahashi does in her "Sakuhin nōto" (Notes on My Works, 1975), whether the eponymous relationships in "We Are Lovers" are, in fact, those of the human and animal couples, or whether they are not the two relationships between K and Mika and L and Yanni. It is clear that in this novella Kurahashi blurs the boundary between human and nonhuman.[34]

The norm of heterosexuality is subverted by the homosexual couple of P and Q in "Mikkoku" (Betrayal, 1960) and by the lesbian inclinations in the relationship between a well-known, aging novelist L and a young, rising writer M in "Warui natsu" (Bad Summer, 1960), the setting of which is based upon Thomas Mann's "Death in Venice." Other elements of homosexuality in Kurahashi's work center on the jazz café called "Monk" in *Sei shōjo* (Divine Maiden, 1965): male homosexual and lesbian couples frequent this café and the owner, Miki, has a lesbian relationship with a woman called M.

A most spectacular exploration of lesbianism, *Amanon koku ōkan ki* (Round Trip to the Amanon, 1986), presents an all-women country of Amanon (with the exception of eunuchs and men kept for the purpose of reproduction), in which female VIPs enjoy erotic relationships with their secretaries.[35]

The most recurrent motif in Kurahashi's works—incest—challenges the legitimacy of exogamy. The theme of sibling incest, which recurs in earlier stories of Kurahashi,[36] becomes central in *Yume no ukihashi* (The Floating Bridge of Dreams, 1970), in which the allegedly half-siblings Keiko and Kōichi decide not to marry each other due to their parents' objection and try instead to consummate their relationship by swapping sexual partners after marrying others.[37] The issue of incest is most radically foregrounded in *Divine Maiden*, which presents two incestuous couples: the heroine Miki and her father Papa and the narrator K and his elder sister L. The novel explores their "antinatural" incest, contrasted to the physical conjunction between close relatives that takes place "naturally" due to their physical closeness and affinity. The main point of Kurahashi's presentation of incest, however, is to examine the question of self and other. Incest, to K, is a form of self-reflexivity in which one loves one's second self and thus undermines the foundations of an exogamy that presupposes the "otherness" or extraneousness of a companion.

The juridical legitimacy of monogamy is transgressed against by partner swapping, polyandry, and polygamy. *Yume no ukihashi* presents the long-term swapping of sexual partners between two married couples, Keisuke and Fumiko and Yūji and Mitsuko. Keiko, the legal daughter of Keisuke and Fumiko, and supposedly the biological daughter of Yūji, starts another round of swapping when she and her lover, Kōichi, Yūji's son, marry others. Virginia in "Vaazinia" (Virginia, 1969) sleeps with most of her male classmates at the university. We see male counterparts in *Divine Maiden* (K), *Amanon koku ōkan ki* (P, the only male allowed to have freedom in the country Amanon), and *Popoi* (Kei). *Kurai tabi* presents a similar reciprocal polyandry in that the heroine, You, and her fiancé, He, make a contract in which both are forbidden to have sex with each other and yet are entitled to sleep with any other man or woman.

Such subversive sexual acts do not merely break taboos and norms but also challenge stable, constative, and substantial notions of selfhood. The self can be defined only in its relationship to others: thus "abnormal" relations presuppose "abnormal" selves. To borrow the words of the narrator of "Vaazinia," echoing a statement in André Breton's *Nadja,* "Who one is depends upon who one is related to."[38] The identity of self is thus by definition relational, not constative, in Kurahashi's works.

WITH/DRAWING LINES: QUESTIONS OF
HOMOGENEITY, AUTONOMY, AND IDENTITY

Selfhood is identified through the binary oppositions implied in the sexual relationships I have examined: man or woman; human or nonhuman; alive or dead; natural or artificial. Kurahashi's subversive selves, however, often do not fall on either side of the oppositions; rather they trespass the borderlines between opposing categories. Three recurrent motifs—hermaphrodites, surgery, and metamorphoses—are the most evident examples of Kurahashi's blurring of the dichotomies.

"Uchūjin" (An Extraterrestrial, 1964) contains the most radical sexual transgressions of the norm in its themes of bisexuality and incest. Bisexuality is embodied in the figure of a hermaphroditic extraterrestrial whose vagina makes it possible for the male adolescent narrator, K, to have sex with him/her, and with whose penis, as K observes, K's elder sister L enjoys sexual intercourse. One night, K and L even have sex with the extraterrestrial being simultaneously, sandwiching him/her between them. On another occasion, K performs both homosexual and heterosexual acts in turn with the extraterrestrial, being troubled by his/her penis when he treats him/her as a woman. K here uses him/her as a substitute for L, with whom he wishes to have an incestuous affair. L is married to a practical man, S, through an arranged marriage, and she comes back to K on the very night of the wedding. K anticipates his wish for incest will now come true, but L tells him that they should enter another world inside the extraterrestial being to consummate their relationship. The story ends with K watching L throw herself into the vast nothingness spread inside the hermaphrodite and falling headlong like a comet into the universe.[39] The hermaphrodite in "An Extraterrestrial" is supernatural in that s/he comes from nowhere on earth. Another androgynous being is manufactured in "Ningyo no namida" (Tears of a Mermaid, 1982), a pastiche of Hans Christian Andersen's "Little Mermaid." Toward the end of the parody, the sea witch, at the mermaid's request, cuts both the mermaid and the prince who loves her in half and grafts the mermaid's lower body onto the prince's upper body. The prince remains single all his life, petting (masturbating?) his female, grafted lower body. This seemingly absurd story presents an "artificial" hermaphrodite and thus questions the unitary and consistent nature of selfhood.

The Adventures of Sumiyakist Q (1969) presents the motif of surgery, which recurs in many other stories, such as "Rinne" and *Popoi*. Doktor, whom the protagonist Sumiyakist Q encounters, operates upon each instructor at the reformatory where he works, even when there is no medical necessity. The most popular of his operations is castration which, again, is an attempt to cross the conventional border of gender. One of the instructors, Bukka, who has already been subjected to plastic surgery, indulges in a nightmarish desire to have all his limbs amputated, himself emasculated, and all his memories erased. P, the polygamous hero of *Amanon koku ōkan ki*, who applies his sexual experience and medical knowledge to initiating virgins in Amanon, is eventually castrated by his favorite girl, Himeko, and sympathizes with eunuchs in the female-governed country. Such surgery attempts to "denaturalize" "nature" and, by so doing, to question the distinction between "nature" (God-made) and "art" (man-made), as well as the solid subject/object relationship between the creator and his creatures and the authority of the Creator God. Kurahashi claims consistently that man made God, not the other way round, challenging Judeo-Christian monotheism.

The third motif—metamorphosis—suggests pre-Christian (Greco-Roman) and non-Christian (Chinese and Japanese) animism. The transformation of human beings into plants often takes place in Kurahashi's fiction. "Aporon no kubi" (The Head of Apollo, 1986) is its most prominent example. In this short story, the female narrator discovers the severed head of a beautiful boy and grows it hydroponically, succeeding in making it bloom and bear fruits. The text refers to Giuseppe Arcimboldo's four seventeenth-century panel paintings *The Seasons,* in which a human head is drawn with a bunch of flowers in bloom, fruits, and so forth, showing the seasonal changes of plants.[40] The transformation of human beings into animals occurs in "Kemono no yume" (Dreams of Beasts, 1986), whose narrator-protagonist, while dreaming, keeps discovering the people around him to be animals; eventually his dreams are proved to be "reality" and he finds himself to be a beast. Such supernatural phenomena cannot be accounted for by modern Western science but were considered quite "natural" in premodern Europe as well as in Asia.

UNDOMESTICATING KURAHASHI

By now it may be apparent that Kurahashi's concerns are similar to those of poststructuralist literary theory. Indeed, Kurahashi's novels unite three presently popular fields of critical inquiry and may be illuminated by reference to poststructuralist critical texts. In her exploration of (gender) identity as performance

—as a masquerade— Kurahashi's work parallels recent developments in gender studies exemplified by Judith Butler's *Gender Trouble*. In her celebration of the death of the Author and her insistence upon the performative nature of textuality, Kurahashi resembles theorists such as the later Roland Barthes, Julia Kristeva, and Michel Foucault. In her demonstration of the narrative as performance, Kurahashi comes closest to Barbara Herrnstein Smith.

The notion of performativity, which is vigorously displayed in Kurahashi's fiction, has been examined primarily in the field of linguistics. Performativity as a linguistic notion is explored by J. L. Austin's speech-act theory. In contrast to the Saussurean linguistic model, which presupposes the stability of a signifying system and the precedence of the addresser over the message itself, speech-act theory gives precedence to the act of speech. The agent and content of the message are merely two of many variables in the act's context, all subordinate to the speech act itself. The concept of performativity, then, destabilizes notions of agency or content. Austin's concept of performativity seems close to Kurahashi's own perception of language, agency, and content. L, the heroine of Kurahashi's "Kekkon" (Marriage, 1965), argues with her husband, who is eager to discover the "real" L: "Do you think that I, apart from my words, different from my words, exist somewhere, just like an object itself?"[41] Agency or content does not precede expressions; rather, expressions constitute the fictional artifact of the agent and content.

In recent theoretical inquiry into sexuality, the notion of performativity has been used by the feminist theorist Judith Butler to indicate the theatrical nature of gender itself. Unlike many earlier feminist analyses that make a distinction between biological sex and culturally encoded gender, Butler says that all aspects of sexuality bear the mark of gender:

> Gender proves to be performative—that is, constituting the identity it is purported to be. In this sense, gender is always a doing, though not a doing by a subject who might be said to preexist the deed. . . . There is no gender identity behind the expressions of gender; that identity is performatively constituted by the very "expressions" that are said to be its results.[42]

Here Butler seems to echo Austin's tenet that there is no preexisting agent prior to expression.

The negation of the "abiding substance"[43] of gender identity echoes the interpretation of femininity made by You in *Kurai tabi*. After menarche, which she interprets as "a castration" executed by the world, You makes the decision to "perform the role of a woman" now that nature has declared her to be a woman.[44] Thus she tries to "denaturalize" an anatomically constructed feminine identity through performance. Getting to know He, who, like her, indulges in performativity, You disclosed that she is "not a woman, merely pretending to be one." In He's words, You "happens to be performing the role of a woman, but is or is not a woman from moment to moment."[45] You transcends the substantial, "naturalized" gender identity that is culturally ascribed to the anatomical female and constitutes a variety of identities by specific expressions upon specific occasions. Thus You confuses convention-bound people with her unidentifiability. In Butler's terms, which in their original context describe drag performance, You "plays upon the distinction between the anatomy of the performer and the gender that is being performed."[46] In other words, there is no "gender core" that exists prediscursively, sustainedly, substantially. Thus Kurahashi's subjects in her fiction, especially in *Divine Maiden*—Writer, Miki, L—embody internal nothingness. Subjects are "identified" only as absences. Writer smiles in a variety of ways without inner necessity, suggesting that there is no "her-self" apart from temporary, contingent expressions such as smiles.

The modern notion of the self that Judith Butler deconstructs—the notion of a substantive and sustained identity that precedes any particular act the self makes or any particular attribute the self displays—is challenged by the performative subjects in Kurahashi's texts (such as the female beggar, Masuda, Satoko, and other characters in *Shunposhion*) and by the severed head and Mai in *Popoi*.[47] Rather than expressing inherent qualities, each character takes up many roles, displays many attributes, and engages in any act that a specific context requires him or her to do—all without any "inner" reason, since the characters have no inner core of meaning. Different subjects show identical attributes and engage in identical acts without reason, questioning, through their actions, whether the self preexists attributes and acts. Rather, "selves" in Kurahashi's texts are traces of others who are either inside or outside the text and are associated with the metaphorical links that, borrowing Barthes' terminology, I have called "indices." The themes of second-self *(Kurai tabi)*, incest *(Divine Maiden; The Adventures of Sumiyakist Q;* "The Long Passage of Dreams"; *Shunposhion)*, amnesia *(Divine Maiden)*, masturbation *(Kurai tabi; Divine Maiden; The Adventures of Sumiyakist Q;* "The Long Passage of Dreams"), the severed head and brain death *(Divine Maiden; Popoi)* radically question the romantic view of the self as an autonomous, substantive individual being.

The theme of the performative self is inseparable from Kurahashi's two major compositional methodologies: indices and pastiche. By discussing emphatically the two methods, my critical approach may come closer to that of Roland Barthes in *S/Z*. Here Barthes develops structuralist terminology to break down Balzac's "Sarrasine" into discrete units in order to examine its construction. His intention in doing so, however, is poststructuralist in that he denies the existence of innate, unchanging structures within texts: "We must renounce structuring this text in large masses, as was done by classical rhetoric and by secondary-school explication: no construction of the text: everything signifies ceaselessly and several times, but without being delegated to a great final ensemble, to an ultimate structure."[48] What he appreciates instead of structure is "plurality" or "multivalence" of the text. While positing the text that is "unimpoverished by any constraint of representation" as the ideal plural text, "a galaxy of signifiers, not a structure of signifieds,"[49] Barthes proposes to apply "connotation" as a tool to "modestly plural" texts. Connotation is defined as "a feature which has the power to relate itself to anterior, ulterior, or exterior mentions, to other sites of the text (or of another text)."[50] Therefore, connotation within the particular text may be what Barthes calls "indices" in "Introduction to the Structural Analysis of Narratives,"[51] in which "a narrative unit [is] linked to other units in the same sequence or action in terms other than chronological or causal (say, thematic)."[52]

Indices, or metaphorical associations, rather than descriptions, are employed to present subjects in Kurahashi's fiction. "What is the point of describing Miki's face, body, and clothes?"[53] the narrator of *Divine Maiden* comments, negating the significance of description, which presupposes the existence of substance to be described. Instead subjects are perceived to be similar to other subjects within and outside the text, whether such similarities are explicitly mentioned by subjects in the text or implicitly constituted as such by the reader. Being merely traces of others, subjects are not independent, unique selves but are subject to others.

Kurahashi's network of word associations is not restricted to any particular work but extends beyond it. Her texts are full of references and allusions to other texts, and words thus function associatively within the scope of a larger discourse. The notion of the text as an autonomous verbal artifact is subverted by Kurahashi's extensive and intricate use of pastiche. Especially in *Shunposhion* and *Popoi*, allusions to anterior texts are made explicit. And thus the texts demonstrate the intertextuality that, according to Julia Kristeva and Michel Foucault, among others, is inherent to any text. Texts are echoes of others, just as selves are traces of others. Or rather: different texts share the same words, which precede texts, just as attributes and acts precede selves. We may recall Kristeva's comments that "any text is constructed as a mosaic of quotations" and that writing is invariably "a reading of the anterior literary corpus," applying Mikhail Bakhtin.[54] Accordingly, the notion of the author as an individual or unique genius who exists prior to the text —a construction that extends from romantic to realist and even as far as modernist poetics—is demolished. Kurahashi achieves this first by the demonstration of pastiche and then by the use of the metafictional paradoxes found in *Divine Maiden* and *Shunposhion*. Both texts feature characters who allude to Kurahashi herself, thus questioning the author's precedence over what are usually considered to be the objects of her creative genius.

Foucault's "What Is an Author?" similarly stresses the precedence of act over agent, as do Austin, Butler, and Smith in different contexts. Claiming that "the author is not an indefinite source of significations which fill a work; the author does not precede the works,"[55] Foucault maintains:

> Referring only to itself, but without being restricted to the confines of its interiority, writing is identified with its own unfolded exteriority. This means that it is an interplay of signs arranged less according to its signified content than according to the very nature of the signifier. Writing unfolds like a game *(jeu)* that invariably goes beyond its own rules and transgresses its limits.[56]

Kristeva and Foucault seem to propose that intertextuality is universally found in any text. Kurahashi's pastiches make the reader conscious of intertextuality by giving indications of, and references to, other texts. They merely perform the attributes of other texts. Her texts are thus not constative but performative; they claim to be fictions of fictions, not representations of truth.

The notion of performativity in linguistics is applied to narrative studies by Barbara Herrnstein Smith in her essay "Narrative Versions, Narrative Theories" (1980). She intends to propose a new approach to narratives based upon speech-act theory, as opposed to structuralist narratology, exemplified by Gérard Genette and Seymour Chatman, which draws its model from Saussurean linguistics. Smith defines the Saussurean view of language, which has been the major model of language in Western intellectual history, as "a conception of discourse as consisting of sets of discrete signs which, in some way, correspond to (depict, encode, denote, refer to, and so forth) sets of discrete and specific ideas, objects, or events." In contrast to the traditional perception of language, she states that "an alternative conception of language views utterances . . . as verbal responses—that is, as acts which, like any acts, are performed in response to various sets of conditions." She then contrasts two views of narratives based respectively upon the two linguistic models:

> In accord with this alternative view of language, individual narratives would be described not as sets of surface—discourse-signifiers that represent (actualize, manifest, map, or express) sets of underlying-story-signifieds—but as the verbal acts of particular narrators performed in response to—and thus shaped and constrained by—sets of multiple interacting conditions. For any narrative, these conditions would consist of (1) such circumstantial variables as the particular context and material setting (cultural and social, as well as strictly "physical") in which the tale is told, the particular listeners or readers addressed, and the nature of the narrator's relationship to them, and (2) such psychological variables as the narrator's motives for telling the tale and all the particular interests, desires, expectations, memories, knowledge, and prior experiences (including his knowledge of various events, of course, but also of other narratives and of various conventions and traditions of storytelling) that elicited his telling it on that occasion, to that audience, and that shaped the particular way he told it.[57]

Smith's view of narratives is useful in noting the features of Kurahashi's narratives. Hers are not monologic narratives with an omniscient narrator who assumes the authority to represent truth, reality, and nature. Rather, Kurahashi contextualizes narrative authority and responsibility by multiplying narrators, incorporating addressees of the narrative into the narrative, and making the narrative conscious of itself. Kurahashi's narratives illustrate Smith's view of narrative in several ways. The second-person narrative of *Kurai tabi,* which enables the narratee to create the narrative, suggests that narrative is not a tool for the narrator to express his or her message. Further, the novel's collage form lacks any rigid narrative structure and hence destabilizes notions of narratorial control.

That the narrative is an interaction between narrator and narratee—and is thus context bound—is demonstrated in *Divine Maiden,* in which characters perform the acts of writing and reading narratives. The two narrators of the novel, "I" and Miki, are never omniscient; nor are they ever neutral. "I" has limited knowledge and misunderstands the circumstances under which Miki writes her secondary narrative. Miki herself has specific intentions to narrate and deliberately fabricates her own life in her fiction. These features of the novel suggest that narrative is not meant to convey an ultimate truth possessed by an omniscient narrator. Instead, narrative is an interaction of various conditions, or "variables" in Smith's terminology, and thus is elusive, flexible, without any ultimate structure containing any specific message from the narrator.

The Adventures of Sumiyakist Q, a third-person narrative, has an extradiegetic narrator who intrudes into the flow of the narrative to make comments; at the same time it is implied that one character, Bukka, may be the "real" narrator. The fact that the narrative continues after Bukka disappears from the story denies the narrator's omnipresence and responsibility for closure.

Shunposhion, another multidiegetic narrative that has more than one level of narrations, one embedding another, demonstrates the notion of narrative as a performance that arises from, and is bound by, a specific context in a similar manner to *Divine Maiden*. Like that novel, *Shunposhion* features embedded narrative —in this case Satoko's narrative, which is written with specific intentions and for a specific reader, Akira, within the primary narrative. The primary narrative of *Shunposhion* is a third-person narrative with an extradiegetic narrator, unlike *Divine Maiden* and like *The Adventures of Sumiyakist Q*, but s/he is, like "I" in *Divine Maiden,* bound within the context in which characters engage in narrative performance, just as narrators in *monogatari* are. Thus the notion of the narrator as an unbiased, neutral, and omniscient origin of the narrative, preceding the narrative, a notion that is predominant in realist novels, is subverted, as is the notion of narrative as a rigid structure.

By embedding a narrative within another narrative, Kurahashi diffuses the power of narration. By incorporating the reader into the text, she demonstrates that what is presented as the text is something that is not only written but also read—not mere representation but rather the perception of perception. The dissonance between what is called "story time" and "discourse time" in narratology denaturalizes the naturalized linear temporality, as well as the very presupposition of complete correspondence between the world and language.

Viewed as a whole, Kurahashi's fictional practice seems to indulge in a performance of the same issues radically questioned by poststructuralist criticism. Thus it seems that we may describe Kurahashi's work as "postmodern" in that she subverts what is "modern." The negation of reality in Kurahashi's texts and its replacement of multilayered perceptions formed out of past cultural constructs conform to Frederic Jameson's definition of the postmodern. The presuppositions of the truth, searches for meaning, and teleological worldviews that postmodernists radically question are, as we have seen, the very things that Kurahashi deconstructs in her novels. Kurahashi certainly "denaturalizes" naturalized concepts of the self, narrative, text, and authorship in romantic, realist, and modernist poetics—concepts that have dominated not only Western critical discourses before post-structuralism but also the Japanese literary establishment.

Kurahashi rejects the conventional novel writing that would have canonized her. Instead she seeks the antinovel—which, while subverting the norm of the realist novel, has not established its own norm or, rather, does not attempt to establish one. The very fact that she has not been fully recognized as significant suggests both the intellectual limits of the literary establishment of Japan and her accomplishments as a contemporary postmodernist. And in her challenges to the modern Japanese norm themselves lie her reason for existence. Kurahashi exists in modern Japanese literature—in her absence therefrom, that is.

NOTES

I would like to thank the following persons for commenting on earlier versions of the chapter: Philip Gabriel, Philip Holden, Sharalyn Orbaugh, Stephen Owen, and Stephen Snyder.

1. I owe the English title to the translation of the story by Samuel Grolmes and Yumiko Tsumura in *Mundus Artium: A Journal of International Literature and the Arts* 14(1) (1983): 103–113.

2. Two English translations of the story are available. One is by Samuel Grolmes and Yumiko Tsumura in *New Directions in Prose and Poetry* 26 (1973):8–22; the other, by Yuko Tanaka and Elizabeth Hanson, is included in *This Kind of Woman: Ten Stories by Japanese Women Writers 1960–1976* (New York: Putnam, 1982), pp. 1–16.

3. I owe the title to Victoria V. Vernon's translation in *Daughters in the Moon: Wish, Will, and Social Constraint in Fiction by Modern Japanese Women* (Berkeley: University of California Press, 1988), pp. 229–240.

4. Karatani's original volume of essays in Japanese was published by Kōdansha in 1980. For an adapted translation with some additions for English-speaking audiences, see Brett de Bary et al., trans., *Origins of Modern Japanese Literature* (Durham: Duke University Press, 1994).

5. Note, however, the twenty-four-year gap in the two most recent instances of her prize winning. It is in fact during this interval that she produced novels such as *Seishōjo* (Divine maiden, 1965), *Sumiyakisuto Kyū no bōken* (The adventures of Sumiyakist Q, 1969), *Yume no ukihashi* (The floating bridge of dreams, 1971), *Shiro no naka no shiro* (The castle within the castle, 1981), and *Shunposhion* (Symposium, 1986). In other words, the literary establishment failed to acknowledge the author's productivity at all.

6. For the evaluative statements on "Partei" and "The End of Summer" made by the Akutagawa Prize Selection Committee, see respectively "Akutagawa Ryūnosuke shō kettei happyō," *Bungei shunjū* (September 1960):292–298, and "Akutagawa Ryūnosuke shō kettei happyō," *Bungei shunjū* (March 1961):272–279.

7. The fact that Kurahashi wrote a B.A. thesis on *Being and Nothingness* by Jean-Paul Sartre suggests her interest in French existentialist philosophy. Other authors she read around the same time include Albert Camus, Arthur Rimbaud, Paul Valéry, and Maurice Blanchot. A remarkable difference in their reception of Sartre is that Kurahashi was disillusioned with him much earlier than Ōe. While Ōe advocated commitment to the student movement against the U.S.-Japan security treaty as a faithful observer of Sartre's "engagement," Kurahashi remained aloof from overtly political movements and came to detest Sartre.

8. Hirano states in his literary review in *Mainichi shimbun* that Kurahashi's "Parutai" (Partei, 1960) had impressed him in the same manner as Ōe's "Kimyōna shigoto."

9. Examples include " 'Parutai' ronsō" (Debate upon "Partei") between Hirano Ken and Niwa Fumio, a writer of autobiographical novels, as well as "Riarizumu hihan" (Criticism on realism), a debate between Okuno Takeo, a famous Japanese literary critic and enthusiastic reader of Kurahashi, and Nakamura Mitsuo, a professor of French at Meiji University and also an influential critic, regarding Kurahashi's two stories "Hebi" (Snake, 1960), an existentialist story in the style of Kafka and Abe Kōbō, and "Mikkoku" (Betrayal, 1960), written in the style of Jean Genet.

10. Kurahashi does use her biographical details in her fiction, but not for the same purpose as *shishōsetsu* writers. She uses them just as she uses parts of others' fiction—namely, to parodize them.

11. Kurahashi Yumiko, "Shōsetsu no meiro to hiteisei," in *Watashi no naka no kare e* (For him inside me) (Tokyo: Kōdansha, 1970), p. 286. Translations of Kurahashi's essays are all my own. For a partial translation of this essay see Dennis Keene, Introduction to "To Die at the Estuary," in *Contemporary Japanese Literature: An Anthology of Fiction, Film and Other Writing Since 1945,* ed. Howard Hibbett (New York: Knopf, 1977), p. 248.

12. "Shōsetsu no meiro to hiteisei," p. 294.

13. Nakamura, "Bungei jihyō" (Literary review), *Asahi shimbun,* July 19, 1960; quoted in Okuno Takeo, "Riarizumu e no gimori: Nakamura Mitsuo hihan," in *Bungakuteki seiha* (Tokyo: Shunjusha, 1964), p. 17.

14. "Shōsetsu no meiro to hiteisei," p. 294.

15. Ibid., p. 291.

16. This overview may give an impression that Kurahashi relies upon Saussurean/structuralist dichotomies between the signified and the signifier and between content and form. She does so only when she has to refute romanticist views of linguistic activity. As we shall see, Kurahashi's view of language resembles that of J. L. Austin and her understanding of the narrative that of B. H. Smith. In short, Kurahashi tries to deconstruct the dichotomies, not reinforce them.

17. *Watashi no naka no kare e,* p. 178.

18. "*Kurai tabi* no sakusha kara anata ni" (From the author of *Blue Journey* to you), *Tokyo shimbun,* February 8–9, 1962, evening ed., p. 8.

19. *Shinchō* (August 1961):204–209.

20. *Watashi no naka no kare e,* p. 167.

21. Ibid., p. 107.

22. Ibid., p. 292.

23. Ibid., p. 26.

24. Ibid., p. 31.

25. Ibid., p. 184.

26. Ibid., p. 301.

27. Ibid., p. 286.

28. Ibid., p. 295.

29. Ibid., p. 132.

30. Ibid., p. 233.

31. See note 18.

32. *Watashi no naka no kare e*, p. 31.

33. *Yume no kayoiji* (Tokyo: Kōdansha, 1989). Three stories from the anthology— "Kuroneko no ie" (The house of the black cat), "Haru no yo no yume" (Spring night dreams), and "Yume no kayoiji" (The passage of dreams)—have been translated in Atsuko Sakaki, trans., *The Woman with the Flying Head and Other Stories of Kurahashi Yumiko* (Armonk, N.Y.: Sharpe, 1997). Kurahashi has experimented with the motif of sex with ghosts in many short stories such as "Yūrei yashiki" (The mansion of ghosts, 1986).

34. The translation is found in Sakaki, *Woman with the Flying Head*. Bestiality also occurs in "Yōjo no yōni" (Like a witch, 1964), which is a parody of "Mitsu no aware" (The heartrending fate of honey) by Muroo Saisei (1899–1962). In Muroo's novella, a male writer has an intimate relationship with a female goldfish; in Kurahashi's, a female novelist caresses her male dog into ecstasy.

35. For an extensive discussion of this work see Susan Napier, *The Fantastic in Modern Japanese Literature* (London: Routledge, 1996), pp. 170–180. The list of bisexual characters continues with the widow in her forties, Keiko, in *Kōkan* (Pleasure exchange, 1989), who sleeps with Machiko, her late husband's mistress, while having an affair with a man, Prime Minister Irie; Yukiko, in *Shunposhion* (1985), is separated from her husband and makes advances to both the man (Akira) and woman (Satoko) of a pair of heterosexual lovers.

36. The incestuous siblings L and K in "Sasori tachi" (Scorpions, 1963), "Himawari no ie" (A house of sunflowers, 1968), and "Kamigami ga ita koro no hanashi" (A tale from the age when gods existed, 1971) commit themselves to the murder of their mother. The plots of these stories are drawn from the well-known story of Electra and Orestes, who engage in incest and kill their mother, Clytemnestra, as a punishment for her infidelity to her husband, Agamemnon.

37. Though their incestuous relationship remains unconsummated in the novel, it is consummated in the sequel, *Shiro no naka no shiro* (1980).

38. *Kurahashi Yumiko zen sakuhin*, vol. 6, p. 73.

39. A translation of this story is included in Sakaki, *The Woman with the Flying Head*.

40. See Giuseppe Arcimboldi, *The Four Seasons* (1573), in Former Cornelia Collection, *The Arcimboldo Effect: Transformations of the Face from the 16th to the 20th Century* (New York: Abbeville; Milan: Fabbri, 1987), p. 109.

41. *Kurahashi Yumiko zen sakuhin*, vol. 5, p. 55.

42. Judith Butler, *Gender Trouble: Feminism and the Subversion of Identity* (London: Routledge, 1990), p. 25.

43. Ibid., p. 24.

44. *Kurai tabi* (1961; Tokyo: Gakugei shorin, 1969), pp. 122, 128.

45. Ibid., pp. 132–133.

46. Butler, *Gender Trouble*, p. 137.

47. See Napier, *The Fantastic in Modern Japanese Literature*, p. 92.

48. Roland Barthes, *S/Z*, trans. Richard Miller (New York: Hill & Wang, 1974), p. 12.

49. Ibid., p. 5.

50. Ibid., p. 8.

51. Roland Barthes, "Introduction to the Structural Analysis of Narratives," in *The Semiotic Challenge*, trans. Richard Howard (New York: Hill & Wang, 1988), p. 107.

52. Gerald Prince, *A Dictionary of Narratology* (Lincoln: University of Nebraska Press, 1987), p. 43.

53. *Kurahashi Yumiko zen sakuhin*, vol. 5, p. 93.

54. Julia Kristeva, "Word, Dialogue, and Novel," in *Desire in Language: A Semiotic Approach to Literature and Art*, trans. Thomas Gora, Alice Jardine, and Leon S. Roudiez (New York: Columbia University Press, 1980), pp. 66 and 69.

55. Michel Foucault, *Textual Strategies: Perspectives in Post-Structuralist Criticism*, ed. Josué V. Harari (Ithaca: Cornell University Press, 1979), p. 159.

56. Ibid., p. 142.

57. Barbara Herrnstein Smith, "Narrative Versions, Narrative Theories," *Critical Inquiry* 7(3) (Autumn 1980): 213–236 and 225–226.

8

MURAKAMI HARUKI'S TWO POOR AUNTS TELL EVERYTHING THEY KNOW ABOUT SHEEP, WELLS, UNICORNS, PROUST, ELEPHANTS, AND MAGPIES

Jay Rubin

Murakami Haruki would be an important figure in contemporary Japanese letters if only for his extensive translations from American fiction (F. Scott Fitzgerald, Truman Capote, John Irving, Tim O'Brien, the complete works of Raymond Carver). But with the enormous popularity of his own fiction drawing attention to his work as a translator, and his translation work providing depth to his broad knowledge of Western and especially American literature, in less than ten years following his widely heralded 1979 debut he became a one-man revolution in Japanese fictional style, nurturing new, urban, cosmopolitan, and distinctly American-flavored tastes in Japanese writing. Dissatisfied with his initial attempts at fiction until he tried writing in English and translating himself back into Japanese, Murakami has created an original, immediately recognizable style marked by humor, lightness, simplicity, and clarity. Bold imaginative leaps and startling imagistic juxtapositions certify his many novels and stories as products of a new sensibility far removed from the traditional Japanese mainstream of autobiographical realism and seemingly liberated from the ghosts of World War II. At first glance apolitical, his works can be read as a spiritual history of his generation: from sixties idealism, to seventies ennui, to eighties late capitalism, to a nineties reassessment of the country's dark recent history in which Japan is no longer seen as a mere victim of war.

Murakami was born on January 12, 1949, in Kyoto and spent his early years in the Kyoto–Osaka–Kobe area with its ancient cultural, political, and mercantile traditions. An only child, he spoke the region's dialect and he heard his schoolteacher parents discussing eighth-century poetry and medieval war tales at the dinner table. For the young Haruki the cradle of imperial culture was an immense disappointment, however, sending him to the pages of Tolstoy and Dostoevski in his early teens and to Ed McBain, Raymond Chandler, F. Scott Fitzgerald, and Kurt Vonnegut when he was not editing the Kobe High School newspaper. An international trading capital, Kobe had many bookstores with foreign residents' used paperbacks, making literature in the original available at less than half the price of their Japanese translations. Haruki was hooked: "It was such a tremendously new experience for me to be able to understand and be moved by literature written in a language acquired after childhood."

That language could hardly have been anything but English. Despite his earlier attraction to Russian literature, Murakami had grown up during the American occupation of his country, which still admired the United States for its wealth and the energy of its culture. America's indigenous music was another source of attraction for him: after hearing Art Blakey and the Jazz Messengers at a live concert in 1964, he would often skip lunch to save money for records. Murakami's encyclopedic knowledge of jazz and many facets of American popular culture are immediately apparent to even the most casual reader. Murakami has been called the first writer completely at home with the elements of American popular culture that permeate present-day Japan.

Although he was an active contributor to his school newspaper and thought of becoming a scenario writer while studying film at Waseda University beginning in 1968, Murakami by no means followed a straight-line path to becoming a novelist. His college years were disrupted by the student riots of 1969, and when he graduated in 1975 with a thesis on American film, he was the owner of a successful jazz bar in a Tokyo suburb. Reluctantly he let the place go in 1981 to begin writing full time after the success of his first two novels. It was only after he finished the third, *Hitsuji o meguru bōken* (A Wild Sheep Chase; trans. 1989), at the age of thirty-three, that he felt he had made the right choice of profession. "Prolific" would hardly do justice to the stream of novels, stories, essays, and translations that have flowed from his pen—or, rather, his word processor—ever since. With the publication in 1994–1995 of the three-volume novel *Nejimakidori kuronikuru* (The Wind-Up Bird Chronicle), a more somber Murakami emerged to present his readers with horrifying images of Japanese depredations in Asia.

■

Oh Danny Boy, the pipes the pipes are calling
From glen to glen and down the mountain side,
The summer's gone, and all the roses falling,
'Tis you, 'tis you must go and I must bide.
But come ye back when summer's in the meadow,
Or when the valley's hushed and white with snow,
It's I'll be here in sunshine or in shadow,
Oh Danny Boy, oh Danny Boy I love you so!

■

Awash in the sentiment of a traditional Irish melody, the inner hero of *Sekai no owari to haadoboirudo wandaarando* (Hard-Boiled Wonderland and the End of the World, 1985) reclaims the connection to his heart through music and sets up resonances between himself and the hero of the outer world, his conscious self, in one of the most moving passages in Murakami Haruki's richly imaginative novel.[1]

Murakami is a lover of music—music of all kinds: jazz, classical, folk, rock. Music occupies a central position in his life and work. The title of his first novel commands the reader to "Listen to the Wind's Song": *Kaze no uta o kike* (translated as *Hear the Wind Sing*),[2] and one magazine went so far as to publish a discography of all the music mentioned in his writing.[3] Murakami owned a jazz bar for seven years, he continues to add to his collection of over six thousand records, and he is constantly going to concerts or listening to recorded music. It is a wonder that he did not become a musician himself—though, in a way, he did. Rhythm is perhaps the most important element of his prose. He enjoys the music of words, and he senses an affinity between his stylistic rhythms and the beat of jazz.[4]

As he employs it in his fiction, music is, for Murakami, the best entry into the deep recesses of the unconscious mind, the timeless other world within each psyche. There, at the core of the self, lies the story of who each of us is: an inaccessible, fragmented narrative that transcends time and that we can only know through images. Dreams or other semiconscious states are one way to come in contact with these images, but more often they surface unpredictably in our waking lives to be apprehended by the conscious mind and then to return just as unpredictably to their place of origin. The novelist tells stories in an effort to bring out the story that lies within, and through some kind of irrational process these stories send reverberations to the stories inside each reader. The process is as subtle as déjà vu and just as indefinable. We see it played out in full in *Hard-Boiled Wonderland and the End of the World* as tiny echoes from the protagonist's core inner story, titled "The End of the World," manage to reach the outer world of his consciousness.

In a literature so full of music and storytelling, the ears play an important role. Murakami's characters take extraordinarily good care of their ears. They clean them almost obsessively to keep in tune with the unpredictable, shifting music of life—so that they can continue to *Dance Dance Dance*.[5] The incredibly beautiful ears of one character, the nameless girlfriend in *Hitsuji o meguru bōken* (A Wild Sheep Chase),[6] who is given the name "Kiki" (Listener) in that novel's sequel, *Dance Dance Dance*, turn out to have almost supernatural powers. And "Boku" (I)—the central character of virtually all of Murakami's stories and novels—is another for whom the ears are important, because his primary function is to listen to stories.

In Murakami's fifth novel, for example, *Norway no mori* (Norwegian Wood, 1987), there is a moment when the hero/narrator Boku remarks: "It felt like a very long day."[7] The statement rings true for a simple reason. This day has occupied more than seventy pages of the novel, in the course of which we have not only followed the narrator's actions but, for part of the time, listened to a story. The wrinkled old woman Reiko (she is all of thirty-nine years old) has been telling us the story of her life—her youthful dreams of becoming a concert pianist, the onset of the mental illness that shattered those dreams, her recovery through marriage, the birth of a daughter, the reestablishment of a music career as a piano teacher, but then her encounter with a malevolent new pupil who threatens to destroy her equilibrium. Just as this new element enters the story, however, Reiko realizes how late it is and leaves Boku and the reader hanging. Boku compliments her as a Scheherazade, and together we look forward to the continuation of her tale in volume two. This is where we learn about Reiko's seduction by a beautiful young lesbian pupil, the shattering of her precariously reestablished life, and her descent into the madness that has brought her to the insane asylum where she tells her tale to the narrator. It is a compelling, heartbreaking tale, and we have been hanging on every word—thanks to the active involvement of the narrator, who speaks up at crucial moments to ask Reiko the questions that we would ask. His timing and intelligence are remarkable. He is just as curious, just as sensitive, just as intelligent and sympathetic as *we* are!

Not only does Murakami Haruki know how to tell a story: he knows how stories are told—and heard. He is awake to the rhythms of exchange between teller and listener, and he is conscious enough of the mechanics of this process that he can recreate it—which he often does—in a fictional setting. In 1985, he went so far as to publish an entire volume of short stories purporting to be mere records of life experiences told to him by various acquaintances—a narrative setting that he later confessed to be entirely fictional, the listening narrator modeled on Fitzgerald's Nick Carraway.[8] Another of Murakami's Bokus describes the storytelling process this way in book three of *Nejimakidori kuronikuru* (The Wind-Up Bird Chronicle), a huge novel crammed full of stories told to the narrator: "I discovered that Nutmeg [the name of his present interlocutor] was an extremely accomplished listener. She was quick on the uptake, and she knew how to direct the flow of the story by means of skillfully-inserted questions and responses."[9]

Nutmeg may be a good listener, but she is primarily of interest to the reader for the story she is telling Boku, thus allowing Boku to convey to us events that go far beyond the limits of his experience. As strange as the stories he encounters may be, Boku himself speaks to the reader in a voice that feels familiar—and, in a way, distanced from the events in the tale—as if a friend were telling us of his own personal experiences. Murakami's consistent use of the friendly, approachable "Boku" is central to his narrative strategy. Boku is usually passive in his own life, but as a listener he is 100 percent active. This is how he describes himself in the opening of *Pinball, 1973:*

I used to have a pathological fondness for listening to stories of places I had never known or seen.

At one time, some ten years ago, I used to go around collaring anybody I could find and listening to stories of where they were born or the places they grew up. Maybe it was a time when the type of person was in short supply who would take the initiative to listen to other people's stories, because everybody—just everybody —would tell me theirs with kindness and enthusiasm. Complete strangers would hear about me and seek me out to tell me their stories.

They would tell me all kinds of stories as if they were throwing rocks into a dry well, and when they were finished, every one of them would go home satisfied. . . . I listened to their stories with all the seriousness I could muster.[10]

If not exactly a therapist, Boku provides a reassuring voice and a sympathetic ear. Undoubtedly this tone accounted for much of Murakami's immediate success. Narrated by a kindly twenty-nine-year-old elder brother describing how he has survived his twenties, Murakami's early novels constituted a kind of guidebook for readers just embarking on the journey through that frightening decade of their own lives.

Much of what has been said here may be seen as an explanation of Murakami's popularity. And there is no doubt that Murakami is a very popular writer—primarily in Japan, of course, but his works have been translated into all the major literary languages and some minor ones as well. In Japan, the Kōdansha publishers have brought out Murakami's eight-volume "complete works," *Murakami Haruki zen sakuhin 1979–1989,* marking the first decade of a writer who began publishing at the age of thirty and who, by forty-eight, had added over twenty new volumes of fiction, nonfiction, and translation to those supposedly "complete" works.[11] Murakami's substantial writings demand attention. And a good many Japanese critics, including the eminently serious Karatani Kōjin,[12] have recognized this.

Many commentators, most of them far senior to Murakami's main readership, seem to take the writer's popularity as a sign that there is something wrong—not only with Murakami's writing but with all of contemporary Japanese literature. Lamenting the current state of literature in Japan, Donald Keene has said in reference to Ōe Kenzaburō's receipt of the Nobel Prize for his "solid" novels: "If you go to a bookstore here, unless it is a very big bookstore, you won't find a real solid literary work. Authors today are writing for the passing tastes of a young audience."[13] Another outspoken critic of Murakami who compares him invidiously with Ōe is the ever argumentative Masao Miyoshi. According to Miyoshi, "Ōe is too difficult, [Japanese readers] complain. Their fascination has been with vacuous manufacturers of disposable entertainment, including the 'new voices of Japan,' like Haruki Murakami and Banana Yoshimoto." Like Mishima, says Miyoshi, Murakami custom-tailors his goods to his clients abroad. Where "Mishima displayed an exotic Japan, its nationalist side," Murakami too exhibits "an exotic Japan, its international version"; he is "preoccupied with Japan, or, to put it more precisely, with what [he] imagine[s] the foreign buyers like to see in it." Miyoshi discusses Murakami entirely in these terms—as a cynical entrepreneur who never wrote a word out of any such old-fashioned motives as inspiration or inner need. To frighten off skittish academics who might be tempted to take Murakami seriously, he warns: "Only a very few would be silly enough to get interested in deep reading."[14] With all due acknowledgment of this admonition, I would like here to attempt a reading—though perhaps not a deep reading—of an early Murakami story.

If we look only at Murakami's novels, it appears that something new started to happen in the third one, A Wild Sheep Chase, first published in 1982. The first two novels, Hear the Wind Sing (1979) and Pinball, 1973 (1980), seem more nearly autobiographical. All three books look back to scenes of disillusionment and alienation following the brief epiphany of the 1968–1969 student uprisings.[15] They feature brooding loneliness, impersonal sex, troubled relationships, suicide, and, above all, boredom. At the end of Sheep Chase, however, a ghost appears, and there are elements of spirit possession that hark back to Genghis Khan, all involving a mysterious sheep. Miyoshi warns us not to search for symbols, and Murakami himself seems to support this view. To an interviewer he once said: "I believe that if the novel does in fact succeed, it is because I myself do not know what the sheep means."[16] Whatever it might or might not mean, clearly Murakami from this point seems to have felt free to use elements of the supernatural—the inexplicable—in his novels that force the reader to respond to him in a whole new way.

If we look at the stories, however, we find Murakami daring to cross the line from realism into fantasy at an earlier point—in fact, in his second story, published December 1980, with the title "Binbō na obasan no hanashi," a title I would translate as "A 'Poor Aunt' Story," with quotation marks around the phrase "Poor Aunt." It is one of those early works in which a writer still fresh to his craft provides something of a key to his later method. It is also one that Murakami felt compelled to rewrite for the complete works in order to clarify his original intent, "lending a hand from the present to my past self."[17]

"After I had finished rewriting them," says Murakami of "A 'Poor Aunt' Story" and the others anthologized in Chūgoku yuki no surōbōto (Slow Boat to

China, 1983), "I realized that . . . most of what we could call my world is presented in this first story collection of mine."[18] In some ways it could be said that, in rewriting "A 'Poor Aunt' Story," Murakami clarified too much—stating too baldly in the later version what he had only hinted at in the earlier one—but the later "Poor Aunt" is still full of those strange, evocative Murakami images that perhaps no one will ever fully explain.[19] In any case, we have Murakami's "Poor Aunt" in two forms,[20] and although the latter is not a massive reworking, it does indeed tell us how Murakami goes about the business of telling stories.

The "Poor Aunt" is that rarity among Murakami works, however common it may be in modern *shōsetsu* in general: a story about a writer trying to write a story.[21] Most of Murakami's protagonists are men stuck in boring, mundane jobs—ad copy writers and the like, people who have lost their sixties idealism and accommodated themselves to the Establishment. The single greatest difference between the two versions of the story is the clarification of Boku's work and the insistence that being a writer makes him different from all nonwriters. In the first version, Boku tells us he wants to write something about a poor aunt but never says that he specifically wants to write a *shōsetsu* or that writing fiction is what he does; the later version says explicitly, "Boku wa shōsetsu o kakō to shite iru ningen na no da" ("I am one of those people who try to write stories")—almost as if "those people who try to write stories" belong to a different species.[22]

The events experienced by both Bokus, however, are the same. Suddenly one beautiful July day he feels an inexplicable urge to write about a poor aunt. The word *"obasan"* could, of course, mean any mature woman and not specifically "aunt," but clearly Boku and his girlfriend have relatives in mind, those family members who have to be invited to weddings and funerals but whose presence is more an embarrassment than a pleasure: "Almost no one bothers to talk to her. Almost no one introduces her to anyone else. No one asks her to give a speech," and so on.[23]

While Boku and his companion quickly move the discussion into the realm of the real world, where "poor aunts" are problematic family members, the text makes it clear from the start that Boku's attention is taken up not with the social phenomenon but with the phrase itself, the very words *(kotoba) "binbō na obasan"*:

> *A poor aunt?*
>
> I scanned the area again, then looked up at the summer sky. Come and gone.
>
> Like the transparent path of a bullet, the words *(kotoba)* had been absorbed into the early Sunday afternoon. . . .

I tried [the words] out on my companion. "I'd like to write something about a poor aunt."[24]

After Boku has brooded on the phrase *"binbō na obasan"* for some weeks, a shadowy, transparent *"binbō na obasan"* materializes on his back and stays with him wherever he goes. She depresses his friends, reminding them of things and people they had long since forgotten, and they begin to avoid him. Briefly, in the funniest section of the story, he attracts the attention of the mass media, but these soon tire of him when he refuses to sensationalize her. Late in autumn, after seeing a sad little girl on a train, he notices that the *"obasan"* is gone from his back. As he begins to wonder where she could have gone, he indulges in a fantasy of a world, ten thousand years in the future, peopled entirely by poor aunts. The story ends, in both versions, with the winter of reality descending upon Boku's world, the quirky humor leavened with a touch of sorrow.

What, then, is a *"binbō na obasan"*? Boku's explanation to a television talk show host is so simple and straightforward that no one in the studio can accept it: " 'The poor aunt is just words,' I said, 'just words.' " This produces only a stunned silence, so he continues:

A word is like an electrode connected to the mind. If you keep sending the same stimulus through it, there is bound to be some kind of response created, some effect that comes into being. Each individual's response will be entirely different, of course, and in my case the response is a kind of a sense of independent existence. . . . What I have stuck to my back, finally, is the phrase "poor aunt"—those very words, without meaning, without form. If I had to give it a label, I'd call it a "conceptual sign" or something to that effect.[25]

Murakami is a writer for whom the unpredictable process of creating something out of nothing, in words, is endlessly fascinating. When he first wrote the story, he was still the owner-manager of a Tokyo jazz bar uncertain what role writing was to play in his life. With the publication of his "complete works" after ten years of dramatic success in print, he was less hesitant to identify himself as a writer— or at least, in retrospect, as a budding writer—"one of those people who try to write stories."

In a booklet published with the "complete works," Murakami notes that most of his stories start out from their titles. A phrase spontaneously *(jihatsuteki ni)* brings an image to mind, and he "pursues" the image in writing without knowing where it will lead him. Sometimes the process is a failure and he gives up, but usually the image will suggest an opening scene from which the rest of the story develops. "As I write, something of which I was unaware makes itself evident to me. I find this process tremendously thrilling *(suriringu)* and interesting," he says. "Binbō na obasan" is one of these stories. Indeed, "it is a story that takes as its motif the very process of beginning a story from its title. . . . The story has a double structure: it consists simultaneously of 'A "Poor Aunt" Story' and 'The Making of "A 'Poor Aunt' Story." ' " In this case, the phrase *"binbō na obasan"* came up in the course of a conversation, he says, and suddenly struck him. He more or less apologizes in the booklet for tampering with his early works, but he declares that "Binbō na obasan no hanashi" is particularly important to him, and he suspects he will want to rewrite it yet again when he is older.[26]

The spontaneous process of becoming intrigued with an image is described in the story as Boku and his girlfriend sit by a pond where they can see a pair of bronze unicorns, "their four front hooves thrust out in angry protest against the flow of time for abandoning them in its wake."[27] The unicorns are symbols of something that has come to exist in the real world—created by an artist working in bronze—as a product originating entirely in the imagination: representations of the timeless core of the unconscious mind. Readers of *Hard-Boiled Wonderland and the End of the World* will immediately recognize the importance of unicorns to Murakami. In that book they live in the story that comprises the core of the protagonist's identity, a world out of touch with the flow of events in everyday life and therefore—although a narrative—timeless.

Whenever a Murakami Boku comes in contact with the timeless world of memory, something funny seems to happen to time in the "real" world. But this was an element of his "other world" that Murakami had not worked out so clearly when he first wrote the story. The new version tells us that before the poor aunt enters Boku's conscious life, "Time moved like the breeze: starting and stopping, stopping and starting." Immediately the world of mundane reality and the world of story and legend begin to interpenetrate: "Soft-drink cans shone through the clear water of the pond. To me, they looked like the sunken ruins of an ancient lost city."[28] Later in this version, Boku and his girlfriend discuss the role of the poor aunt in his life: "She [the girlfriend] kept folding and unfolding a sweatshirt on her knees. Folding and unfolding. As if she were turning time backward or urging it ahead."[29] Boku describes the perfection of that July day, and then, without warning, says:

Why a poor aunt, of all things, should have grabbed my heart on such a Sunday afternoon, I have no idea. There was no poor aunt to be seen in the vicinity, nothing there to cause me to imagine her existence. She came to me, nonetheless, and then she was gone. If only for a hundredth part of a second in between, she had been there, in my heart . . .

I tried the words out on my companion. "I'd like to write something about a poor aunt."[30]

When, in the earlier version, the girlfriend asks him why he wants to write on such a subject, he remarks: "Not even I knew the answer to that. It was just that something had passed through me, like the shadow of a little cloud." In the later version we find: "Not even I knew the answer to that. For some reason, things that grabbed me were *always* things I did not understand."

By the time he wrote this, Murakami had proved to himself that he could, indeed, function as a writer by purposely cultivating those very areas of his mind that he did not understand: by pursuing an unknown "something" with little idea where it would lead him. The turning point for him came with *A Wild Sheep Chase,* the first book he wrote as a full-time novelist. Still uncertain of his powers when writing his second novel, *Pinball, 1973,* he worried all the way through that book. But he was convinced that the next one would work out:

> I made no story outline for *Sheep Chase* other than to use "sheep" as a kind of key word and to bring the foreground character "I" and the background character "Rat" together at the end. That's the book's entire structure. . . . And I believe that if the novel does succeed it is because I myself do not know what the sheep means.[31]

In a talk he gave at the University of Washington in November 1992, Murakami revealed (probably for the first time) the source of the sheep image and his retrospective view of what it might signify. The novelist Takahashi Takako had criticized Murakami for describing some bushes as looking "like grazing sheep" in *Pinball, 1973.* This, she said, was "an inappropriate figure of speech because there are no sheep in Japan." Certain that there must be sheep in Japan, Murakami began to do research in Hokkaido. He described this investigation in a talk the following week at Berkeley:

> I learned that there had not always been sheep in Japan. They had been imported as exotic animals early in the Meiji period. The Meiji government had a policy of

encouraging the raising of sheep, but now sheep have been all but abandoned by the government as an uneconomical investment. In other words, sheep are a kind of symbol of the reckless speed with which the Japanese state pursued a course of modernization. When I learned all this, I decided once and for all that I would write a novel with "sheep" as a key word.

These historical facts regarding sheep turned out to be a major plot element when it came time for me to write the novel. The character I call The Sheep Man is almost surely a being that floated up out of that vast historical darkness. At the time I was deciding to write a novel on sheep, however, I knew nothing about such facts. The Sheep Man was a product of a great coincidence.[32]

I think we must take such statements at face value. Pressed by interviewers for the "meanings" of his symbols, Murakami stubbornly insists that he himself does not understand them. They come out of his unconscious, he says, almost like "automatic writing," and any reader's interpretation of their meaning is as valid as his own.[33]

Murakami said much the same thing when attending a class of Howard Hibbett's at Harvard in April 1991 for a discussion of his story "Pan'ya sai shūgeki" (The Second Bakery Attack, 1985).[34] The undersea volcano in that story was not a symbol, he insisted: it was just a volcano. Clearly, however, within the context of the story, the undersea volcano is very much a symbol of unresolved problems from the past: issues that linger in the mind and threaten to explode and destroy the order of the present. As far as Murakami was concerned, however, by calling it a symbol and defining it one could only drain it of its potential power. He would prefer to leave it a volcano and let it do its work, undefined, in the mind of each reader.

Still, Murakami is not above nudging the reader's interpretation in a direction he finds congenial. After Boku has explained to his TV interviewer that "binbō na obasan" is just words, he is asked whether he is free, then, simply to expunge them. "No," he says in both versions, "That is impossible. Once something has come into being, it continues to exist, independent of my will." In the later version, he adds: "It's like a memory. You know how a memory can be— especially a memory you wish you could forget. It's just like that."[35]

The "binbō na obasan," then, has something to do with memory—nagging, unpleasant memories in particular. The new version gives a hint of that near the beginning of the story, where the narrator sets the scene. Both versions tell us (with only slight differences in the text): "The breeze carried snatches of music from a large portable radio set on the grass: a sugary song of love either lost or about to be." The new version adds a significant note of uncertainty: "I seemed to recognize the tune, but I could not be certain I had heard it before."[36]

It is this borderline area of consciousness that most interests Murakami: the "place" where déjà vu occurs. The song that signals "her" appearance is one that Boku half-knows; when "she" is gone a few moments later and the twinge of half-forgotten memory has ended, Boku hears another song on the radio, and again the newer version sharpens the parallel with memory: "The portable radio started playing a different tune, much like the first one, but this I didn't recognize at all." Here the original version has only: "The portable radio started playing a different tune. The world must be full of love that is lost or about to be."[37]

By having Boku fixate on the phrase *"binbō na obasan,"* Murakami in effect gives us a memory we never had. He makes us experience déjà vu ourselves by inventing a cliché—a phrase that takes on uncanny familiarity as it is repeated until we begin to think that it is one of those idiomatic expressions we've known most of our lives but have never bothered to clarify in our own minds.[38] Murakami makes his new cliché stand for everything unpleasant we push out of our minds by subtly suggesting things we ought to know about but have managed to suppress. When Boku's friends see the *"binbō na obasan"* on his back, they see her in different forms: a nagging mother, a grammar school teacher with terrible burn scars from the war, a pet dog that died of cancer. For us the "poor aunt" may be a homeless panhandler on the street, or Salvadoran children crippled by American-made bombs, or tortured political prisoners, or simply relatives we avoided because we didn't like their table manners: "Each individual's response will be entirely different, of course," as Boku explains it.[39]

Murakami often speaks of the writing of short stories as a kind of game: he starts with a phrase and pursues it to see where it will lead him.[40] But the contents of the game can be surprisingly serious, depending on the original hint and the way the writer's mind reacts to it. Once the phrase "binbō na obasan" came up in a conversation with his wife (who, like Boku's companion, did have a poor aunt in her family, unlike Murakami, who found the phrase fascinating precisely because he did not have one and therefore had no concrete image attached to the phrase),[41] Murakami found himself extending the lugubrious overtones of the "poor" image.

The phrase arouses in Boku not only pity but a degree of guilt that derives from a feeling of helplessness—of being unable to assuage the suffering or loneliness of any kind of "poor aunt" in the real world. At the entrance of an imagined community of poor aunts, there would stand a sign: "No Admittance Except on Business." Murakami says: "Those who dare to enter without business, of course, receive an appropriately tiny punishment. . . . Perhaps it was the tiny punishment that had been prepared for me. A poor aunt—a little one—was stuck to my back."[42]

What is it about the poor aunts of the world that so disturbs us? Boku concludes that they sensitize us to the impact of time:

> Time, of course, topples everyone in its path equally—the way that driver beat his old horse until it died on the road. But the thrashing we receive is one of frightful gentleness. Few of us even realize that we are being beaten.
>
> In a poor aunt, however, we can see the tyranny of time before our eyes, as if through an aquarium window.[43]

A "binbō na obasan" is a symbol, but a transparent one that may or may not be filled in with specific equivalents by the reader. The important thing for Murakami is how it feels in the mind of each reader. It should have a sense of déjà vu. It should feel strange and familiar at the same time. Perhaps no other writer concerned with memory and the difficulty of reclaiming the lost past—not Kawabata, not even Proust—has succeeded as well as Murakami in capturing the immediacy of the experience of déjà vu. When a Murakami narrator tells you he is uncertain about his recollections, you can be sure he is pointing to the heart of the story.

Karatani Kōjin seems to overlook this element entirely in his eagerness to label names in Murakami's works as "arbitrary." If, for example, the nickname "Nezumi" (The Rat) is not a source of an identity crisis for the character so named in Murakami's first three novels, as it is in Ōe Kenzaburō's *Man'en gannen no futtobōru* (The Silent Cry), then it is nothing but an arbitrary sign *(kigō)* used to differentiate one character from another. Karatani overlooks the fact, however, that Nezumi has "forgotten" how he got the name and that it was given to him long ago *(zuibun mukashi no koto sa)*. In "The Rat," we find a wry self-portrait of a writer a-borning. Bearer of a nickname so "old"—so embedded in the psychic primordial slime of once-upon-a-time—that he himself has "forgotten" how he got it, this self-absorbed young man is identified as a dark, unnerving creature that burrows into shadowy hidden spaces.[44]

After she has clung to Boku's back for some months, the poor aunt suddenly disappears. The trigger is another incident involving memory:

It was late in autumn when the poor aunt left my back. Recalling *(omoidashite)* some work I had to complete before the onset of winter, I and my poor aunt boarded a suburban train.[45]

On the train Boku sees a little girl being treated unfairly by her mother, and his heart goes out to her. The scene echoes an earlier discussion between Boku and his companion concerning the origins of "poor aunts" in the real world:

"I sometimes wonder what kind of a person becomes a poor aunt. Are they born that way? Or does it take special poor aunt conditions—like some kind of huge bug that laps up everybody passing by a certain street corner and turns them into poor aunts?"

She nodded several times as if to say that my questions were very good.

"Both," she said. "They're the same thing."

"The same thing?"

"Uh-huh. Well, look. A poor aunt might have a 'poor aunt' childhood or youth. Or she might not. It really doesn't matter."[46]

The little girl on the train may be a "poor aunt" in the making. Or she may not. It really doesn't matter. What does matter is that she is as much of a "poor aunt" figure for Boku right now as the dog or the teacher or the mother is for his friends. What matters is that someone out there, in the real world, has aroused his sympathy (and the reader's: the scene is quite touching) and thus released Boku from his obsession with the phrase in his mind.

The obsession has interfered with his personal relations as well. While he has been living his inward-turned life, his companion on that first fateful Sunday in July has become a peripheral figure for him (much as the protagonist's obsession with the disappearing elephant interferes with a love relationship in the story "Zō no shōmetsu" (The Elephant Vanishes):[47] they do not see each other for three months, and winter is coming by the time they talk again. Telephoning her is the very first thing he does after the poor aunt disappears from his back. He is relieved to find that she is "still alive," so far removed has she been from his thoughts, but she is not ready to respond to him with an open heart just yet. A hunger of metaphysical proportions suddenly overtakes him when their call ends inconclusively. And to fill that hunger, he turns with almost shocking desperation to his readers, addressing them indirectly at first, and then directly, in the second person:

I'd go mad if I didn't get something to eat. Anything. Anything at all. If they'd give me something to put in my mouth, I'd crawl to them on all fours. I might even suck their fingers clean.

Yes, I would, I would suck your fingers clean. And then I'd sleep like a weathered crosstie. The meanest kick wouldn't wake me. For ten thousand years I'd be sound asleep.[48]

What follows is a rhapsody of imagination, a free plunge into the world of word and image association that perhaps only the writer can experience—and perhaps only in those moments when he is slightly out of control, when he chooses to accept whatever his unconscious produces, unedited, unanalyzed, and weirdly beautiful:

If, ten thousand years from now, a society came into being that was peopled exclusively by poor aunts, would they open the gates of their town for me? In that town would be a government and town hall run by poor aunts who had been elected by poor aunts, a streetcar line for poor aunts driven by poor aunts, novels for poor aunts written by poor aunts.

Or, then again, they might not need any of those things—the government or the streetcars or the novels.

They might prefer instead to live quietly in giant vinegar bottles of their own making. From the air you could see tens—hundreds of thousands of vinegar bottles lined up, covering the earth as far as the eye could see. And it would be a sight so beautiful it would take your breath away.

Yes, that's it. And if, by any chance, that world had space to admit a single poet, I would gladly be the one: the first honored poet laureate of the world of poor aunts.

Not bad. Not bad.

And I would sing in praise of the resplendent glow of the sun in the green bottles, sing in praise of the broad sea of grass below, sparkling with the morning dew.[49]

Here, it seems, he can at last provide salvation for all the poor aunts, the cancerous dogs, the scarred teachers of the world. He can sing for them as poet laureate, compensate them somehow for their loneliness, and try, as well, to salve the guilt he feels for having turned away from them.

Salvation is only momentary, however. The story concludes:

But this is looking far ahead, to the year 11,980, and ten thousand years is too long for me to wait. I have many winters to survive until then.

The story has begun on a beautiful July day and ended with the approach of winter. (Murakami says his concern with the seasons is an element that marks him as a Japanese writer.)[50]

The disappearance of the poor aunt has been as unpredictable as her materialization. "I had no idea when it happened. Just as she had come, she had gone before anyone noticed. She had gone back to wherever it was that she had originally existed."[51] This original place (here called *"somo somo sonzai shite ita basho"* but in most other Murakami works *"moto no tokoro"*) is where memories reside, the place from which they leap out and grab us and to which they return, just as the twins in *Pinball, 1973* go "back to where we came from."[52] Murakami had not worked things out so clearly in the first version: "Just as she had come, she had gone before anyone noticed. I had no idea where I should go from here."[53] The new version:

> Just as she had come, she had gone before anyone noticed. She had gone back to wherever it was that she had originally existed, and I was my original self again.
>
> But what *was* my original self? I couldn't be sure any more. I couldn't help feeling that it was another me, another self that strongly resembled my original self. So now what was I to do?

Murakami would go on after "Binbō na obasan" to explore this indefinable area of the mind, this "original place," the very foundation of his writing. In this connection, the references to Proust in both *Sheep Chase* and *Hard-Boiled Wonderland* are by no means accidental. Let's look first at *Sheep Chase*. Whether we view Boku's successful reunion with his dead friend as "real" or a product of delirium, it is the culmination of his quest. Through a detective-novel search, he has escaped from anaesthetic boredom to recapture his lost past: "the old days" *(mukashi)*.[54] When Boku catalogs his boring existence for the girl with the beautiful ears, he says: "I've memorized all the murderers' names in every Ellery Queen mystery ever written. I own the complete *A la recherche du temps perdu,* but I've only read half."[55] The use of the French title may strike an American reader as somewhat affected for the normally unpretentious Boku. But what we have here is an alert translator's signal to us that the mention of Proust is more than just an illustration of boredom. The English version, *Remembrance of Things Past,* would simply not do here. In the far more accurate Japanese, Proust's title (since retranslated as *In Search of Lost Time*) sounds like pure Murakami: *Ushinawareta toki o motomete*—"searching for lost times," and that is exactly what Boku has been doing in his "adventure surrounding a sheep."

In retrospect, it seems almost inevitable that Murakami would have written *Hard-Boiled Wonderland and the End of the World.* If not so clearly in his first novel, *Hear the Wind Sing,* with its Martian wells, certainly by the following year's *Pinball* he was thinking in terms of a timeless "original place" within the deep wells of the mind, a place of legend and dream inside each individual that is not accessible to the rational faculty but from which highly idiosyncratic images and words associated with a particular lost past (and things and people lost through death in the past) emerge mysteriously and unpredictably, travelling down dark passages and occupying the conscious mind for a while before returning to that original place.

The image of the well is flashed at the reader on the first page of *Hard-Boiled Wonderland,* and soon the protagonist Watashi (another word for "I") is walking down a long, gloomy corridor. The scent of cologne fills him with "a nostalgic yet impossible pastiche of sentiments, as if two wholly unrelated memories had threaded together in an unknown recess,"[56] at which point the young woman showing Watashi down the corridor forms the word "Proust" on her lips. This typical Murakami-ism (try reading the single word "Proust" on anybody's lips, especially outside of any context, and more especially in the Japanese pronunciation, "Purūsuto") diverts us from the possibility that what Watashi is embarking on now is a journey into the "unknown recesses" of his own memories as serious as anything Proust ever attempted. Murakami is apparently confident that he is forging into Proustian territory and that no one would ever suspect him of harboring such pretensions.

Considering the possibility that he has misread her lips, Watashi begins to experiment with "meaningless syllables": *"urūdoshi"* ("intercalary year"—a word connected with ancient ways of keeping time); *"tsurushi ido"* ("dangling well"— a word Murakami seems to have made up to add to his inventory of wells); and *"kuroi udo"* ("black *Aralia cordata"*—a subterranean vegetative image):

> One after the other, quietly to myself, I pronounced strings of meaningless syllables, but none seemed to match. I could only conclude that she had indeed said, "Proust." But what I couldn't figure out was, what was the connection between this long corridor and Marcel Proust?

Perhaps she'd cited Marcel Proust as a metaphor for the length of the corridor. Yet, supposing that were the case, wasn't it a bit too whimsical—not to say inconsiderate—as a choice of expression? Now if she'd cited this long corridor as a metaphor for the works of Marcel Proust, that much I could accept. But the reverse was bizarre.

A corridor as long as Marcel Proust?

Whatever, I kept following her down that long corridor. Truly, a long corridor.[57]

With his literary credentials thus both established and denied in a single stroke, Murakami sets his protagonist upon a new but familiar quest down the long corridors leading to the core of the unconscious.

We see much the same thing happening in *The Wind-Up Bird Chronicle,* Murakami's three-volume examination of World War II as it exists in the minds of Japanese living in the mid-1980s. In this novel the war is presented, not as facts experienced by Boku, but as part of the psychological baggage carried around half-consciously by Japanese of Murakami's generation and later. For most Japanese, the war exists in the same realm of the half-known as the Rossini opera *The Thieving Magpie (La Gazza Ladra),* the title of which occurs on the first page of the novel and indeed in the title of the entire first volume. Again and again the overture is mentioned, until, on page 558 of the 611-page translation, we encounter this:

What kind of opera *was* "The Thieving Magpie?" I wondered. All I knew about it was the monotonous melody of its overture and its mysterious title. We had had a recording of the overture in the house when I was a boy. It had been conducted by Toscanini. Compared with Claudio Abbado's youthful, fluid, contemporary performance, Toscanini's had had a blood-stirring intensity to it, like the slow strangulation of a powerful foe who has been downed after a violent battle. But was "The Thieving Magpie" really the story of a magpie that engaged in thieving? If things ever settled down, I would have to go to the library and look it up in a dictionary of music. I might even buy a complete recording of the opera if it was available. Or maybe not. I might not care to know the answers to these questions by then.[58]

The overture is featured prominently in the book not because a knowledge of the opera's contents will provide a key to the novel but precisely because of its place on the foggy periphery of consciousness. (We often hear parts of the overture in TV commercials; some might recognize it from the film *A Clockwork Orange.*)

Murakami, then, examines World War II as a psychological phenomenon shared by generations too young to have experienced it firsthand: as history: as story.

In the two versions of "A 'Poor Aunt' Story," we see an author writing initially from his unconscious and returning a decade later to clarify his vision as he himself has come to understand it more fully. After all, the writer who revised the story had behind him the experience of having examined that "original place" on the scale of *Hard-Boiled Wonderland and the End of the World,* which in some ways can be seen as Japan's most elaborate and imaginative I-novel. For when Boku decides not to escape to the "real" world but to keep his heart and remain an outcast in the forest—a timeless (and deathless) world of song and memory that he has created for himself—he is opting for the role of the outside observer of society *(bōkansha)* as defined in the Meiji period by writers such as Sōseki, Ōgai, Katai, and Tōson. Boku, the active listener, is, finally, "one of those people who try to write stories."

We should keep on the lookout for future revisions of "A 'Poor Aunt' Story." If Murakami does indeed choose to revise this important work yet again, it will undoubtedly tell us much about what he has learned in the meantime.

NOTES

1. *Sekai no owari to haadoboirudo wandaarando* (Tokyo: Shinchōsha, 1985), in *Murakami Haruki zensakuhin 1979–1989*, vol. 4 (Tokyo: Kōdansha, 1990–1991) [cited hereafter as *MHZ*]; translated by Alfred Birnbaum as *Hard-Boiled Wonderland and the End of the World* (Tokyo: Kodansha International, 1991). For "Danny Boy" passages, see *MHZ* 4:17 and 542; Birnbaum, pp. 3 and 368. An earlier version of this chapter appeared in Dennis Washburn and Alan Tansman, eds., *Studies in Modern Japanese Literature* (Ann Arbor: Center for Japanese Studies, University of Michigan, 1997), pp. 307–319.

2. *Kaze no uta o kike* (Tokyo: Kōdansha, 1979); translated by Alfred Birnbaum as *Hear the Wind Sing* (Tokyo: Kodansha English Library, 1987).

3. *Murakami Haruki bukku: Bungakukai* (April 1991), pp. 103–114.

4. "In a word, my style boils down to this: First of all, I never put more meaning into a sentence than is absolutely necessary. Secondly, the sentences have to have rhythm. This is something I learned from music, especially jazz. In jazz, great rhythm is what makes great improvising possible. It's all in the footwork. To maintain that rhythm, there must be no extra weight. This doesn't mean that there must not be *any* weight at all—just no weight that isn't absolutely necessary. You have to cut out the fat." From Murakami's Una Lecture, "The Sheepman and the End of the World," delivered in English at Berkeley, November 17, 1992.

5. *Dansu dansu dansu* (Tokyo: Kōdansha, 1988); translated by Alfred Birnbaum as *Dance Dance Dance* (Tokyo: Kodansha International, 1994).

6. *Hitsuji o meguru bōken* (Tokyo: Kōdansha, 1982); translated by Alfred Birnbaum as *A Wild Sheep Chase* (Tokyo: Kodansha International, 1989).

7. Murakami Haruki, *Norway no mori*, 2 vols. (Tokyo: Kōdansha, 1987), 1:236; translated by Alfred Birnbaum as *Norwegian Wood*, 2 vols. (Tokyo: Kodansha English Library, 1989), 1:243. The narrative of this day starts on 1:165 of the original and 1:172 of the translation.

8. *Kaiten mokuba no deddo hiito*, in *MHZ* 5:239–401, especially pp. 243–247. The confession can be found in the supplement to vol. 5, "Jisaku o kataru: hosoku suru monogatari gun," pp. 9–12. One story from that collection, "Lederhosen," and the related story "Chinmoku" (The silence) have been translated by Alfred Birnbaum in *The Elephant Vanishes* (New York: Knopf, 1993), pp. 119–129 and pp. 291–306, respectively.

9. *Nejimakidori kuronikuru*, 3 vols. (Tokyo: Shinchōsha, 1994–1995), 3:120; translated by Jay Rubin as *The Wind-Up Bird Chronicle* (New York: Knopf, 1997), p. 410.

10. *MHZ* 1:123; *1973 nen no pinbōru* (Tokyo: Kōdansha, 1980); translated by Alfred Birnbaum as *Pinball, 1973* (Tokyo: Kodansha English Library, 1985).

11. *MHZ* 4:17 and 542; Birnbaum, *Hard-Boiled Wonderland*, pp. 3 and 368.

12. Karatani Kōjin, "Murakami Haruki no 'fūkei,' " pts. 1–2, *Kaien* (November 1989): 296–306 and (December 1989):236–250. In this interesting study, Karatani rejects the postmodern label for Murakami, seeing instead parallels between Murakami and the "romantic irony" of Kunikida Doppo (1871–1908). Karatani cites only Murakami's more abstract philosophical passages, however, never the vinegar bottles.

13. Quoted in James Sterngold, "Japan Asks Why a Prophet Bothers," *New York Times*, November 6, 1994, p. 5. Several decades ago Keene was eager to introduce the world to Dazai Osamu, much of whose readership was of high school age.

14. Masao Miyoshi, "Kenzaburo Oe: The Man Who Talks with the Trees," *Los Angeles Times*, October 19, 1994, p. B7; *Off Center* (Cambridge, Mass.: Harvard University Press, 1991), p. 234.

15. Kuroko Kazuo, *Murakami Haruki: za rosuto waarudo* (Tokyo: Rokkō shuppan, 1989), discusses the political and historical importance of the year 1970 to Murakami.

16. Kawamoto Saburō, " 'Monogatari' no tame no bōken," *Bungakukai* (August 1985): 64.

17. "Jisaku o kataru: Tanpen shōsetsu e no kokoromi," *MHZ* suppl., p. 3.

18. Ibid., pp. 3–4.

19. The origin of the umbrella stand *(kasa tate)* that pops up suddenly at the end of part 2 may, however, be traceable. Asked about it by a student in Charles Inouye's class at Tufts University on December 1, 1994, Murakami mused that it might have come to him because the umbrella stand in his jazz bar was a constant source of trouble for him at the time. Angry customers would complain to him whenever their expensive umbrellas disappeared.

20. Originally printed in *Shinchō* (December 1980) and anthologized in *Chūgoku yuki no surōbōto* (Tokyo: Chūō Kōron sha, 1983), the older version is quoted here from the paperback *(bunkobon)* version of that collection (Tokyo: Chūkō bunko, 1986), pp. 43–73. The newer version is in *MHZ* 3:41–67.

21. *Kaze no uta o kike* deals with such material indirectly.

22. *Bunkobon,* p. 46; *MHZ* 3:44.

23. *Bunkobon,* p. 50; *MHZ* 3:47.

24. *Bunkobon,* p. 46; *MHZ* 3:44. Translated from the *MHZ* text. There are a few stylistic changes here, but the word *"kotoba"* appears in both versions.

25. *Bunkobon,* p. 59; *MHZ* 3:55.

26. "Jisaku o kataru: Tanpen shōsetsu e no kokoromi," *MHZ* suppl., pp. 4–6.

27. *Bunkobon,* p. 48; *MHZ* 3:46.

28. *Bunkobon,* p. 45; *MHZ* 3:43.

29. *Bunkobon,* p. 62; *MHZ* 3:58.

30. *Bunkobon,* p. 46; *MHZ* 3:44; for this and the following lines.

31. Kawamoto, "Monogatari," pp. 63, 64.

32. "The Sheepman and the End of the World," November 17, 1992.

33. Kawamoto, "Monogatari," p. 38.

34. For my translation of this story see *The Elephant Vanishes,* pp. 35–49.

35. *Bunkobon,* p. 59; *MHZ* 3:55.

36. *Bunkobon,* p. 46; *MHZ* 3:43–44. The entire translation here is based on the *zensakuhin* version.

37. *Bunkobon,* p. 48; *MHZ* 3:45.

38. Unfortunately for anyone attempting a translation, readers encountering the story in English assume that the phrase "poor aunt" must refer to some Japanese cliché and feel that they are missing something.

39. *Bunkobon,* p. 59; *MHZ* 3:55.

40. John Solt's Amherst class, November 17, 1994; Tufts class, December 1, 1994.

41. Tufts class, December 1, 1994.

42. *Bunkobon,* pp. 52–53; *MHZ* 3:49–50.

43. *Bunkobon,* p. 65; *MHZ* 3:60.

44. Karatani, "Murakami Haruki," pt. 1, pp. 297–298; *MHZ* 1:17.

45. *Bunkobon,* p. 66; *MHZ* 3:61.

46. *Bunkobon,* pp. 63–64; *MHZ* 3:59. Only the girlfriend's nod and the comment on it are new in the *MHZ* version.

47. For my translation of this story see *The Elephant Vanishes,* pp. 307–327.

48. *MHZ* 3:66; in *Bunkobon,* p. 72, the hunger is described in less gargantuan terms.

49. *Bunkobon,* pp. 72–73; *MHZ* 3:67.

50. Remark made in the Tufts class, December 1, 1994.

51. *MHZ* 3:64–65.

52. *MHZ* 1:253; Birnbaum translation, p. 178. The phrase is *"moto no tokoro"* here.

53. *MHZ* 3:64–65 for this and the following lines.

54. *MHZ* 2:345; Birnbaum translation, p. 276.

55. *MHZ* 2:57; Birnbaum translation, p. 35.

56. *MHZ* 4:25; Birnbaum translation, p. 9.

57. *MHZ* 4:26; slightly altered from Birnbaum translation, p. 10.

58. *Nejimakidori kuronikuru* 3:397–398; Rubin translation, p. 558.

9

EXTREME IMAGINATION: THE FICTION OF
MURAKAMI RYŪ

Stephen Snyder

Murakami Ryū was born in 1952 and grew up in the port city of Sasebo
in western Japan near a large U.S. naval base. His parents were school-
teachers, and much of his youth was apparently spent in rock and roll
bands and mild forms of rebellion. While attending Musashino College
of Art in Tokyo, he entered *Almost Transparent Blue* in a *shinjin* (new
writer) contest conducted by the literary monthly *Gunzō*. When published as a book the following year, the novel became a best-seller and was
awarded the Akutagawa Prize for 1976.

Since this debut, Murakami has continued to publish fiction, report-
age, and commentary at a rapid pace while also working as a radio and television host, international sports reporter (often for tennis), and, more
recently, as a film director. His films, notably *Topaz: Tokyo Decadence,*
have achieved a fair amount of positive critical attention. In addition to
Almost Transparent Blue (1976; 1977), his novels include: *Coin Locker
Babies* (1980; English translation 1995), *69 Sixty-nine* (1987; English translation 1993), *Ai to genshō no fuashizumu* (1987), *Gofungo no sekai* (1994),
Piasshingu (Piercing, 1994), and *In za miso suupu* (In the Miso Soup,
1997), which was awarded the Yomiuri Prize. His collected essays were
published in three volumes in 1991.

Although he was the subject of a special issue of the scholarly journal *Kokubungaku*, Murakami has played something of a trickster's role in his relations with the Japanese literary establishment, functioning as critic, outsider, lampoon artist, and lightning rod for controversy. Shimada Masahiko has called him "Japan's Smerdyakov."

•

Normalcy is a sign of poverty of the spirit.

— Karl Jaspers

•

The protagonist of Murakami Ryū's recent science fiction novel, *Gofungo no sekai* (The World Five Minutes After, 1994), is snatched inexplicably from his life in contemporary Japan into a parallel world (five minutes after our own) in which Japan never surrendered in the Pacific War but fights on fifty years later from a warren of tunnels dug beneath Mount Fuji. He is taken prisoner by the Japanese side and subjected to humiliating interrogations, forced marches, and a bloody battle at the gate of one of the tunnels leading to the subterranean fortress. Finally, due to a misunderstanding, Murakami's hero, Odagiri by name, is about to be summarily executed when his guard, who seems to realize that the prisoner is not from "around here," asks him what he thinks of the place ("Koko o dō omou?"). "In a word," Odagiri answers, "I like it." Despite all the mayhem he has seen in the parallel world, he prefers it to his own:

> Where I was before, everybody was always butting in where they weren't wanted, shooting off at the mouth. Somebody was always telling you what to do and where to go. In train stations, there were loudspeakers yelling "Danger! Keep away from the tracks!" or "Watch your step! Wide space between the train and platform!" "Keep your arms and head in the car. . . . " And it did no good to tell them to leave you alone; that only brought the meddlers in swarms. Money was everything back there, and yet people didn't even know what they wanted to buy with it; they just bought what everybody else was buying, wanted what everybody else wanted.[1]

Murakami's character indicts what he sees as Japan's social ills: a lack of respect for individual privacy, overregulation, mindless consumerism. But his hero's choice, in fact, reveals as much about Murakami's narrative practice as it does about the reality of contemporary Japanese life. Odagiri, like virtually all Murakami characters, prefers the violent, hazardous, extreme world "five minutes after" to the bland, innocuous everyday place he has come from—prefers high-tech firefight, that is, to waiting for a train. Nor is it merely that the former, as anyone would agree, is more exciting than the latter (and more narratable, which of course it is); for the people who populate Murakami's fictional world, the mundane represents a kind of threat from which they must flee, an anxiety for which they seek therapy in violent conditions and degraded situations. Murakami's is a fiction of what Jean Baudrillard calls "extreme phenomena"—a fiction, in effect, of evil—and as such is positioned in opposition to the totalizing, accelerating (and, for Murakami, deadening) flow of everyday life in late-century Japan.[2]

For Baudrillard, and for Murakami, contemporary experience constitutes a postliberation orgy of "transparency" and "reversibility" in which all difference is erased and everything becomes instantly convertible to anything else: sexuality is indistinguishable from politics, which is, in turn, revealed to be a form of economics, which has become a matter of aesthetics. The radical Other (the "opposite" sex, the "Evil Empire") is erased by cloning—Baudrillard's metaphor for the leveling of cultural and sexual difference, making both travel and sex impossible. Theory as well is rendered impracticable as all fields of inquiry expand beyond themselves:

> Each category is generalized to the greatest possible extent, so that it eventually loses all specificity and is reabsorbed by all the other categories. When everything is political, nothing is political any more, the word itself is meaningless. When everything is sexual, nothing is sexual any more, and sex loses its determinants. When everything is aesthetic, nothing is beautiful or ugly any more, and art itself disappears.[3]

The resulting figures are interchangeable: transpolitics, transsexuality, transaesthetics. Finally, even distinctions between subject and object collapse, rendering desire itself nothing more than a reproduction of simulated desire, freed for uninterrupted circulation. It is against this total flow that a fiction such as Murakami's becomes a kind of narrative cataract: by thematizing excess (sexual, political, aesthetic), by staging a kind of linguistic terrorism or contagion, by forefronting violence and desire of all kinds, in short, by imagining "evil," Murakami's work attempts to staunch the torrents of everyday reality, to resist the leveling tendency of contemporary life. As Baudrillard puts it:

In the face of the threats of a total weightlessness, an unbearable lightness of being, a universal promiscuity and a linearity of processes liable to plunge us into the void, the sudden whirlpools that we dub catastrophes are really the thing that saves us from catastrophe. Anomalies and aberrations of this kind re-create zones of gravity and density that counter dispersion.[4]

Or somewhat more metaphorically:

One is put in mind of a fluid travelling at increasing speed, forming eddies and anomalous countercurrents which arrest or dissipate its flow. Chaos imposes a limit upon what would otherwise hurtle into an absolute void. The secret disorder of extreme phenomena, then, plays a prophylactic role by opposing its chaos to any escalation of order and transparency to their extremes.[5]

If contemporary Japan is a place of escalating order and transparency, of unlimited and utterly promiscuous image exchange (a proposition that can be readily confirmed by an afternoon watching the "Wide" shows on television), then Murakami's fiction constitutes a prophylaxis of chaos and anomaly. Murakami's fiction insists on aberration, on difference, on the irreconcilable. It is replete with the very things erased by contemporary culture: desire, sexuality, terror, and art (as opposed to their ubiquitous simulated versions).

The "evil" in Murakami's work takes a variety of forms and serves a variety of narrative and ideological ends. But at least two thematic strands of "extremity" run through a productive career that will soon span two decades. *Kagirinaku tōmei ni chikai burū* (translated by Nancy Andrew as *Almost Transparent Blue;* hereafter referred to as *Blue*), which won the Akutagawa Prize in 1976, inaugurates one of these strands—namely, the themes of "evil" sex and the deviance from the societal norm it entails. Sex is the narrative topos responsible for the extreme celebrity of *Blue* and a number of subsequent Murakami novels (and films), and it is reworked and refined in a series of novels dealing with sadomasochism Murakami began publishing in the 1980s, including *Topaz, Ibisa,* and the recent *Piercing.* Murakami's other "evil" interest, which might be called his "fantasy of evil," concerns the possibilities for experiencing the extreme (and thereby escaping the mean) in the landscapes of science fiction. The principal works of this group, to date, are *Coin Locker Babies, Ai to genshō no fuashizumu,* and *Gofungo no sekai.*

Murakami has remarked that all his works have been written as if to say to the reader: "You may not know it, but there are incredible [*'sugoi,'* that is, 'horrible,' 'unearthly,' 'superb'—'extreme'] worlds such as this out there."[6] In effect, he has self-consciously presented his work as an investigation/celebration of the "secret disorder of extreme phenomena." His "mission" (to use a term seemingly inappropriate to Murakami's authorial persona), then, has been to confront a complacent Japanese collectivity with unsettling images of itself or what it can become —images drawn from the realms of marginal and dangerous sexuality or alternative fantasy universes. Before examining the range of such realms in a bit more detail, however, it should be noted that any "confrontation" staged in a Murakami work must, of necessity, be bracketed; Murakami Ryū is, in many senses, a visionary writer, but his vision is colored by a very personal ironic filter that, more often than not, tends to distance him from his material. His narrative habit, as I have suggested, is one of hyperbole and excess, of enthusiastic absolutes, and yet these excesses are perpetually in danger of being rendered, collapsed, as it were, into the mundane. In the 1987 novel *69 Sixty-nine*, for example, ironic deflation becomes a narrative principle whereby the protagonist repeatedly (pathologically) elaborates a set of dire circumstances only to reveal them, almost immediately, as fabrication, as excess for its own sake:

> My grades had been dropping at a steady and alarming rate ever since I'd entered high school. There were various things one could blame for this—my parents' divorce, my younger brother's sudden suicide, the effect that reading Nietzsche had had on me, and the shock of learning that my grandmother had come down with an incurable disease—but none of them were true. The simple fact was that I hated studying.[7]

Divorce, suicide, disease—and Nietzsche, with Sade, the original theorizer of evil. Murakami invokes his own thematic universe only to add to it the (perhaps even more disturbing) possibility that catastrophe itself may not be something to take seriously, may not be separable from the narrative it interrupts.

Murakami Ryū's debut was, or staged itself as, a kind of cataclysm. The selection of *Blue*, which Karatani Kōjin has called a "basically base novel based upon the base,"[8] for the Akutagawa Prize was not, even for the selection committee, an easy choice.[9] Futhermore, the award enraged critics such as Etō Jun, who called the selection "nonsense," and no doubt shocked a wide segment of the reading public.[10] In the first place, it is unlikely that an Akutagawa Prize novel had ever before (or perhaps since) featured such explicit sex; but much more damning no doubt were the "outlaw" nature of this sex (at turns, violent, interracial, homoerotic, and polymorphous) and the general atmosphere of disaffection among the people having it. Take, for example, the following emblematic conversation between the narrator, Ryū, and one of his familiars after a night of drinking:

> As we walked back inside, Yoshiyama said, "Hey, Ryū, when I heave like that, you know, and my guts are all mixed up and I can hardly stay on my feet and I can't see good, you know, that's the only time I really want a woman. Well, even if there was one around, I couldn't get it up and it'd be too much trouble to open her legs, but anyway I still want a woman. Not in my prick or in my head, but my whole body, all of me, is just squirming for it. How about you? Do you get what I mean?"
>
> "Yeah, you want to kill her, rather than fuck her?"
>
> "That's it, that's it, squeezing her neck like this, tearing her clothes off, ramming a stick or something up her butt, a classy chick like the kind you see walking on the Ginza."[11]

The irony of the furor over this repellent passage (and numerous others like it) is not, however, its misogynistic, antisocial nature but the fact that it cites a similar sentiment in another famous coming-of-age fiction, Ōe Kenzaburō's *A Personal Matter.* Ōe's Bird, on two different occasions, imagines virtually the same act Murakami's character does:

> His eyes closed still, Bird groped for his trousers and felt his erect penis through the cloth. He felt wretched, base, rueful; he longed for the ultimate in antisocial sex. The kind of coitus that would strip and hold up to the light the shame that was worming into him. Bird left the [bus] line and looked for a taxi with eyes brutalized by the light, seeing the square as though in a negative, with blacks and whites reversed. He intended to return to Himiko's room, where the light of day was shut out. If she turns me down, he thought irritably, as if to whip himself, I'll beat her unconscious and fuck her then.[12]

The resemblance between the form that "antisocial sex" *(hanshakai teki na seikō)* takes in Murakami and Ōe's imaginations is remarkable for the difference between the ultimate reaction that these scenes and novels evoke. While Ōe's book is hailed (if not immediately then eventually) as an inaugural work in a *junbungaku* career that culminates with a Nobel Prize, Murakami's is excoriated as pornographic "nonsense." No doubt the difference in evaluations is due in large part to the difference in the respective endings of the works and the retrospective light they throw on the scenes. Bird's sudden (some would say unrealistic) conversion in the final pages of *A Personal Matter* rehabilitates his earlier behavior: he is restored to the heart of the familial structure, to the role of father that Ōe has cultivated in any number of fictions since. In essence, the ending of *A Personal Matter* restores order to the social (and narrative) universe, acknowledging the values of family, responsibility, and collectivity over the tempting chaos represented by deviant sex with Himiko or flight to the dreamscape of Africa.[13] *Blue*, on the other hand, ends with the smell of rotting pineapple and a letter, written four years after the action of the novel, from the protagonist, Ryū, to another character assuring her that he is unchanged, that the disorderly world depicted in the novel continues, unreconstructed and perhaps irredeemable.

Despite their ultimate contextualization, these two narrative moments are similar to the extent that in both cases the (young) novelist deploys an "evil" sexuality (and undisguised misogyny) not only to disrupt the flow of the narrative (which becomes difficult for the reader to naturalize in the face of such extreme horror) but to decenter the novel form itself (and, by implication, the society it represents). For Murakami this act of decentering—creating fissures in the everyday by tossing narrative bombs into the calm of our smoothly functioning representational circuits—has continued throughout his career. And the thematization of aberrant sexuality has been one of his chief strategies. Fuse Hideto has observed that Murakami's fiction is the "last stronghold of overflowing carnality" in a world where the flesh is vanishing before an onslaught of technology.[14] (Technology is, in essence, the driving engine of the accelerating flow.) But, he adds, it is the addition of violence (the catalyst of "evil"), from *Blue* on, that allows Murakami to develop sexuality into a significant theme.[15] This addition is performed in works such as *Topaz, Ibisa,* and *Cocksucker Blues,* but perhaps nowhere is it more interestingly realized than in the recent novel *Piercing.*

Ueshima Keiji points out that Murakami's *Cocksucker Blues,* among other works, is so larded with sex that the reader is left confused: Is this pornography, or exactly its opposite? What, in fact, are we to make of such a text?[16] In reading *Piercing,* however, there is simultaneously both this strong sense of bewilderment—this is a truly troubling, indeed "evil," work depicting a sadistic sexuality that is difficult to recuperate as "art"—and a kind of disturbing clarity of structure and execution (not found in *Cocksucker Blues*) that suggests Murakami is perfecting the mechanism of disruption. Sekii Mitsuo describes Murakami's narrative process as an "inversion" (Karatani's *tenkō*) of the "realism of the 'modern'

Japanese novel into a phenomenology of the body," out of which he "reconstructs the world that has been cut to pieces [by that inversion]."[17] In *Piercing,* the "real" world (the world of narrative realism) fragments under the stabbing ice pick wielded by the protagonist, and the world Murakami constructs in its stead is of a piece with the one he had created in *Blue:* a radically disturbed and disturbing place.

The novel is predicated on a simple, but devious, conceit: the chance encounter between a suicidal woman (who happens to be an S&M sex worker) and a homicidal man. The choreography of their interaction is at times worthy of a 1940s movie script or an Oscar Wilde comedy of manners, and the dialogue is filled with double entendre as each fails to grasp the other's intentions. The man, Kawashima, fighting an inexplicable but overwhelming urge to stab ("pierce") his infant child and wife, decides the only way to spare them is to stab someone else. In desperation he plans a "perfect" crime: the ritualized murder of a prostitute done with elaborate precautions to conceal his identity and ensure the crime goes undetected. In preparation for the deed, he moves into a hotel room and writes, in explicit detail, all the particulars of the crime he intends to commit, in effect doubling the author's creative process by narrativizing his own actions. Finally, however, it is this *written* crime, or his crime of writing, that becomes the driving force of the narrative, since it is in this narrative form—concretely the notebooks in which Kawashima records his plans—that the crime is *imagined* in its most extreme detail and the real horror of Murakami's "psychothriller" is created.

Yet the power of this novel comes from a very different source than that of *Blue,* for example. In the earlier work, the language used to describe the sexual deviance of Ryū and his companions itself becomes a kind of "extreme phenomenon." Moreover, it is not merely the descriptions of sexuality that obtain this status; excess contaminates the whole of the narration, rendering even ordinary descriptions pornographic:

> Cherry cheesecake, grapes in black hands, steaming boiled crab legs breaking with a snap, clear sweet pale purple American wine, pickles like dead men's wart-covered fingers, bacon sandwiches like the mouths of women, salad dripping pink mayonnaise.[18]

Murakami manages, with this sort of virulent language, to infect not only Japanese syntax but the very world it is used to model. The "base" sexuality of *Blue* becomes a means of rendering everyday existence a mere diseased shadow of itself. Yet by the time he writes *Piercing*, Murakami has found a more subtle means of destroying assumptions.

The language of much of *Piercing* is flat by comparison—not unlike the "toneless, rather catatonic narrative voice" that John Aldridge identifies in American minimalist fiction.[19] Indeed, it is in the sinister sadomasochistic pairing itself and the remote, icy detachment with which the murderer formulates his plans that readers locate their disgust with the novel. In the afterword, Murakami emphasizes that all the characters are "ordinary people," that what happens to them "could happen to anybody."[20] In other words, here is a "normal" salaryman, a good family man who happens to use his hard-earned vacation days to plan the brutal stabbing of a call girl; moreover, the same skills that make him a success at work—attention to detail, a creative imagination—can conveniently be put to good use in this "hobby." The immediate and explosive language that made *Blue* so controversial is replaced by an equally devastating detachment. As Kawashima plans his murder, for example, it occurs to him that he will have to specify to the S&M service that he wants a Japanese woman. He realizes that killing a foreigner—someone from Southeast Asia, for instance—would be safer in the sense that a foreigner's disappearance might attract little attention, incite only a cursory search, but this factor is outweighed by others:

> Her skin has to be white. I have to stick the ice pick into *white* skin. A foreigner is no good. We have to be able to talk in Japanese, and then she has to scream out her fear and her agony in Japanese.[21]

Kawashima fills page after page of his notebook (just as Murakami fills page after page of his novel) with such chilling calculations. A bit later on, for example:

> When I come after her with the ice pick, she's going to try to get away. And she'll scream. I'm not planning to stab her in the heart, so she's not going to die from just one wound. Ideally, I'd prefer to watch her bleed to death slowly, but I doubt much blood actually comes out of little puncture wounds like an ice pick makes. I suppose she could die from the pick hitting an organ, but that's dull since you can't *see* it.[22]

The tone is perhaps not unlike the famous "cool" of Murakami Haruki's ubiquitous narrator,[23] but here it is put into service to narrate a very different sort of material with very different effect. While in Haruki's work it could be argued (as Miyoshi among others has done) that the style, the detached bemusement of the narrator, finally is the *point* of the work, that it ends by overwhelming the content, in Ryū's work the psychotic detachment of the narrator simply emphasizes the horror of the content of his speech.

In effect, the power of *Piercing* depends on the fact that violence has supplanted sexuality; reversing Fuse's formulation, eroticism itself has all but given way to a vaguely eroticized violence. Perhaps even more significant for the development of Murakami's powers as a writer, the violence itself is now largely *imagined* mayhem, taking place almost exclusively on the pages of Kawashima's notebook (that is, *represented* imagination or imagination doubled in the sense that Kawashima himself is already a product of Murakami's imagination).

In the event, when Kawashima attempts to put his plan into effect, the woman who arrives is herself suicidal and tries to kill herself before he can murder her. This unforeseen development puts Kawashima at risk of discovery and forces him to put his plans on hold and seek help for her, at least until he can determine a "safe" way to kill her. She, in turn, mistakes his concern (spurred largely by his fear that she may have read his notebook) for affection and the resulting misunderstandings propel the plot to an ambiguous conclusion. In the final analysis, neither the anticipated erotic encounter nor the elaborately planned murder in fact take place; *Piercing* focuses instead on the possibilities offered by the creation of anticipation of such extreme phenomena. In the final analysis, however, the effect of *Piercing* is essentially consistent with that of earlier texts: these "normal" people come equipped with extreme emotional disorders which radical chance exacerbates into a demented set of coincidences that undermine the notion of everyday experience. The emotionally misshapen (if formally perfect) story is, as Sekii suggests, something that might be reconstructed from the shards of a shattered realism.

Developed in tandem with the theme of deviant sexuality is Murakami's fascination with other worlds—with imagined alternatives to an oppressively "normal" Japan. In a sense *Blue* is the precursor of this development, as well, in that the drug-induced, visionary squalor, the surreal orgies and late-night jaunts to hallucinatory jet landing strips, are represented as escapes from the "straight," "square," constricted reality of the high-growth period. Still, Ryū (the narrator) and his friends inevitably wake up the next day confronted with everything they had temporarily left behind: landlords, the police, the necessity of earning some sort of living. Their encounters with the extreme are a repetitive cycle, modeled on the monotonous coitus of pornography or the addict's vacillation between euphoria and the desperate search for the next fix. The S&M fictions, *Piercing* included, in many senses reenact this cyclic form. Murakami's fantasy fiction, on the other hand, effectively breaks the cycle, allowing for more radical examination of what Julia Kristeva calls the "powers of horror."[24] In *Gofungo no sekai*, to take the latest example, the otherness of the imagined world is absolute. The parallel universe may reflect back ironically on the "real" one—for instance, the war being waged at the secret gates of Japan's underground fortress is humorously similar to contemporary economic competition, with the dollar gaining ground against the yen every time the United States wins a battle—but in essence it is a wholly other place, a landscape of unrelieved violence and adventure where Odagiri would prefer to die rather than return to the train platforms of "real" Japan.[25] *Gofungo no sekai* is remarkable for a Murakami novel in that there is virtually no representation of sexuality—as if the violence and exotic features of the place where Odagiri finds himself are enough to overcome the dangers of the normal.

Murakami's most ambitious effort to date in the fantasy/science fiction genre, however, is *Coin Locker Babies*. It is also the book cited by readers as the Murakami work that has affected them most.[26] The plot is a double-helix structure tracing the lives of two boys, Kiku and Hashi, who are abandoned at birth in train station lockers. (The idea is developed from a rash of actual incidents of abandonment in the late 1960s and early 1970s.) Raised as brothers, they set out on separate but equally destructive paths, looking to repay in kind both the women who abandoned them and the society they perceive as utterly hostile. Unlike the radically altered world of *Gofungo*, however, the society Kiku and Hashi want to destroy is, in most senses, recognizably that of contemporary Japan or, more specifically, Tokyo. Indeed, one of the startling, no doubt disturbing, things about *Coin Locker Babies* is the fact that the surreal, often terrifying cityscape Murakami depicts is so very familiar, even to relatively secure Tokyo dwellers. (The fascination of Ridley Scott's Los Angeles in *Blade Runner*, for example, is no doubt the same, rooted not in difference but uncomfortable similarity.) The Japan of *Coin Locker Babies* is a troubling admixture of the evil and the everyday.

The primary locus of this mixture, however, is one of Murakami's most memorable spatial creations: a barbed-wire-enclosed waste dump in the heart of Tokyo labeled "Toxitown."[27] In accepting the Noma New Writer's Award in 1982, Murakami announced that the book represented his effort to "demolish his relationship with the novel form." "Beyond the rubble left from that demolition," he added in characteristically metaphorical fashion, "there was something wriggling and squirming," and that something was "creating a place *(basho)*—not scenery *(fūkei)*, I no longer intend to describe scenery—I want to talk about *places.*"[28] Toxitown is the first of these "places." It was created, in the shadow of the cluster of high-rises in Shinjuku, by a toxic waste spill that left the area virtually uninhabitable—at least by "normal" people. Sealed off and patrolled by guards in protective uniforms, it becomes a haven for the city's outcasts, who gather there

> precisely because it was the one place in Tokyo where police jurisdiction didn't extend. And once the area had been colonized by gangsters and hoods, other types began to collect there too; drifters and vagrants, the deinstitutionalized mentally ill, low-class whores, male prostitutes, wanted criminals, degenerates, cripples, and runaways all took up residence in Toxitown, and an odd sort of society began to form. In the end, apparently, even the police preferred to look the other way thanks to an unexpected side effect of so many marginal types gathering in one spot: the crime rate, particularly for sexual offenses, began to fall sharply in other parts of the city.[29]

Toxitown, like a modern-day Yoshiwara, is an *akusho,* an "evil place" designed to siphon off the dangerous contagions of the city: sexuality, criminality, deviance, in a word, difference.[30] In a way, it is this setting of difference that comes to dominate the narrative of *Coin Locker Babies.* This "place," in Murakami's strong sense, assumes greater significance than character or plot—taking on, in essence, the status of theme. And this supplanting is accomplished by conflating the vital elements of the plot into a single overlapping "place."

Sekii Mitsuo notes a similar sense of physical location that pervades the controlling metaphor of the novel:

> [Kiku and Hashi] believe in the physical sense *(shintai no kankaku)* of the coin locker; that is what they are storing up. And through this sense, they heap up destruction, and continue with the actions that cause cracks in the structure of the everyday. This is because, for the two of them, this physical sense is conceived as a place of "danger."[31]

This is, indeed, a telling reading of the significance of the lockers. But it does not go far enough. The physical sense of place that Kiku and Hashi experience as a form of "danger" merely begins with the lockers, which become the paradigm for the novel's other evil places, principal of which is Toxitown. There is, moreover, a third "place," coextensive with the lockers and Toxitown, that completes the topography of Murakami's novel: namely, the body. In a sense, as Sekii has remarked of Murakami's work in general, "the body is the subject" (as well as the object).[32] The bodies of the babies, stuffed like objects into the lockers, the bodies of their mothers for which they search, the bodies of the inhabitants of Toxitown that are eaten through by the chemicals in the soil—all are examples of Murakami's "material" *(busshitsu teki)* imagination,[33] what Karatani Kōjin calls an attempt to "divine the germ of 'meaning' from an overwhelming animality."[34] It is from this animality *(dōbutsusei),* the sheer physical horror of much of Murakami's fiction, that the disruptive "evil" is derived.

The "evil" to which I have repeatedly referred may be a familiar, if not hackneyed, concept to students of the modern. (Hannah Arendt speaks of evil's "banality.") And Murakami's obsession may not seem, at first glance, to differ substantially from the literary projects of Céline, Jean Genet,[35] Baudelaire, or their great predecessor Sade. In fact, however, the terms of engagement are substantially altered in Murakami's case. While earlier writers invoke "evil" in opposition to some sort of "good" (which they, in some sense, affirm by the act of negation),[36] Murakami lives in an age when "evil" no longer exists in any conventional sense, at least not as the opposite of anything that can be labeled "good." "The principle of Evil," notes Baudrillard, "is not a moral principle but rather a principle of instability and vertigo, a principle of complexity and foreignness, a principle of seduction, a principle of incompatibility, antagonism and irreducibility. . . . It is a vital principle of disjunction."[37]

In other words, it is a principle of opposition to the seamless conjunctions that characterize contemporary society (those between politics and business, between advertising and art, between individual identity and collective will). The long search in *Coin Locker Babies* for a way of countering these convergences, of destabilizing the stable, comes to an end in a scene that is an example of what Julia Kristeva labels the "ultimate of abjection."

The scene in question, the last one in the novel, depicts Hashi wandering the empty streets of Tokyo. Kiku, the other coin locker baby, has released a cloud of the nerve agent Datura, and the inhabitants of Tokyo are mostly dead or evacuated. In essence, he has generalized the poisons of Toxitown to the city at large, demonstrating on a practical level the disjunctive power of the extreme. Datura endows its victims with an absolute rage and superhuman strength before killing them, and Hashi is beginning to experience these symptoms as he comes upon the only other survivor in the area, a dazed pregnant woman. His imagination takes over:

In his mind, he could see himself putting one hand on either side of her mouth and tearing her head apart like a ripe fruit. Rip her open, he said to himself. Rip her! He noticed the way her throat bobbed as she swallowed, and he could hear himself laughing—a rasping, gargling, laugh. A wave of excitement broke over him and he reached for his groin, spraying a wad of cum almost instantly, merely from the pleasure that surged up in him from the hot pavement.[38]

Murakami, who has, both before and after this scene, searched for the ultimate vision of degradation, here seems to be closing in on it. Sexual ecstasy conflates with physical violence, all clustered around the violation of the most inviolable of images, the pregnant female body:

He ran his fingers through the woman's hair, and then, closing them into a fist, pulled her out of the ditch. Before she could cry out, he shoved his right hand into her mouth. Sour bile leaked from the back of her throat and her tongue curled into a tight ball as he let go of her hair and wrapped his left hand around her jaw. . . . Beside himself, he went on pulling, but just as the corners of her mouth began to tear, a shudder ran through his body. He'd heard it: the sound of a heart beating! Of course! It had to come, the heartbeat, surrounding him, enfolding him at the peak of pleasure, as he put this woman heavy with an unborn child to death.[39]

Hashi (and Murakami) have been obsessed with the body of the mother (both Hashi's mother specifically and mothers in the abstract). The "overwhelming animality" of which Karatani speaks is heaped on the mother's body: the body that commits the affectless, incestuous rape of the infamous first lines of the novel; the body that is turned to red pulp in the murder that ends the first volume; the body that generates the heartbeat that haunts Hashi throughout. It is this body, which is metaphorically giving birth (to him), that he must reenter (hallucinogenically) for a proper rebirth to counter the experience of the coin locker.

But suddenly he knew: "It's you. You're the one who left me in that locker," he whispered, reaching out again to tear her chest open. In he dived, pushing aside other organs until he came to a warm, slippery, twitching red lump: her heart.[40]

Having discovered the source of the sound, his mother's heart, he is able to forgive her, to release unharmed the pregnant woman who has served as surrogate for this exorcism, and move on, reborn, as it were:

He took a deep breath, soothing his tongue and throat with the cool air. The message that the heartbeat carried to the child within was one that never changed. He drew another breath, feeling it refresh his lips, and then a sound emerged—the cry of a newborn baby. . . .

Hashi let his hands fall from the woman's mouth. Leaving her, he walked into the heart of the deserted city, his cry melting into a song.

"Can you hear?" he whispered to the towers in the distance. "Can you hear? It's my new song."[41]

The scene that Murakami is invoking is that of childbirth: the body of the pregnant woman is opened so that Hashi can enter to be reborn, to cry the newborn's cry, his "new song." The scene, of all Murakami's violent scenes, has a kind of liberating energy, for reasons that Julia Kristeva identifies in a work by Céline with a similar moment:

When Céline locates the ultimate of abjection—and thus the supreme and sole interest of literature—in the birth-giving scene, he makes amply clear which fantasy is involved: something *horrible to see* at the impossible doors of the invisible —the mother's body. The scene of scenes is here not the so-called primal scene but the one of giving birth, incest turned inside out, flayed identity. Giving birth: the height of bloodshed and life, scorching moment of hesitation (between inside and outside, ego and other, life and death), horror and beauty, sexuality and the blunt negation of the sexual.[42]

Murakami has come to this moment of extreme liminality, this moment "horrible to see," as an endpoint to an investigation of the possibilities of abjection. And what he has discovered is that while "evil" may not be a "solution" per se, may not resolve itself neatly into some other category (such as "beauty," as it might have done for Tanizaki or Genet), it does provide a kind of filter that may be superimposed over any phenomenon to prevent transparency—a "scorching moment of hesitation" to disrupt the free flow of "meaning" in our information age, to keep us at bay, temporarily paralyzed by our horror. What Kristeva says of Céline, again, one might say of Murakami: that he

speaks from the very seat of . . . horror, he is implicated in it, he is inside of it. Through his scription he causes it to exist and although he comes far short of clearing it up, he throws over it the lacework of his text: a frail netting that is also a latticework, which, without protecting us from anything whatsoever, imprints itself within us, implicating us fully.[43]

The irony of the fact that Murakami's most powerful treatment of evil to date comes in the form of fabulation and science fiction is that, of late, these fictions seem to be in the process of becoming fact. The "point" of *Coin Locker Babies* is, in effect, to imagine the unimaginable destruction of Tokyo under a cloud of Datura, the scene that Murakami has said was the "only thing that was in his head" from the moment he started writing the novel.[44] But, of course, what might have been unimaginable in 1980 is happening with some regularity in Tokyo in the 1990s. In the face of the terrorist sarin gas attacks of March 1995 and a general spread of violence and paranoia, it would seem that, symbolically at least, the order that once characterized Japanese society is being disrupted by actual versions of Ryū's narrative incursions.[45] Revelations about underground antigovernment, antisocial activities suggest that things are not as cohesive nor as transparent as they seem; and the schemes of Asahara Shōkō, leader of the Aum Shinrikyō cult, himself a kind of self-beatified coin locker baby, go well beyond anything that Murakami might have been capable of imagining.

What this life-imitating-art drama may show, however, is that the kind of narrative resistance (through the foregrounding of "evil") that Murakami began staging two decades ago has already become impossible in today's world. As Fredric Jameson has suggested, what once qualified as the most extreme forms of evil have long since been naturalized into our understanding and are already part of the ineluctable flow of information and images. Thus even the most "offensive features" of the "postmodern revolt"—which range from "obscurity and sexually explicit material to psychological squalor and overt expressions of social and political defiance" (that is, all the key elements of Murakami's fictional economy) —"no longer scandalize anyone and are not only received with the greatest complacency but have themselves become institutionalized and are at one with the official or public culture of Western society."[46]

Indeed, there is a sense that the "psychological squalor" of *Blue* or novels such as *Topaz* or *New York City Marathon* (1986) is no longer shocking, no longer outside of mainstream literary expression. Likewise, as I have just suggested, the deviance depicted in *Coin Locker Babies* pales in comparison to the images of the Aum Shinrikyō affair—gassings, stabbings, kidnappings—recycled endlessly on daytime television. And Murakami himself, despite continued attempts to construct genuinely disturbing, disruptive texts (most recently in *Piercing*), has been willingly and readily absorbed into mass culture, hosting a TBS talk show called "Ryū's Bar" in the 1980s, directing reasonably successful commercial films, publishing in various forms (including frequent roundtable discussions, or *taidan*)[47] and almost unlimited quantity, and in general functioning as the literary equivalent of *tarento* (a "celebrity"). The imaginer of extreme phenomena, then, is co-opted into the total system. The "evil" of Murakami's texts is not antithetical to the political or social flow at all but a logical consequence of it, an aspect necessary to its maintenance. As Baudrillard puts it:

> The actual catastrophe may turn out to be a carefully modulated strategy of our species—or, more precisely, . . . our extreme phenomena, which are most definitely real, albeit localized, may be what allow us to preserve the energy of that *virtual* catastrophe which is the motor of all our processes, whether economic or political, artistic or historical.[48]

Unfolding across dozens of works in various media, Murakami's "virtual catastrophe," his ongoing paean to the extremes of sexual and political violence, his narrative virus, may, in the end, be yet another way of preserving the integrity of the body politic it infects. But don't try telling him that.

NOTES

1. Murakami Ryū, *Gofungo no sekai* (Tokyo: Gentōsha, 1994), p. 102. All translations are mine unless otherwise indicated.

2. Jean Baudrillard, *The Transparency of Evil: Essays on Extreme Phenomena*, trans. James Benedict (London: Verso, 1993).

3. Ibid., p. 9.

4. Ibid., p. 69. Baudrillard's examples of "catastrophe" include terrorism, cancer and the AIDS epidemic, transvestism, financial crashes, and computer viruses—all of which share a kind of family resemblance in that they are all forms of "disease" that infect the systems of which they are part (that is, they are not "foreign" to those systems). All result in what Baudrillard calls "superconductive events," which are "untimely intercontinental whirlwinds which no longer affect just states, individuals or institutions, but rather entire transversal structures: sex, money, information, communications, etc." (p. 37).

5. Ibid., p. 68.

6. Murakami Ryū and Ijuin Shizuka, "Bokura no erosu no genten," in *Shōsetsu Subaru* (January 1995):123.

7. Murakami Ryū, *69 Sixty-nine*, trans. Ralph F. McCarthy (Tokyo: Kodansha International, 1993), p. 9 (first published by Shūeisha, 1987; p. 7). This tendency to undercut

Stephen Snyder

one's own narrative is prevalent also in the works of Murakami Ryū but pervasive in those of Murakami Haruki.

8. Karatani Kōjin, "Sōzōryoku no beesu," in *Ryu Book* (Tokyo: Shishosha, 1991), p. 84. See also Murakami Ryū and Sakamoto Ryūichi, *E.V. Cafe* (Tokyo: Kōdansha bunko, 1989), p. 204.

9. The selection committee consisted of Yoshiyuki Jun'nosuke, Niwa Fumio, Nakamura Mitsuo, Inoue Yashushi, Nagai Tatsuo, Takii Kōsaku, and Yasuoka Shōtarō. Of the seven, Inoue is perhaps the most supportive. Yoshiyuki and Nakamura offer fairly positive comments. Yasuoka is the most negative, confessing that he has no clue what the author of *Blue* is trying to say and would just as soon have not given the prize to the novel. For their comments see "Dai 75 kai, Shōwa 51 nendo jōhanki Akutagawashō kettei happyō," *Bungei shunjū* (September 1976):381–385.

10. See, for example, Etō's "Murakami Ryū, Akutagawa-shō jushō no nansensu," *Sandei Mainichi,* July 25, 1976, pp. 136–138. Etō says, in effect, that *Blue* merely "reflects a subculture" instead of "expressing the culture as a whole," which is the job of real fiction. He remarks, quite perceptively, that the experience of reading *Blue* is more akin to the "passive" *(ukemi)* watching of a film than the "active" *(nōdōteki)* reading of a novel (pp. 136–137). Subsequent readers of Murakami's fiction have noted the "antiliterary" quality of the work. See, for example, Fuse Hideto, "Dennō jidai no bungaku: Murakami Ryū no shōsetsu o megutte," *Kokubungaku* 38(3) (special issue on Murakami Ryū) (March 1993): 49. And, of course, Murakami himself now prefers to be seen as a film director.

11. Murakami Ryū, *Almost Transparent Blue,* transl. Nancy Andrews (Tokyo: Kodansha International, 1977), p. 34; originally published as *Kagirinaku tōmei ni chikai burū* (Tokyo: Kōdansha, 1976), pp. 52–53.

12. Ōe Kenzaburō, *A Personal Matter,* transl. John Nathan (Tokyo: Tuttle, 1969), p. 104; originally published as *Kojinteki na taiken* (Tokyo: Shinchō bunko, 1964), pp. 122–123. See also p. 64 (p. 80), where Bird has similar thoughts.

13. Whether or not Ōe's work as a whole represents such an affirmation of order and control is a very different question. (Ōe himself might argue that it is an attempt to construct alternate, marginal models of order in opposition to the central, hegemonic models.) The present comments, limited to *A Personal Matter,* are simply meant to address the difference between the ways Ōe's and Murakami's works contextualize the antisocial impulse they deploy.

14. Fuse, "Dennō jidai no bungaku," p. 49.

15. Ibid., p. 49.

16. Ueshima Keiji, "Murakami Ryū to sekushuariti: *Kokkusakkaa burūsu* o megutte," *Kokubungaku* 38(3) (special issue on Murakami Ryū) (March 1993):51.

17. Sekii Mitsuo, "Murakami Ryū—Supōtsu, shintai, onna no imeeji," *Kokubungaku* 38(3) (special issue on Murakami Ryū) (March 1993):57.

18. *Almost Transparent Blue,* p. 37 (p. 57).

19. John Aldridge, *Talents and Technicians: Literary Chic and the New Assembly-Line Fiction* (New York: Scribners, 1992), p. 65.

20. Murakami Ryū, *Piasshingu* (Tokyo: Gentōsha, 1994), p. 193.

21. Ibid., p. 40.

22. Ibid., pp. 40–41.

23. See, for example, Masao Miyoshi's description of Murakami Haruki's narrative voice in *Off Center: Power and Culture Relations Between Japan and the United States* (Cambridge, Mass.: Harvard University Press, 1991), pp. 234–235.

24. Julia Kristeva, *Powers of Horror: An Essay on Abjection,* transl. Leon Roudiez (New York: Columbia University Press, 1982).

25. In the event, Odagiri is not executed in the passage cited earlier. Instead he is taken below to the Japanese fortress, and there follows a detailed description of the idealized, elitist, quasi-heroic military society of the tunnels—a tiny fraction of Japan's best and brightest who survived the Allied invasion of Japan and continue to resist with their superior technology and moral fiber. The nostalgia and xenophobic nationalism in the rhetoric of this section of *Gofungo no sekai* is odd for Murakami. One looks for signs of irony in pronouncement after pronouncement echoing right-wing propaganda; such signs are difficult to detect if they in fact exist. It will be interesting to see whether this tone marks a new development in the author's thinking.

26. This conclusion is based on anecdotal evidence. In a poll conducted by a suburban Tokyo department store in 1994, however, thirty-seven of ninety-six respondents identified *Coin Locker Babies* as their "favorite" Murakami work; *Blue* was named second most frequently, or fourteen times (original surveys in my possession). *Ai to gensō no fuashizumu* (Love and illusory fascism) (Tokyo: Kōdansha, 1987), 2 vols., is an enormous and complex work that in many ways prefigures *Gofungo no sekai* in terms of mood and theme. It is, however, less accessible and less compelling than *Coin Locker Babies.*

27. Murakami Ryū, *Coin Locker Babies,* transl. Stephen Snyder (Tokyo: Kodansha International, 1995); originally published as *Koinrokkaa beibiizu* (Tokyo: Kōdansha, 1980), 2 vols. Murakami uses the coinage *"yakujima,"* literally Medicine Island, for the place that has been loosely translated as "Toxitown."

28. Murakami Ryū, "Noma Bungei Shinjin-shō jushō no kotoba," in *Murakami Ryū zen essei* (Tokyo: Kōdansha, 1991), vol. 2 (1982–1986), p. 13.

29. *Coin Locker Babies,* p. 53 (pp. 65–66).

30. See, for example, Takahashi Toshio's discussion of the Yoshiwara as *akusho* in *Nagai Kafū to Edo bun-en* (Tokyo: Meiji shoin, 1983), p. 158.

31. Sekii, "Murakami Ryū," p. 58.

32. Ibid., p. 57.

33. Ibid., p. 56.

34. Quoted in Sekii, "Murakami Ryū," p. 58.

35. There seems, in fact, to be evidence that Murakami has been influenced by Genet's work. The general outline of the character who narrates Genet's *The Thief's Journal,* trans. Bernard Frechtman (London: Penguin, 1967), is similar to that of the character Hashi in *Coin Locker Babies:* both are abandoned as children and grow up to lives of crime and homosexual prostitution, followed by great success as artists. There are, in addition, at least two scenes in *Coin Locker Babies* that closely echo episodes in *Thief's Journal:* in one, the abandoned child encounters an elderly vagrant woman he imagines to be his mother

(*Coin Locker Babies,* pp. 202–203; *Thief's Journal,* pp. 14–15); in the other, characters muse on the attractions of the planet Uranus, where the strong gravity keeps everything close to the ground (degraded), a kingdom of creeper ferns and alligators, in both Genet's and Murakami's description (*Coin Locker Babies,* pp. 49–50; *Thief's Journal,* p. 35).

36. For a discussion of this notion in the works of Genet and Sade see Georges Bataille, *Literature and Evil,* transl. Alastair Hamilton (New York: Marion Boyars, 1985). Julia Kristeva's study of Céline in her *Powers of Horror* makes much the same point. (Genet, it seems to me, is in fact looking for a certain form of beauty in evil—see, for example, his discussion of evil in the opening pages of *Thief's Journal.*)

37. Baudrillard, *Transparency of Evil,* p. 107.

38. *Coin Locker Babies,* p. 391 (2:219).

39. *Coin Locker Babies,* p. 391 (2:219–220).

40. *Coin Locker Babies,* p. 392 (2:220).

41. *Coin Locker Babies,* pp. 392–393 (2:221).

42. Kristeva, *Powers of Horror,* p. 155.

43. Ibid., p. 156.

44. Murakami Ryū and Murakami Haruki, *Walk Don't Run: Ryū versus Haruki* (Tokyo: Kōdansha, 1981), p. 79.

45. In another, equally sinister, real-life replication of Murakami's fiction, the *Coin Locker Babies* scene in which Hashi beats a mentally impaired homosexual man in a public bathroom in a park in Sasebo (pp. 175–177; original pp. 208–210) was tragically echoed by the 1993 murder of Allen Schindler, a homosexual U.S. Navy sailor who was beaten to death by other sailors in a public restroom in a Sasebo park—yet another example of what Karatani meant by a "basically base novel based upon the base."

46. Fredric Jameson, *Postmodernism: Or, The Cultural Logic of Late Capitalism* (Durham: Duke University Press, 1991), p. 4.

47. See Masao Miyoshi's useful critique of this form of literary production in *Off Center,* pp. 219–231.

48. Baudrillard, *Transparency of Evil,* p. 69.

10

DREAM MESSENGERS, RENTAL CHILDREN, AND THE INFANTILE: SHIMADA MASAHIKO AND THE POSSIBILITIES OF THE POSTMODERN

Philip Gabriel

Shimada Masahiko was born in Tokyo in 1961 and moved at the age of four to Kawasaki City, where he grew up near the Yomiuri Land theme park. After graduating from the Kawasaki Prefectural High School, he entered the Tokyo University of Foreign Languages, where he majored in Russian. His graduation thesis was on the fiction of the Soviet writer Zemyatin (known for his science-fiction novel *We*). While in university he was active in the school's Soviet Union/Eastern Europe Study Group and began writing fiction. His first work, the 1983 novella *Yasashii sayoku no tame no kiyūkyoku* (A Divertimento for Gentle Leftists), written while he was still a student, depicts the activities of a lethargic pseudo-leftist student group and was noted by some critics as reflecting the political apathy of the generation of 1980s Japanese students. *Yasashii sayoku* was nominated for the Akutagawa Prize, the first of six of Shimada's works to be nominated for this prestigious award in the space of three years, a total that gives Shimada the dubious distinction of tying the record for most unsuccessful nominations for the award. It should be noted, though, that Shimada has had his share of literary awards: he won the Noma New Writer's Award for the novella *Muyū ōkoku no tame no ongaku* (Music for a Somnambulant Kingdom, 1984) and the Izumi Kyōka Prize for *Higan Sensei* (1992).

After his graduation from university in 1984, Shimada has continued to publish prolifically. Among his works of fiction are *Bōmei ryokōsha wa sakebi tsubuyaku* (Cries and Mutters of the Refugee Travelers, 1984), *Boku wa mozō ningen* (I Am an Artificial Man, 1985), *Tengoku ga futte kuru* (Heaven Is Falling, 1985), *Donna Anna* (1986), *Mikakunin bikō buttai* (Unidentified Shadowing Object, 1987), *Yumetsukai* (1989; translated as *Dream Messenger,* 1992), *Rococo-chō* (Rococo-Ville, 1990), and *Ryūkeichi yori ai o komete* (From Exile with Love, 1995). Shimada has published a number of essay collections, as well, including *Shokuminchi no Arisu* (A Colonial Alice, 1993), and has written and produced two plays: *Ulalume* (1988), based on the poem of the same name by Edgar Alan Poe, and *Luna* (1990). Shimada has appeared in several plays as well, including a cameo appearance in a 1990 production of *Ulalume.*

Shimada's fiction is peopled by youthful rebels, refugees, and orphans and is characterized by a playful yet intellectually engaged style influenced by his own wide reading of writers as varied as Dante, Natsume Soseki, and Witold Gombrowicz. His stories touch on such themes as national identity, artificial intelligence, genetic engineering, and AIDS. In addition to *Dream Messenger,* three other stories by Shimada have appeared in English translation: "Momotaro in a Capsule" (1990), "A Callow Fellow of Jewish Descent" (1990), and "Dessert Dolphin" (1997).

■

Innocent as a child, perhaps unaware—perhaps—that in his play he wrecks the elegant rooms of history, threatens the idea of cause and effect itself. . . . Will Postwar be nothing but "events" newly created one moment to the next? No links? Is it the end of history?

—Thomas Pynchon, *Gravity's Rainbow*

"Utopia is just the flip side of hell."

— Shimada Masahiko, *Rococo-chō*

■

I n what is perhaps the most often cited article on Japan and the postmodern, "Infantile Capitalism and Japan's Postmodernism: A Fairy Tale," Asada Akira sketches a vision of capitalism's "global trajectory" encompassing three stages: elderly capitalism, adult capitalism, and infantile capitalism. In contrast to the model proposed by Maruyama Masao and others of the formation of the mature adult *shutai* (individual subject) as the enabling condition of Japan's modernity, Asada identifies in contemporary Japan less a process of maturation than a country growing "progressively more infantile" at the same time that its capitalist economy soars:

> In Japan, there are neither tradition-oriented old people adhering to transcendental values nor inner-oriented adults who have internalized their values; instead, the nearly purely relative (or relativistic) competition exhibited by other-oriented children provides the powerful driving force for capitalism. Let's call this infantile capitalism.[1]

Contemporary Japan is a country of childlike obsessions—for machines by engineers, for wordplay, parody, and "childlike games of differentiation" by advertisers and consumers. It is both a "playful utopia and at the same time a terrible 'dystopia,' " dystopic in that the image of Japan as mammoth theme park describes one reality and conceals another:

> In fact, children can play "freely" only when there is some kind of protection. They always play within a certain protected area. And this protected area is precisely the core of the Japanese ideological mechanism—however thinly diffused a core. It is not a "hard" ruling structure which is vertically centralized (whether transcendental or internalized), but "soft" subsumption by a seemingly horizontal, centerless "place."[2]

The word "seemingly," of course, is key here. Such an ideology conveniently disguises the still vertical nature of power relations in postmodern Japan: for there to be protectees, in other words, there must also be *protectors* whose project it is to delineate the boundaries of the "protected area" and the rules governing the seemingly free play that ensues therein—the adults watching over the children in the playground, as it were. One is reminded of Alan Wolfe's characterization of the postmodern as "postnarrative":

> For nations and peoples in daily struggle with Western and Japanese imperialism, it must come, if they hear about it, as a surprise to learn that the game or story "is over." For the third world, the idea that Japan or the first world has no system, no structure, no content, no signifieds does not induce apathy so much as vigilance; the view of the postmodern as a postnarrative, hence postpolitical, stage is itself a dangerous narrative ploy designed to defuse the potential of political struggle.[3]

The political struggle Wolfe refers to, of course, is the Third World struggle for survival, including the struggle against an imperialist Japan with designs to "control increasingly large realms of the world's necessity."[4] In much the same way that this depiction of the postmodern plays itself out by potentially blinding and diffusing resistance on an international scale, the "soft" core of the Japanese ideological mechanism Asada identifies—with its vision of horizontal, equalitarian relations—acts domestically to counter resistance.

If we accept Asada's twin notions of infantilization and a free zone of protected play as reflective of certain realities of contemporary Japan, we should not be much surprised to find expressions of both in the writings of some of Japan's younger writers. And indeed such is the case. Here I want to examine the works of two such writers—briefly Shimizu Yoshinori and at more length Shimada Masahiko, both of whom are consistently called Japan's leading postmodernists—and ask the question (in Shimada's case) of what makes this work "postmodern." Taken as a whole, Shimada's "Sei Akahito den" (1984), *Yumetsukai* (1989), and *Rococo-chō* (1990), which thematize this notion of Japan and the infantile, reveal an unstable, slippery stance toward this subject—a stance that illustrates Linda Hutcheon's definition of postmodernist art as paradoxical and contradictory, a "curious mixture of the complicitous and the critical."[5] Shimada's rapid alternation between what Fredric Jameson calls the "celebratory posture" and the "moralizing gesture" vis-à-vis Japan's contemporary "infantilism" allows us not only to characterize his work as particularly postmodernist but to understand the possibilities of the postmodern.[6]

First, though, I would like to look at the work of Shimizu Yoshinori, Japan's most deliriously productive master of pastiche. Shimizu has explored Japan and the infantile in such stories as "Guroingu daun" (1989; Growing Down, trans. 1993) and "Eien no Jyakku & Betei" (1988; Jack and Betty Forever, trans. 1993).[7] "Growing Down" is the story of a high school student, Taka, who, along with the rest of the world, is "growing down"—that is, steadily growing younger, finding that the day after today is not tomorrow but, incredibly, *yesterday.* The setting is 1964, some thirty years after time, for some unexplained reason, began to flow backward, leading to a series of absurd situations: Taka enjoying the closing ceremony of the Tokyo Olympics before the opening ceremony; dreading the first day of high school since it will be the last time he'll ever see his girlfriend, whom he met that day; looking back wistfully at the day he regained his virginity. Near the end (beginning?) of "Growing Down," as they struggle against a creeping infantile forgetfulness, Taka and his cousin review the various theories proposed for the sudden reversal of time. Rejecting the idea of parallel worlds and a mass dream-state, Taka speculates that a fin de siècle fear of crossing the barrier represented by the year 2000—coupled with the increasingly violent, right-wing nihilism of the younger generation that his generation (the "last truly antiwar generation") finds abhorrent—led to a mass realization: "People seemed to be turning into something they weren't supposed to turn into. The old days were better, we decided. We wanted to go back to the old days."[8] This mass thought, implanted in the minds of millions of Taka's generation, then, in a kind of wish fulfillment, may have caused the mid-1990s reversal of time. There is, of course, no proof of this, and all Taka can be sure of is that "growing down"—an infantilization of the world—is far preferable to the alternative.

Shimizu's choice of time periods is significant: the story, written at the tail end of the 1980s bubble economy, envisions the near future (the mid-1990s) as a period of great unease—and indeed soon after Shimizu wrote the story the economic bubble burst and the Japanese economy went into a prolonged period of retrenchment that continues to this day. In the story, this period of mid-1990s unease stands in stark contrast to the year 1964, the present of the story and the standard designated starting point of Japan's economic "miracle," which is bathed in a rosy nostalgia. Huddled around a black-and-white TV, entranced by the flickering images of the Tokyo Olympics drawing to an opening, Taka and his family are happy in a way they never were before—in the future:

> Even my dad saw a huge drop in his income when we went through the period of high economic *reverse* growth, but that hasn't made our lives more depressing

or anything. We're still having a good time. Our refrigerator disappeared from our kitchen, but we get ice for our ice box from a house next door. Actually, we've become friendlier with our neighbors than we were before. . . .

All I can say is that I like the way things are now. We're getting poorer, but that doesn't bother me. And it feels great to keep getting younger.[9]

In contrast to the "progressively more infantile" Japan as driving force for its present-day capitalist economy that Asada outlines, Shimizu, then, in his typically playful and comic way, sketches a different vision of a retreat from high growth —a reversal toward a more penurious, though satisfying, infantile state that predates Japan's great economic growth. Shimizu is not alone in expressing this sort of nostalgia for a formerly infantile Japan. Such sentiments are shared by Murakami Haruki in his 1992 best-selling novel, *Kokkyō no minami, taiyō no nishi* (South of the Border, West of the Sun; trans. 1999).[10] Here the protagonist in his late thirties, a successful owner of two nightclubs in the tony Aoyama district of Tokyo, finds his life progressively pointless and empty. Though ostensibly a depiction of a typical midlife crisis coupled with a rekindled desire for his first love who suddenly reenters his life, the novel deals principally with two dynamics: the protagonist's disillusionment with late-1980s-style Japanese affluence (brought to a head by a confrontation with his wealthy father-in-law's insider stock trading) and his aching nostalgia for when he was twelve, the year 1963. Though the novel is clothed in the genre of a love story (and so marketed), the reader soon realizes that the ghostly nature of the protagonist's lover is closely linked to his desire for the ghost of Japan's not-so-distant past: the period predating the emergence of Japan's affluence.[11]

If both "Growing Down" and *Kokkyō no minami* present a return to an infantile state as a preferable alternative to Japan's own present and future, Shimizu's earlier story "Jack and Betty Forever" contrasts Japan and its Other—the United States—and comes to a radically different conclusion: that a present-day infantile Japan is far preferable to any "mature" society, here represented by the United States. Jack and Betty are Japan's equivalents of Dick and Jane—characters in junior high school English readers used extensively throughout Japan in the 1950s. The comedy in the story lies in their imagined reunion thirty-four years later when they are both fifty—principally in the contrast between their mature thoughts and their inability to speak to each other in anything more than the stilted, childish dialogue of the readers:

"Are you alone?"

"Yes. I am alone."

"Let us drink a cup of coffee, or a cup of tea."

"Yes. Let us do that."

Jack invited Betty to a local coffee shop. When they were inside, he asked, "Is this a table?"

"Yes, this is a table."

"Is that a sofa?"

"No. That is not a sofa. That is a chair."

"Please sit down."

"May I sit down, too?"

"Yes, you may sit down."[12]

As with the running gag in "Growing Down"—the temporal confusion engendered in both the reader and the protagonist with events turned upside down—Shimizu makes the most of the absurd spectacle of a couple of fifty-year-olds hopelessly confined to a *Cat in the Hat* vocabulary. As in "Growing Down," though, the playfulness of "Jack and Betty Forever" barely disguises a critical edge that makes it much more than just an inventive romp. This is revealed in the coffee shop dialogue as Jack and Betty catch up on what has happened in each other's lives in the intervening years. What we learn is grim. Jack, a lawyer for an automobile company, has lost his job because the flood of Japanese imports has bankrupted the company. ("And now, thirty years later, I lose my job because of some Japanese who learned English from that . . . textbook [modeled on our lives].")[13] He was married but got divorced after the surrogate mother of his child won custody of their child; his brother is suffering from AIDS; his sister ran away from home and ended up in hardcore porno films, her whereabouts now unknown. Betty's father ran a shop that couldn't compete with McDonald's; he took to drinking and was killed in a drunken car wreck; her sister became "neurotic" and committed suicide. Betty was married to a mentally unstable Vietnam vet who killed eight hostages in a supermarket before being shot by police. She has one son, a drug addict and rapist:

"Does your son play baseball?" [Jack] asked.

"No, he does not play baseball."

"Does he play football?"

"No, he does not play football."
"Does he play the piano?"
"No, he does not play the piano."
"What does he do?"
"Sometimes he does drugs and rapes women."[14]

Turning to their old junior high school in hopes of finding a brighter subject, Jack reveals that it was torn down and replaced by a nuclear power plant where a near meltdown came close to producing a "China Syndrome."

Though on the surface a cataloging of America's woes since the halcyon Ozzie and Harriet days of the 1950s—as well as Americans' desire for a return to that past, a country that wasn't "beset by crack, drive-by shootings, and serial-killer chic,"[15] in the words of James Wolcott—the subtext of the Jack and Betty story for the Japanese reader is unmistakable: present-day Japan—unlike the United States—is most decidedly *not* a country rife with unemployment, drug addiction, hardcore porn, AIDS, or police shootouts with crazed vets. Japan did not experience the fracturing psychological and social consequences of Vietnam, nor is it torn apart by rampant divorce and litigation. In short, a "mature" and ailing America is depicted in unspoken, yet clear, contrast with a Japan that is neither mature, nor sick, but a nation combining an innocent, childlike state with an aggressive and triumphant economic dominance.[16]

Jack and Betty, we must remember, are inextricably linked with the master/pupil relationship obtaining between the United States and Japan at the time they appeared in textbooks (and, arguably, until very recently). At the time the textbooks were in widespread use, America was indeed for many Japanese an idealized country: the maturing superpower tutoring the "nation of twelve-year-olds." In Jack's not uncommon dilemma of losing his job to his former "pupils," we now witness a reversal, for the story drives home an idea much in line with Asada's analysis of postmodern Japan: economic success and an infantile state—in this case, an idyllic state of purity—are reinforcing realities. The "twelve-year-olds" have won.

∎

Probably no other contemporary Japanese writer has explored the notion of the infantile more than Shimada Masahiko, Japanese literature's own enfant terrible.[17] Influenced heavily by the work of Witold Gombrowicz, whose classic *Ferdydurke* (1937) traces the reduction of an adult into childishness, Shimada at times seems intent on rewriting Gombrowicz into the postmodern era his work anticipates.[18] Declaring his own interest in the notion of being a "domestic refugee" *(kokunai bōmeisha),* eternally "in between" Japan and the rest of the world,[19] Shimada in his fiction explores a variety of such refugees: adolescents caught between childhood and a fixed identity and, in some cases, heading back toward the infantile. The work that launched his career, *Yasashii sayoku no tame no kiyūkyoku* (A Divertimento for Gentle Leftists, 1983), for instance, reduces traditional radical student politics from an adult's deadly serious struggle to a childish game. The main character, Chidori, who sees himself as a *henkaya* (perhaps translated as "quick-change artist"), is a member of a university *akai shimin undō* (red citizens' movement). Participating in the activities of the "circle" is much like commuting to work from the suburbs; the activities are safe, almost like a hobby, and they demand not the ideologies of the past, or ideology of any sort at all, but rather "gentleness" *(yasashisa).* "Their activities were laid back," the narrator tells us. "They'd always been taught that political movements were festivals, or plays."[20] After an abortive attempt at real politics, the circle ends up attracting public support through the use of fashion, producing badges to act as their "trademark" that intellectuals, then the "citizens," wear. Far from being bound together by belief in a cause, intellectuals and the people are linked through the wearing of an accessory; in this circle of relationships the badge and the citizens' movement come to be surface phenomena with no more depth or content than meets the eye.

Paralleling this story of the reduction of politics to fashion and childish play is the subplot of Chidori's interest in a girl, Midori. While at first imagining himself driving a wedge between Midori and authority (her father) in order to liberate her (the typical "citizen"), in the end Chidori envisions himself snug and safe in a return to the womb she represents—the "triangular area," *sankaku chitai,* Midori's vagina—which becomes his "safe zone" *(anzen chitai).* The story ends with these words:

> "Don't think. Thinking makes you worry. If you don't want to worry or feel bad, they say it's best to just stop thinking."
> So said Midori—Chidori's guardian god, his Virgin Mary, the vessel big enough for him to fit inside. These were words to save not him alone—but all humankind.[21]

In the Japan of the 1980s, then, the realm of change is limited to the introduction of a new fashion—to a play of surfaces—and the ultimate goal is to be fashionable, cheerful *(akarui)*, and to have fun. And for men, at least, a kind of "growing down" applies to both politics and sexual relations: the ideal is to live, unthinking, in a combined state of dependency *(amae)* and mother fixation *(mazakon)*.[22]

Shimada's 1984 story "Sei Akahito den" (The Legend of Saint Akahito) extends his vision of the infantile to encompass an entire metaphoric country: a thinly disguised Japan. At the very end of the story, the narrator, an old classmate of Akahito's who has followed his career with dread, attempts to assassinate his longtime nemesis, Akahito, the supreme ruler of Taijinkoku (written "Adult Land" but probably closer to "Land of Giants"). Approaching the platform where Akahito is addressing an audience of his literally hypnotized subjects, the narrator lifts up a chunk of concrete he plans to hurl at Akahito. Instead, inexplicably, he hits himself on the head and loses consciousness. This last holdout against the power of Akahito has finally succumbed to the mesmerizing power of this totalitarian leader. Upon regaining consciousness, the narrator finds himself no longer an adult but a helpless infant, in a cradle, unable to articulate anything other than a pathetic "Manma"—a plea to be fed. And hovering over him are his wife and Akahito:

> I was given milk to drink. My wife was changing my diapers. My crotch was bereft of a single pubic hair, and all I had was a tiny white penis the size of a little finger. I couldn't even ask whether this was a dream or reality—all I could do was groan. What had happened to me? Did somebody attach my head to a baby's body? My wife flicked at my helpless little penis with her finger. Along with the pain, my whole body was enveloped in a pleasant sense of floating in a gravity-free space.[23]

The story reaches its conclusion with these words, the protagonist defeated, confused, yet strangely content. In brief the story traces the rise to power of Akahito, son of the most powerful behind-the-scenes leader in the country. Akahito's ascent is no longer in question once his so-called Hypnotism Squad has mesmerized the citizens and helped turn the country into one large amusement park —a "Nonsense Zone" where thinking adults are turned into children more concerned with mud fights than questioning authority. These developments are all seen through the eyes of a narrator who, as leading social critic, rails in his writings against the steady infantilization of the country. As the amusement park threatens to spill over and engulf the entire land, the protagonist writes a piece called "The Season of Childhood Regression":

A society is upon us which urges citizens towards a regression into childhood, disguised in the pleasant countenance of Alice's Wonderland. It is all an exciting show presented in simple words anyone can understand. But there is nothing as awful as utopia. An amusement park where police serve as guides. Where the brainwashed become a trompe l'oeil, a hidden attraction. This is Akahito's Utopian Hell.[24]

Before this regression takes place, though, the story details the ways in which Akahito carefully orchestrates this national mental meltdown. From the very first, power and play are linked: by harnessing the people's dissatisfaction with the "democracy" introduced by Akahito's father and with their increasingly materialistic lifestyle—and guiding it into infantile "play" in his Nonsense Zone—Akahito gains complete control over the nation. At first this zone is dubbed the "Love Zone":

> Love is power [says Akahito]. A zone in which everything is accepted vaguely is a love zone. Not excluding any foreign substances, but including them all. My dream is to rule over Taijinkoku by turning it into a Love Zone.[25]

Excluded from this all-inclusive zone, however, is knowledge of who and what is truly behind it. After gaining enormous wealth through marriage to the daughter of a tycoon, after accumulating both his Hynotism Squad and an elite squad of high-tech specialists (computer programmers, special-effects technicians, chemists specializing in mind-control drugs), Akahito appears, after a three-year absence, in the sky aboard a "castle in the air." Hovering over a crowd outside the Diet demonstrating against a stagnant economy, he declares himself an alien from the planet Sartorenus whose role it is to "transform Taijinkoku into a utopia."[26] He then has mud poured over the crowd of five thousand and a huge mud fight ensues, with salarymen and OLs ("office lady" clerical workers) happily tackling passersby. Akahito next turns to sex to relieve the people's "confusion" by organizing cheap brothels with discount coupons. He has a sci-fi spectacle filmed called "The Seven Days of Creation," the story of a man from outer space creating a paradise on earth. The movie has hypnotic effects built in, the surround-sound of the rhythm of the mother's womb to lull the viewers, and a gas like sodium pentothal released into the theater—all designed to implant in the viewers' minds the hypnotic notion that a "superintellect alien has come to change the history of their country."[27] Finally, anticipating Kobayashi Kyōji's massive *Zeus gaaden suibōshi*

(History of the Decline of Zeus Garden, 1987) and Shimada's own *Rococo-chō,* Shimada introduces the notion of nation-as-giant-amusement-park.

"Sei Akahito den" depicts the end of the country's "Dark Ages" with the construction of a series of new cities built by Akahito, all of them like enormous amusement parks. Fences around established amusement parks are torn down, allowing them to infiltrate nearby residential neighborhoods. In new suburbs without amusement parks, roller coasters, ferris wheels, and the like are brought in: "Once a town took on the function of an amusement park, the personalities of its residents became childish *(kodomoppoku naru).* Once under the sway of Akahito," the narrator tells us, "everyone awoke to a wild, infantile state, easily discarding reason and culture."[28] In a sort of Bakhtinian display of the carnivalesque, all sorts of weird *matsuri* (festivals) spring up, as do miniature cities-within-cities: miniature Dublins appealing to alcoholics and terrorists; imitation Soho districts peopled by artists, sculptors, and architects; and "Barcelona Town," where AIDS patients live out their final days.

"Sei Akahito den" can easily be read as Shimada's thinly disguised history of Japan since the war, ending his negative view of Japan in a postmodern world. In a word, the citizens of Adult Land are anything but adults; their critical powers have been dulled as they spend their days wandering in a vast array of amusement parks where they can play to their hearts' content. The Nonsense Zone of superficial diversity and free play is seductive, Shimada tells us, but dangerous; what appears as a decentered, horizontal world of freedom and equality blinds us to the truly vertical nature of the society: Akahito, backed by the power of multinational corporations, is pulling the strings for his own ends. This is, in short, the Postmodern Condition as dystopic utopia.

This view of the postmodern world as hellish dystopia, however, is notably muted in Shimada's 1989 novel *Yumetsukai* (Dream Messenger, 1992). Instead we are overwhelmed by something quite different: a more positive vision of the postmodern condition that thoroughly (if only temporarily) displaces the earlier vision. In *Dream Messenger,* Shimada shows us the world—Tokyo and New York, in this case—as Akahito's Nonsense Zone, significantly minus any menacing figure like Akahito and his band of hypnotists. It is a more grown-up and mellow vision of the world as stage for postmodern play: the infantilized narrator of "Sei Akahito den" is replaced by the figure of the adolescent Rental Child; the menacing figure of Akahito is supplanted by the grandfatherly Japanese expatriate Katagiri whose orphanage is a front for the training of Rental Children.

Dream Messenger is subtitled "The Rental Child's New Tale of Two Cities," the two cities being New York and Tokyo. A reviewer in the *New York Times* finds affinities between this novel and shaggy dog stories;[29] more accurately it should be read as a decentered novel—or, as Shimada himself does, as a novel-as-opera, a series of arias sung by a vast array of characters who take the stage, sing their piece, and fade away.[30] This is not to imply that there is no recoverable plot— there is a detective-like search for the long-lost son Matthew by his mother—but this main story line soon loses its urgency. Instead we become engrossed in the passing parade of offbeat characters involved in the search for Matthew.[31] As in many Shimada novels (one thinks of *Yasashii sayoku* with its characters Chidori/Midori and another character, Muri, a gloss of which might be "impossible"), there is a decided playfulness regarding the names of characters. "Rokujō Maiko" literally means "a *maiko* (a type of geisha) from Rokujō (a place-name in Kyoto, calling to mind Lady Rokujo of *The Tale of Genji*)"; "Upper West Side Call Girl" might be as close as one might come to translating the cultural equivalent in contemporary English. The "Amino" in "Amino Mika" is a conventional surname, yet its homonym "amino" as in "amino acid" is one Shimada underscores —an appropriate bit of wordplay considering Mrs. Amino's role as progenitor of the life (Matthew/Masao) around which the novel revolves. "Kubi Takehiko" in romanization fails to catch the wordplay of the original: Takehiko sounds like a man's straightforward given name, but combined with the surname it contains the word "Kubittake," meaning "to be head over heels in love" or crazy about someone. (Kubi Takehiko was Shimada's pen name in college.) Finally, the name "Katagiri," while an ordinary surname, came to prominence when an emotionally disturbed captain of a Japan Airlines jet with that name nose-dived his plane into Tokyo harbor in the early 1980s, an incident hinted at in the novel when Maiko first meets Katagiri.[32]

The book ends on a happy note as Matthew reunites with his mother after a monthlong search and, quite predictably, has fallen in love with Maiko, the woman who tracked him down. Interwoven with this third-person narrative is a first-person narrative in Matthew's voice taking us back into his past at the Rental Child agency, where he and other talented children were raised together to be rented out to "Orpharents"—adults who need a child, usually to replace their own who have died. In his present life in Tokyo, he rents himself out to both men and women as a Professional Friend and Lover. Much of Matthew's narrative is in the form of a dialogue with Mikainaito, his alter ego, who allows him to visit the dreams of others, and there are several dream sequences that allow us to define the Japanese title: *Yumetsukai*.[33] Matthew (through the agency of Mikainaito) is the Dream Messenger capable of breaking the barriers between dream and reality, self and other, all in the name of gently helping others achieve happiness and calm. By day, in other words, he soothes the bodies of his clients; by night, he soothes their unconscious. As his very name indicates—he has two names plus an alter ego—Matthew is a subject for whom traditional boundaries of identity do not obtain. He is the American Matthew, the Rental Child and Dream Messenger, but at the same time that he is the lost Japanese boy Masao—and Mikainaito. He is bilingual, bicultural, and bisexual—a person for whom the boundaries of self and other, of nation, of culture, of language, of dream and reality, are no barriers at all.[34]

But standing behind Matthew is another character: Katagiri. Matthew is Katagiri's most successful disciple—the fulfillment of Katagiri's dream to create a new world order peopled by Rental Children. As Ian Levy notes in his Japanese review of *Yumetsukai,* perhaps Katagiri more than Matthew is the most compelling character in the novel.[35] It is the vision of Katagiri, an elderly expatriate Japanese obsessed with his hatred of the emperor system and modern Japan, that guides both Matthew and the novel. Though *Dream Messenger* may at first appear to be an uncritical look at the contemporary world, scattered throughout the work are a variety of characters' harsh words for Japan's politicians, its financial world and salarymen, and even its youth. Tokyo, for instance, is described as a "desert island without a history," an amnesiac city filled with brain-dead young men and women "born in Disneyland, raised in Harajuku, nurtured on McDonald's."[36] All of these comments, though many of them are spoken by Matthew and other characters (or the narrator), emanate from the worldview of Katagiri.

In the long chapter, centering on Katagiri's view of life, that forms both the physical and moral center of the book, we find him a gentle yet bitter man whose hopes are pinned on Matthew and his other former Rental Kids. Hope for the future of Japan, indeed of the world, lies in the creation of an advance guard of Rental Kids—eternal children at play who become leaders of a new order. "A rental child is no one's child, and at the same time everyone's child," he says. "My dream was to raise children like that who could make it without parents, without God, even. . . . All children should by nature be free orphans."[37] By the end of the book, his vision of a new world of Rental Children begins to look like more than an old man's pipe dream. Matthew, now reunited with his wealthy mother, toys with the idea of opening his own Rental Child agency in Tokyo and playing the role Katagiri played for him. The final section of the novel, "Creation," which is Matthew's dream in which he recreates the universe in three days, seems a tacked-on ending until we remember the status of dreams in Matthew's world —only a thin, porous membrane away from reality.[38] This "creation" section ends with these words:

> We are still in the second day of creation. But the morning of the third day will surely come. . . . As long as we stay mired in the night of the second day, this sense of powerlessness and despair can never be wiped away. . . . The world wasn't created according to some plan of an all-knowing, all-powerful god. It came about by accident, through the gods' wasted effort, through unprogrammed, free play. A million gods loved each other, hated each other, grew jealous, went insane, got sick, fought battles, formed conspiracies, were transformed, died and were reborn. And dreamed. And before anyone knew it, the world was born.
>
> Until the evening of the third day, creation is not complete. On the morning of the third day, the rental child will join the gods at play. And the world will never be the same.[39]

Katagiri's vision (as filtered through his disciple Matthew, an appropriate name for a disciple) stands in contrast to that of the earlier character Akahito. Akahito's Nonsense Zone is the result of hypnotism: the product of a forced regression to an infantile state wherein the citizens of Akahito's land are blinded to the truth of their enslavement as they play in his Utopian Hell. What better control technique could there be, "Sei Akahito den" tells us, than to mesmerize citizens into believing they occupy a decentered, horizontal world of free play and equality? But Katagiri is no Akahito, and the world of the Rental Child is far from that of the babbling infant at the end of the earlier work. Instead of an infantilization of the adult, *Dream Messenger* depicts the *maturation* of the Rental Child. The truth of the world is not covered, as with Akahito, but uncovered. Katagiri is not a hypnotist but a meditator, calmly seeking out and releasing the hidden truth. And his truth as spread by Matthew is this: When the Rental Children come into their own, the original nature of no less than the earth itself will be revealed, and we will all act in a chaotic harmony with it—when we *all* become as children at play.

One could, of course, argue that *Dream Messenger* should be read in a much more negative way: as the next step in Akahito's nefarious project, wherein even the unconscious can only work within the confines of a Nonsense Zone. We cannot, in other words, even *dream* ourselves beyond the dystopia we occupy. The dominant tone of the two stories' depiction of the postmodern world—one negative, the other positive—reveals the ways in which Shimada's work shifts between these two quite different stances. Reading "Sei Akahito den," followed by *Dream Messenger,* is an experience very much akin to reading postmodern theory—following up a sober, critical session with Jameson and Eagleton, for example, with some of the more delirious examples of postmodernizing. We should note, too, that such a contrast in Shimada's two works reveals itself not just in content but in stylistic differences as well. "Sei Akahito den" is presented as a single-voiced, first-person history of someone who sees himself as the last rational voice of opposition: an attempt to preserve a historical consciousness in the face of a growing amnesia. *Dream Messenger* is something else again: an explosion within a traditional genre—the detective novel—a decentered parade of enough voices (first, third, and otherwise) to satisfy even the most hardcore Bakhtinian dialogist. Reviewers in the United States, with their "shaggy dog" remarks, see this as merely sloppy writing, as if Shimada still needed a few more years of apprenticeship before he mastered the novel; this shortsighted view, however, misses the fact that Shimada is doing something new with prose fiction, something that goes beyond the institutionalized postmodern quirks he occasionally employs—having himself as one of the characters, having other characters question their fictional status, and the like. In *Dream Messenger* the content and the form work upon each other skillfully: the master narrative is dead; those who were enslaved to it are freed.

If we were to abandon this incomplete survey of Shimada's fiction at this point, we might conclude that Shimada's career is a clear-cut linear development: a progression from skeptic to cheerleader for postmodern infantilism. As one might expect of Shimada, something of a quick-change artist himself, though, this is not the case. In the novel that soon followed *Dream Messenger,* the 1990 *Rococo-chō,*[40] Shimada returns to a position closer to his earlier, dystopic vision of the postmodern. Rococo-chō is the name of a semisecret amusement park, a sort of parallel Tokyo, that the narrator visits and eventually comes to accept as his home. The novel has a certain aura of Michael Crichton high-tech gloss lacking in Shimada's other novels—much of the story revolves around a supercomputer and an operation to realign human genes—but readers expecting the cyberpunk technical sophistication of William Gibson's work (the immediate influence on the novel) will be disappointed. Though less densely populated than *Dream Messenger,* Shimada's *Rococo-chō* combines the earlier novel's preference for a varied cast of eccentric characters, each taking turns telling his or her story, with "Sei Akahito den" 's first-person narrative of resistance to infantilization and the allure of the postmodern space of free play. In *Rococo-chō* we meet a high-tech "shaman" whose computerized helmet is connected to a mainframe, a woman who sleeps with men to help them recover after their genes have been "rearranged," an information peddler linked to a worldwide computer network, and an all-female "Venus Corps" engaged in unmasking the romantic hypocrisies surrounding love. Shimada, known for recycling older material (as if the novelistic process itself was a kind of recombining of "genetic material"), does the same in *Rococo-chō:* the novel combines the amusement park motif of "Sei Akahito den" with Kubi Takehiko's plan for a "Stateless Floating City," a sort of floating Las Vegas in the middle of Tokyo Bay, and, like *Dream Messenger,* ostensibly involves the search for a missing person—in this case the narrator's friend B, a computer genius whose plans for a city of the future have been realized in Rococo-chō.[41]

The narrator of *Rococo-chō*—identified only as M.S. (one of many possible "Masahiko Shimadas," one is to assume)—after much travail makes it to Rococo-chō, where he believes B lives. We soon learn that this is no ordinary town. The narrator must descend a slide into Rococo-chō, symbolic of the return to childhood, the first step in the "education" of its inhabitants. The first scene he encounters is that of a woman being raped. But here, as elsewhere in the town, appearances are deceiving, for the woman turns out to be a professional rape victim to whose thriving business the narrator has temporarily put a halt. This first encounter is significant, for Shimada often uses sexual metaphors in describing encounters with cities. Matthew in *Dream Messenger,* for instance, was "sexually assaulted" by Tokyo; other characters are urged to "have sex" with the city. This sexual encounter also presages the "Sei Akahito den"–like orientation of the narrator's experience in Rococo-chō—the carnivalesque series of mud fights, orgies, and generally chaotic, infantile behavior he encounters.

The professional rape victim becomes the first of the narrator's many guides to Rococo-chō. The novel overall is a kind of bildungsroman as it traces the "education" of the narrator—specifically the gradual breakdown of his resistance to the lifestyles of the town and his eventual decision to undergo genetic realignment. And this he does in a remarkable chapter. This chapter of *Rococo-chō* amplifies the kind of multiple consciousness approach seen briefly in *Dream Messenger* in the following passage:

> Before him [Kubi] saw the entire country, Japan, millions of people, drinking, spewing out their complaints, their misery and jealousy and fatigue enveloping them like mist.

. . . rotten things at work the boss is a pain my husband is cheating on me why go to school just to get picked on better locked up in a Zen temple him or my career? what do you think? I miss him got to be better men around how is one supposed to act gross-looking but helpless office girls falling all over I'm a much better actress but do I ever get a good part? the manager must be plotting against me how could that hack win? . . .[42]

In *Rococo-chō,* in some of the most innovative writing he has done, Shimada expands this technique to encompass an entire chapter. In chapter five, free of his physical body, the narrator flies over Tokyo in a dreamlike, astral-projection sort of state. He eavesdrops on conversations of pigeons; he is inhaled by people, entering their consciousness for an instant; he rides telephone lines, electric waves out into space, enters others' dreams; and finally he is sucked into the artificial intelligence we later learn contains the mind of his friend B.

In many ways in *Rococo-chō* we are revisiting an updated Akahito-like "Nonsense Zone." Becoming a full-fledged citizen of Rococo-chō (and the narrator is informed that the world is full of Rococo-chōs) involves an infantile regression similar in many ways to that in "Sei Akahito den." The narrator sees the town as a vampire: "It makes people regress to being infants, planting in them powerlessness and dependence." A little later he remarks: "I've already completed the final step in Rococo-chō education. In other words, I've regressed to being a helpless infant. Mama, I'm scared."[43] These remarks reveal the stages of his regression and resistance to it: first resistant, later somewhat resigned, yet afraid, by the end of the book he is a budding proselytizer for the place. While in "Sei Akahito den" the adult is reduced to a helpless, infantile state, a child's body attached to a drugged and unresisting adult mind, the final state one reaches in Rococo-chō is that of pure consciousness: attached to a huge artificial intelligence, Ephemera 2014, B's mind, we are told, is floating in one of many possible worlds, most likely a "heaven" of sorts. The narrator, while still hesitant to join B, is given the job of collecting data B sends back from the beyond.

Where "Sei Akahito den" shows a sudden, unexplained reversal of the ever resistant narrator, *Rococo-chō* details in step-by-step fashion the enticements and temptations of infantilization: the narrator's own "growing down" and gradual embrace of what can only be explained as a thinly disguised totalitarianism. He is not hypnotized but a willing participant. Not content to reduce people to physically helpless infants, here the vision concerns a desire to control their consciousness as well. Proclaiming not the freedom *of* the individual, but the much more intriguing freedom *from being* an individual, there is nevertheless no freedom in Rococo-chō. As one character tells the narrator: though we believe the self equals past memories and present position, it is really a machine to "reproduce genetic information";[44] it is when one willfully disrupts this tyranny of the genes that one is able to create an infinite number of possible *different* selves, rather than being but one small link in the endless replication of similar selves. Individuality is but a "myth" of an absolutist state bent on confining "human chaos to a narrow framework."

Rococo-chō, however, harnesses this chaos to produce its own form of absolutism. The supposed dialogic liberation of many consciousnesses that Rococo-chō's genetic realignment promises is, in the final analysis, a *monologic* vision of the subsuming of these by *one* consciousness (Ephemera and B). When the narrator enters Ephemera in chapter five, it is not just one more consciousness he briefly visits, but a glimpse of the single consciousness in control of Rococo-chō. The narrator and all the other citizens of Rococo-chō end up as fragments in the dream of Another—unaware, like characters in a dream, of their very presence within it. In this sense Shimada's version of cyberpunk differs from that of his precursor, William Gibson. Jameson views Gibson's work as an expression of high-tech paranoia "in which the circuits and networks of some putative global computer hookup are narratively mobilized by labyrinthine conspiracies of autonomous but deadly interlocking and competing information agencies in a complexity often beyond the capacity of the normal reading mind."[45] While Gibson's global computer and information networks are certainly echoed in *Rococo-chō,* cyberpunk's conspiracy theory and autonomous agencies are notably muted. We are left, instead, with Asada's blissful (or blissed-out) "protected area": the "seemingly horizontal, centerless 'place' " within which children play—cheerful, unthinking, drained of all power to resist.

In his chapter on theories of the postmodern in *Postmodernism,* Jameson outlines four general positions on the meaning and value of postmodernism (and, inevitably, modernism). These range from Tom Wolfe's pro-postmodernist/anti-modernist stance (an absence of any "Utopian celebration of the postmodern" combined with a "passionate hatred of the modern"); to Hilton Kramer's celebration of classical modernism and denigration of the "fundamental irresponsibility and superficiality" of the type of postmodernism represented by Wolfe; to Lyotard's pro-modernist/pro-postmodernism (which views the postmodern as "the triumphant reappearance . . . of some new high modernism endowed with all its older power and with fresh life"); to Manfredo Tafuri's anti-modernist/anti-postmodernist position that questions the " 'Utopian' substitution of cultural politics for politics proper."⁴⁶ As Linda Hutcheon would have it, however, any stance on the postmodern must take into account postmodernism's character as a divided phenomenon—a "doubleness" that itself is in constant flux between the critical and the reactionary:

> The basic defining feature of postmodernism . . . [is] its paradoxical, not to say, contradictory nature. In both formal and ideological terms, as we have seen, this results in a curious mixture of the complicitous and the critical. I think it is this "inside-outsider" position that sets the postmodern up for the contradictory responses it has evoked from a vast range of political perspectives. What frequently seems to happen is that one half of the paradox gets conveniently ignored: postmodernism becomes either totally complicitous or totally critical, either seriously compromised or polemically oppositional. This is why it has been accused of everything from reactionary nostalgia to radical revolution. But when its doubleness is taken into account, neither extreme of interpretation will hold.⁴⁷

The term "infantile," of course, is a loaded one, carrying with it a fully negative evaluation of the contemporary, and it is in this sense that Asada employs it in his "fairy tale" critique. In Shimada's fiction the infantile becomes not only a critical view of the postmodern condition in line with the dystopic state Asada describes but also a celebration of such a state. And it is precisely this doubled state of his fiction—neither totally critical nor totally complicitous—which makes it particularly postmodern. Certainly it is no difficult task to categorize the three works in line with a critical/celebratory stance in regard to Japan and its "infantile" society: "Sei Akahito den" and *Rococo-chō* critical of an infantilized Japan, *Dream Messenger* quite the opposite; the first two works "moralizing" on the present state of a Japanese "protected area," the last work blissfully, seemingly uncritically, immersed in a "Nonsense Zone." Thus one can see, in Shimada's writings, an on-again, off-again, on-again shift between works. But with fiction such as Shimada's, a more nuanced reading is called for. What makes Shimada's works truly postmodern is the "doubleness" within.

There is a curious formalistic difference between *Dream Messenger* and *Rococo-chō* which indicates that all is not as it seems. *Dream Messenger,* the postmodernist text (in the sense of both its stylistic dialogism and surface celebratory "message"), is structured in the supremely "modernist" genre—detective fiction—while *Rococo-chō,* with its monologic style and surface "message" of modernism's warning against the excesses of the postmodern, is situated within the very "postmodern" genre of science fiction.[48] Further complications, predictably, muddy any attempt to undo this doubleness. For *Dream Messenger* quickly unravels the traditions of the detective story (the missing person is located almost from the start), while *Rococo-chō* introduces the trappings of science fiction and cyberpunk only to deflect any steady focus on them, turning into a much more compelling detective story. Beyond these, of course, are the surface "messages" of the two texts: *Dream Messenger*'s complicity in infantilism, *Rococo-chō*'s critical stance, both of which are undercut by opposing tendencies. In *Rococo-chō*, a critical view of an infantile state is countered by the insistently seductive "feel good" message of the town to which the narrator gradually succumbs. Shimada's fiction always has a decidedly sexist bent: any amusements it catalogs are those of the male (the professional rape victim; the women who use sex to resuscitate post-gene-realignment males). For the male reader at least (one imagines in particular the stressed-out salaryman packed into a sweaty subway car), it is hard to discount the visceral appeal of "letting go" in carnivalesque Rococo style—a way of acting severely circumscribed in modern Japan. One is tempted to say that ultimately Shimada comes down on the side of "letting go"—his narrator, after all, completes his education and ends up sending off letters to entice others to join him (including one to his "extremely curious" friend, the writer Shimada Masahiko).[49] There is, however, a notable ambivalence about him—his reluctance to follow the path of B and join the Ephemeral, for instance, and the curious way in which he is, after all the fuss about gene realignment, left with pretty nearly the same identity with which he began.

Dream Messenger reverses these dominants. From start to finish it displays little reluctance to jump into the fray and feel good. Instead of being plugged into the world through one's consciousness (upper half), Shimada's Dream Messenger and Rental Child knows the world through his lower half. As Shimada puts it in his afterword:

> In the nineties you have to train the lower half of your body. The strong yen makes the lower half wither away. Fulfilling your curiosity through money is not the way to go. The world must be known through the legs, and the genitals. Friends and lovers are the best media for learning about the world, something money cannot buy. It's something you create with your lower half. Just like Matthew.[50]

Behind this life-as-movable-feast approach, however, lies a deeply paradoxical vision: one that involves one of the more contentious areas of postmodern theory—history. Critics on the left have critiqued postmodernism as ahistorical; its cultural products, they say, are a pastiche of disembodied, uncontextualized remnants from earlier periods organized in schizophrenic fashion as disconnected moments in time. Those more sympathetic to postmodernism see its relation to history quite differently: postmodernism is "resolutely historical," containing a "historical consciousness mixed with an ironic sense of critical distance." [51] *Dream Messenger* appeals to both evaluations. In one sense *Dream Messenger* embodies a search for history: the main plot involves a woman's search to recover her son, her relationship with him, and her past. As postmodernist "historiographic metafiction" tells us, though, the recovery of the past is always a problematic undertaking—a point that Shimada's novel underscores: traces of her long-lost child that Mrs. Amino detects in the grown-up Matthew are always mixed with the rewritten history she has inscribed over the years (the "illusion of love" that had "created for her a whole new son"),[52] as well as the reality of the present-day Matthew who, in good Rental Child fashion, sees the infinite possibilities in this renewed relationship, among which is the rewriting of the mother/son relationship as one of woman/lover.

More important, *Dream Messenger* juxtaposes yearnings for historical stability with the disconnected and provisional and contrasts the desire for grounded identity with the untethered life of the Rental Child. The Rental Child is by definition a person without history—or, more accurately, a person with multiple created histories (the fiction of belonging for a time to each new family) who discards the past with each new assignment:

> When a new job came up and we rental kids went off into a new family, we had to erase from our minds all experiences with families we'd known before. Each family had its own ways, and if we wanted to fit in, we had to wipe our slates clean. It was as if nothing at all had happened, and a new story could begin.[53]

Katagiri's dream of a world of orphans, freed from authority, chameleon-like in their ability to confine previous identity and history to oblivion, is countered throughout the book by a desire for history and personal grounding. Matthew's words that, like Gulliver in Lilliput, the world is "here for children to play with," are immediately challenged by his lament over lost history:

> There's nothing around now that can help you get a handle on the history of Tokyo. If you go into the back alleys where the boutiques and restaurants are, it's

all old people and ghosts exhaling their musty breath; they know something about history, but they don't touch anybody, and nobody touches them. Slums are buried one layer underground, with the postmodern structures by Tange and Isozaki pushing down on them like stone weights in tubs of pickling vegetables.[54]

One notes the mention of the postmodern here—and how, in the guise of its most famous emblems, postmodern architecture, it is crushing out the history of Tokyo. Tokyo, as quoted earlier, is an "amnesiac city set in a desert"; Japan is a "desert island with no history." But the second city in this "New Tale of Two Cities," New York, is lauded as the site of a genuine sense of history. Matthew notes:

Katagiri, though, had his own history. I knew why he'd ended up in New York. It's what you call historical consciousness. In New York each person has his own history, his own nation, his own god. New York is where all these things bump up against each other, get mixed together like in a stew. In a place like New York, your sense of history gets focused and sharpened. [p. 59]

Dream Messenger is the story of a wake-up call for Tokyo. Matthew, as well as Kubi and several other characters, are set to transform the city into Shimada's version of New York—a blend of childlike play and cultural diversity on top of a sense of history, mixed in with the fluid identity of the Rental Child. Reveling in this paradoxical mix of a desire for history, a desire for its erasure, plus the fore-grounding of personal history as ever-shifting construct, Shimada's novel refuses to be pinned down.

In this slippery stance of Shimada's toward his subject matter (both the infan-tile and history) lies his (and, I would argue, postmodernism's) ethical moment: a continued resistance to a fixed identity. Just as one thinks one has identified his stance, Shimada, like Matthew, slips from one's grasp. Tatsumi Takayuki, writ-ing on "avant-pop," has characterized the Rental Child as a "typically realistic frag-ment of Japanese postmodern life that not only naturalizes the loss of identity but also capitalizes on this loss."[55] This negative "loss" and subsequent "hypercapital-ization of identity" are certainly at work in *Dream Messenger,* and one notes that Shimada's Rental Children just barely predate the emergence of the actual "rental family" companies in Japan. At the same time, though, the fictional Rental Child in Shimada's world remains a positive model of resistance to fixed identity—or, more accurately, a continually evolving reworking of identities along the lines of the parody of Genesis, the new beginning that ends the book.[56] One is tempted to contrast the figure of the Rental Child (and its grown-up equivalent the Professional Friend) with some of Ōe's fictional children and see in them a shorthand for the differences between the modernist (Ōe) and postmodernist (Shimada) artist. Frog, for instance, the protagonist of Ōe's "The Catch," in line with Ōe's fascination with the figure of Huck Finn, is thrust into a position as outcaste; no longer child, yet spiteful of the adult world, he will be eternally an outsider at a critical remove from society. But Shimada's Rental Child, in keeping with the paradoxical "insider-outsider" of the postmodern, stands totally immersed in the world yet is able to maintain a critical edge. It is here that we find the paradoxical possibilities of the postmodern.

NOTES

1. Asada Akira, "Infantile Capitalism and Japan's Postmodernism: A Fairy Tale," in *Postmodernism and Japan,* special issue of *South Atlantic Quarterly* 87(3) (Summer 1988):631.

2. Ibid., p. 632.

3. Alan Wolfe, "Suicide and the Japanese Postmodern: A Postnarrative Paradigm?" in *Postmodernism and Japan,* special issue of *South Atlantic Quarterly* 87(3) (Summer 1988):587.

4. Ibid., p. 587.

5. Linda Hutcheon, *A Poetics of Postmodernism: History, Theory, Fiction* (New York: Routledge, 1988), p. 201.

6. Fredric Jameson, *Postmodernism: Or, The Cultural Logic of Late Capitalism* (Durham: Duke University Press, 1991), p. 66.

7. Both of these stories are translated by Fredrik L. Schodt in Yoshinori Shimizu, *Jack and Betty Forever* (Tokyo: Kōdansha Eigo Bunko, 1993). Translations from these stories are from this edition.

8. Ibid., p. 53.

9. Ibid., pp. 32 and 53, respectively.

10. For my translation of *Kokkyō no minami* see *South of the Border, West of the Sun* (New York: Knopf, 1999).

11. The ghostly quality of the female protagonist, Shimamoto, is discussed in Yokoo Kazuhiro, *Murakami Haruki 90 nendai* (Tokyo: Daisan shokan, 1994), pp. 1–38. In a personal conversation in January 1995, Murakami lent further credence to such a reading by telling me that the novel was influenced by his reading of the ghost stories in *Ugetsu monogatari.*

12. Shimizu, *Jack and Betty Forever,* p. 8. I have changed the translation of the first two lines to read more accurately.

13. Ibid., p. 9.

14. Ibid., p. 12.

15. James Wolcott, "Beyond the Values of the Supervixens," *New Yorker,* February 13, 1995, p. 90.

16. One should be cautioned, though, that with the recent Aum Shinrikyō terrorist attack on the Tokyo and Yokohama subways, the standard, even smug, contrast drawn by many Japanese between their safe society and that of a fractious, frightening United States may be eroding.

17. The phrase appears in the title of Shimizu Yoshinori's (no relation to the writer discussed here) essay at the end of Shimada Masahiko, *Donna Anna* (Tokyo: Shincho bunko, 1986), p. 198: "Anfuan teriburu no seijuku" (The maturing of an enfant terrible).

18. Shimada presents his own views on Gombrowicz and his influence on his writing in the 1986 essay "Chikasitsujin kara entoropii ningen e," reprinted in *Katarazu, utae* (Don't talk, sing!) (Tokyo: Fukutake bunko, 1991), pp. 52–82.

19. See the interview with Shimada, *"Yumetsukai* o megutte," *Subaru,* January 1990, pp. 156–169, especially p. 169.

20. Shimada Masahiko, *Yasashii sayoku no tame no kiyūkyoku* (Tokyo: Fukutake bunko, 1985), p. 30.

21. Ibid., p. 155.

22. For another view of this story see Isoda Koichi, *Sayoku ga sayoku ni naru toki* (Tokyo: Shūeisha, 1986), chap. 8.

23. Shimada Masahiko, "Sei Akahito den," in *Donna Anna* (Tokyo: Shinchō bunko, 1990), p. 85.

24. Ibid., p. 74.

25. Ibid., p. 59.

26. Ibid., p. 66.

27. Ibid., p. 69.

28. Ibid., p. 70.

29. Julia Just, "In Short" column, *New York Times,* December 27, 1992, p. 15.

30. Shimada, *"Yumetsukai* o megutte," p. 158.

31. To name a few of the prominent ones: Matthew's mother, Amino Mika, a Japanese-American living in Kamakura, heiress to a real estate fortune left by Tanaka Kakuei's right-hand man; Rokujō Maiko, a beauty-queen-turned-securities-analyst-turned-detective who is hired to track down Matthew over two continents; Kubi Takehiko, an ex-novelist and former mental patient whose dream is to float a huge tanker in Tokyo Bay and convert it into a foreign country within Japan; Katagiri Yūsaku, expatriate Japanese in New York who ran the Rental Child agency where Matthew grew up and who dreams of destroying Japan and repopulating it with Rental Kids; Yamashita Tarō, ex-Red Army member, now a bum on the streets of Shibuya in search of descendants of the lost Heike clan; and Nishikaze Tetsuya, paranoid rock star from a tiny southern island who wants to turn the imperial palace into the site of a rock concert and who ends up staging a bloody mini-coup d'état. And tying all of these characters together, however loosely, is the figure of Matthew (also called Masao) and his alter ego, Mikainaito.

32. Shimada discusses some of these names in the afterword to *Yumetsukai* (Tokyo: Kōdansha, 1989), p. i.

33. Shimada speaks of the term *"yumetsukai"* as having a double meaning: both the idea of "dream magician," one who can make good use of dreams, and "dream messenger" *(yume*

no shisha); see "Yumetsukai o megutte," p. 157. What the name "Mikainaito" means is open to interpretation. Shimada says it is the name used by the son of a friend of his for his imaginary friend (*Yumetsukai*, p. i). In the context of the novel (with the mother, Mika, looking for the lost son), "Mikainaito" evokes the Japanese phrase "Mika inai to . . . ," that is, "If Mika [mother] isn't here . . . ," with its implication of a child's longing to be reunited with his mother. (This interpretation is raised by Shima Hiroyuki in the interview "*Yumetsukai* o megutte," p. 160.)

34. It is in this sense that Ian Levy calls it a "bi" novel. See Riibi Hideo, " 'Zai' to 'bai' to, Katagiri no me," *Bungakkai,* March 1990, pp. 313–316.

35. Ibid.

36. Shimada, *Dream Messenger,* trans. Philip Gabriel (Tokyo: Kodansha International, 1992; New York: Warner Books, 1995), p. 205.

37. Ibid., pp. 106–107.

38. This creation section, incidentally, with its view of the world created in half the time of the Bible—as if by stressed-out *sarariimen* working overtime—is strangely at odds with the relaxed tenor of other events in the Rental Child's world. Shimada mentions this section and its status as "tag ending" in "*Yumetsukai* o megutte," p. 167.

39. Shimada, *Dream Messenger,* p. 293. I have taken some liberties with the final sentence, which literally reads: "And stir up the world created by the gods on the second day." Despite the emphatic repetition of the original (English is perhaps less amenable to such repetition in prose), as translator I decided the final sentence needed more impact.

40. The title puns on Rococo "Ville" and Rococo "Style."

41. Rental Children are mentioned in *Rococo-chō* as well (p. 101).

42. Shimada, *Dream Messenger,* p. 193.

43. Shimada, *Rococo-chō* (Tokyo: Shueisha, 1990), pp. 75 and 79.

44. Ibid., p. 74.

45. Jameson, *Postmodernism,* p. 38.

46. Ibid., pp. 55–66.

47. Hutcheon, *Poetics,* p. 201.

48. Brian McHale discusses these genres and their connection with an "ontological dominant" (postmodernism and science fiction) and an "epistemological dominant" (modernism and detective fiction) in his *Postmodernist Fiction* (New York: Methuen, 1987), especially p. 59.

49. Shimada, *Rococo-chō,* p. 243.

50. Shimada, *Yumetsukai,* p. vi.

51. Hutcheon, *Poetics,* pp. 4 and 201.

52. Shimada, *Dream Messenger,* p. 14.

53. Ibid., p. 136.

54. Ibid., p. 58.

55. Tatsumi Takayuki, "Creative Masochism: Abe, Auster, Shimada, Erickson, Numa, or an Approach to Comparative Avant-Pop," unpublished paper, 1993, p. 5.

56. Shimada mentions this idea of work in progress and anti-apocalyptic view of the world in the interview "*Yumetsukai* o megutte," p. 167.

11

ARGUING WITH THE REAL: KANAI MIEKO

Sharalyn Orbaugh

Kanai Mieko was born in 1947 in the city of Takasaki in Gumma prefecture. After graduating from Takasaki Girls' High School, she embarked immediately upon her literary career. In the year following her graduation, 1967, Kanai published several poems in prominent journals; by the end of the year her combined poetry publications had been awarded the eighth annual Contemporary Poetry Notebook Award. During that same year, her first published short story, "Ai no seikatsu" (Love Life), was the runner-up for the third annual Dazai Osamu Prize for fiction. Since that strong beginning Kanai has continued to publish poetry, fiction, essays, and criticism. She is one of very few writers of any generation to remain active on such diverse literary fronts.

Kanai's work has been nominated for nearly every major literary prize. Her 1970 story "Yume no jikan" (Dream Time) was nominated for the Akutagawa Prize. "Puratonteki ren'ai" (Platonic Love, 1979) won the seventh Izumi Kyōka Prize for Literature. The 1987 novel *Tamaya* was awarded the Women's Literature Prize. Her earliest fiction takes the form of short (sometimes extremely short) stories and is notable for its graphic and fantastic scenes. Her short fiction from the 1980s is characterized by themes associated with fantasy or science fiction; it explores postmodernist and deconstructionist techniques and theories. She recently completed a fifteen-hundred-page novel, *Ren'ai Taiheiki* (Love *Taiheiki*), which critics have compared to Tanizaki Jun'ichirō's *The Makioka Sisters*.

Only three of Kanai's short stories have appeared in English so far: "Rabbits" ("Usagi," 1972); "Platonic Love" ("Puratonteki ren'ai," 1979); and "Rotting Meat" ("Funiku," 1972). The two stories discussed in this essay are both from 1982: "1 + 1" and "Ryōseiguyūsha(tachi)" (The Hermaphrodite(s)).

·

Kanai Mieko's work defies easy categorization. Much of her early prose was very short and full of scenes of blood, cannibalism, dismemberment, incest; her recent prose takes the form of full-length "novels of manners" in the style of Jane Austen. As the late Nakagami Kenji pointed out, since her debut in 1967 Kanai Mieko has been remarkable for remaining active on the three fronts of poetry, fiction, and literary criticism.[1] Although still young, and not among the most conspicuous figures in the *bundan* (literary society), Kanai has been writing and publishing longer than any other Japanese writer born after the war. She is knowledgeable about Anglo-European literary and cultural theory—her critical essays cite Lacan, Barthes, and Deleuze—but she revels in pop culture too: a recent book of short essays about the cinema includes a piece on the relative "kissability" of the mouths of Cary Grant and Gary Cooper. (Grant comes out ahead.)[2] I know of no one who has explicitly classified Kanai's work as science fiction, or even fantasy, yet her characters constantly contravene both the normal laws of physics and the normal laws of narrative realism. In bookstores that shelve *"joryū bungaku"* (women's literature) separately—and this still includes most of the bookstores in Japan—Kanai is defined thereby as a "woman" writer. But she herself disavows the characterization "feminist" and says that she has no interest in books written by women for women. Nonetheless, some critics have argued persuasively that, whatever her intent may be, much of her work is feminist in effect.[3] To my knowledge only three of her short stories and one poem have appeared so far in English translation, but she already has a three-volume *zenshū* (complete collected works) of her short fiction.[4] In the scope of this essay I cannot do justice to the many facets of Kanai's writing. Nor, considering the length of her career so far (thirty-one years) and its various changes in focus, can I hope to construct more than a general overview of her work. I will therefore confine

myself to a brief explanation of her background and publications before discussing two stories, written in the 1980s, that are characteristic of her work of that
period.

■

Kanai Mieko was born in 1947. Japan was only two years beyond the end of
World War II and still under the authority of the Allied Occupation, headed by
Supreme Commander Douglas MacArthur. The occupation lasted until 1952.
Thus Kanai grew up in a society that was in recovery from a devastating war and
the almost equally traumatic peace. Although she rarely refers directly to Japan's
specific historical circumstances in her stories, one should keep in mind the discursive context within which her education took place and against the background of which her writing began.

With the loss of the war and its horrific destruction, and spurred by the not
so subtle "encouragement" of the Allied Occupation, Japan in the late 1940s and
early 1950s began a radical questioning of its most fundamental values. The
assumptions that had provided the implicit underpinning for the social structure
were challenged and, in some cases, permanently altered. One example of this was
the relative status of the emperor and the individual Japanese citizen. Whereas
the prewar juridical/social/political conceptualization of "personhood" located the
individual citizen as a lower-ranking element in a hierarchy of sovereignty headed
by a divine emperor, the postwar constitution (in imitation of the U.S. democratic
model) elevated the individual to the position of final repository of state sovereignty
in a secularized political system. The constitution that embodied and enacted this
concept was written by American officers of the occupation and imposed upon
the Japanese. But even after the occupation ended, the provision relating to the
status of the emperor, though much debated, was not revised. Other significant
changes of the period included the enfranchisement of women as full legal citizens and the guarantee of equal rights in marriage. Although one may argue that
much of Japan's prewar epistemic legacy was gradually restored in the fifty years
following World War II, the questioning of fundamental social concepts in this
period had a lasting effect on those who lived through it, particularly those who
were children at the time. The concern of a writer such as Ōe Kenzaburō with
the relationship of emperor to individual can be traced to these immediate postwar questions. Interrogations of the meaning and status of the designation
"woman" appear in the work of many postwar women writers; this questioning
may have been influenced by occupation-period changes as well.

Kanai's father was an avid reader particularly fond of Tanizaki Jun'ichirō. Her mother loved movies, and Kanai accompanied her to the theater from infancy. One event that seems to have had a profound influence on Kanai's life and writing career was the death of her father when she was six years old. Kanai has commented that for her the act of reading was a way of escaping the "nightmare of dark death and absence" engendered by the loss of a parent.[5] Kitada Sachie goes further and attributes the origins of Kanai's writing, particularly her obsessive concern with the meaning of writing itself, to the attempt to escape from the "uneasiness of absence into the unreality of a 'world of enchantment.' "[6] In any case, Kanai began writing both stories and poetry in elementary school and decided at that point to become a writer. In junior high school she went to the movies as often as twice a week and continued her writing. In high school her preferred reading included Ishikawa Jun and Sakaguchi Ango. She began reading modern poetry during this period as well.

After graduating from Takasaki Girls' High School, Kanai embarked immediately upon her literary career. She felt that the preparation for college entrance exams was a waste of time and that college-level studies would not contribute significantly to her writing. In the year following her graduation, 1967, Kanai published several poems in *Gendai shi techō* (Contemporary Poetry Notebook) and elsewhere; by the end of the year her combined poetry publications had won her the eighth annual Contemporary Poetry Notebook Award. During that same year her first published piece of fiction, "Ai no seikatsu" (Love Life; *Tenbō* 8 [1967]) was the runner-up for the third annual Dazai Osamu Prize for prose fiction.

After this auspicious beginning, Kanai continued to publish prolifically. In the first half of the 1970s she published two poetry collections—*Madamu juju no ie* (Madame Juju's House, 1971) and *Haru no e no yakata* (The Hall of Spring Pictures, 1973)—as well as two volumes of short fiction: *Yume no jikan* (Dream Time, 1970) and *Usagi* (Rabbits, 1973). The story that gave *Yume no jikan* its title was nominated for the prestigious Akutagawa Prize. Between 1975 and 1980, she published three more collections of short stories: *Akashiya kishidan* (Acacia Knights, 1976), *Puratonteki ren'ai* (Platonic Love, 1979, winner of the seventh Izumi Kyōka Prize for Literature), and *Tangoshū* (Vocabulary List, 1979). In 1974, Kanai produced her first full-length novel: *Kishibe no nai umi* (Sea Without a Shore). Nakagami Kenji praised the work for its "absolute refusal to pander to popularity" and its "utter smashing of the lukewarm *monogatari* (tale)" tradition.[7] But, perhaps not surprisingly, *Kishibe no nai umi* did not achieve the popularity to which it refused to pander. It was not until eleven years later that Kanai returned to the long-fiction format.

During this first full decade of her career, Kanai's idiosyncratic voice and themes emerged and developed. As Kitada Sachie points out, all the stories in the *Yume no jikan* collection feature a female protagonist who is searching for the missing *"ano hito"* (him/her/that person), who is named only as "P." In this first collection of her stories, she was already exploring the theme of the search for "the absent," the unrecoverable, which Kitada associates with Kanai's search for the origins of writing itself (and which may more mundanely be associated with the search for the lost, unrecoverable father).[8] The next collection, *Usagi,* was more varied in theme and structure, but here too the stories are concerned with the search for an absent lover and the connection of that search with the act of writing or creativity. The story that gives the collection its title, "Usagi" (Rabbits; trans. 1982), opens with a writer putting aside her pen to go out for a walk. That walk leads to an encounter with a remarkable young woman, dressed entirely in rabbit skins, whose obsessive love for her father has left him dead and herself half-blind. The story is violent and extremely disturbing. But as I have argued elsewhere, its main concern is the nature of gender roles and the possibility of transcending those roles through performance (such as narrative).[9]

The final three collections of this decade focus on the metafictional theme of writing. Kanai is concerned in these stories with the relationship between writer, reader, and text—or, rather, she is concerned with the impossibility of distinguishing these roles according to some unique function. The reader of a story "writes" it as she reads; the writer of a story "gets it" from somewhere impossible to identify and claim as her own (perhaps even from the letters of "the real" author, the woman who continually claims to have originated the writer's stories in "Puratonteki ren'ai" [Platonic Love; trans. 1985]); and the story itself exists only in the mise-en-abyme sense of a production that is constantly re-produced, and differently, by each reader and has no existence outside that unceasing re-production. In the *atogaki* (afterword) of the *Puratonteki ren'ai* collection, Kanai explains it like this:

> Considering the fact that a person reading a text will shave away some parts by skipping over them, and will write in new things by reading words that aren't there, it is not merely the person called the writer who writes a text, the reader also "produces" a text. The writer of the resulting story is certainly not "I."[10]

In fact, in all of the "afterwords" of the story collections from this period, Kanai discusses her complex attitude toward the act of writing. In the *atogaki* to *Akashiya kishidan* Kanai likens the writing of a text to Penelope's weaving of cloth. Believing that her husband Odysseus was still alive, Penelope put off the many suitors for her hand by promising that she would choose among them as soon as she had finished weaving a certain piece of cloth. Although she could be seen working steadily on the cloth every day, she secretly undid the weaving at night to gain time. In Kanai's case, she explains, the "unweaving" at night of what she has written by day is not deliberate: it occurs through dream, through the passage of time, and through the resulting distance from whoever she was who wrote yesterday. Rather than a piece of weaving that deliberately is not completed, her work is a piece of "weaving" that cannot be completed. It continually unravels on its own.[11] Kanai has written that *"watashi no 'ai' "*—probably "my 'I'," but also possibly "my 'eye'," or even "my 'love' "—must become aggressive when faced with this situation: in a world where a sentence unravels as soon as it is written, the most admirable writing is that which questions the act of writing itself.[12]

Given this complex, even deconstructionist, view of fiction, it may easily be imagined that Kanai's stories do not offer the reader a simple or straightforward "reading experience." Upon first reading of a story, it is often difficult to distinguish who is "speaking" at a given moment and what the discursive location of that speaker might be. Kanai often avoids the kind of obvious punctuation markers or paragraph divisions that are usually used to indicate changes in speaker or other significant narrative junctures. And since Kanai's plots are not necessarily bound to physical reality or narrative realism, events may be related that strain the reader's normal suspension of disbelief. I will offer some examples of this practice later in the essay when I discuss two of Kanai's stories in detail.

Between 1978 and 1982 Kanai ran a regular column of critical essays in the journal *Umi*. These were collected and published in 1983 as *Kotoba to "zure"* (Language and "Disjunction"). The essays address topics from literature to film to the general intellectual climate and also cover a range of registers from playful to dense and theoretical. Throughout the 1980s and into the 1990s, Kanai continued to write short stories and critical essays, but she also began devoting more of her time to longer fiction. She published several more collections of short stories: *Ai no seikatsu* (Love Life, 1981), *Kuzureru mizu* (Crumbling Water, 1981), *Ai no yō na hanashi* (Stories Like Love, 1984), and *Akarui heya no naka de* (In a Bright Room, 1986). The grotesquerie and graphic violence of her early stories gradually faded from her work in this period, but Kanai was as relentlessly "transgressive" as ever in her exploration of difficult and often troubling themes—such as sex/gender roles or the nature of subjectivity—through her relentlessly antirealist prose style. Several of her "short story collections" during this period seem designed to transgress generic boundaries as well. *Kishi no machi* (Déjà-vu Town, 1980), for example, includes both short prose pieces by Kanai and photographs by Watanabe Kaneto. *Hanabi* (Fireworks, 1983) mixes prose and poetry. Hasumi Shigehiko has called Kanai's short fiction *"geijutsu tanpen"* (artistic short works) in an effort to describe the provocative, complex, antirealist nature of her texts.[13] These collections, too, are extensions of that will to artistic expression and resistance to the easy assignment of categories that characterizes so much of Kanai's short fiction.

Her longer works, however, are narrated differently: more accessibly. In them she builds worlds that reflect realistically, though with great irony, the lives of urban intellectuals. These novels include *Bunshō kyōshitsu* (Composition Class, 1985), *Tamaya* (1987, winner of the Women's Literature Prize),[14] *Indian samaa* (Indian Summer, 1988), *Dōkeshi no koi* (A Clown's Passion, 1990), and *Ren'ai Taiheiki* (Love *Taiheiki*, 1988–1994). In response to the discovery by several critics of various links between *Ren'ai Taiheiki* and the long novels of Tanizaki Jun'ichirō, particularly *Sasameyuki* (The Makioka Sisters, 1948), Kanai has said that her intent was closer to the novels of manners of Jane Austen than to Tanizaki.[15] And in response to further critical questioning about her future intentions, Kanai has replied that she will continue to pursue both tracks of prose fiction: long realist novels and the short *"geijutsu tanpen"*—which I prefer to think of as her "arguments with the real." In the remainder of this essay I want to concentrate on Kanai's short fiction and the ways it constantly challenges the grounds of both narrative and "real-life" cognitive structures.

•

The title of this essay, "Arguing with the Real," is taken from a chapter of Judith Butler's *Bodies That Matter: On the Discursive Limits of "Sex."* Butler's discussion concerns sex/gender as performativity, a subject about which she has written extensively. She sees performativity not as "the efficacious expression of a human will in language" but as "a specific modality of power as discourse." Discourse, in her terms, "materialize[s] a set of effects," and these effects are "vectors of power." At the risk of oversimplifying Butler's complex discussion, I want to focus on one particular aspect of her model of discourse and the performance of identity or subjectivity.

The acquisition of a (seemingly) stable, unchanging personal identity is an imperative in contemporary postindustrial capitalist societies. The materialization of this identity is effected through a set of related imperatives: the imperative to be "sexed" as either male or female, for example. (In addition, the acquisition of identity in many societies includes the imperative to be "raced" or "tribed" or "languaged" or "religioned" or "casted"; different imperatives configure the identificatory parameters of different societies.) We may hardly be aware of these imperatives because they form the most elemental basis for each person's understanding of the discursive universe (the specific cultural and historical context) within which he or she lives. As Butler puts it: "The power of discourse to materialize its effects is thus consonant with the power of discourse to circumscribe the domain of intelligibility."[16] These identificatory imperatives are not, however, stable or exhaustive; nor are they necessarily invisible, even though we rarely stop to analyze them. The identificatory systems within which we live—such as a culture's gender system—are no more than metaphors or discursive paradigms; they are not "natural" and therefore inviolable. Yet, living within such a system, we are subject to its power to "circumscribe intelligibility." Talking specifically about the materialization of "sex," Butler writes:

> This imperative, this injunction, requires and institutes a "constitutive outside"—the unspeakable, the unviable, the nonnarrativizable that secures and, hence, fails to secure the very borders of materiality. The normative force of performativity—its power to establish what qualifies as "being"—works not only through reiteration, but through exclusion as well. And in the case of bodies, those exclusions haunt signification as its abject borders or as that which is strictly foreclosed: the unlivable, the nonnarrativizable, the traumatic.[17]

It is precisely these margins, these "abject borders," that Kanai's stories relentlessly explore. As Butler indicates, it is the paradoxical power of these excluded elements simultaneously to secure and to fail to secure the borders of materiality. An exploration of the ways that the excluded continues to "haunt" signification provides the basis for many of Kanai's *"geijutsu tanpen,"* or arguments with the real.

In 1982, Kanai published two stories that directly address the constitutive imperatives of contemporary subjectivity: "1 + 1" and "Ryōseiguyūsha(tachi)" (The Hermaphrodite(s)).[18] Both stories were included in the 1984 collection *Ai no yō na hanashi*. In a 1991 interview with Suzuki Keiji, Kanai commented that these two stories were similar to each other in several ways and both were somewhat different from the rest of her work at that time—the main difference being the obvious science fiction or fantasy quality of the stories.[19] When "The Hermaphrodite(s)" first appeared, Abe Kōbō, Japan's most famous writer of this genre, called Kanai to compliment her on the story. Kanai tells Suzuki that this alarmed her somewhat: she evidently had not intended to produce something that would attract the attention of sci fi or fantasy professionals. In this interview Kanai relates that the title for "1 + 1" was inspired by the Godard film but says the idea for its theme came from Flaubert's (unfinished) *Bouvard et Pécuchet* (1881).[20]

∎

"1 + 1" opens with a voice telling us that it is the time of day and time of year when the secretary of the office turns on the light before she leaves:

> This isn't an area that ever gets completely dark, but [I] had the feeling that there was still some time to go before the sun completely disappeared and the long dim dusk turned into a darkness appropriate to nighttime.[21]
>
> Outside the window was dyed a dusty yellowish gray, no, rather than dyed, the blue color of the sky was fading, and someone, no, not someone, it was of course the female employee in her black rimmed glasses—farsighted—who was office girl and receptionist and accountant and PR person, and who even, when the need arose, served as our *(bokura no)* private secretary, who pressed the switch next to the entry door for the fluorescent light.
>
> Regarding pressing the switch, there was always an argument. She said that a switch is something you "turn on," while we always insisted that a switch is something you "press." [pp. 258–259][22]

In the next paragraph the female employee argues that most household appliances, for example, have "on" and "off" written by the switch. The person/people identified so far only by the pronoun "we" *(bokura)* reply that these terms refer to the electric source within the appliance—whether the electric flow is on or off—whereas their use of the word "press" refers to the action performed on the switch itself. "Neither is wrong, it's just a difference in where you choose to aim your words," *bokura* conclude (p. 259).

Like the beginnings of many Kanai stories, this is all very perplexing. The narratorial voice is clearly first person, and as soon as we reach the first actual pronoun, *"bokura,"* we realize that it is first-person plural (and masculine).[23] This plural narrator is itself fairly unusual in narrative fiction. (And in every other case I can think of, plural narrators work sequentially, taking turns narrating in first-person singular voice different aspects or points of view of a story.) But another difficulty arises when we try to situate ourselves as the audience to which this odd narratorial voice is directed. *"Bokura"* are simultaneously explaining things to us that we could not be expected to know—such as the nature of the female employee's job and the recurring argument over proper diction—and at the same time narrating as if we already know quite a bit. The first paragraph ends with the words *"ki ga suru,"* which would usually be interpreted to mean (particularly in the absence of any personal pronoun) "I thought," or "I felt." It is not until the middle of the next paragraph that the narratorial voice is revealed to be plural. And yet there is no attempt either here or at any point in the text to make explicit the nature of that plurality. It soon becomes clear that we will have to figure that out for ourselves.

These opening paragraphs do, however, suggest models for the kind of thinking that may illuminate the nature of that plural narrating subject. The seemingly trivial discussion about the proper verb to use when talking about the daily act of turning on a light is concluded by *bokura* commenting that the difference between the two opinions merely reflects a different conceptualization of what constitutes the act, and neither conceptualization is more "true" or "accurate" than the other. The different conceptualizations focus on different levels of "the real" —one focusing on the internal workings of the invisible animating source (the flow of electricity) and the other on the most superficial and visible action that produces the desired result (the movement of the switch from one position to another). When conceptualizing subjectivity, too, it is possible to speak of different levels that do not necessarily reveal themselves in the same way in discourse—levels that may, in fact, appear entirely contradictory when brought into comparison with each other.

Light, particularly as it changes with the seasons, is one of the recurring concerns of our narrator(s). *Bokura* make it clear, though without saying so directly, that it is not just natural light that reflects seasonal change, but also the myriad of artificial lights with which modern humans surround themselves. Immediately following the discussion about the proper terms for turning on the lights, *bokura* tell us that during this season (spring or fall, evidently) the female employee flips on the fluorescent light switch as she is leaving the office for the day:

> Usually that is the time when we are most absorbed in our work, and so we have
> the fluorescent Z-lamp on our desk turned on the whole time, but around then
> [as the female employee is clearing off her desk preparing to leave] we begin to

feel that the space around our back and shoulders and ears has become dark. During this season that's how it works, but if this were winter, it would be different. The overhead fluorescent light would have been turned on much earlier, and she would not yet have left, but would be bustling about continuing her work. [p. 259]

In the reader's quest to find out more about *bokura* (how many people are in this plurality, where are they located in relation to each other and to the woman, why do they speak with "one" voice?), this paragraph is interesting because it includes the words *"senaka ya ryōkata ya ryōmimi,"* which I have translated as "back and shoulders and ears" but might be more literally rendered as "back(s?) and both shoulders and both ears." Although the distinction between singular and plural nouns in Japanese is often ambiguous, the phrasing here is such that it requires some effort of interpretation to recall that these body parts are meant to refer to more than one physical subject. But in the paragraphs immediately following this one, we are given more "information" about the nature of *bokura*—information that pointedly reminds us that we are dealing with more than one subjectivity. *Bokura* tell us that in response to questions about their work, they always reply that it consists of "collecting and analyzing certain data." When the questioner next asks what those data are:

"Well, generally," one of us answers, "every kind," the other continues, and then the first again, "you might say." [p. 260]

[*"Sō, oyoso" to no ippō ga kotae, "arayuru koto" to ippō ga tsuzuke, mata ippō ga "to, itte mo ii kamo shiremasen."*]

Bokura thus seem(s) to consist of two distinct halves—which, however, share one consciousness. The next question that might occur to the reader, then, is whether they also occupy one body. If so, then we might be dealing with a narrator who presents to the eyes of the world the appearance of a perfectly normal, singular human creature (perhaps someone who is merely confused about his subjectivity or even "mentally ill"). If not—if the two halves of *bokura* are also distinct spatially—then we will have to consider how it is possible for one consciousness to exist simultaneously in two places. (Perhaps it is meant as some sci fi type of creature, not human, in a world where such things are possible.) Are we supposed to read this as realism or as fantasy? How can we tell? From the point of view of "the reading experience" this text (like many of Kanai's short works) is ambiguous and frustrating (or perhaps tantalizing) in the extreme. The frustration is exacerbated by the fact that the text moves from this promising increase in information about the narrator(s) into, once again, a discussion of light in different seasons:

> In this season, after the office girl leaves, we usually work late.
>
> You might think that would have no connection with the season, but nonetheless, when we finish the day's work, get on the train and go home, it suits our taste better if it is already dark outside. In this season, the sky doesn't take on its diluted indigo night color until after 7 o'clock. Lights from the countless windows in the buildings crowding this area and the neon signs flashing off and on like festival fireworks from the tops of the buildings for Instant Curry Mix and cosmetic products and pawnshops, intersection traffic lights, lighting used to illuminate the letters on various billboards, the orange glittering night lighting equipment of the batting center and the rooftop driving range with its green net enclosure, the deep red-dyed large-scale night lighting curving in the shape of a covered bowl in the sky over a faraway amusement park and baseball stadium located on high ground, and of course the counterclockwise and clockwise trains [of the circle line] that get more frequent around that hour turn on their bright inside lights, and all the train-cars pass each other packed tightly with commuters. The long thin lights like movie film shaking and glittering brightly as two trains pass each other go by in violent bursts like an old-fashioned flashlight reflected in the black glass of one row of windows in the building opposite ours where the lights have already gone out, but rather than saying that they "go by" or "rush by," we would say that they scrape by with a deafening noise, leaving invisible, indefinable wounds.
>
> And then from the rooftop beer garden which has been hung round with peach and aqua cocoon-shaped paper lanterns alternately, peach, aqua, peach, aqua, we hear the raucous performance of an amateurish rock band. [pp. 260–261]

Kanai has said that she most appreciates fiction that engages all five of the reader's senses; certainly this passage is evidence that she incorporates that strategy in her own work.

This wild ungrammatical description of lights is designed to evoke the elements of night scenery that are significant to *bokura*, who purposely stay late at work until the world outside exhibits these characteristics. Combining evidence from this descriptive passage and others later in the text, it is possible to identify the location of the story as Tokyo and to narrow that identification to the Mejiro –Ikebukuro–Ōtsuka area. This is, in fact, an extremely accurate description of the material reality in an identifiable urban area. This accuracy of representation lends weight to the reader's desire to read this as "realism"—meaning that *bokura* must be a confused subjectivity inhabiting the normal world-as-we-know-it. But the most arresting and significant point of this passage is its dense "materiality" in all senses of the word. *Bokura* are describing both the natural and man-made/ artificial elements of material reality that surround modern urban inhabitants. Of those man-made elements, nearly all are related to the material wealth of consumer society: food, products, amusements, performances, trade (the pawnshop), transportation, and the "work" that makes consumption possible.

In the next few paragraphs, *bokura* describe a typical day's work, including the overtime mentioned earlier. Then, in a new paragraph, *bokura* comment:

> *Kō kaku to, maru de, bokura ga taihen kinben na ningen de aru ka no yō ni omoware-kanenai ga, mochiron, sonna koto wa nai.* [p. 262]

The most straightforward translation of this passage would have to be: "Having written this, we must surely be thought to be an extremely diligent person, but, of course, that isn't so." Again the nature of *bokura* is thrown into question by the semantic incongruity of "we" and "a person."[24] But for the narratorial voice, that is not the point of this discussion; *bokura* are simply trying to explain their attitude toward their work. *Bokura* go on to tell us that they often amuse themselves by thinking of all the things/people they did not, but could have, become. And in the course of this explanation, we get more information about the nature of *bokura:*

> We were born and raised in different, widely separated places, but we have childhood memories that we share in common, and those memories, oddly enough, are exactly the same down to the very smallest detail. For example, one of the jobs that we didn't choose, but wanted to choose, was that of bicycle racer, and when we try drawing maps or something for each other, we are always surprised at how exactly they match. In the neighborhoods of the castle towns where we were born, there lived a bicycle racer. [p. 263]

Bokura is two people, it seems. As they continue to tell us their common childhood memories, however, the perfect matching of every detail is increasingly unbelievable. This is not the usual "shared memory" of two people born at the same time in a particular culture. *Bokura* both remember how the bicycle racer's brother, who was said to be an idiot, always defeated the local greengrocer's attempts to cheat him. They could have been that idiot, they say. They both remember every feature of the *"abon"* salesman—*"abon"* was their childish word for *"shabon"* (soap). This *"abonya"* always wore a too-short dark-blue kimono and walked the streets pushing a baby buggy containing his cosmetic products. He had a clubfoot and a very peculiar way of hawking his wares. They could have become the *"abonya,"* too, they say. Or else a carpenter, a bicycle store owner, a train conductor, a movie theater projectionist, a librarian; or they could even have been born a woman, they conclude. Any of those alternatives to their current "reality" would have been good:

> In that way we would talk about our own "things we didn't become," "things we couldn't become," "things we wanted to become," and "things we tried to become."
> [p. 264]

At this point *bokura* repeat the opening sentences of the text, changing the order of the clauses only slightly. They talk about the sky slowly darkening into dusk. Then they begin talking about their work, saying that sometimes they are asked about it by a man they frequently see at a bar near their house. He suggests that "the collecting and analysis of data" could be better done by computer. In their turnabout manner of speaking a sentence, *bokura* explain to him why they don't use a computer; they manage this without giving the slightest indication of what their data are or what the goal of their analysis might be. And in the course of this explanation, *bokura* comment parenthetically that the man is sitting between them. Again we are forcefully reminded that this is one consciousness (or two identical consciousnesses?) occupying two separate bodies.

Finally *bokura* decide that we should know more about what their work consists of:

> In this season, about thirty minutes after the sun has set, we put away that day's work, for the time being, arranging it in a-i-u-e-o order in a gray file box, but it must be emphasized that this can only be a temporary arrangement. We use the fifty headings of the a-i-u-e-o system, and each of those fifty headings is further divided into the forty-eight headings of the i-ro-ha system, and each of those

forty-eight headings is further divided into twenty-six headings using the alphabet in capital letters, and each of these is further broken down into twenty-six headings using the alphabet in lowercase letters, and those are further categorized using numbers—this is the method we employ because "This kind of classification method is the only method for making absolutely clear the differences in things . . . , and the reason is that if there is any mistake, more mistakes will grow from that one, and that will further cause one after another, an unlimited number of mistakes . . . "—this is clearly written in the General Research Plan distributed by the high-level people in our company, and it's a real pain. Those people who don't know the situation seem to think that we do nothing but copy out each word and each letter of the stuff we call data, and even the female employee in our office seems to believe that, and frequently sneers at our work. [p. 266; ellipses in the original]

After this explanatory passage, *bokura* return again to the "real time" of the day they are describing. They call a temporary end to their endless sorting task, attend to the details of shutting up the office, and leave the building. After having boarded the small tram, they remember for the first time that tomorrow is a holiday and regret not having left work early to take in a movie. But perhaps they could celebrate the evening in another way:

We discussed the possibility of getting off at a station where we'd never gotten off before and finding a place in that area to eat. But that's kind of a lot of trouble, let's go to the café in our usual neighborhood, said one half of us, and get the B set course, the other half added. The usual routine, the usual life. "And, on the way home" "we'll stop off at that place" "of course, is there any other" "place to go?" [p. 268]

Arriving at the usual café, *bokura* are told that the B set course is sold out; only the A course is left. They know that this is ridiculous: the A course is exactly the same as the B, but it contains more of each item and is slightly more expensive. If the ingredients for A are available, the ingredients for B must also be available. Nonetheless they do not protest and order the A course. "It's depressing to be cheated like this" "but if we pretend that we ordered the A set from the beginning" "we'll feel okay" (p. 268). From there they go to their usual bar and meet the man they usually see there. When they tell him about the A and B set courses at the café, he criticizes their failure to protest to the manager (pp. 268–269):

Saying that we should point out to the manager that it doesn't make logical sense to claim that the B set is sold out when the A set is still available, he says that we should march right over to the café together and have it out with the manager, so we look at each other and chuckle. From the open window of the bar, we can see the small yellow train go by bright and glittering in the light, and because it really does make the sound gatan-goton gatan-goton as it goes by, we laugh all the more, and we laugh so much that the man looks from one of our faces to the other with amazement, and this causes his head to shake gently from side to side.

"Tomorrow's" "a holiday" "right?"

"Let's go" "to the zoo"

■

This is how the "story," if that's the appropriate word for this text, ends—with no final punctuation, no plot, and no resolution. Clearly it has been from the beginning a sort of puzzle or experiment. Kanai sets up a problem for the reader to solve: what is the nature of *bokura*'s subjectivity? As I read through the text attempting to solve that puzzle, I inevitably use my knowledge of what subjectivity is in what I take to be "the real" world. In this case, that reality includes both "real life" in contemporary Tokyo and the "real-ist" possibilities of narrative fiction. Like the protagonists of Flaubert's *Bouvard et Pécuchet* (the unfinished novel that provided the inspiration for "1 + 1"), the narrators of this story are bourgeois, repetitive, and trivial.[25] The unremarkable nature of their observations and comments, the dull, tedious nature of their job, and the simple, commonplace nature of their entertainments lend an almost inescapable air of realism to the story. If they are meant as some sort of fantasy or science fiction prototype for a new subjectivity, it is difficult to imagine what the advantage could be in such a model. Rather, the point of their existence seems to be that, as my own assumptions about the possible or "intelligible" types of subjectivity are confounded at point after point in the story, I am forced to see the parameters of that intelligibility. Kanai makes me think about how the modern subject is constituted both through identity and exclusion, as *bokura* constantly reveal themselves as inhabiting a subjectivity that is excluded from current conceptions of "the real."

The story opens with light and the seasons. Certainly modern conceptualizations of an individual subjectivity include the sense that it moves in a linear way through time toward its own dissolution. In contrast to that one-way movement of inevitable change, the cyclic nature of daylight and the seasons provides a reassuring coherence. Since we move through time in recognizable cyclic patterns of light and dark, cold and hot, we are less conscious of the relentless linear movement toward the end. Moreover, because one day is like another, and one year like the previous one, we become convinced that we are individual subjectivities that also remain stable from one moment or one day to the next: I saw the sun come up yesterday, and I see it come up again today—that "I" must therefore be the same "I." The recognition that "I have done this before" or "I know this pattern" is fundamental to the construction of a sense of the continuation and uniformity of the self.

We often associate these cyclic patterns with changes in natural light, but *bokura* point out the ways that artificial lights fulfill the same function. *Bokura* are extremely conscious of the fact that the hour when the female employee flips on the overhead light changes from season to season, and therefore the length and rhythm of *bokura's* working day also changes. Living within this rhythm is part of what gives *bokura* their sense of continuity. In contrast to this seasonal pattern, the night lights of Tokyo are always the same. They become visible earlier or later depending on the season, but since *bokura* always stay at work until after dark, they always experience the lights in the same way. These lights, too, provide shape for the individual subjectivities that live with them. They illuminate against the darkness all the trappings of modern urban culture: consumer goods, prepackaged amusements, recreation facilities, transportation, and "work." (*Bokura* make the packaged amusement of their local bar into one of the rituals that gives their life shape: "the usual routine, the usual life.") We are stable in our individual subjectivities because we consume and play and move and because we hold specific jobs in a huge economic network in order to make the consumption and play and movement possible. That which consumes must exist, must be "real," we tell ourselves. That which fills a specific economic niche must be identifiable, must have a necessary role in this "real world." The fact that all of these goods and services and buildings are just artificial constructions does not impinge upon their function as comforting, stabilizing markers of a cultural system of reality that includes (at least potentially) a place for each individual subjectivity.

As *bokura* lovingly describe the various lights of their nighttime neighborhood, they connect some of the specific lights with cultural icons from Japan's past. The Instant Curry and cosmetic advertisements are like festival fireworks, they say; the huge lights at the stadium and amusement park are like a covered lacquer soup bowl; the lights from the train windows as they flash by are like an old-fashioned flashlight; the paper lanterns are like cocoons. The festival fireworks are markers for seasonal/cyclic activities, the bowl and flashlight mark inconsequential items of daily use, the cocoons mark the foundations of a traditional craft/industry; these are signs of a previous cultural construction within which subjectivities were controlled, defined, and found a sense of stability. That they have been replaced by these new cultural constructions does not in any way change the fact that material objects—past or present—are used to protect and enhance a sense of coherence and belonging. How could we be said to exist, who or what would we be, if the trappings of our "real life"—urban capitalism—suddenly and permanently disappeared? And yet how can it be that our individual identities are dependent upon these artificial, ever-changing constructions?

The second theme that *bokura* bring into their narrative is the dislocations and gaps and contradictions in language that make it possible for one action to be described accurately using two entirely unrelated verbs: "turn on" and "press." As *bokura* point out, each is perfectly appropriate to one particular model of the workings of electricity, and models are "valid"—that is, both adequately represent the "reality" of electricity as we experience it. It is impossible to refrain from extending this cognitive paradigm to the problem of subjectivity as well. There may be two, or several, or an infinite number of models that reflect the "reality" of subjectivity as we experience it. Each person's preference for a particular model (preferring "press" to "turn on") can be traced to the conceptualization of subjectivity that seems primary to that person. Some might prefer, like the female employee, to valorize the internal workings of the invisible animating source; others might prefer to put the emphasis on the most visible, pragmatic, verifiable model. In either case—or in the potentially limitless number of other possible cases—we are given to understand that neither word, neither model, is monolithic or final.

Bokura return to this theme several times in the text. The bicycle racer's brother, "said to be an idiot," is in fact revealed to be quite clever. The *"abonya"* is really the *"shabonya,"* and it presents a grotesque appearance completely out of keeping with his perfumed, elegant wares. While most people might describe the Yamanote line trains as "passing by" or "rushing by" the window, *bokura* prefer to think of them as "scraping by," leaving long invisible wounds in the air behind them. Aurally, this might be a far more accurate description of the phenomenon. The A set course and the B set course both are and are not really the same thing; but *bokura* view attempts to argue the point a waste of time, even laughable. In both Japanese and English, one of the fundamental characteristics of "the subject" *(shukan)* is a "subjective" *(shukanteki),* unique point of view. In a world where each person's conceptual model of a phenomenon may be different, yet equally "valid," what is the use of attempting to establish an ultimate truth? Yet as *bokura*'s job indicates, the compulsion (to attempt) to reduce phenomena to a nonsubjective, verifiably true form is powerful and seems related to the maintenance of a stable identity.

A stable identity is also constructed and maintained by means of exclusion: *bokura* are who they are partly because of who they are not. They could have become, but didn't, the bicycle racer, his "idiot" brother, the *"abonya,"* or female, or many other things; the shape of what they are now is determined by this set of excluded possibilities. Certainly to be male is in large part to be not-female; to be human is to be not-animal; and so forth. But as *bokura* remind us, identity construction includes choices or performances that do not always take the simple form of conforming to one "half" of a binary model and excluding only that other "half." They list the patterns, the possibilities, they have known in childhood; from such early patterns we choose and exclude and are chosen and excluded, but the result is thought to be one final, stable, identifiable subjectivity. From *bokura*'s "things we didn't become," "things we couldn't become," "things we wanted to become," and "things we tried to become" there emerges the one thing they did become—although just what that is remains somewhat mysterious in this case.

It is often believed that we take our identities in this world partly from what we do—the niche we fill in what is figured as a huge web of production, commerce, consumption. *Bokura*'s work is clearly fundamental: *bokura* identify and classify and file—so carefully and in such detail that there is not the smallest chance for a mistake. Unless, as the directive from the "higher-ups" warns, there should happen to be a mistake—in which case that mistake will produce other mistakes in an endless stream. The imperative to identify, classify, and file comes from this directive of the superiors. And the material that must be collected, analyzed, and filed is "'in general' 'every kind.'" It is partly through this action of classifying—defining the world around them and controlling it through neat categories (although that control is always vulnerable to endlessly proliferating error)—that *bokura* construct and maintain their subjectivity.

It is at least partly through the same kind of compulsion that I construct and maintain mine. It is therefore deeply troubling when I find that I cannot classify and file away the vision of subjectivity presented in this text. At the surface of the story *bokura* narrate a succession of metaphors or analogs for various conceptualizations of identity construction and performance, making clear the tentativeness, unverifiability, mutability, and vulnerability of these conceptual structures. So far so good. But the subjectivity providing this interesting narration incorpo-

rates characteristics that I cannot make consonant with any of the conceptualizations of "selfhood"—even narrative selfhood—that I know of. It is singular but
dual; it possesses one set of memories, one job, one set of preferences, one set of
daily behavior and thoughts and movements, but two faces, two voices, two bodies. It is surprised at the identical nature of its shared memories but takes all its
other surprising shared behavior for granted—at least *bokura* narrate as if their
audience already knows their nature, recognizes this model, and takes it as "normal," as existing in the domain of the intelligible and "real." Among various
models of modern identity there are certainly those that incorporate a "pairing"
of subjectivities: twins, sexual couples, and so on. But *bokura* fit none of these.
Bokura violate the "laws" of physics, one of our most potent touchstones for the
real.

And that, finally, is the point. In being what cannot be, *bokura* reveal the margins of subjectivity. Far more potently than *bokura*'s narrated metaphorical structures (riddled though they are with disjuncture), *bokura*'s narrating "voice" reveals
the discursive limits that materialize subjectivity.

■

The second story from 1982 that I want to discuss here is "Ryōseiguyūsha(tachi)"
(The Hermaphrodite(s)). From the title alone one can guess that this story, too,
is concerned with boundaries that configure identity—in this case "male" and
"female"—and the "violation" of these boundaries. It is as if Kanai has this time
set a problem for herself rather than the reader: to imagine the ramifications of
being able to escape from the polarization of sex/gender.[26] What would it require
and what would it mean for an otherwise human creature to be somehow beyond
or free of gender concerns? How would an entire society of such creatures differ
from the gender-determined world we know? How would such a species reproduce? What would be the myths produced by or about such a society? By what
system would such a society configure moral law or conduct?

This set of questions is remarkably like those used by Ursula Le Guin in constructing her science fiction novel *The Left Hand of Darkness*.[27] Both Kanai and
Le Guin are attempting to explore, through fiction, the possibilities that are
excluded by the constitutive terms of modern society. While I am not aware of
any direct connection between Le Guin's novel and Kanai's story, I will use *The
Left Hand of Darkness* as well as Le Guin's subsequent essays on the process of writing it to illuminate the differing ramifications of posing the questions in the context of Japanese and North American gender systems.

Compared with "1 + 1," the discursive location, or structure, of "The Hermaphrodite(s)" is made clear (or at least clearer) from the beginning. The story opens with an unidentified first-person narrator describing a meeting that she or he attended. (It is impossible to tell the gender of this opening narrator, but this is a "normal," single-sex human being.) As she or he describes the meeting, the reader begins to understand that its purpose was to introduce a "race" or "society" of hermaphrodites to a general (single-sex) audience. The speaker at the meeting was a member of that hermaphroditic "race."[28] The speaker at this gathering was entirely neuter in appearance, we are told by the opening narrator. The members of the audience at the meeting were not physicians or biologists, so they could not pose analytical questions about the body parts that frame sex identity and in which, of course, they were most interested. On the other hand, the narrator comments, because they are not physicians and biologists, it may be that for them sexuality is framed in terms beyond mere anatomy. Of course there was that one woman in the audience from the "Getting to Know the Female Body by Having Women Show Each Other Their Uteruses and Vaginas with a Speculum Group" who tried to convince the speaker that s/he (the hermaphrodite speaker) had a right and duty to show his/her organs and see those of others—the only way to fight the mystification that so long surrounded, for example, the female body. And then there was that man who laughed at her, saying that this kind of "uterus worship" was a sign of mental illness. And after that, the meeting broke up in disarray. And there had been problems all along with the technical systems: the microphone and amplifiers needed constant adjustment, there were shrill bursts of static and times when the microphone went completely dead, so that it wasn't possible to hear everything the speaker said. Nonetheless, the speaker had remained calm and composed through it all. After this introduction, the opening narrator disappears entirely. What we are reading seems to be the narrator's transcript (minus, of course, those inaudible parts) of the speaker's lecture.

Besides establishing for the reader the discursive setup of this story, this opening also introduces the kinds of problems that always arise in a gendered society when we try to analyze the nature of sexual difference or try to imagine an alternative to our polarized gender system. Is gender determined by clear-cut anatomical difference; or is "sex identity framed in terms beyond mere anatomy"? Are women better off with a gender system that makes of them mysterious objects of desire or one that valorizes the demystification of the body through exposing it —including exposing it to ridicule? The fact that it is a man and a woman whose disagreement over these issues causes the meeting to break up in disarray indicates the difficulty of getting one gender to take seriously the other's point of view. And the technical problems parallel the epistemological gaps that inevitably accompany any attempt to think about gender. If a person has achieved adulthood with one particular anatomically and culturally marked gender, how is it possible to know or accurately imagine anything not determined by that gender?[29] The audience could not hear all that the speaker said—just as those of us with an established sex/gender identity would find it difficult to take in all the aspects of a human experience outside our own sex/gender coding. The recurrence of the figure of Tiresias in Western literature is a sign of the desire to reach beyond the sex- or gender-determined limitations of experience—to know what the other knows— and the impossibility of achieving that desire.[30]

Kanai's hermaphrodite speaker begins by warning the audience against taking the notion of hermaphroditism as mere allegory. S/he is real—no matter how much that may seem to run counter to established scientific views, such as the theory of evolution. S/he explains quite clearly the differences between what the audience takes to be normal gender and the situation of his/her own society:

In your world, it is taken as an absolutely "natural law" that switching between the polarized or dualistic sexes of male and female is impossible, that one is endowed by nature with a gender identity and retains that from birth until death. As Freud indicated with his phrase "biology is destiny."

The world, the world of living things, is divided into male and female.

There are of course creatures who do not possess either a male or female sex, such as the primitive organisms that rely on asexual reproduction—that is, who reproduce by simple cell division—but among higher organisms it is thought that the polarized sexes female and male, or to put it another way, the obvious differences identified as female and male, are an extremely logical and rational part of the evolution of living creatures.

When it comes to our case, we do not multiply through simple asexual means like amoebas or molds; we of course multiply, or rather, we have children, through sexual reproduction.

Our uniqueness, then, lies rather in the fact that we are not differentiated into two polarized sexes.

That is to say, in our society, the constitution of a person's sense of coherent self-identity through gender is not possible.

Of course even so, the concepts female and male, or the facts female and male, do exist.

But these do not accompany our sense of the development of a coherent self-identity.

The reason is that we are periodically male, periodically female, or neuter.
[p. 244]

The speaker goes on to talk about the theory of evolution, the molecular biologist François Jacob's theories about the compulsion of primitive organisms to reproduce, and the idea that higher organisms do more than simply replicate themselves: they produce "better" and "stronger" offspring through the combination of different genetic codes. In this respect the hermaphroditic society is the same as that of the audience. In this section of the lecture, in other words, the speaker is setting out for the audience the "scientific" parameters surrounding the exploration of the notion of gender. This is a rhetorically appropriate place to start, given the modern world's intense valorization of scientific, "empirical" explanations as sources of validation and authorization. In this discussion the speaker includes the psychological ramifications of these biological paradigms—another of modern society's sources of authorization. In this respect, the hermaphroditic society does differ fundamentally from that of the audience, but this difference is made more comprehensible by its framing within the paradigms of Freudian psychology.

Next the speaker turns to history. S/he mentions several instances of true hermaphrodites (humans possessing both male and female external genitalia) that appear in the historical records of ancient Greece, medieval China, medieval Europe, and so on. S/he relates how, in many societies, such beings were regarded as freaks and were killed. In other cases, children born with two sets of genitals were assigned a gender by their father or godfather; upon reaching their maturity, they were allowed to choose to retain that gender or switch to the other; but then they must adhere to the identity of that one gender for the rest of their lives. A failure to do so was seen as "homosexuality" and liable to whatever penalties that brought.

Yet the speaker warns that these historical instances are all a matter of a genetic accident or mutation: these hermaphrodites were the children of "normal" parents, and the children of these hermaphrodites were anatomically "normal," too, that is, possessing only one set of genitalia. In his/her hermaphroditic "race," however, all the people were born from hermaphroditic parents and all give birth to hermaphroditic children. In their case it would require a genetic mutation to lead to a single-sex child. Besides the external secondary sex characteristics, all the people in that "race" possess fully functional uteruses and ovaries, as well as the sperm-producing organs within the testicles and so forth. Another feature that distinguishes the speaker's "race" from the hermaphrodites appearing in historical records is the fact that they periodically change from one sex to another. S/he explains that the body naturally changes from male to female, or vice versa, at intervals of between one month and one year. In other words, a person never remains in one sexual configuration for less than one month or for more than one year.[31] While pregnant, the body remains "female" for the duration of the pregnancy and lactation periods. But, as the speaker remarks, it makes no sense to say that the pregnant person is "female," since every adult is capable of attaining that condition. There is no "femaleness," no "motherhood," possible under those circumstances. "And this is also to say that there is no possibility of 'maleness' or 'fatherhood,' nor any social opposition constructed around 'male' vs. 'female'" (p. 248).

Here the speaker has moved from the context of history to that of sociobiology: how bodily functions (such as pregnancy) are framed in structures of social discourse. Ursula Le Guin has written that she took great pleasure in the sentence, "The King is pregnant"—to the extent that it could almost be called the inspiration for the entire society she creates in *The Left Hand of Darkness*. That a king —normally associated with the ultimate in patriarchal, abstract power—could in this society experience pregnancy—normally associated with the essence of gentle motherhood and the inescapable physicality of the female body—was for Le Guin the key contradiction that could usefully confound readers' assumptions about the natural order of society.[32] The impact of the idea that all adults in a society are just as capable of (susceptible to) getting pregnant as they are of impregnating others is weakened somewhat in Kanai's speaker's straightforward statement. Nonetheless, since nearly all theorizing about gender roles returns ultimately to the fact that "women" get pregnant and "men" do not (and therefore it is "natural" to divide social roles along sex/gender lines), the ramifications of Kanai's hermaphroditic social structure are as significant as Le Guin's.

The hermaphrodite speaker continues in the sociobiological vein, extending the discursive or conceptual ramifications of his/her "race's" biological difference. Like the question posed to Tiresias regarding the relative degree of male and female sexual pleasure, the speaker addresses the question of which sex/gender experience is more "complete" *(kanzen)*. Unlike Tiresias, however, the speaker is unable to provide a clear answer. Since his/her society is not unacquainted with the values, religious ideas, morals, philosophy, and science of the outside world, the hermaphrodites are of course aware of the prevalence of this question in "normal" human discourse (and the relentless valorizing of the male experience). Sometimes they will even be struck by the unhappy compulsion to try to answer the question themselves. But if one's self-identity is based from birth upon being both "male" and "female" sequentially for all of one's life, how can such a question have any meaning? As the speaker explains, the physical changes from one sex to the other are quite dramatic and unmistakable: when one is female, one is completely so; when male completely male. How could one of these states be more intense or more complete than the other? The speaker relates how in their own society's past, there were periods when the people would attempt to keep to one sex only, just like those in the outside world. These attempts always led to madness and self-mutilation, proving that for members of the speaker's "race," to be "complete" means to be both sexes, not one or the other.

The speaker then turns to the eroticism of gender in his/her progress through the various discursive contexts within which sex/gender is constructed. Although the hermaphrodite has long been a figure in "normal" society's art and literature and has often been presented as an elegant if slightly perverted object of desire, the speaker warns against seeing his/her society as some utopic, polymorphously perverse playground. In the first place, his/her people are not simultaneously male and female like the hermaphroditic figures in art and literature. At any given moment the people in the speaker's society will be either in their male or their female form. The eroticized hermaphrodites of art and literature have the piquant combination of voluptuous breasts with male musculature and male genitalia or a curvy female figure equipped with an impressive penis: the speaker's "race" is not like that. Neither do they adopt extreme versions of the external trappings that mark masculinity or femininity in the outside world, such as makeup or gender-marked clothing and accessories. And although members of the hermaphrodite society are physically capable of having sexual intercourse (hetero- or homosexual) with single-sex humans, they generally prefer their own kind, the speaker explains.

Next the speaker turns to myth, beginning with myths told within hermaphrodite society about their origins. One myth says that long long ago there was one pair of human beings, one male and one female. They loved each other exceedingly and were ecstatic in their sexual pleasure. But no matter how perfect the ecstasy of melting into one another, there always came a time when they returned to the realization that they were separate. So, thinking they would like to return to the state Plato had talked about when two people had originally been joined together, they prayed to the gods to bring it about.[33] The god who had created them duly granted their wish. But instead of making them one flesh, the god mixed up the parts of their bodies so that each had both kinds of genitals. Thereafter the children of the couple were also born as hermaphrodites.

The speaker points out that this myth frames the origins of the hermaphroditic "race" in terms of a "mistake" caused through an excess of sexual pleasure and desire. Then s/he relates a second myth, one that came along much later. According to this story, originally humans were divided, like the rest of the animal kingdom, into two sexes. Men were strong and brave—like the lion or the peacock, they possessed vivid outward signs of their manliness. Women, too, were clearly marked as female, with rich breasts and soft curving hips and stomachs. And everyone was happy. But then one woman—more lascivious than all the rest—grew dissatisfied at being limited to the pleasures a woman can experience. She wanted to know what it felt like to experience pleasure as a man. She had her husband sacrifice the largest bull in the land and prayed to the gods to change her into a man. Her prayer was answered, but not in the way she had expected: she became a hermaphrodite, retaining her voluptuous female form but also growing a magnificent penis. Unfortunately for her, her husband was disgusted by her new form and divorced her. Neither could she attract any women with whom to try out her new maleness. But eventually, of some young man or woman whom she finally seduced, the "race" of hermaphrodites was started. This myth, too, founds the "race" upon an excess of desire and a mistake. But this time it is one insatiable female, rather than a loving couple, who is responsible.

Having explained the myths of his/her society, the speaker ends with a brief description of their social structure, laws, and morals. Their society has no history of a time when (hetero)sexual intercourse was the only accepted form of sex. From the point of view of creatures who are physically and psychically organized as they are, the idea of one sole legitimate form of pleasure is ludicrous, the speaker explains. And for creatures who switch sexes at least once a year, the idea of a monogamous couple—one husband, one wife—is also patently unworkable. There is no guarantee that both would switch sexes at the same time; in fact it is highly improbable that they would. Therefore, if their society had had moral or legal sanctions against having heterosexual sex outside the confines of a "couple," their race would never have reproduced enough to survive. They do, however, have other sexual prohibitions. For example, although it is in no way prohibited or even frowned upon to have heterosexual sex outside the confines of an acknowledged "couple," it is considered a betrayal and a violation of morals to have sex outside the "couple" with someone who happens to be in the same sexual period (female period or male period) as oneself: same-sex "adultery" is forbidden. But this is an odd prohibition when you think about it, says the speaker, since if the two people involved just wait a short time, one or the other will switch sexes and whatever they choose to do with each other will be sanctioned.

At this point the speaker ends the talk, remarking that s/he was not able to touch upon the "neuter" sexuality of children or the details of pregnancy and birth. Nor was there time to discuss language or religion. But as the very first discussion of this hitherto unknown hermaphroditic society, the speaker hopes that something has been accomplished.

■

This is the way this story ends: with the same set phrases heard at any formal lecture. And presumably it was after this, during the question and answer session, that the meeting eventually fell into disorder and confusion.

One notes that Ursula Le Guin traces a similar path in her creation of a world in which the sex/gender systems are different from our own. Into her narrative she mixes the formal reports of an anthropologist and an ambassador (whose role in explaining his world is rather like that of Kanai's speaker), several different myths and ancient tales, scientific speculation about the origins of the ambisexual humanoids, and so on. Most of Le Guin's book concerns the friendship that develops between a single-sex human male and an ambisexual Gethenian; this dimension is completely lacking in Kanai's much shorter work. Nonetheless, Le Guin's plot cannot stand alone without these various supporting documents, each representing a different discourse of sex and/or gender. Current conceptualizations of the "meaning" of gender tend to configure individual experiences of gender identity; it is pointless to attempt to analyze gender solely in terms of anatomical "facts" (some of which are more ambiguous than is usually acknowledged). And these "current conceptualizations" are constructed through multiple discursive streams, including the myths of one's culture, popular beliefs and stories, and anthropological, linguistic, psychological, sociological, legal, economic, and medical paradigms. To try to imagine one's way out of our sex/gender system requires the untangling of elements from all of these contexts.

I would hesitate to argue that either Kanai or Le Guin succeeds completely in shaking loose the cognitive strictures that accompany gender. But both provide opportunities for provocative speculation. Why does homosexuality remain "off limits" in both imagined worlds (impossible, in fact, in Le Guin's)?[34] Surely the contemporary construction of gender owes nearly as much to oppositional contrasts between gay and straight as it does to contrasts between male and female.[35] Neither pursues the "economic" ramifications of this kind of society. Would industrial capitalism as we know it be possible in a world not configured by differentiated gender roles?[36]

In "The Hermaphrodite(s)," as in "1 + 1," Kanai does not provide a fully formed utopian model for some new kind of subjectivity. She leaves many questions unanswered. But here, as in all of her work, she makes visible some of the paradigms within which we live: the "naturalized," "hegemonic" structures so fundamental to the constitution of individual subjectivity. She makes these paradigms visible by crossing the boundaries that are normally taken as natural and inviolable and making protagonists of those "impossible subjectivities" that cathect the margins of what we take to be "the real." In this sense, it seems appropriate to repeat the opening line of this essay, this time with a different emphasis: Kanai Mieko's work defies easy categorization.[37]

NOTES

1. Nakagami Kenji, "Kōshitsu no kagayaki o hanatsu kotoba" (Language that gives off a hard radiance), in *Kanai Mieko Zentanpenshū*, vol. 1 (insert) (Tokyo: Nihon bungeisha, 1992).

2. Kanai Mieko, *Tanoshimi wa TV no kanata ni: Imitation of Cinema* (Pleasure is far from TV: Imitation of cinema) (Tokyo: Chūōkōronsha, 1994). This is the second collection of Kanai's essays about film. Her first was *Eiga—yawarakai hada* (Movies—soft skin) (Tokyo: Kawade shobō shinsha, 1983).

3. Kitada Sachie makes this argument in her insightful essay on Kanai: "Usagi," in *Tanpen josei bungaku: Gendai* (Short literature by women: Contemporary), ed. Imai Yasuko, Yabu Teiko, and Watanabe Sumiko (Tokyo: Ōfūsha, 1993). See also Komata Yūsuke, "Kanai Mieko—Gengo geemu no hatsuwa," pt. 5, "Feminizumu: Josei kūkan no genzai" (Feminism: The contemporary space among women), *Kokubungaku: kaishaku to kyōzai no kenkyū* 37(13) (November 1992). I have also made this argument at some length in "The Body in Contemporary Japanese Women's Fiction," in *The Woman's Hand: Gender and Theory in Japanese Women's Writing*, ed. Paul G. Schalow and Janet A. Walker (Stanford: Stanford University Press, 1996).

4. *Kanai Mieko Zentanpenshū*, vols. 1–3 (Tokyo: Nihon bungeisha, 1992) (hereafter *ZTP*). In addition, her poetry has been anthologized in *Gendai shi bunko: Kanai Mieko shishū* (Modern poetry library: Collection of Kanai Mieko's poetry) (Tokyo: Shisōsha, 1973), and a selection of her short works has been anthologized in *Chikuma shobō gendai bungaku taikei*, vol. 93 (Tokyo: Chikuma, 1978). Three of her stories have been published in English translation: "Rabbits," trans. Phyllis Birnbaum, in *Rabbits, Crabs, Etc.: Stories by Japa-*

nese Women (Honolulu: University of Hawai'i Press, 1982); "Platonic Love," trans. Amy Vladeck Heinrich, in *The Shōwa Anthology*, vol. 2, ed. Van C. Gessel and Tomone Matsumoto (Tokyo: Kodansha International, 1985); "Rotting Meat," trans. Mary Knighton, *Fiction International* 29 (1997).

5. Quoted in Kitada, "Usagi," p. 153.

6. Ibid. I am indebted to Kitada's work on Kanai for much of the biographical information included here. I have also consulted *Gendai josei bungaku jiten* (Modern women's literature dictionary), ed. Muramatsu Sadataka and Watanabe Sumiko (Tokyo: Tōkyōdō, 1990), and the *nenpyō* (biographical and bibliographical chronologies) and *kaisetsu* (explanatory notes) in the three volumes of the *ZTP*. There are no complete biographical and bibliographical sources on Kanai Mieko; here I have collated information from journal interviews with Kanai, library holdings, and the sources just mentioned. Although this information is as complete as I can make it, it is not comprehensive.

7. Nakagami, *ZTP* 1 (insert):1.

8. Although Kitada does not speculate about this, it is difficult to refrain from associating the initial "P" with the interconnected notions of, in the first place, papa/paternity and, second, penis/phallus. In the Lacanian psychoanalytic schema of child development, the realm of the symbolic, which includes language (and therefore writing), is governed by the "law of the father" and organized around the economy of the phallus. In this regard it is also appropriate to associate the letter "P" with "pen," which Gilbert and Gubar (among others) discuss as a (fetishistic) metaphor for the phallus. In these stories Kanai is constructing a complex narrative web of the relationships between her literal father, patriarchy, and the act of writing.

9. Orbaugh, "The Body in Contemporary Japanese Women's Fiction."

10. The *atogaki* (afterword) is reproduced in *ZTP* 3:602–603. This quote is from p. 602.

11. Reproduced in *ZTP* 3:599–602.

12. Quoted in Kitada, "Usagi," p. 153. Because the word *"ai"* is written with katakana syllabary, rather than with a Chinese character, it is impossible to know which of the three meanings Kanai actually meant. (It is likely that this ambiguity is intentional.) Since katakana is normally used for words of non-Japanese origin, one could argue that the first two possibilities—"I" or "eye"—are the most plausible.

13. Hasumi Shigehiko, *Aratana tenki no yochō no naka de* (Interview with Kanai), *ZTP* 2 (insert):2.

14. Although *Tamaya* may also be considered a group of linked short stories, Kitada classes it among Kanai's *chōhen shōsetsu* (full-length novels) and I have done the same. See Kitada, "Usagi," p. 156.

15. Interview: "Ren'ai Taiheiki no shūmatsu o megutte" (Concerning the completion of *Love Taiheiki*), *Subaru*, December 1994. Interview conducted October 11, 1994; interviewer Yoshikawa Yasuhisa. *Ren'ai Taiheiki* ran serially in *Subaru* from June 1988 to October 1994 (with a few breaks). In all it comprises sixty episodes and 1,500 pages. *Ren'ai Taiheiki*, like Tanizaki's *The Makioka Sisters*, is in three sections *(jō, chū, ge)* and features a family of four sisters and chronicles, among other things, their attempts to find husbands. Kanai remarks that she is certainly familiar with *The Makioka Sisters* and may well have

been inspired by it. She denies, however, any direct or sustained links between it and her novel.

16. Judith Butler, *Bodies That Matter* (London: Routledge, 1993), p. 187.

17. Ibid., p. 188.

18. "The Hermaphrodite(s)" was first published in *Subaru 6*. This special issue of *Subaru*, published in June 1982, was titled "Joryū sannin shū" (Collection of three women's literature writers); besides Kanai, the authors Saegusa Kazuko and Yoshida Tomoko were featured.

19. Although many, perhaps most, of Kanai's works of short fiction involve the "fantastic" violation of some physical or temporal boundary, the two stories in question are actually premised upon an impossibility. Her other stories might be located in the normal, real world, but they involve temporary or eventual transgressions against "the real." Because the categories of fantasy and science fiction have so far been delineated and theorized only in the context of Western-language literature, I hesitate to lean too heavily on the distinction between the two in my discussion of Kanai's work. It is interesting to note, however, that "the fantastic depends for its effects on the uncertainty of vision, a profusion of perspectives and a confusion of subjective and objective," on "play of pronoun function," and on the period of uncertainty before determining whether a story inhabits the real or the supernatural: once it is clearly one or the other, it moves into a new category. This set of definitions is assembled by Carol Clover in *Men, Women, and Chain Saws: Gender in the Modern Horror Film* (Princeton: Princeton University Press, 1992), p. 56, n. 52 and p. 67, n. 4. Here she is summarizing the definitions of Rosemary Jackson, Mark Nash, and Tzvetan Todorov. These characteristics sound extremely close to the key features of "1 + 1" and, in somewhat lesser degree, many of Kanai's other stories. From the beginning of "The Hermaphrodite(s)," however, we are aware that we are in a supernatural context, making it much closer to the classic definitions of science fiction.

20. Suzuki Keiji, "Kannō teki na mono o megutte" (interview with Kanai), *ZTP* 3 (insert):2–3.

21. Kanai Mieko, "1 + 1," *ZTP* 3:258–269; hereafter page numbers are noted parenthetically in the text; all translations are mine. Because Kanai's use of paragraphing and punctuation is often idiosyncratic, I have made every effort here to maintain the diction, punctuation, and paragraph divisions of the original, even when this policy resulted in less than felicitous English. The use of the pronoun "I" in brackets in the first paragraph is meant to indicate that until reaching the first Japanese pronoun, in the middle of the second paragraph, this would be the default assumption of a reader.

22. The word I am translating here as "turn on" is written with the character for *"nyū"* (or *iru/hairu*) and might therefore be more literally rendered as "to flow in" or "to let in." The opposite action, which I translate as "turn off," is written with the character *"kiru"* and might more literally be translated as "to cut off" or "disconnect." The Japanese word used here for "press" is *"osu."*

23. The plurality "we" represented by the pronoun *"bokura"* could include a woman or women, too, so long as the primary speaker of the group were a man. At this point, there-

fore, we have no way of knowing either the number or the genders of this group. Later in the story, however, we discover that *bokura* is only two "people," both of them male.

24. This is partly a problem that becomes noticeable when one translates into English, of course. Nonetheless, a more natural phrasing avoiding all incongruity would be "*Bokura wa taihen kinben de aru.*"

25. Bouvard and Pécuchet do not narrate their own story, it should be noted. The story is told by an omniscient third-person narrator. And the nature of their subjectivities is never in question: they are "normal" people.

26. Contemporary theorists of sex and gender usually make a distinction between the two. "Sex" refers to the physical aspects of this type of categorization—the XX versus XY chromosomal structure—or the clear-cut presence of the primary sexual characteristics—penis and testicles versus vagina and ovaries, for example. (There are, of course, rare instances when these "absolute," material definitions are ambiguous.) "Gender" refers to the masculine and feminine roles that are created within specific historical and cultural circumstances and with which people identify. Gender is marked by clothing, language, and other sorts of "presentation of self." The reason for this differentiation is that some people of one particular "sex" (body type) may have a cultural identification associated with the opposite gender: biological men who feel themselves to be feminine, for example. In this story, as in life, the two are conceptually and experientially intertwined in complex ways. In the hermaphroditic speaker's society, it seems likely that "gender" is much less of an issue than it is in "normal" society: the speaker is completely "neuter" in appearance, we are told. But since s/he is speaking to a gendered audience, the behavior and facts s/he describes call up our own notions of culturally constructed gender identities and roles. I therefore will not attempt to maintain a complete distinction between my use of the terms "sex" and "gender" in what follows.

27. Ursula K. Le Guin, *The Left Hand of Darkness* (New York: Ace Books, 1969). This book won both of science fiction's highest awards: the Hugo and the Nebula awards for best science fiction novel of the year.

28. Kanai Mieko, "Ryōseiguyūsha(tachi)," *ZTP* 3:242–257; hereafter page numbers are noted parenthetically in the text. Although the frame narrator is a "normal" single-sex human, it is not possible to determine his or her sex by any linguistic cues. It is significant that Kanai exploits the possibilities of (written) language to leave this determination ambiguous.

29. Again this question, like the story itself, presumes that the reader has a "normal," stable sex/gender identity. Those whose sex and gender identity is more ambiguous obviously have a very different experience.

30. In Greek myth Tiresias was blind but had the gift of second sight. Because he had spent seven years as a woman (the result of having seen two snakes mating), he was the only creature to know both male and female experience. Zeus and Hera called upon him to settle their argument over whether men or women had more physical pleasure from sex. He replied in favor of women, 9 to 1. (It was for this decision, in fact, that he was blinded by Hera.)

31. The hermaphroditic or ambisexual nature of the Gethenian humanoids in *The Left Hand of Darkness* works somewhat differently. Each Gethenian is sexually neutral for most of the month. Then, for about five days, each person enters an estrous stage, during which sexual satisfaction is the only goal. (During this period each person is excused from work and other responsibilities; the timing of this period is different for each person.) It is impossible to know in advance whether one will spend this sexually active period as a male or a female—that is determined by hormonal changes which take place in response to a potential sexual partner. That partner, too, develops a gender in response to the first person. If the partner who has become female for this period gets pregnant, the body stays essentially female for the duration of pregnancy and lactation. But then it returns to its habitual neutral state and develops no predisposition to becoming one gender or the other during estrus. As in Kanai's model, it is possible for the mother of several children to be the father of several others.

32. Le Guin has written several essays about *The Left Hand of Darkness*. One of the first such ("Is Gender Necessary?" first published in *Aurora*, 1976) defended her decision to retain male pronouns—he, him, his—and male-identified titles—king, brother—to designate the ambisexual humanoids inhabiting the world of Gethen. She argues in this essay that the masculine pronoun is simply more generic than the feminine and therefore did not seriously impede her attempts to describe and inscribe a gender system utterly different from that of late twentieth-century North America. In a later essay ("Is Gender Necessary? Redux," dated 1987; published in Ursula K. Le Guin, *Dancing at the Edge of the World* [New York: Grove Press, 1989]) she analyzes her earlier strongly defensive reaction to the critiques of her novel based on that decision. She acknowledges in this later essay that the use of the masculine pronoun renders all Gethenians "male," if only in a latent sense, rather than the wholly ambisexual model she was striving for. By the mid-1980s, linguists had produced enough evidence that native speakers of English do not read masculine pronouns as "neutral" or "generic" that Le Guin had been convinced. She writes that perhaps she should have tried harder to create a plausible-sounding neuter pronoun to force readers to leave behind their assumptions about gender when imagining the society she described. She remains, however, pleased with the sentence about the king's pregnancy. This problem of pronouns and gender-marked language is one that Kanai is able entirely to avoid. Because the hermaphrodite is delivering a public lecture, s/he (unfortunately I have to use pronouns!) can avoid all gender-specific linguistic markings: the pronoun *"watakushi"* would be appropriate to either sex in such a context, and the polite locutions that might designate female speech in other contexts are used by both sexes in such a formal address.

33. This seems to be a reference to the story in Plato's *Symposium*, told by Aristophanes, of the origin of human desire. According to Aristophanes, originally each human was "double": two heads, two pairs of arms, two pairs of legs, two sets of genitalia. Some were doubled men, some were doubled women, and some had one set each of male and female genitalia. Zeus, fearful of the humans' power, decided to cut each in half. Ever since then, each "singled" human has gone looking for its other half, wishing to be joined together again. Those who are half of what was a doubled male look for another male to complete

them (thus the origin of "homosexual men"); those who are half of what was a doubled female look for another female ("lesbians"); and those that were mixed look for one of the opposite sex to complete them ("heterosexuals"). Evidently the original couple in Kanai's myth wanted to "return" to that doubled state.

34. Just as Le Guin later regretted her decision to use masculine pronouns to identify Gethenians, she also writes that she regrets her failure to consider the possibility of homosexuality in Gethenian culture ("Is Gender Necessary? Redux," p. 14). In fact, both Le Guin and Kanai structure certain of their societies' "arbitrary" moral codes around arguments privileging species reproduction—an argumentative basis familiar in the modern world. In Kanai's hermaphrodite society, sex outside "marriage" is acceptable so long as it might contribute to the continuation of the species: heterosexual sex. Homosexual sex outside the partnership has no such redeeming potential and is therefore "betrayal." That this argument has no "emotional" logic is revealed in the speaker's comment that if the two people who are currently same sex just wait a little while, one will switch sexes and their mutual attraction can be licitly consummated. (It should be noted that there is evidently no injunction against homosexual sex within a partnership when both partners happen to be in the same physical form.) In Le Guin's world, sibling incest is acceptable until the first child of such a union is born; then the pair must split forever. The sexual joining of full siblings is not a moral issue. What is at issue, evidently, is the sufficient mixing of genes to ensure a hardy species. Too much incest would be a detriment to the species' long-term health, this law suggests.

35. For readable discussions see, for example, Eve Kosofsky Sedgwick, *Between Men: English Literature and Male Homosocial Desire* (New York: Columbia University Press, 1985); or Gayle Rubin, "The Traffic in Women: Notes on the 'Political Economy' of Sex," in *Toward an Anthropology of Women*, ed. Rayna R. Reiter (New York: Monthly Review Press, 1975).

36. This question may have particular relevance in contemporary Japan, where the remarkable success of the postwar economy is often attributed to the strict bifurcation of gender roles.

37. I would like to thank the graduate students at the University of California, Berkeley, with whom I first read Kanai's work: Andra Alvis, Kim Kono, and Mary Knighton. Kathryn Sparling and Joshua Mostow kindly read this essay in draft form and contributed valuable suggestions. I am also grateful to the editors of this volume and two anonymous readers for useful comments in the revision process.

12

JAPANESE WITHOUT APOLOGY: YOSHIMOTO BANANA AND HEALING

Ann Sherif

Yoshimoto Banana's (b. 1964) first novel *Kitchen* (1987) became an instant best-seller. Immensely popular with young audiences, Banana has continued to produce appealing fiction such as *Bubbles/Sanctuary* (Utakata/Sankuchuari, 1988), *Tsugumi* (1989), *N.P.* (1990), *Lizard* (Tokage, 1993), and *Amrita* (1994). She has won a number of literary prizes including the Izumi Kyōka Prize and the Yamamoto Shūgoro Prize. Yoshimoto's devotion to popular fiction contrasts with the philosophical and scholarly emphases found in the writings of another famous member of her family: her father, writer Yoshimoto Takaaki. Banana is a pen name; her real name is Yoshimoto Mahoko.

∎

Every era has to reinvent the project of "spirituality" for itself. (Spirituality = plans, terminologies, ideas of deportment aimed at resolving the painful structural contradictions inherent in the human situation, at the completion of human consciousness, at transcendence.) . . . In the modern era, one of the most active metaphors for the spiritual project is "art."

— Susan Sontag, "The Aesthetics of Silence"

Time may enhance what seems simply dogged or lacking in fantasy now because we are too close to it, because it resembles too closely our own everyday fantasies, the fantastic nature of which we don't perceive. We are better able to enjoy a fantasy as fantasy when it is not our own.

— Susan Sontag, "Notes on Camp"

Like Ōe and Mishima, Murakami's works concern themselves with finding meaning in a seemingly empty and desolate world, even a world on the brink of destruction. Like Ōe but even more so, Murakami's works are filled with ghosts whose vivid presence . . . suggest a lost something (the past, the sublime), which cannot be recovered and yet which still must be looked for.

— Susan Napier, *The Fantastic in Modern Japanese Literature*

■

Doctor Machizawa Shizuo, a psychiatrist in Tokyo, reports that he is troubled professionally about the darkness of much of modern Japanese prose narrative. He notes that suicidal individuals frequently stumble into his office clutching copies of Dazai Osamu's novels and say: "This is exactly how I feel. I'm sorry that I was born" *(Sensei, watashi no kimochi wa kore desu. Umarete, sumimasen).*[1] In addition to the high incidence of suicide among Japanese novelists, the works themselves, Machizawa asserts, glorify suffering, negativism, and death. The doctor finds an exception in the writings of Yoshimoto Banana (b. 1964), such as the best-seller *Kitchen* (1987), *N.P.* (1990), and *Lizard* (Tokage, 1993). Even his most melancholy patients feel encouraged by Yoshimoto's novels, he says, and find in them an optimism and brightness absent in their own lives. Indeed, in the majority of her writings Yoshimoto Banana exhibits an interest in troubled people *(komatta hito),* individuals whose lives have been nearly devastated by acts of random violence, loss, illness, and troubled families. Yet her writings do not harbor the darkness of much other modern Japanese fiction because her narrative concerns the processes of grieving and healing and exhibits a steadfast belief in the possibility of reintegration into society, even after extreme alienation or trauma. She handles serious subjects with a remarkably light hand or even, as many critics have noted, a studied nonchalance.

While still in her twenties, Yoshimoto Banana won numerous literary prizes, and her novels, essays, and short stories have sold tens of millions of copies. Several of her novels and short stories have been translated into other languages as well, including Chinese, Italian, German, French, English, and Spanish, and have sold exceedingly well outside of Japan. In Italy, Yoshimoto was prominently featured in an anthology of interviews with that country's best-loved female authors. In the United States, the prestigious *New York Times Book Review* and the *New Yorker* have featured reviews of Yoshimoto's novels and short stories. Japanese and American scholarly journals have devoted pages and even entire issues to criticism of Yoshimoto Banana's fiction and analysis of the meteoric sales and critical fury over novels written by a youngish female author regarded by many as redolent of mass society and mass culture.

Indeed, serious critics find themselves puzzled, and perhaps even slightly embarrassed, at having been seduced by Yoshimoto Banana's fiction. One can propose several reasons for such conflicting feelings. In the first place Yoshimoto openly acknowledges her debt to decidedly popular genres of narrative, such as the *manga*, or adult comic book, as well as her general devotion to popular culture of the world. Moreover, many critics and writers—most notably Nobel Prize winner Ōe Kenzaburō—invoke the question of quality in relation to her works, because they regard her command of language as less than mature and her style as undistinguished. Yet because of the mind-boggling sales of her books, the internationally successful effort to market her, and the critical attention paid to her, Banana came to be regarded as a cultural phenomenon, even an indicator of paradigmatic shifts in Japanese society. While Ōe's scorn for Yoshimoto is understandable, given his convictions about the ideological and social meanings and uses of literature, Yoshimoto has made her mark on literary and commercial history.

Readers have repeatedly visited Yoshimoto Banana's early fiction for a variety of ends: as a site for discovering new, oppositional female identities; as the locus of the construction of the fetishized *shōjo*, or girlhood utopia; or as a means of probing into postoedipal cultural logic instrumental in managing libidinal and economic desires in the postmodern, postindustrial global economy.[2] In this chapter I venture into the narrative realm of the (slightly more) mature Banana —in particular the fiction and essays she produced during the middle and late 1990s—for the purpose of elucidating other reasons for the phenomenal popularity of her writings.

Yoshimoto's popularity and acceptance by a wide spectrum of readers both inside and outside Japan, I would argue, derive from her construction of a social imaginary centering on a Japan innocent of the Bomb, a Japan inured to the taint of wartime guilt. The older critical establishment's use of Yoshimoto's fiction as an occasion to divest itself especially of seriousness and orthodoxy and to embrace

the supposed innocence and utopian views of female adolescent, or *shōjo,* culture
stems not so much from an adoration of the supposed consumer impulse of the
shōjo or from the nonheterosexual, nonproductive narcissistic eroticism attributed
to the *shōjo.* Rather, the quest aims at a state of being unthreatened by the cluster of meanings that burden adulthood, and especially male maturity, almost to
the breaking point (whether in narrative or in social practice). This includes an
anxious awareness of the nuclear age, despair over Japan's spiritual heritage and
its potential uses and abuses in the present day, and alienation from adulthood.

Although Yoshimoto Banana's novels teem with women and androgynous
men (or even transsexuals), there is a conspicuous absence of heterosexual males
and fathers.[3] Critic John Treat attributes this lack primarily to Yoshimoto
Banana's (and by extension the *shōjo's*) privileging of nonreproductive sexuality.
Yet the reader cannot help but notice the understated yet constant threat of
unbridled and potentially violent male sexuality and self-assertion in Yoshimoto's
works. Even in *Kitchen,* Eriko, the man who has willingly relinquished his phallus to become a woman, ends up as victim of a crazed heterosexual man who goes
into a rage when he discovers that Eriko is transsexual. Eriko, however, has the
last word. When, fatally wounded, she smashes her attacker over the head with
a metal pipe, she screams: "They'll say it was self-defense, won't they?"[4]

By Yoshimoto's day, rejection of heterosexual reproductive sex was far from
a new topic in fiction. And by no means is it the exclusive domain of the adolescent female, as has been claimed. Ōe Kenzaburō, for example, explores repeatedly
the liberating nature of "what might be called deviant sex often involving pain and
sacrifice," as Susan Napier points out in Chapter 1 of this volume. Such assertively
nonreproductive sex "is clearly linked to an almost utopian dream of connection
and perfection," or the sublime, even as far back as Ōe's *A Personal Matter* (Kojin-
tekina taiken, 1964). As Sharalyn Orbaugh has discussed, the novelist Kanai
Mieko likewise explores nonorthodox sexual experiences in her prose.[5]

In addition to highlighting the hints of same-sex attraction in Yoshimoto's stories (in *Kitchen,* for example, and the protagonist of the story "A Strange Tale from
Down by the River" [Okawabata kidan, 1993]), one must recognize an even more
predominant pattern in Yoshimoto's writings. Specifically, the writer returns
repeatedly to the theme of women's quest for transformation and transcendence
facilitated by spiritually potent male/androgynous figures. Most often, it is a
woman who willingly steps into the liminal space inhabited by a male with extraordinary spiritual powers and vision.[6] As we shall see, examples of this dynamic
include Hachi in *Hachiko's Last Lover* (Hachiko no saigo no koibito, 1994), the

little brother in *Amrita* (1994), and Orange in *Marika's Sofa* (Marika no sofua, 1997). In the short story "Lizard" (Tokage, 1992), however, Yoshimoto inverts the formula and depicts the male narrator as finding solace in his girlfriend Lizard, who practices Asian herbal medicine, acupuncture, and faith healing. The goal for the characters does not lie in permanent union with their lover: their presence is understood as temporary, or they are unsuitable as partners. Instead the men resemble a bodhisattva in their ability to bring the women to a higher level of understanding of themselves.

Beyond these spiritual pairings, Yoshimoto emphasizes spirituality or transcendence by invoking spaces for what she views as their sacred potential—especially Asian venues outside of Japan, such as Bali, the Middle East, and India. Her use of the "Orient" as exotic Other and beautiful backdrop resonates with many other cultural practices, such as the contemporary marketing of Asia to Japanese tourists as spiritual home. Yoshimoto never denies the spiritual potential of Japan: at the end of the story, Lizard and her boyfriend take the train to the temple at Narita, outside of Tokyo. Only there, at the gate of the temple, are the two able to confess their deepest secrets and fears to each other. A counterexample to the positive influence of Asian space is the corrupting influence of the West in the novel *N.P.* (1990).

A NOTE ON *SHŌJO*

Variously denigrated as narcissistic and nostalgic infantilism and exalted as a splendid escape from the rigidity of adulthood for all Japanese, regardless of age and gender, *shōjo* (adolescent female) identity/subjectivity became inextricably identified with Yoshimoto's writings. Ogura Chikako names three defining characteristics of the late-twentieth-century construction of the *shōjo*: "(1) because *shōjo* are not adults, they can perceive things that those in control of the society cannot; (2) because they are not young men, they can see things that those who will someday rule society cannot see; and (3) because they are no longer children, they are fully aware of who controls Japan."[7] Kanai Yoshiko notes that modern society has obviated the possibility of adolescence as a rite of passage and a warm, nurturing stage of life that "enables one to individuate and to accept difference," so the idea of the *shōjo* in Banana's works became a "symbol or fantasy of that missing time or space."[8]

During the 1980s a public debate raged over *shōjo* culture, spurred on by the sudden popularity of *Kitchen*. Most of the opinions emanated from the pens of male critics and authors. Much of the despair over Yoshimoto Banana's sup-posed "baby talk" babble style resulted more from generational anxiety and less from a careful reading of her novels.[9] Male critics appeared especially eager to legit-imize their fascination with a novel of the ilk of *Kitchen* and the related cultural realm of discursive practices (fiction, media, *manga,* advertisement) originally aimed at and often generated by a younger female population of readers/con-sumers/citizens. As Kanai Yoshiko has commented, until the age of Banana, such *shōjo* discourse had been despised by orthodox critics as being "too sweet" *(ama-sugiru)* to merit serious attention, yet it flourished among a certain community of readers. A critical maneuver was required to allow mature male and female read-ers to enter legitimately into the sociolinguistic realm of the *shōjo* and regard the texts and cultural practices therein as fodder for their critical exercises.

Several aspects of Banana's early fiction facilitated such an integration of the separate/marginalized realm of the *shōjo* with that of the orthodox heterosexual journalist and critical establishment. And, furthermore, this process of integration and acceptance was predicated on the objectivization and theorization of *shōjo* as oppositional (antiheterosexual, anti-oedipal, artistic, lyrical, humanist, sensitive) and utopian by establishment critics. The literary marketplace and the critical establishment have facilitated the legitimization and canonization of the for-merly despised *shōjo* by reconceptualizing her in terms of postmodernism, con-sumerism, and the political economy. Part of this strategy took the form of celebrating the gendered aspects of *shōjo* culture (supposedly feminine values such as cuteness, innocence, naïveté, nostalgia, consumerism) while at the same time seizing this imagined cultural realm and its codes as the prerogative of men of all ages, not only of adolescent boys whose sense of fashion and style had already merged with that of the *shōjo* in the *manga* and fashion/style/taste world.

THE LAST GOOD MAN

Although imagining the realm of the adolescent female as a positive world has become a virtual industry in Japan, it would be futile to portray the *shōnen,* or ado-lescent male, in utopian terms. This is because masculinity and the male social realm are so politically and historically tainted and male members of society so burdened as future economic animals. Such negative associations have obviously not, however, led to overt questioning of patriarchal rule. Values such as ambi-tion and self-sacrifice for the group and male domination of financial and polit-ical power still loom large in Japanese society in the late twentieth century. They are, however, conspicuously absent in Yoshimoto's narratives. Instead she portrays sensitive males who hover on the margins of the power structure and society.

The general affluence of postwar society, even now that the bubble has popped, has made viable, even desirable, Yoshimoto's ubiquitous female orphan characters. Equally appealing are their spiritually potent male counterparts, who similarly have no desire for material opulence, no visible means of support, but also no concerns about where their next meal will come from. The female protagonist Mao in *Hachiko's Last Lover* relishes her life most when she is sharing an apartment with her boyfriend, spending her days painting pictures, and eating only when she feels like it. Oblivious to brand names and high fashion consumerism, Mao thrives on the spiritual and artistic fulfillment she experiences and is not bothered that her spare diet has caused her to lose weight. Similarly, in *Kitchen* the orphaned Mikage identifies food with social and erotic communion, not nourishment for the body. Movement toward closure in both of these novels involves the women's decision to become productive members of society, with or without their men.

AN UNLIKELY FATHER AND DAUGHTER PAIR?

Initially one reason that Banana stood out from the brat pack of younger writers was because she had an exceedingly famous father in the world of letters. Her father, critic and poet Yoshimoto Takaaki, functioned as a link between older readers and the young, suddenly wildly popular daughter. The familial connection also served as point of reference for readers not of Banana's age group and cultural milieu. While one cannot reasonably expect that artistic or rhetorical talent will be inherited, readers of Takaaki's generation, or closer to it, appeared mildly shocked that his daughter would be seemingly ignorant of Japan's past glories and ignominious deeds. Such attitudes reveal as much about the father as the daughter, however. Yoshimoto Takaaki became notorious during the 1960s and 1970s for his polemics and vitriolic attacks on other writers about their complicity, guilt, and responsibility during Japan's imperialist expansion into Asia and military aggression during World War II. Yoshimoto Takaaki also sat in the streets and was arrested with the students during the protests of the 1960s, yet later he criticized the anti–Vietnam War protests. He aggressively, almost excessively, questioned and explicated the emperor system. Never one to shy away from major issues, he did not hesitate to take on the Bible, Marx, and the leftist establishment.[10]

Yoshimoto Banana both benefited from and paid the price for being the daughter of this well-known man—especially in the eyes of an audience that expected writers to be serious and follow the moral high road. Indicative of the influence of Yoshimoto's family background on the readings of her fiction is the title of a book of essays by poet Matsuoka Tsuneo (b. 1951): *The Passing of Asia: Between Yoshimoto Takaaki and Yoshimoto Banana* (Ajia no shūen: Yoshimoto Takaaki and Yoshimoto Banana no aida, 1990). Matsuoka begins his book with the words: "To me there is a huge, dark sinkhole between Yoshimoto Takaaki and Yoshimoto Banana."[11]

Kanai Yoshiko states pointedly that the critical and readerly response to Banana has been exaggerated because of the "ambivalence" of Takaaki's generation to his writings. Among feminists, Banana has been regarded with caution because she was raised by a father who at times made antifeminist pronouncements such as: "If feminism gains more currency than it currently has, the birth rate will drop to zero." Kanai concedes that the Yoshimoto household was perhaps not a den of reactionary misogyny after all and even concedes that Takaaki acknowledges the importance of feminism, and thus his daughter should be forgiven.[12]

Somewhat ironically, Yoshimoto Banana claims a greater influence from her father than one might expect. Her assertions, however, strike the reader as vague: she reports in an interview that her connection with her father has "enabled me to look at my own works with a degree of objectivity . . . and I can feel the tenor of the age with my skin. . . . [Thanks to him,] I know how to step back and analyze my feelings, even if I'm feeling totally overwhelmed and swallowed up by those feelings."[13]

THE HORROR OF THE PATRIARCH

Yoshimoto's maturation as a writer can be seen in her increasing willingness to confront the specter of violent masculinity and her narrative attempts at evoking a viable alternative. Being Japanese without guilt becomes possible, she implies, if one refuses to construct a positive vision of mature (hetero, reproductive, adult) manhood and instead only embraces a fantastic androgynous male presence. John Treat has noted the absence of the "terror of the father" in *Kitchen*. But in other works one discovers a profoundly destructive male presence: the suicidal novelist in *N.P.*; the incestuous brother in *N.P.*; the criminally violent and abusive father in *Marika's Sofa*.

Yoshimoto's novella *Marika's Sofa* (1997) concerns, more than any other of her works to date, the dismal consequences of the untamed, brutal paternal pres-ence.[14] After a childhood of sexual, physical, and emotional horror at the hands of her sadistic father and alcoholic mother, Marika finds solace in the home of a woman named Junko and her husband. Marika's emotional turmoil and pain manifest themselves in the presence of multiple personalities: a troubled young girl named Pain (Pein), rambunctious Happy, kindly older woman Mitsuyo, and a brainy, gentle thirteen-year-old boy named Orange. It is the last of these personalities that stays with Marika the longest. For both Marika and Junko, Orange signifies a desirable and innocent masculinity, bordering on androgyny, a positive alternative to the monster father who prostituted Marika, molested her, and did violence to her reproductive organs. Once her cruel father is in prison and her irresponsible mother is dead, Marika spends her days either with her grand-mother or in mental institutions. Over the many years that Marika comes to seek solace in Junko's home, mostly by sleeping on a sofa in her living room, Junko recognizes a gradual improvement in Marika's emotional state. Eager to encour-age Marika's interest in the world outside, Junko decides to travel with her to Bali. The novel describes this trip—especially the women's encounter with Bali as a sacred and mystical space—as well as the last appearance of the appealing boy Orange (in the form of Marika).

Rather than treating Marika as a freak or presenting her various personalities in a sensationalist manner, Yoshimoto creates a compassionate portrait of the over-lapping psychological and spiritual worlds of both Marika and Junko. Junko is a maternal figure who not only seeks to help Marika heal her many wounds but acknowledges the reality of Marika's multiple personas, especially the endearing Orange. Mature and caring, Junko works comfortably in the role of Junko Sen-sei (Dr. Junko), as Marika likes to call her, recognizing the nature of the younger woman's illness and carefully monitoring her progress toward wellness. Yet the vivid reality of Junko's interactions with Orange leave her unable to dismiss his presence as a psychological aberration or to discount him as the product of a young woman's overactive imagination. She finds herself in the uncanny position of look-ing forward to a meeting with Orange and mourning his final disappearance. In a humorous passage, Junko confesses her surprise that only one of Marika's per-sonalities breaks out in hives if she drinks milk whereas the others love milk and consume it without any ill effect.

Over the course of the narrative, she wonders whether Marika and Orange are like twins, or if Orange is part of Marika, or if they are conceivably separate people. And what will happen to this seemingly viable Orange, his individuality *(kosei),* when Marika's mental condition improves? Indeed, the novel hinges on our willing suspension of disbelief in a world of spirits that overlaps with the realm of the subconscious. Junko puzzles over the source of the personalities: "Has Marika created them, or has she called them from somewhere?"[15] In a passage narrated by Marika herself, the young woman confesses that she calls herself Marika "because that's what everyone else calls me," not because she believes in the sanctity of individual identity.[16]

Junko at last concludes that although Orange may not appear again, his "life" *(inochi)* will most definitely not disappear (p. 67); Marika acknowledges that Orange still resides somewhere deep within her in a place she cannot reach. Marika, in her innocence, mourns the disappearance of Orange, because he meant many different things to her. He was her friend, her lover; she wished she could have married him. After years of abuse by her father, Marika has created for herself the ideal man, so desirable and gentle that she imagines sex with him might have been good, even "not painful." In a moment of celebration of androgyny, Junko speculates that Orange was "Marika's ideal friend," the "opposite sex who was one with her" *(tanin dewanai isei),* whom she created for the purpose of escaping from the coming of adolescence."[17] Once Orange has completely disappeared, Marika confesses to Junko that he was constantly with her. The older woman reacts by proposing that their unity resembles a fetus in its mother's womb: "Maybe Orange was your baby?" Junko asks.[18] Marika also believes that her spirit can leave her body. The last instance of this in the novel occurs in a dream sequence in Bali in which a doglike creature called Baron comes to fetch Marika's spirit from a dangerous place and guides her back to Orange, who dwells in her body.

Other modern writers have evoked spirits or souls wandering outside the body. Enchi Fumiko in her 1958 novella *Masks* (Onnamen), for example, brings Heian-period belief in spirit possession and supernatural beliefs to life in a postwar social context, but she does so cautiously by introducing them as objects of academic interest of the main characters, who pursue research on the tenth-century romance *The Tale of Genji.* Yoshimoto, seemingly innocent of the *Genji* character Lady Rokujō, whose vengeful spirit wanders uncontrollably outside her body, cites no particular source for her evocation of spirits on the loose, although her well-known interest in New Age beliefs may have inspired her.

As well as questioning the unity of body and spirit, Yoshimoto emphasizes the fluidity of the concept of personality and the power of the spiritual. Even Junko finds herself transformed by her interactions with the kindly Mitsuyo, the childish Marika, and especially by Orange. When she and Marika eat a magical Bali omelette, filled with psychedelic mushrooms, she becomes a young carefree girl *(shōjo),* laughing with Marika, but then virtually at the same moment she regards Marika as a bodhisattva: a compassionate being dedicated to the salvation of others. Junko later dreams of the future possibility of intimacy with Marika "soul to soul, in a deep place under the vast starry sky, caring for each other like two children" (p. 103). When Marika's psychological condition has improved, Junko compares the grown-up Marika to a Buddhist stone statue: perfectly whole though slightly chipped. Similarly, Junko has a satisfying, almost blissful, encounter with Orange during which she becomes both mother and childhood friend to this perfect boy, as they walk hand in hand beneath the night sky. It is the sick girl in her charge who has helped Junko to find different sides of herself and who challenges her by proposing that each individual is ultimately made up of different people.

Yoshimoto renders Marika's psychic and spiritual instability viable by several means. First, in a somewhat Orientalist move, she portrays the mythical process of disintegration, spiritual and psychological wandering, and finally reintegration as all happening on the exoticized South Pacific island of Bali. In the novel, spirits are somehow evident in Bali and the place is magically beautiful and filled with temples and sacred spaces. To Junko, everything is extreme: the colors are brilliant; dark and light are more pronounced than she has ever known. The Balinese people dance trance dances, whip up magic mushroom omelettes for willing Japanese visitors, and sell handwoven cloth that will ward off evil. In the printed edition of the novella, brightly colored paintings of Balinese scenes by Yoshimoto's illustrator, artist Hara Masumi, are interwoven with the text. Since Yoshimoto's 1994 novel *Amrita,* in which a young woman and her brother visit Saipan and sense the spirits of dead soldiers (recalling Japanese battles there during the Pacific War only indirectly), the writer has been interested in the supernatural potential of exoticized Asian otherworlds.

Lest the narrative sound excessively psychological, Yoshimoto has filled it with images of light and darkness, water and sky, to decided effect. The reader repeatedly encounters in the novel the images of a gorgeous pool at Junko and Marika's hotel in Bali, waterfalls, the ocean, the dark of the night, the brilliance of the tropical sun. As is often the case in Yoshimoto's fiction, light is associated with enlightenment and water with the unconscious:

"Doesn't it seem really dark all of a sudden?" asked Orange. "Look over there. It's pitch black!"

"You're right. How strange."

Orange's white shirt was the only thing that stood out clearly and plainly in the dark. It was hard to see where we were going. I noticed that even the motorcycles had slowed down. The road lit up only when they rode by, and then it would be all black again as the single threads of headlights receded into the distance.

"It's kind of spooky, like a haunted house," I proposed.

"But look, once your eyes get used to it, you can see *that* many stars. Unbelievable."

Huge diamonds of light sparkled across the jet black sky. At that moment, I truly felt as though I were with a small boy, my son. I couldn't imagine him as anything but my own precious child.

"Orange, how long have you been here? Where did you come from?" I blurted out, though it may seem that I might have asked that same question many times before.

"From some dark place. Marika called me and so I went inside of her," Orange told me with complete honesty.

"What about before that?"

"I don't remember. All I know is that I was sucked into Marika from some dark space. I heard her calling, and she sounded like she was in so much pain that I just couldn't stay away. Oh, wow, look, Sensei. Look over at those lights over there."

I felt Orange tug at my sleeve, and we both stopped and stood side by side, gazing up at the sky.

I turned and saw all the shops magically illuminated by the glow of electric lights and framed by red and green strings of tiny lights going on one after another. Then, as if on signal, all the street lights and the lamps . . . went on too, just like lights on a Christmas tree. [pp. 49–50]

Although Junko had been assigned the role of helping to cure Marika, she accompanies Marika on her journey to the depths and darkness of her psyche and willingly enjoys the "light" (good health, enlightenment) that Orange/Marika points out.

LANGUAGE AND CONTAMINATION

If the distant destination of Bali can bring promises of healing and enlightenment, on the other side of the Pacific darkness and defilement lie in wait for the Japanese in Yoshimoto's novel *N.P.* The work concerns grief, loss, and recovery. One summer the narrator Kazami meets three people who have a connection to her old boyfriend Shōji and to the novel *N.P.* that Shōji was translating at the time of his death. Two of these new acquaintances, Saki and Otohiko, are the children of Takase Sarao, author of the (fictional) novel called *N.P.* Sui, whom they meet for the first time as adults, is their stepsister (same father, different mothers). Through new friendships with these three, Kazami comes to understand some of the events and relationships that led her boyfriend Shōji to commit suicide while translating *N.P.*, as well as those surrounding Takase, the author of *N.P.* Takase, a Japanese, had written the novel in English while living in the States. He too had taken his own life. Kazami, as well as Takase's three children, manage to distance themselves from the powerful (lethal?) text and carry on with their lives.

Yoshimoto's novel *N.P.* promotes an essentialist view of Japanese national identity. By essentialist, I mean that it expresses the attitude that there exists an inborn and unique quality in Japan, its culture, people, and language. This notion contrasts with a constructivist outlook that emphasizes the role of history, culture, and narrative in the formation of a discourse of uniqueness or difference. Although Yoshimoto's novels are marketed and conceived of as fresh and new, at their core lurks a profound conservatism. In *N.P.*, contact with the world outside of Japan brings with it the possibility of corruption and contamination. In other words, morality is suspended outside of Japan for the Japanese characters in the text. When individuals portrayed in the novel leave the comfort of the womb that is Japanese culture, they abandon their family roles and the family structure itself dissolves. This topos of foreign contamination appears not infrequently in modern Japanese literature, even as early as Mori Ōgai's Meiji novella *The Dancing Girl* (Maihime).

This rhetoric of contamination permeates *N.P.* Many of the characters who leave Japan go to hell. The novelist Takase, for example, leads a totally dissolute life in Boston, sleeping with young Japanese women who could be his daughter. One such object of Takase's corrupt passion turns out in fact to be his stepdaughter, Sui, who is yet another lost Japanese abroad. Sui subsequently has a sexual relationship with her stepbrother Otohiko. Once out of Japan, these people forget—or pretend not to know—their roles in the family and the norms and taboos that define family life. In contrast to Yoshimoto's earlier fiction, such as *Tsugumi* (1989), in which the reader encounters instances of pseudo-incest, *N.P.* introduces people who are related by blood but who do not, or pretend not to, acknowledge that fact and enter into intimate sexual relations. Sui and Otohiko seem oblivious to the moral implications of their sexual relationship. Even when their familial relationship is confirmed, they react not by separating but instead by fleeing Japan for Boston, where they aspire to live a "normal life" together. Finally, after talking with the level-headed Kazami, the incestuous siblings consciously acknowledge that they have transgressed acceptable limits of familial relations.

In linguistic terms, the novelist Takase sets off a chain of disastrous events when he dares to write prose in a foreign language (English) rather than in his native Japanese. He loses his mind and kills himself; Shōji and two other would-be translators of the novel commit suicide as well. Kazami, who herself attempts to translate Takase's novel, triumphs as the sole survivor of this linguistic and cultural transgression. As a means of explaining the puzzling deaths of the other would-be translators, she presents the following thesis:

It probably has something to do with the process of putting his English into Japanese. . . . [Whenever I tried to translate his novel], a black vapor would fill my lungs. I simply couldn't get the feeling out of my head. I felt as if I were walking out into the ocean with my clothes on, the waves pounding on my body, and then swimming out toward the horizon, with nothing to hold me back. Like that sensation of wet clothes clinging to my body.[19]

Eventually Kazami decides that she must quit translating the novel and concludes that this is the "proof of a healthy mind."[20] Later she analyzes her contact with the potentially lethal text written by Takase:

What would be an appropriate metaphor to explain my feelings when I was doing the translation? An endless meadow of golden pampas grass swaying in the wind, or a coral reef beneath a deep, brilliant blue ocean. That utter stillness you feel when you see a whole bunch of tropical fish swimming by, all in bright colors, and they don't even look like living creatures.

You're not going to last long with that kind of world in your head. I looked at Otohiko and thought of the devastating sadness of his father's life.

[Otohiko said,] "Japanese is a strange language. It really is. This might contradict what I said before, but I feel as if I've lived a very long time since I came to Japan. The language even affects the way you think. It wasn't until I moved over here that I understood that my father was indeed Japanese and that, even when he was writing in English, his true home was the Japanese language. That's why such disastrous things happen when someone tries to translate his English into

Japanese. Father's strong sense of longing for his homeland is a fundamental part of his writing. He should have written it in Japanese from the start."[21]

Kazami's ability to resist the moral taint of Takase's betrayal of the native tongue stems from her family's correct and disciplined relationship to language, native and foreign. Not coincidentally, it is Kazami's mother who enables the family to resist moral chaos. Thus only Kazami and her sister are exempt from Yoshimoto's discourse of contamination, because their contact with the other, the alien, is tempered by linguistic control in the form of their mother's realization of the power of language and subsequent teaching of "the pleasures of English" to her children. The mother herself has good reason to be distraught and desperate —her husband abandoned her—but even so she refuses to give in to depravity. Rather than allowing the foreign tongue to render her life chaotic, the mother takes control over it and uses it as the tool of her trade, making a living as a translator. Even though Kazami's sister lives in London with her British husband, she too is protected from contamination because she too has been trained well by her mother and understands and is in control of the "pleasures of English."

Here the reader encounters a linguistic and cultural rupture caused by a Japanese person who writes in a language other than Japanese in a place other than Japan. In conception this resonates with the discourse of *kotodama,* or language filled with "limitless power."[22] The contaminating influence of Takase's act proves to be far-reaching: three people choose death rather than complete the ordeal of putting the stories into Japanese, the language originally violated by Takase when he chose to be unfaithful and dip his pen elsewhere. It is ironic that Yoshimoto Banana—regarded by readers and critics as supremely modern and universal in appeal—should espouse myths of uniqueness about Japanese language and the geographic space that is called Japan and the power and inescapability of these forces.

EROTICIZING THE MUNDANE, DOMESTICATING THE MARGINAL

While some readers may find comfort in discovering yet another affirmation of the uniqueness of the Japanese language and culture in Yoshimoto's works, there is another reason for the appeal of her writings: the frequent appearance of morally and socially controversial topics. From coin locker babies to sadomasochistic sex, provocative topics have become commonplace in postwar Japanese literature—world literature, for that matter—whether presented sensationally for shock value or employed metaphorically to comment on social and ideological configurations of the late-twentieth-century world. Yoshimoto's tendency to evoke taboo subjects in an indirect, unthreatening manner, her disarming and comic pen name, and the long-held perception of this author as representative of *shōjo* (adolescent) female culture are all elements that have contributed to the critical establishment's refusal to regard her writings as "serious" literature.

In most of her novels and stories, the manner of delivery hovers between casual and deadpan. Many critics have noted the apparent lack of affect in the reaction of Mikage (the heroine of *Kitchen*) to her grandmother's death and her realization that she has no family left in the world: "I was so surprised" *(bikkuri shita)*. Yoshimoto's narrators characteristically treat the occurrences that surround them—incest, suicide, drugs, murder, transsexuality, lethal violence—with utter nonchalance. This is partly because Yoshimoto shies away from the familiar techniques of delivering vivid first-person accounts or extreme-close-up third-person depictions of shocking events. Instead she frequently cushions the readers from direct impact by creating a sympathetic narrator or character who experiences trauma indirectly (as a friend, observer, or companion to the troubled parties).

Kitchen's Mikage experiences firsthand the shock of having family die in a car accident or natural death, for example, but she observes only indirectly (through hearsay) the violent murder of Eriko. Kazami comes from a broken family, but she encounters greater—or perhaps more shocking—misfortune only secondhand in the form of the Sarao family's bouts of incest and suicide. In *Tsugumi*, Tsugumi suffers from physical and psychological difficulties, but the real plot and drama of the novel centers on her friend Maria. In *N.P.*, although incest and Takase's insanity have wrecked havoc on many lives, the mediating gaze—the narrator Kazami—views it all with complete calm. Her strongest reaction to Sui's incestuous relations with her father is: "Didn't you get a little too close?"

Ever sensitive to her readers' opinions, Yoshimoto Banana has communicated publicly her awareness of the seriousness of real social problems and asserted elsewhere that she does not intend to condone sexual violence or abuse by such portrayals.[23] From her earliest to her more mature works, however, the emphasis is not on delving into the depths of unconventional sexual situations or celebrating the breaking of taboo. Rather, Yoshimoto exhibits consistent interest in the possibility of recovery from trauma and in the healing process itself. When Mikage, the narrator of *Kitchen*, for example, learns that her friend Yuichi's mother is in fact a transsexual, she dwells very little on this revelation. Instead she latches onto the fact of Eriko's astonishing beauty, which in turn distracts her from her own grief and displaces the anxiety over suddenly becoming an orphan. Yoshimoto thus naturalizes the marginal.

Yoshimoto's novels and stories characteristically open with a revelation of the sensational and then quickly shift to evocation of the mundane rhythms of life. Uncharacteristic in late-twentieth-century fiction, Yoshimoto's works rarely describe sex and violence directly or explicitly. Rather, the reader finds people describing incidents secondhand or recalling (and attempting to recover from) disturbing or sometimes bizarre incidents or encounters. This therapeutic function and the promise of recovery offered by her narratives, though often overlooked, is certainly one of the reasons for Yoshimoto Banana's popularity. Often criticized by older critics and readers for being "too sweet," Yoshimoto diverges not in the range of her subject matter, which by no means precludes controversial social topics, but in her impulse to domesticate the very subjects that are sensationalized or made strange by her literary contemporaries. In turn, this treatment renders many subjects palatable to the reader.

At the same time, Yoshimoto's texts transform the mundane into an object of desire. In the novel *Kitchen,* for example, Mikage finds solace in her kitchen after she has lost her last blood relative. The utensils in her kitchen, even her purring refrigerator, become sources of comfort, objects of desire. In contrast to Mikage's loss of her entire family, she can at least have total control over food, physical space in the kitchen, and the tools of culinary work and pleasure. The text contains many passages of loving, longing description of this vegetable peeler, that glass, and the famous delicious, glistening bowl of *tonkatsu* (breaded fried pork on rice).[24]

Despite the centuries of cultural baggage that conventionally burdens Japanese kitchens *(daidokoro),* linking such domestic spaces with the confinement of women, uncompensated labor, and conventional gender roles, Yoshimoto gives rise to a sense of wonder and sensuality by presenting a revisionist reading of this space and its contents. Yoshimoto signals this from the very cover of the book— by employing the term *"kitchin"* derived from English rather than the Japanese *daidokoro.* As Mizuta Noriko has pointed out, a crucial element behind this transformation of the kitchen into the site of play, security, and pleasure is the absence of the father in the novel. In other words, a kitchen can be exorcized of the ghosts of the social structure that force women to labor, unrewarded, if there is no father who sits and waits for the fruits of the mother's labor.[25]

THE PROMISE OF SPIRITUALITY

In the 1990s, Yoshimoto exhibited a growing obsession with searches for spiritual meaning in her fiction. This compulsion does not emanate from the anxieties of life in the nuclear age and only to a limited degree from any awareness she may have of social issues and the contradictions of life in postindustrialist capitalist society in general or those pressing issues specific to Japan's postdefeat, postsurrender age. Certainly there is no overt mention of politics and history in the novels and stories. Moreover, a number of extratextual events promote this view that Yoshimoto's conceptual origins stem largely from discursive and aesthetic practices. In the collection of essays titled *About a Dream,* Yoshimoto included a short piece called "Hey, Old Queen, Where Are You Off To?" in which she explains that her creation of *Kitchen*'s Eriko was more narrative, or literary, in nature than it was a comment on the social realities of gays and transsexuals in society:

I recently recalled—though I had never really understood it before (!)—the controversy over the character Eriko (the father who has the appearance of a mother) in my novel *Kitchen*. When I was writing the novel, I had conceived of Eriko as a sort of parody of the archetypal mother-in-law, rather than as a meditation on gay people. Indeed, Eriko was not gay; he was simply a man who dressed in women's clothing.

Soon after the novel came out, however, I had many new experiences in my life, including having a gay friend for the first time. My friend's name was Mr. Koide. Once he got through that initial period of "shyness toward women" typical in queer men, he became very friendly to me, and he taught me many things about the gay world.

Koide had his own bar in Takadanobaba. The gentleman (lady?) usually spoke in the same language that women usually use, but he could turn into a man instantly if the occasion demanded it: "Hey, what in the hell do you think you're doing? Not in my place, buster." I thought he was completely adorable. . . . Koide died this past November. The last time I saw him was in September, when a friend and I visited him. He was gaunt and pale, and looked as if he had been drinking all day. Barely able to stand up straight, he leaned on the bar and told me that he planned to sell the bar and spend the rest of his days drinking. . . .

My friend went to Koide's bar once after that. . . . When he told Koide that he thought the place stunk of death, Koide apparently replied, "No way, darling!" I really admired his attitude. . . . [26]

Yoshimoto's initially naive understanding of transsexuality as men wearing costumes is striking, as is her desire to subvert archetypal patterns of the evil mother-in-law in her narrative.

For many members of Ōe Kenzaburō and Yoshimoto Takaaki's generation, spirituality and religion in postwar Japanese society remain tainted by the ghosts of prewar and wartime uses of state Shinto. Yoshimoto Banana, however, displays a constant and unapologetic interest in spirituality in her works. In her story "Blood and Water" (Chi to mizu, 1991), a young woman flees the life her parents have chosen as members of a village/commune run by a New Religion sect for the secular world of Tokyo, only to discover that her need for belief and spirituality remains strong:

> When I was younger, I used to think that the occult, religion, New Age, Kitarō, channeling, and all that kind of stuff was really stupid. . . . But I don't feel that way now. I guess that I feel more comfortable about spirituality. . . . I guess that it all goes back to my parents. Both of them are such kind, honest people—too good for this world, like saints. But then, one day when I was a little girl, something terrible happened to them. Some guy stole all their money, every cent they had worked so hard for. The man was an old friend of my father and his business partner, and then he did something like that to them. What were they supposed to do? Say that they forgave him? Even they couldn't do that, and instead they got involved in a religious sect, one based on Esoteric Buddhism. . . . By the time I was eighteen, I couldn't stand it anymore, and so I ran away . . . I suppose that I felt pessimistic about the beliefs that kept my parents alive and happy, and the effect they had on me. At some point, it struck me that the village and my parents reeked of defeat, and that I did too.[27]

But eventually, after she moves to Tokyo, the woman enters into a relationship with a man who makes good luck charms (*omamori*) that look like jewelry but have exceptional powers to bring good fortune to the wearer. In "Lizard," a counselor of emotionally disturbed children and his girlfriend go to a large Buddhist temple to pray. It is one of the first times that the girlfriend, an aerobics instructor turned faith healer, has shown any interest in things outside her narrow, intense devotion to helping the sick and dying.

In contrast to Ōe Kenzaburō's references to biblical narrative and tradition, Yoshimoto's stories emphasize a vague, amorphous brand of spirituality. At the same time, she exhibits considerable skepticism vis-à-vis organized religions and especially the New Religions.[28] Yoshimoto's version of spiritual belief has close links with gender. Most often a female character will seek transformation, transcendence, and education through the guidance of a spiritually potent male/androgynous figure. Examples include "Blood and Water," discussed earlier, Hachi in *Hachiko's Last Lover,* Orange in *Marika's Sofa,* and the clairvoyant little brother in *Amrita.*

Desirable men are too good to last: indeed, in *Hachiko* Mao enjoys a year of utter sexual, spiritual, and social bliss and healing with her spiritual lover/teacher Hachi. But Hachi's destiny compels him to decide to leave Japan and return to the religious life in India by the end of the year. Evidently no place exists for such a superior man in Japan. Unlike cherry blossoms, which are bound to fall and perish, Hachi is destined for a higher place: the spiritual realm of the "Indian" mountains. In contrast to the same-sex attractions evident in earlier works, in *Hachiko* Yoshimoto rejects the vision of lesbian sexuality as liberating. Indeed the work opens with a description of a less than satisfying sexual encounter between the inexperienced fifteen-year-old narrator Mao and a slightly older but still teenaged woman that Mao calls "Mother" (Okaasan). Drug-loving "Mother" lives with Hachi, but late one night when he is out with friends, she creeps into Mao's bed and asks permission to kiss her. Their sexual encounter ends abruptly when "Mother" confesses her limited knowledge of female intimacy ("I never know what to do next . . . ") and insists that they get out of bed and go out to buy Italian lemon ice ("At 3:00 in the morning?" Mao objects). Generously, "Mother" gives Mao permission to sleep with her lover Hachi a couple of times, or as many times as she wants, in the event that "Mother" dies in a motorcycle accident in the Hakone mountains. And that is precisely what happens—but only after "Mother" has left with the parting words: "But if you let another woman do it, I'll put a fatal curse on you."[29] Aside from this brief and surprising opening passage, the rest of the novel concerns the heterosexual relationship between Mao and Hachi.

In a plot similar to that of the short story "Blood and Water," Mao seeks to escape the shallow spirituality of the religious cult that has grown up around Grandmother and to which her mother has devoted herself. The story also plays out her Grandmother's prediction that Mao will become a talented painter, as well as her mysterious vision that her granddaughter will be "Hachiko's final lover." In this way, Yoshimoto does not take issue with individual expressions of belief or practice but objects, rather, to organized religion, especially in its cult form, which leads to abuses.

When Mao meets Hachi, he strikes her as a "typical Japanese guy," so she is surprised later to discover that Hachi was raised in India by Indian parents. His Japanese parents, frustrated with their own spiritual search in India, had abandoned him there. Hachi seems very different from the undistinguished group of men she has met and even had relations with. One result of insufficient faith in organized religion, Yoshimoto suggests, is the breakdown of the family: Hachi's parents abandon him when their quest for enlightenment in India does not meet with their satisfaction. Mao's own experience growing up in a cult meant that the entire group was defined as her family. Moreover, her mother had relations with a number of men in the cult, and the identity of her father remained unclear. Thus familial and social roles become confused. When Mao and Hachi are disrobing to make love for the first time, for example, Mao is watching him as he spreads out the futon and thinks to herself:

> I don't have a father, but I thought that Hachi seemed like my father. Then I realized that, though there were many adult males around when I was growing up, all of them were Father, and none of them were just "men." . . . I was watching Hachi take off his clothes, and then it suddenly occurred to me that I was always just watching. I was watching, and I wasn't there at all, like a wandering spirit, like a stuffed animal slumped in the corner of a room."[30]

As in *Marika's Sofa*, Yoshimoto Banana makes extensive use of vivid imagery such as light and water. Her texts are accessible to readers of many cultures because the imagery does not have to be read as culture-specific—especially not as evocative of traditional/exotic/non-Western Japan or the Anglo-European world. Instead it is generally suggestive of spiritual, mythical, and psychological categories of transcendence, enlightenment, and the unconscious. While her novels have a vaguely New Age tone, Banana always pulls back from endorsement of, and in fact regards with a critical eye, the syncretism of the New Religions.

A TEMPORARY SENSE OF HOPE

Yoshimoto Banana is only one of many best-selling authors in Japan during the last several decades of the twentieth century. Even so, her career has been distinguished by the surprising degree of attention her works have been given by the Japanese critical establishment, which often ignores popular writers, as well as by the foreign press and readers, which had previously lavished praise only on canonical male authors and Nobel Prize winners. Recalling the words of Doctor Machizawa, the mental health professional cited earlier, readers cannot help but be pulled into Banana's promise of group therapy for her fans.

Yoshimoto is offered to the world as an acceptable representative of Japanese culture. Domestically her consumption is marked by deft maneuvers aimed at rendering comprehensible to the critical establishment the previously unpalatable fiction of a younger female writer. Shying away from the stench of popular culture in her fiction, the critics attempt to transcend "the nausea of the replica" by reading Banana as indicative of a paradigm shift and generational fissions.[31] Some even attempt to naturalize Banana's novels by comparing them to premodern Japanese literature. Fukazawa Tōru and Katō Norihiro, for example, find common links between the tenth-century discursive *Pillow Book of Sei Shōnagon* and Banana's styles—both styles of which are "full of holes, like swiss cheese" (to use Banana's own phrase)—and contend that both texts constitute "discourse without an addressee, except for the narrator herself."[32]

The terror of the father, death, abandonment, abuse, suicide—all occupy central positions in Yoshimoto's writings. But the author broaches these weighty topics in ways that have variously been described as cheerful and matter-of-fact. I would add that, in a literary world of the 1980s and 1990s that celebrates graphic and disturbing evocation of similarly serious themes—suicide, sodomy, S&M, violence (one need look no farther than canonical authors such as Mishima, Ōe, and Kōno Taeko)—Yoshimoto's approach to the same topos strikes the reader as astonishingly tame. Perhaps it is Yoshimoto's refusal (many might claim inability) to join in this normative discourse, which deliberately aims at disturbing the reader, that has made her palatable, indeed wildly attractive, to millions of readers. Her consistent vision of a realm where spiritual concerns are viable and not redolent of the tainted spiritual past of prewar and wartime Japan, a realm where recovery from personal trauma is possible, has undoubtedly contributed to her success. Yet this optimism does not sit right with many critics and generations of writers whose dystopic visions inevitably lead to the end of the world—the logical conclusion of the nuclear age.

But it is precisely this combination of bright spiritualism and blissful ignorance of Hiroshima, in all its manifestations and significance, that has rendered Banana marketable in so many countries around the world. It is more these emphases than it is consumerism or postindustrial capitalism—which are shared or at least aspired to everywhere Coca Cola is sold and are hardly unique to Japan—that have made Yoshimoto Banana an international writer. Americans can read Banana and not feel guilty about the *Enola Gay;* we can celebrate a discursive Japan that does not seem, at least as Banana would have it, devoid of spiritual values, a hopelessly patriarchal, sexist society, much less conformist than the media has made us believe, where transvestites and lesbians are heroines in her best-selling novels. But while her works entertain us and give us a temporary sense of hope for the world, the nuclear threat that Yoshimoto Banana so blissfully ignores remains steadfastly by our sides, for other authors to recall.

NOTES

1. Machizawa Shizuo, "Yoshimoto Banana o yomu," *Frau* 5 (1991):116.
2. Nobuko Awaya and David P. Phillips, "Popular Reading: The Literary World of the Japanese Working Woman," in *Re-Imaging Japanese Women,* ed. Anne E. Imamura (Berkeley: University of California Press, 1996), pp. 244–270; John Whittier Treat, "Yoshimoto Banana Writes Home: Shōjo Culture and the Nostalgic Subject," *Journal of Japanese Studies* 19(2) (1993):353–387; John Whittier Treat, "Yoshimoto Banana's *Kitchen,* or the Cultural Logic of Japanese Consumerism," in *Women, Media, and Consumption in Japan,* ed. Lisa Skov and Brian Moeran (Honolulu: University of Hawai'i Press, 1995), pp. 274–298. These essays offer extensive discussions of Yoshimoto's earlier novels, especially *Kitchen* and *Tsugumi.*
3. Treat, "Cultural Logic," pp. 290–296.
4. One of the two film versions of *Kitchen* omits Eriko's murder and self-defense entirely and instead domesticates the character by locking her up in a pleasant mental hospital, where she finds a boyfriend.
5. Sharalyn Orbaugh, "The Body in Contemporary Japanese Women's Fiction," in *The Woman's Hand: Gender and Theory in Japanese Women's Writing,* ed. Paul Schalow and Janet Walker (Berkeley: University of California Press, 1996), especially pp. 127–152.
6. For an excellent discussion of a similar yet distinct quest in Takahashi Takako's fiction see Maryellen Toman Mori, "The Quest for Jouissance in Takahashi Takako's Texts," in *The Woman's Hand,* pp. 205–235.
7. Quoted in Mitsui Takayuki and Washida Koyata, *Yoshimoto Banana shinwa* (Tokyo: Aoyumisha, 1989), pp. 69–70. Mitsui and Washida also construct a literary genealogy that links Yoshimoto Banana's fiction to *manga* (romantic young adult fiction) as well as to the coming-of-age novels of 1970s writers such as Murakami Haruki and Murakami Ryū (pp. 71–75).
8. Kanai Yoshiko, "Feminizumu no me de 'Banana genshō' o yomeba," in *Kokubungaku kaishaku to kanshō—bekkan: Josei sakka no shinryū,* ed. Hasegawa Izumi (May 1991), p. 270.
9. Masao Miyoshi, for example, quoted in Treat, "Cultural Logic," p. 285.
10. Lawrence Olson, *Ambivalent Moderns: Portraits of Japanese Cultural Identity* (Savage, Md.: Rowman & Littlefield, 1992), pp. 84–111.

11. Matsuoka Tsuneo, *Ajia no shūen* (Tokyo: Yamato Shobo, 1990).

12. Kanai, "Feminizumu," pp. 266–271.

13. Yoshimoto Banana, *B-kyuu Banana/Yoshimoto Banana dokuhon* (Tokyo: Fukutake Shoten, 1995), p. 45.

14. Yoshimoto Banana, *Marika no sofua/Bari yume nikki* (Tokyo: Gentosha, 1997).

15. Ibid., p. 12.

16. Ibid., p. 24.

17. Ibid., p. 44.

18. Ibid., p. 99.

19. Yoshimoto Banana, *N.P.* (Tokyo: Kadokawa Shoten, 1990), p. 31.

20. Ibid., p. 31.

21. Ibid., pp. 31–32.

22. Thanks to Joshua Mostow for linking this aspect of *N.P.* with the notion of *kotodama*.

23. "Afterword" to *N.P.*, second printing.

24. See Treat, "Cultural Logic," for a detailed, insightful reading of *Kitchen*.

25. Mizuta is quoted in Ishihara Chiaki, "Seibetsu no aru basho," in *Kokubungaku kaishaku to kanshō—bekkan: Josei sakka no shinryū*, ed. Hasegawa Izumi (May 1991), pp. 298–299. At the same time, Ishihara notes that some critics claim that Mikage regards the refrigerator as her mother, a mechanical mother.

26. Yoshimoto Banana, "Oita okama yo doko e iku?" in *Yume ni tsuite/About a Dream* (Tokyo: Gentosha, 1994), p. 52.

27. Yoshimoto Banana, "Blood and Water," in *Lizard* (New York: Grove Press, 1995), pp. 93–95.

28. An older yet familiar contrasting image is Natsume Sōseki's powerful, secularizing image in *Mon* (The gate) of a troubled man who sits at the gates of a Buddhist temple but is unable to pass through them to enter the spiritual realm. See especially Susan Napier's essay in Chapter 1 of this volume concerning Ōe's search for the sublime.

29. Yoshimoto Banana, *Hachiko no saigo no koibito* (Tokyo: Metarogu, 1994), pp. 7–10.

30. Ibid., pp. 41–42.

31. Katō Norihiro, *Gengo hyōgenhō kōgi* (Tokyo: Iwanami Shoten, 1991). The "nausea of the replica" is from Susan Sontag.

32. Fukazawa Tōru, "Makura no sōshi: gensō no nyōbō bungaku toshite," *Kokubungaku: Kaishaku to kanshō* 62(5) (1997):37–42.

CONTRIBUTORS

DAVINDER L. BHOWMIK earned her doctorate in modern Japanese literature at the University of Washington where she concentrated on regional fiction. Her research focuses on questions of history, memory, and representation in atomic bomb fiction, and issues of language, identity, and culture in Okinawan fiction. She currently teaches Japanese literature at the University of California, Berkeley.

PHILIP GABRIEL is associate professor of Japanese literature at the University of Arizona. He is the author of *Mad Wives and Island Dreams: Shimao Toshio and the Margins of Japanese Literature* (University of Hawai'i Press, 1998), and translator of two novels *Dream Messenger*, by Shimada Masahiko (1992), and *South of the Border, West of the Sun*, by Murakami Haruki (1999). He is at work on a study of postmodern Japanese fiction and a translation of a novel by Kuroi Senji.

VAN C. GESSEL is professor of Japanese and dean of the College of Humanities at Brigham Young University. His publications include *The Sting of Life: Three Contemporary Japanese Novelists* (1989) and *Three Modern Novelists: Sōseki, Tanizaki, Kawabata* (1993). He is coeditor of *The Shōwa Anthology* (1985) and has published six translations of the works of Endō Shūsaku, most recently *Deep River* (1995). Presently he is working with J. Thomas Rimer to edit an anthology of modern Japanese literature.

ADRIENNE HURLEY is a Ph.D candidate in Japanese literature at the University of California, Irvine. Her work focuses on the fiction of Ohba Minako.

SUSAN J. NAPIER is associate professor of Japanese literature and culture at the University of Texas at Austin. She has published two books, *Escape from the Wasteland: Romanticism and Realism in the Fiction of Yukio Mishima and Kenzaburō Ōe* (1991), and *The Fantastic in Modern Japanese Literature: The Subversion of Modernity* (1996), and numerous articles on subjects ranging from popular culture to constructions of gender in modern Japanese literature and film. She is currently writing a book on Japanese animation.

SHARALYN ORBAUGH is associate professor of Asian Studies and Women's Studies at the University of British Columbia. Her work engages theories of vision and the body as represented in various narrative media.

JAY RUBIN is professor of Japanese literature at Harvard University. He is the author of *Injurious to Public Morals: Writers and the Meiji State* (1984) and translator of two novels by Natsume Sōseki. He has translated Murakami Haruki's *Nejimakidori kuronikuru* as *The Wind-Up Bird Chronicle* (1997) and recently completed a study of Murakami tentatively titled *Haruki Murakami and the Music of Words*.

ATSUKO SAKAKI is associate professor of Japanese literature at Harvard University. Her publications include *The Woman with the Flying Head and Other Stories by Kurahashi Yumiko* (1998) and *Kōi to shite no shōsetsu: Naratorojii o koete* (1996). Her *Recontextualizing Texts: Modern Japanese Fiction as Speech Act* is forthcoming.

ANN SHERIF is assistant professor of Japanese literature at Oberlin College. She is the translator of Yoshimoto Banana's *N.P.* (1994) and author of a book on Kōda Aya forthcoming from the University of Hawai'i Press.

STEPHEN SNYDER is assistant professor of Japanese literature at the University of Colorado at Boulder. He is coeditor of *In Pursuit of Contemporary East Asian Culture* (1996) and has published translations of work by Ōe Kenzaburō, Murakami Ryū, and Tsuji Kunio. His *Fictions of Desire: Narrative Form in the Novels of Nagai Kafū* is forthcoming from the University of Hawai'i Press.

MARK WILLIAMS is senior lecturer in Japanese studies at the University of Leeds, U.K. His work focuses on the influence of Christianity on twentieth-century Japanese literature, and he has published articles in both Japanese and English on Endō Shūsaku and related topics. He is the translator of two novels by Endō, and his monograph, *Endō Shūsaku: A Literature of Reconciliation*, is due to be published in early 1999.

EVE ZIMMERMAN is assistant professor of Japanese literature at Boston University. She is currently working on a book about myth, violence, and language in the fiction of Nakagami Kenji, and her translation of "Misaki" and other stories by Nakagami is forthcoming.

INDEX